THE
OFFSHORE
SOLUTION

"The Offshore Solution" is an important contribution to anyone's library. An engaging book that provides clarity on how an individual can safely and legally harvest enormous rewards by moving assets offshore. It is a must read for anyone with wealth."

J.J. Childers, JD, author of the *"Secret Millionaire Series."*

"Terry Neal's best book yet! He is well-known and well respected in this arena and I heartily endorse his latest contribution to the offshore industry."

Dr. Larry Turpin author of *"How and Why Americans Go Offshore"*

"A masterfully written book on the offshore world. No one knows the ropes better than Terry, he has provided efficient, knowledgeable fiduciary services to so many of my offshore clients that I can confidently say that he is truly a master of the "ins and outs" of the offshore world."

Arnold S. Goldstein, JD, LLM, Ph.D.
Author of *"Offshore Havens"* and *"How To Protect Your Money Offshore."*

"An excellent book that explains why and how people go offshore. "The Offshore Solution" shares alarming trends that are bound to affect us all and teaches readers tried and tested strategies and how to stay clear of the hazards."

Kevin L. Day, JD, co-author of *"Offshore Money Strategies"*
and *"The Ultra-Privacy Guide."*

"Terry Neal's remarkable insight and powerful writing style once again validate his extensive knowledge of offshore concepts and strategies. A well-written book that should be read by everyone serious about taking charge of their financial future. Every professional I know should have this book close by as it contains a wealth of up to date reference information."

Kevin R. Andersen, CPA, MS (Taxation)
Author of *"How To Reduce Your Taxes to Zero."*

"The Offshore Solution" is outstanding! It contains not only Terry Neal's considerable grasp of the forces that drive the offshore marketplace but also illustrates how individuals can safely and legally improve their lives, take back their privacy, invoke premier asset protection strategies and have higher and safer returns on their investments."

Cort Christie, CEO, National Audit Defense Network
Author of "1-800-AWAY-IRS."

"… a superb summary of the relatively brief history of the so-called tax havens up to the present. It helps greatly for anyone who has any interest in "going offshore" and it clarifies a lot of diverse cross-currents that can be confusing to anyone who wants to understand the political disputes and issues affecting tax havens."

Vern Jacobs, CPA, author of "Offshore Press"
and "Research Press" professional newsletters.

"Having read most every book on going offshore or asset protection, I didn't greet the appearance of another book with too much enthusiasm. I was mistaken! Terry's "The Offshore Solution" is a refreshing new look at the present offshore dynamic environment by an offshore entrepreneur. It is contemporary, addressing the pressures on the offshore jurisdictions from banning banking privacy to a total transparency and destructive tax reforms."

Arnold L. Cornez, JD, author of "The Offshore Money Book"

"Once again, Terry Neal's clear perspective and robust writing style has demonstrated his superior grasp of offshore concepts and strategies. This is a well-written contribution that should be read by everyone serious about taking charge of their financial future."

Michael J. Potter, Esq., Tax and Asset Protection Attorney, co-author
of "Offshore Money Strategies" and "The Ultra-Privacy Guide."

"An important work that provides significant insight whilst serving the industry professional as a desk handy reference manual. A must read for those of us in the legal profession. Accountants and financial planners should also keep this book close by."

Stephen ffrench Davis, Barrister-at-Law, contributing author
of the Nevis International Exempt Trust Legislation.

A quiet revolt is festering within developed nations today.
This revolution is not about blood and bullets.
It's about education and economics.

– T.L.N.

THE OFFSHORE SOLUTION

PRIVACY
ASSET PROTECTION
TAX SHELTERS
OFFSHORE BANKING AND INVESTING

TERRY L. NEAL

MASTERMEDIA PUBLISHING CORP.

Contact:

MasterMedia Publishing Corp.
1005 Terminal Way, Suite 110
Reno, NV 89502
Phone: 800-334-8232 Fax: 503-668-0494

Library of Congress Cataloging-in-Publications Data:
Neal, Terry, 1946–
        The Offshore Solution: Privacy, Asset Protection, Tax Shelters,
Offshore Banking & Investing/Terry Neal.
        ISBN 1-57101-457-8

Title page photo: Copyright 1999 - David J. Lenertz/Carib-Photo
Photos pp. 15, 31, 111, 151, 277 and 338 © 2001 www.arttoday.com

Manufactured in the United States of America

Dedication

To Maureen Neal, my life partner for 38 years,
mother to our eight children, grandmother of 24
and a pillar of strength and support to all.
She is the wonderful woman who brings the
beauty to my life. Thanks to her, I consider
myself one of the luckiest men alive.

Disclaimer

The Offshore Solution includes specialty reference materials, including the *Offshore Directory*, which is an interpretation and summary of the legislative status of numerous offshore jurisdictions, as the author understands them. This book also includes a section entitled *Business Terms and Abbreviations*, which the author believes to be pertinent and accurate, but certainly not exhaustive.

The Offshore Solution includes a paper entitled *Expatriation* provided by legal counsel trained in this narrow legal arena for which the author of the book provides no comment.

This book includes the *Offshore Tax Guide*, which is a summary of the Internal Revenue Code as it relates to the treatment of various offshore legal entities, their structure, intent, and other information pertinent to their taxation. It is provided with the understanding that the authors and publishers are not engaged in rendering legal, accounting, or other professional advice to the reader. We strongly recommend that before relying on any of the information contained herein, competent professional legal advice and opinions should be obtained. This summary contains information on the laws and regulations of the United States government and its agencies that is very technical in nature and which is subject to change at any time. Therefore, the authors and publishers make no guarantee as to the accuracy of this information insofar as it is applied to any particular individual or situation. The information contained in this summary is believed to be accurate in the opinion of the authors at the time this summary was completed.

The authors and publishers specifically disclaim any liability, loss or risk, personal or otherwise, incurred as a consequence directly or indirectly of the use and application of any of the information in this summary. In no event will the author, the publisher, their successors, or any resellers of this information be liable to the purchaser for any amount greater than the purchase price of these materials.

Reservation of Rights

This information is sold to you, the purchaser, with the agreement that you have a right to non-exclusive use of these materials for your own educational purposes. Your right to use these materials is non-transferable. You agree that you will not copy or reproduce any of the information contained herein, in any form whatsoever, and that you will not sell, lease, loan, or otherwise make these materials available to third parties or permit anyone else to do the same.

Terry L. Neal

Table of Contents

Acknowledgements

Many individuals have contributed to the writing of this book, and the author is honored to express appreciation to: Lee Morgan and Aaron Young, business associates and men of insight and integrity, Quinn Sutton whose intelligence and background seem limitless and Felix Reuben who has provided unfailing support and encouragement. Chuck Carter and Kevin Andersen, both CPA's with extensive offshore background have contributed ideas and checked information contained within these pages. Dr Sherry L Meinberg, my sister an author of several books herself, who is always an inspiration, and Dr Evan Ames who patiently read the manuscript and provided comments and grammatical corrections.

A special thanks goes to Matt Blackman for providing technical research and part of the draft for Chapter 6 entitled "The Offshore Evolution."

Dr. Arnold Goldstein, Kevin Day, Stephen Holmes, Arnold Cornez, Michael Potter, Stephen ffrench Davis, and Ben Knaupp, are all lawyers that are widely published on asset protection and the offshore world and men who have been of personal assistance. Dr Larry Turpin and Vernon Jacobs CPA are also both widely published on offshore matters and whose help I appreciate. Rebecca Eddy, a U.S. lawyer living in Grenada has been of considerable support in proof checking and expanding upon the Offshore Directory, which is included as Chapter 13 and drafting information on Grenada. Without the help, influence, and friendship of these valuable business associates, this book would not be the rich source of information and financial guidance that it is.

Many thanks to Albert Yokum, editor and publishing consultant, who personally converted the manuscript into a book and who has provided invaluable expertise in this publication and two of my prior books entitled *The Offshore Advantage*, and *Barter & The Future of Money*.

There are many more that have directly or indirectly contributed and I thank them all, and hope that my efforts measure up to the invaluable contributions they have so freely given.

Introduction

In my prior book *The Offshore Advantage*, the preface began with the following: "Independence Day 1998 my family and I watched the largest July 4th fire works display on the U.S. West Coast from the motor yacht Zarahemla anchored in the Columbia River between Portland, Oregon and Vancouver, Washington. Three generations of Americans on board thrilled to the magnificent aerial display that has come to commemorate our country's birthday. Sunday morning July 5th our church service began with the singing of "God Bless America." It ended as we stood and sang our national anthem "The Star Spangled Banner." These were passionate events that brought tears to our eyes and made us feel ever so blessed to have been born in the greatest nation on earth and to be a part of this very special country which was founded on a freedom formed by a visionary people to ensure the inalienable right of liberty for all."

Notwithstanding my love and passion for America I live and work in the international community. And, although this book is written to Africans, Asians, Australians, Canadians, Europeans, and Latinos as well as U.S. persons, the rationales that drove Americans to race offshore in the eighties and nineties are even more in evidence today than they were at that time. Like it or not, many of those in power within the U.S. government view America as the King of the World and at their bidding Lady Liberty has become the instigator for many or most of the reasons people are today searching for new solutions beyond prying eyes and grasping hands.

We should all fear for America because as she goes, so goes the world. America is no longer what she was, her principals have been sullied, her objectives unclear. I have discovered first hand that information and education can be easily manipulated to achieve the objectives of those in power. The American free press, the cornerstone and guardian of liberty, has largely become a tool of the elite. Greed and power have made the "Spinmeister" the ultimate professional for the overlords of America and much of the developed world.

Some of the information we will cover together may be familiar to you. For most, the truth comes as a shock. You may wonder why this information is not common knowledge or why it isn't highlighted in the media. The fact is that the truth is frequently overshadowed by rhetoric.

11

And it is best one keep in mind that advertisers drive the media.

Perhaps a small example may help to illustrate the growing conflict the major media consortiums have with truth. Some years ago I had a discussion with a rather famous producer for the investigative television program known as "20-20." He was in hot pursuit of scandalous information for a program he was then producing. When discovering some very positive information about the industry he was preparing to "trash," and in response to my question as to whether or not he would include it in his program, he said, —"If you want good news buy advertising; scandal generates ratings, good news is boring."

That comment speaks volumes, but do you think that "20-20" or any other investigative program would be allowed to waste the advertisers that keep them on the air? The reason for their concentration on scandal is largely an issue of ratings. Higher ratings mean advertisers pay more to get their message out to viewers. Programming is ratings and advertising driven.

Much of what you're going to read in this book is not taught in school, but it should be. In most countries the central government ultimately approves educational curriculum. And instruction in truth outside the sciences, is not always helpful to those in power. There are few sources you can consult to learn what is offered in these pages. My objective is that you gain new insights, understand what's going on, and use this information to your considerable benefit.

As to the reasons "WHY" people go offshore, there have been many legislative, judicial, and social changes in the past three years that dramatically effect rationales. Most of these changes have strengthened the argument for utilizing offshore resources. However a wicked backlash by power focused bureaucrats, led by U.S. regulators, have had a dramatic effect on the offshore industry as a whole. Great rewards may lie offshore, but now even greater care must be taken to ply these waters.

What is it about the word "offshore" that stirs the emotions of almost anyone who hears it? Isn't it amazing that almost everyone has an opinion about offshore banking, for example, and few know much about it? Notwithstanding the glamour associated with international travel, the percentage of people who have a working knowledge of offshore financial centers is small, particularly when contrasted with the huge amount of "misinformation" and many times "disinformation" put forth on the subject. This book is designed to clear up the mystery.

Outright warfare between larger, stable, first world countries is not the threat it once was, but first world countries seem everywhere engaged in class revolution. This revolution is not about blood and bullets. It is about education and economics. And, when I say education, I mean what it used to mean – clear knowledge about a subject, not the confusion we so frequently encounter in the make-news media of talking heads, or the feel-good curriculum of our enlightened educational communities. With real knowledge one is prepared to make and implement solid plans and increase the separation between those that know and those that think they do.

Why another book on the loss of privacy and the need for asset protection? Because the problems are real and getting worse and more people need to know the critical position they may be in and what they can do about it. Do people really care about the erosion of personal rights, given the current financial strength of the world economy? Many do, many do not, but those of us who champion freedom need to be better informed and learn how to use this information productively.

This book is not about a particular political platform nor has it been written as a white paper rationalization. It does not pretend to be a news article or some form of annotated essay. I assume complete responsibility for the information contained herein and believe that my sources are accurate but cannot be certain of more than I know first hand. The conclusions herein are mine and I only cite sources when I believe it is particularly informative or where the reader may wish to follow a given line of thought.

If after you've read this book, you're not motivated to talk about it with friends, and you don't believe it's really necessary to reorganize your affairs, it means that I've failed to put across the need and urgency for you to take action. Those who take the time to learn something beyond the party line and carefully and prudently act upon their newfound knowledge, move rapidly beyond the rank and file. These are those that literally become members of a new class of enlightened, self-directed, financially solvent, independent, free citizens.

Please devour this book. Read it with pen in hand and scribble all over it. I hope you find it valuable and that you use the information to your best benefit.

Terry L. Neal

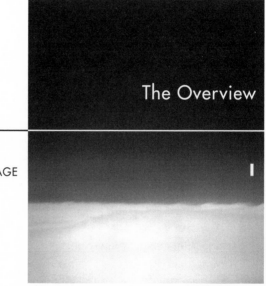

The Overview

THE OFFSHORE ADVANTAGE

I

Important Notice

There are many advantages to offshore strategies, including guaranteed privacy, premier asset protection, reduced regulatory interference, tax benefits, access to global markets, and higher and safer investment returns. But before you launch into the offshore world, you should contact a qualified professional to ensure your plan is valid and meets the standards set by law.

For a professional referral contact *The Sovereign Crest Alliance* at 869-466-3794 (www.sovereigncrest.com). The Sovereign Crest Alliance is a commercial trade association comprised of legal, accounting, and financial professionals working in concert with a consortium of licensed offshore service providers. They will organize a private telephone consultation with a member professional.

If you practice tax law or are skilled in offshore estate planning or accounting matters, another excellent source of information is the International Tax Planners Association at 44.1534.855488 (www.itpa.org), they comprise a network of professional members from all over the globe and they provide continued training and updates on offshore matters.

The Offshore Advantage

"Over and over again courts have said that there is nothing sinister in so arranging one's affairs as to keep taxes as low as possible. Everybody does so, rich or poor; and all do right, for nobody owes any public duty to pay more than the law demands; taxes are enforced exactions, not voluntary contributions. To demand more in the name of morals is mere cant."

Judge Learned Hand
U.S. Court of Appeals

Reality Check

The purpose of this book is to provide the reader with an improved reality map on a number of related subjects both economic and philosophical. It culminates in a practical working knowledge of offshore solutions, including both the why's and how's of going offshore.

M. Scott Peck, in his wonderful book *The Road Less Traveled,* observed that "People find new information distinctly threatening, because if they incorporate it they will have to do a good deal of work to revise their maps of reality, and they instinctively seek to avoid that work. Consequently, more often than not they will fight against the new information rather than for its assimilation." This insightful comment speaks volumes and provides the backdrop against which the reader may want to measure what is set forth herein.

The Underlying Force

If you've ever seen the aftermath of a tidal wave, you can't help but be moved by its devastating power. Boats smashed to pieces and scattered on the shore, buildings collapsed — a vast scene of destruction and disarray. And yet, if you have boating experience and are out to sea, you know that a tidal wave can move right beneath your hull and you might never know the difference. That's the way it is with the truly massive changes in the world. They seem to happen with sudden fury, but in reality the big transformations move beneath us so silently we rarely know what is happening.

A tidal wave is sweeping under us today. Money has burst through the floodwalls of national borders and now flows freely wherever it will. People with money recognize that no single country is a safe haven for their wealth and now send it wherever they get the best return.

This change is part of the process that may end up causing the death of national governments. A change that is inevitable if governments can't control the exodus of money. Feeling the threat, bureaucracy reacts with

17

ever-harsher means of exacting wealth from the people whom government was created to protect. Nation states are being superseded by a host of overlapping quasi-governmental bodies while at the same time national borders are uncontrollable — open to a flow of drugs, illegal immigrants and cash. Nationality has more meaning now as an ethnic preference than a political persuasion.

The alert individual is claiming personal sovereignty as nation states lose their authority. Slowly, quietly, as if waking from a dream, we take control of our lives and make the decisions that are best for us. Governments seem no longer to be fully capable of delivering what they promise — protection and security. It is the task of the autonomous individual to assume more of these responsibilities.

It's been said that there are three kinds of people in the world: those who make things happen; those who watch things happen, and those who wonder what happened. Continuing with the nautical theme above, we might suppose that those who steer their ships safely to harbor are the ones who "make things happen;" those who never get off the dock are the ones who "watch things happen;" and those whose ships get dashed on the rocks for lack of understanding and direction are the ones who simply "wonder what happened."

By understanding the processes that are in play, the self-directed individual who makes things happen has the opportunity to place assets in secure locations where they may grow more rapidly beyond the grasping hands of predators. These pages tell how to chart that course and make good your destination.

Thinking Offshore

If you are reading this book the concept of "going offshore" is an option you are evidently prepared to consider. For my nautical friends the term "going offshore" means blue water cruising, heading out there where the timid don't go. And yet those familiar with yachting understand that a boat kept in harbor deteriorates faster than one under way. Educated sailors know that boaters who hug the shore and never learn the skills or have the courage to sail deep water, actually have more boating failures than those who learn the ropes and move boldly beyond where the average will go. So it is with entrepreneurial enterprise.

From a business perspective "going offshore" is not a nautical term and will likely have little to do with where you live and work, instead it relates to your desire to improve your personal and business privacy, invoke a serious asset protection program and implement forward thinking tax and estate planning strategies. Some of those seeking offshore benefits want access to higher yield investments not available in their home country, whilst others want greater freedom of action and less governmental constraint. Of course there are those for whom the anticipation of actually living on a tropical island in the Caribbean, South Pacific or Indian Ocean provides all the motivation they need to conjure up images of paradise. And, although this book does not champion expatriation as a normal business alternative, the concept may represent a real option for those few wanting a complete lifestyle change. (In the Appendices you will find a paper entitled "Expatriation" prepared for inclusion in this book by Stephen Holmes, a partner in the law firm of Holmes and Greenslade in B.C. Canada.)

The information contained within these pages is directed to the upper middle class and the wealthy. If you are a U.S. person then you likely have assets at risk, a family income of over $80,000 per year, (or have committed to be there), have assets of a million dollars or more (or have reason to believe this goal will be achieved.) If you are European, Australian, or you live in Latin America, Asia or Africa, you may be driven by a different set of financial and personal objectives. Possibly a professional has referred you to this publication for background information.

This is a book about privacy and the lack of it. This is a book about today's most frightening predators: governments and contingency litigators. This is a book about asset protection, the need for it and how to get it. This is a book about tax havens, why they exist and how they work. And, this is a book about offshore investing, and what you probably don't know about it.

This first chapter is designed to summarize some of the points as to WHY and HOW people go offshore. Or as multinational organizational expert Stephen R Covey might say, "Begin with the end in mind."

Offshore Financial Centers

Twenty years ago there were few offshore financial centers and their use was surrounded by reports of drug money and other illicit activities so frequently repeated and expanded upon that they became more fictionalized than true and eventually took on the characteristics of modern mythology.

Today the offshore industry has developed into a major business spanning all quarters of the globe, and involving in one way or another, a third of the world's total currency and half of the world's financial transactions by value. Of course criminals can be found in the offshore world, just as they can in any other environment, but in my experience the level of criminality on a relative basis is much greater in the Middle East, Russia, and the United States than found in the typical offshore financial center.

An offshore financial centre (OFC), also referred to as an international financial center (IFC), is the professional name used to identify a legal tax haven. An IFC is a nation or independent legal jurisdiction that has passed important legislation to protect and attract international clients. At present there are approximately sixty-five jurisdictions throughout the world that have taken steps to position themselves as an offshore or international financial center. Recent legislative actions taken in five U.S. states have been designed to encourage non-U.S. funds to flow into these low population areas, so if these jurisdictions are included in the total count for offshore financial centers, there are seventy such jurisdictions. In all of these locations U.S. dollar accounts are available to banking customers in addition to accounts held in the currency of that nation. In many of these locations multi-currency accounts are readily available.

The use of offshore jurisdictions is considered by sophisticated global money managers to be a safe and reasonable way to conduct business. Every day more people discover the benefits of taking at least a part of their assets offshore. In fact, according to Dr. Arnold Goldstein, a widely published expert in offshore matters:

> "... about one in four who earn over $100,000 a year now enjoy use of one or more safe haven jurisdictions."

The offshore industry was once the bastion of the world's financial elite, for only they could afford the advice it took to successfully implement an offshore strategy. Today strategy and implementation costs are down and trillions of dollars are kept offshore as a rising number of knowledgeable business people, concerned about asset protection and draconian tax rates, join the financial elite in their trek to more friendly financial climes. Yet for all the money being invested abroad, most people who could benefit by utilizing an offshore strategy are simply confused. After all, what does going offshore really mean?

An offshore jurisdiction is essentially anywhere outside of one's own country of residence. As an example Canada is considered an offshore jurisdiction for a Norwegian or anyone else that is not a Canadian or a person that does not reside there. Nevis, Switzerland, the Bahamas, Ireland, Austria and so forth are offshore to the U.S. Likewise the U.S. is considered an offshore jurisdiction for Canadians, Europeans, and anyone who is not a citizen of the U.S. or it's territories.

Going offshore means nothing more than utilizing a country other than one's country of residency or citizenship in which to hold assets or from which to conduct business and financial affairs. Where you go offshore, what to look for and why, and how to do it, are the primary subjects of this book.

Why Go Offshore?
Companies and individuals move assets to offshore jurisdictions in order to better protect themselves, improve privacy, increase return on investments, and reduce risks, taxes, and costs.

People of moderate net worth are increasingly using the resources of offshore trust companies to form and operate legal entities based in attractive jurisdictions and take advantage of opportunities unavailable in their home country. The offshore industry is a huge growth business with an estimated 140,000 new offshore corporations formed in the Caribbean for citizens of other countries during 2000 alone. Motivating factors may include:

- An offshore company can invest in global securities including top performing funds not available to citizens of certain countries. For example, U.S. persons are restricted, not by law, but by virtually all of the world's top performing offshore mutual funds, from participating in their collective investments. (Strange but true and more about this later.)
- Privacy is often integral to risk planning. Offshore typically means greater confidentiality in business affairs to protect business strategies.
- Asset Protection. Assets held offshore are essentially immune from seizure and hostile litigation.
- Offshore companies are generally tax-exempt in their resident country.
- Offshore jurisdictions are less business invasive allowing for aggressive and unrestrained enterprise with lower overhead.

There are so many benefits to being offshore it should come as no surprise that tens-of-thousands of business owners and professionals implement offshore strategies each year. A staff report commissioned by the United States Congress several years ago and reprinted in numerous publications sums up the value in going offshore:

"The offshore financial market has many advantages for rational economic operations. The reasonable expectation, when one learns that an entity is engaged offshore, is that it is there for honest economic reasons, buttressed by whatever advantages privacy holds. The major categories for offshore use are to profit from higher interest rates when lending, to enjoy lower interest rates when borrowing, to escape taxation, to enjoy greater business flexibility by avoiding regulation in an efficient market, to enjoy the protection of confidentiality when engaged in activities…"

Other Motivators

Many countries have some form of inheritance tax; in the United States inheritance tax, (commonly referred to as "the death tax") can consume as much as 55 percent of an estate. Today's fortunes are frequently made through family businesses and the value is often trapped in the equity of these enterprises. The death of the family Patriarch or that person who founded and controlled the family business, can spell big trouble for beneficiaries. Confiscatory estate taxes destroy these generators of wealth as the business is often pried out of the hands of families and sold to big corporations in order to satisfy inheritance taxes.

The death tax is not far from unwarranted seizure (more about this later) and essentially constitutes double tax jeopardy, after all taxes were paid on the accumulation of such wealth and to tax it again without leaving the nuclear family constitutes a double taxation scenario. Such inequity has spawned the Kill the Death Tax Coalition (www.60plus.org) and other groups to oppose inheritance taxes by lobbying for legislative reform. For example, in 2000 a bill passed both houses of the U.S. Congress to eliminate this inequity but was vetoed by President Clinton. Sheldon D. Pollack, professor at the College of Business and Economics at the University of Delaware, pointed out:

> "To the extent that we insist on imposing this double tax, we should not be surprised that investors enter into contorted financial transactions to lower the after-tax rate of return on their investments."

There are alternatives to losing family-built enterprises to government abuse. Such alternatives often involve using offshore investment vehicles for privacy, asset protection, and legal tax avoidance or deferral.

Why Asset Protection?

Predatory litigation, or lawsuits on a commission basis, was originally a U.S. phenomenon whose horrible example is now being copied to some degree in Canada and at least one European jurisdiction. This is bad news for Europeans who have laughed at the ridiculous judgments and blackmailing activities pursued by less scrupulous law firms and their something-for-nothing clientele. These people seek victims from which to garner high settlement penalties and unfortunately all too often they are successful in this game of legal extortion.

A quick look at the growing predatory litigation phenomena, everywhere present in the United States, pretty much tells the story of why business owners and professionals are worried about the need for asset protection:

5% or less of the world's population reside in the U.S.
20% or thereabouts, of the world economy is U.S.
70% of the world's lawyers reside in the U.S.
94% of the world's lawsuits are in the U.S.

Lawsuits performed on a commission basis is against the law in most countries but anyone doing business with a U.S. person, regardless of where they live and work is not exempt from this risk. Regrettably in North America contingency litigation is a major growth industry and the primary targets are business owners, professionals and publicly traded companies.

Money held offshore is immune from most forms of judicial proceedings from one's home country and in some jurisdictions it is completely resistant to judgments from abroad. There are literally millions of the financially astute that maintain offshore accounts in safe harbor jurisdictions and sleep better at night for it. More about predatory litigation in Chapter 5.

Too Much Success?

Due to pressure from the U.S. and subsequently the other G-7 countries, jurisdictions around the world have been forced to enact anti-avoidance legislation designed to reduce the use of tax haven countries. It is interesting to note, however, that the very existence of many safe harbor jurisdictions began as an effect of British, and eventually American and Canadian efforts to reduce aid to specific developing nations. Instead of providing foreign aid, legislation was passed to grant tax incentives for multinational corporations to invest in target offshore locales. Once entrepreneurs spotted these attractive options they determined ways to use these same legislative concessions to benefit individuals.

In an effort to block what they see as abusive tax schemes the U.S. Internal Revenue Service, followed quickly by England and the European Union, has taken the position that if "the" primary reason an offshore option is invoked is taxation based, this motivation is sufficient grounds to deny tax benefits. It is important therefore that anyone considering an offshore business opportunity do so for reasons OTHER than simply tax issues alone. Yes, the tax issue may be "a" reason for going offshore but it should not be the "only" or principal reason for doing so.

Notwithstanding efforts by high tax governments to reduce the use of tax-friendly offshore jurisdictions, offshore centers have become a critical part of the tax planning strategies of individuals and corporations throughout the world. Corporations based in an OFC may derive substantial tax benefits from their activities provided they know the rules and follow them carefully. But the simple act of setting up an offshore corporation does not automatically reduce tax liability for the individual. For example, were you a U.S. person, the implications of your offshore company being designated a "*Controlled Foreign Corporation*," a "*Foreign Personal Holding Company*" or a "*Passive Foreign Investment Company*" are matters that should be addressed by an informed accountant or tax attorney. More about government's legislative response to the success of offshore financial centers is contained in Chapter 6. And, included in the Appendices is the

2001 Offshore Tax Guide (for U.S. persons) which was provided by the offshore consulting firm of Morgan Carter & Young and prepared by Benjamin D. Knaupp, international tax lawyer.)

Privacy & Confidentiality

Keeping financial transactions private in some countries is against the law; in other countries it is a violation of law to reveal anything about anyone's private banking or financial activities. Of those countries claiming its citizens are free, the largest and most recent source of personal privacy violation has been the countries that most prominently espouse freedom. Government agencies focused on the desire for greater power and control are leading the onslaught against personal privacy, and the champion of this regrettable trend is the United States closely followed by England and the European Union.

A pertinent example of America's rapidly expanding citizen control laws is that financial institutions must automatically report to government on the banking, bartering, credit card, real estate transactions, and securities business of its private citizens. Everyone is being watched and profiled. Like the once infamous KGB of the former Soviet Union, U.S. taxing and regulatory authorities now receive automatic reports on their citizens.

An interesting quote by Frank Murphy provided by Tax Analysts in Arlington Virginia says:

"It is wise to remember that the taxing and licensing power is a dangerous and potent weapon which, in the hands of unscrupulous or bigoted men, could be used to suppress freedoms and destroy religion unless it is kept within appropriate bounds."

From Newsweek magazine (Jan 15, 2001) comes this persuasive quote by Whit Diffie made during a U.S. Senate hearing regarding the FBI's infamous snooping device code named the Clipper Chip:

"The legitimacy of laws in a democracy grows out of the democratic process. Unless the people are free to discuss the issues — and privacy is an essential component of many of those discussions — that process cannot take place."

Privacy is an essential ingredient to freedom and when rights to personal privacy are invaded by government the liberty of the people are directly at risk. Chapter 2 examines this critical subject in some depth.

Carnivore

In 2000 it was discovered that the U.S. Department of Justice had developed and implemented in secret, a surveillance system code-named

Carnivore being used and tested without the courts permission and without seeking or receiving warrants to intercept and examine private communications. The circumstances of its development and the political intrigue surrounding its evolution was widely reported and became the basis of multiple news articles over a several month period.

Carnivore is a combination hardware and software system with far-reaching electronic snooping capabilities that can access, read and collate any person's emails from virtually anywhere on the planet. An oft-quoted phrase coined by Lord Acton, an international citizen born in Naples and educated in England, Scotland, France and Germany, seems appropriate to the Carnivore revelation:

"Power corrupts and absolute power corrupts absolutely."

The good news is that a recent report on Carnivore states that the use of an email encryption system can defeat this horrific example of one government's snooping into the private communications of companies and individuals throughout the world. Incidentally you can access a good encryption email system for free at www.hushmail.com.

Echelon

On the 3rd of November 1999 the British Broadcasting Corporation reported that an Australian government official had finally confirmed what both the Americans and British had consistently denied — that the super-secret spy network code-named Echelon did in fact exist. As it turns out, Britain, Australia, Germany, Japan, and surprisingly the People's Republic of China are jointly operating Echelon, a global spying network whose existence was first revealed by Duncan Campbell at a symposium held in Luxembourg.

The vast international global eavesdropping network Echelon is said to be able to monitor ALL, as in EVERY one, of the world's telephone and fax transmissions and sift out messages it finds interesting. According to published reports it is alleged that computers are now automatically analyzing every phone, fax, and data signal, and can also identify calls to say, a target telephone number in London, no matter from which country the call originates. Originally designed to snoop on the Russians the system has been expanded to eavesdrop on domestic citizens of all nationalities and it is now believed that much of the work appears to be focused on commercial and private civilian targets. (More on Echelon later.)

The erosion of personal privacy coupled with the alarming increase in citizen control laws has been achieved under the cover of fighting the "war on drugs." The assault on personal rights, including privacy, is justified with convincing arguments about the common good and how the state is "improving" the quality of the protection it provides its citizens.

On closer examination one may observe coincidentally, that the "common good" always happens to benefit the political concepts of those in power and that the individual's loss of personal power is quickly transferred to the bureaucracy. (More about this in Chapter 3)

In an increasingly hostile environment privacy is essential to risk planning. The clientele of licensed offshore trust companies, the engines of offshore commerce, almost always seek confidentiality in their affairs to protect assets from disasters, unwarranted third party interference, and to reduce an ever-growing burden of unnecessary disclosure. It is a trust company's business to provide legal structures, private banking and other financial services to protect client assets, insure privacy, and reduce risk, taxes, and costs.

Offshore Investments

Contrary to popular belief, offshore mutual funds and unit trusts frequently outperform the pooled asset investments of funds based in more highly regulated environments. Offshore funds are generally based in tax-free and low-overhead jurisdictions such as Luxembourg. This does not mean they are less safe or less liquid, but it may mean they are not permitted to offer their investments in the country of your residence. For example, U.S. regulators require mutual funds to provide exhaustive and extremely expensive registration filings before an investment may be offered in the States.

Many of the world's top-performing funds find some countries' registration costs unnecessarily demanding and uneconomical. Instead, offshore based funds may invest the money saved and improve overall profitability. The result of this choice for greater returns and less legal hassle is that top performing funds outside the U.S., for example, are simply unavailable to citizens of the United States.

The Standard & Poor's Guide to Offshore Investment Funds (www.intl-offshore.com) reports on 6,800 offshore funds including an in-depth survey of the top 350 performing investments. Some of these funds have achieved five-year returns of 800% to 900%. Standard & Poor's reports that the common factor these 6,800 funds share (other than their being pooled investments) is their policy to refuse U.S. investors. Offshore funds as a group could care less if you are an Afghan freedom fighter, a Cuban dissident or an escapee of Communist China; they simply want to avoid harassment from taxing and regulatory authorities of the United States. Even though many of these funds are fully vested in U.S. stocks, they insist that their participants NOT be U.S persons.

On Private Banking

Although the concepts of private banking can be traced to the earliest recorded history, the Swiss are generally accredited with developing the process into an art form. For several hundred years the Swiss government was not allowed to force disclosure of business secrets, or discover the existence of trust property, nor could private property be expropriated. Due to inalienable personal property rights, the rights to privacy, and the encouragement of free enterprise, the concepts of private banking matured.

Most large banks throughout the world have a system for providing the affluent with special services. However, private banking means something quite different today in England, Canada, France, and the U.S., than it may in Austria, Bahamas, Cayman Islands, Grenada or Nevis. For starters, American banks operate in an environment where personal privacy is no longer regarded as a "right" and therefore the very name "private banking" is a misnomer. The U.S. form of "private" banking is in reality "personal" banking, or traditional commercial banking with added personal service. There is absolutely NO privacy left to private banking in the United States. And unfortunately, this example is now being rigorously pursued by other G-7 countries. Private offshore banking is explored in greater depth later on.

Offshore Trust Companies

An offshore trust company is generally empowered with the rights to form International Business Companies, Limited Liability Companies, International Exempt Trusts, Asset Protection Trusts, etc., in the jurisdiction(s) in which they are licensed. Some trust companies are also empowered to open and operate bank accounts for third parties, act as a registered agent, trustee, nominee shareholder, or director, and generally provide the various services of a private banker.

For those unfamiliar with these kinds of services, the concept may seem a bit scary and unsafe. Nevertheless, according to information on money movements provided by the U.S. Federal Reserve System, about one half of all the daily money transactions worldwide by value are handled through international financial centers, the home of offshore trust companies. This amounts to almost two trillion dollars in business that flows through offshore centers daily! The numbers are huge, and precisely because they are so incredibly large, no emerging financial jurisdiction can afford to let a scandal destroy it's reputation and interrupt this growth industry.

Of course bank failures do happen, both offshore and in your home country. For example, there have been some rather huge bank failures in England, the U.S. and Japan, in the recent past, not to mention Russia, Antigua, and one in the Cayman Islands, etc. But, the most dismal record for banking failures goes to the U.S. for the great Savings & Loan debacle of the eighties. Yes, some countries are historically safer than others and interestingly enough the banks with the best safety record are those domiciled in the tax haven jurisdictions of the longest duration, ie: Switzerland, Austria, Liechtenstein, and so on.

Having an Offshore Company

The world of offshore is surrounded in its own mystique and language and for some this aura can be disconcerting. It is worth remembering however that the real differences between an offshore jurisdiction and one considered onshore are relatively few. Any person with a reasonable grasp of their domestic business practices is equipped to begin navigating the world of international financial centers provided they are based in British Commonwealth jurisdictions. Why use British Commonwealth jurisdictions when going offshore? Because they all adhere to the underlying principals of British Common law, a legal system well understood by most of the world, and the traditional British offshore domiciles are English language based. On the other hand, if you are French or Hispanic you may prefer using a legal jurisdiction based on Napoleonic law such as Panama or Uruguay.

Forming a corporation offshore and structuring its activities correctly will assure an individual increased privacy and greatly improved asset protection. And, were you able to implement a single tax benefit it might easily pay for the entire process and put you on the trail of huge future savings. Once one has an offshore business in place there are multiple other options to increase asset base, earn greater returns, possibly enjoy tax-deductible offshore travel, and so forth.

The decision to utilize a licensed trust company to form and operate an offshore corporation is easy to implement and the costs are generally reasonable. But you should note that the taxing authorities of several countries have recently made quite clear that if the only reason you have for going offshore is to achieve some form of tax avoidance you may lose the value you seek and end up with fines or penalties to boot. On the other hand, estate planning, asset protection, access to otherwise unavailable financial investments, and other similar rationales are generally considered valid business reasons for going offshore. If there are tax benefits let them be the sweetener for your move to safer grounds — not be the primary motivating force. Tax issues can be tricky and one should expect obstacles that must be dealt with carefully prior to taking action on a tax avoidance strategy. Thankfully there are an increasing number of skilled tax attorneys and offshore accountants that focus on these matters.

If your goal is to gain personal and business privacy, implement a globally focused estate plan, access new markets, take advantage of business and investment opportunities that are unavailable in your home country, protect assets from frivolous and predatory litigation, or to reduce regulatory reporting when and where possible, AND to avoid or defer taxes, the use of an offshore corporation can reap extraordinary benefits.

What Your Financial Advisor Should Know

The American Institute of Certified Public Accountants, (AICPA) is the U.S. equivalent organization that represents Chartered Accountant designees in much of the rest of the world. In late 1999 and again in 2000, the AICPA advised accountants across America as follows:

> "To prepare for the 21st century, CPA's must be aware of the hottest, most important tax-savings and asset protection devices. Once thought of as reserved for the very rich, offshore planning is available for virtually all clients, and should be part of overall planning."

This announcement by THE accounting authority in the U.S. and possibly the most influential accounting authority in the world, appears to have caused a governmental backlash of regulative and legislative measures designed to stop U.S. persons from seeking offshore options.

It is a right guaranteed to the citizens of virtually all democratic countries that they may conduct business, maintain bank accounts, travel to and from virtually anywhere in the world, with the exception of North Korea, Iraq, and perhaps a couple of other rogue states alleged to support terrorism. (Americans are restricted from most business activities in Cuba although Europeans, Canadians, etc., generally are not.)

This leaves about 200 countries open as potential locations from which to base platforms for business and investment activities, not that most of them ought be seriously considered as a wise place from which to conduct your affairs. But, the point is that it is your right to shop around and go virtually anywhere in the world you wish and carry out your business and personal objectives under whatever set of laws to which you wish to submit.

On the other hand, everyone should be aware that there is a serious attack under way against the rights of the individual driven primarily by American politicians and bureaucrats overstepping the bounds of the U.S. Constitution. Their objectives are such that every U.S. person's financial and business activities will be kept directly under the government's scrutiny, power and control. And, because they are not able to stop U.S. person's from accessing offshore options they instead are doing all they can to interrupt offshore financial centers from working with and for U.S. persons. (Much more on this subject ahead.)

Evidently due to legislative changes and governmental posturing, by late 2000 the AICPA had redesigned their offshore training programs three times in less than one year in order to better instruct accountants on how to evaluate and implement offshore strategies for their respective clientele. The AICPA remains unrepentant for strongly recommending that accountants learn and pass-on the benefits of offshore options. Offshore training workshops are now routinely available for CPA's and similar training programs are available for lawyers and financial advisors from their respective associations.

You may want to refer your personal financial advisor, your lawyer or your accountant to an organization known as the International Tax Planners Association (www.itpa.org), they are a professional trade association with hundreds of members from all over the globe to whom they provide extensive training and other resources focused on tax minimization strategies.

Another excellent offshore association is the Sovereign Crest Alliance (www.sovereigncrest.com). Members of the Alliance form an interactive commercial group of offshore financial service providers and professional firms focused on privacy, asset protection, tax and estate planning and global commerce. The Sovereign Crest Alliance provides referrals to qualified professionals in several countries.

The battle lines have been drawn - the entrepreneurial among us, supported by legal and accounting professionals worldwide, are exploring and choosing to implement offshore options. Bureaucrats and predatory litigators are unhappy with this trend as their access to your resources is reduced. The socialistic, and those absorbed by their special access to power, are personalities present in all government bureaucracies. These character types would have you believe that anyone who seeks privacy in their personal or business affairs has something nefarious to hide. The reality is quite different and history teaches us a dissimilar lesson. If we do not preserve our rights to privacy, freedom cannot long endure, as we shall see in the next chapter.

The Dilemma

2

Freedom Requires Privacy

"The right to be left alone is the most comprehensive of rights, and the right most valued by civilized men."

Justice Louis Brandeis
U.S. Supreme Court - 1928

Privacy is Paramount

Privacy and freedom are irrevocably linked, remove one and the other is soon lost. For those who espouse principals related to individual free agency and believe that each of us should have the right to think and act for ourselves, there follows a moral imperative that we protect one's right to privacy. According to Richard A. Spinello, associate dean of faculties at Boston College, "A world where privacy is in short supply will undermine our freedom and dignity and pose a grave threat to our security and well-being."

Spinello is one of many scholars and observers who report on the loss of privacy and its corollary, the consequent loss of freedom. He points out that many people feel as though their financial life has become part of the public record, a result of the "Information Age." He suggests many of us feel that we "are the powerless victims of technology that has stripped away our privacy without our ability to recognize what has happened."

Globalization moves us steadily towards one multicultural - multiracial society. We have come to learn that to be Argentinean, Brazilian, Chilean, or what have you, has nothing to do with the color of your skin or your economic status. Those of us who live and work outside our homeland are quick to discover that even our residence does not determine whether one is a Canadian, Austrian, or an American. For example, a Frenchman living in England is most assuredly aware that living in England does not make him English. Nor is the reverse true.

The land or nationality with which we feel most connected is usually a consequence of our family heritage. However, as strong as family ties are, the rights to privacy and its resultant liberty, followed by the prosperity that eventually follows, is the magnet that pulls us towards the bright light of economic freedom.

To be an enlightened citizen from whatever country or nationality you hail is to be a person who understands that it is his or her responsibility to protect the rights of the individual. The right to privacy is core because it most closely evokes the concept of individual sanctity. All other rights will simply not exist for any length of time if and when those in power are permitted to abuse this fundamental of all civil liberties, the right to privacy. Robert S. Peck provides this insight as to our basic need for privacy:

> "The chilling effect of the loss of privacy is an undesirable incentive to conform to societal norms rather than assert one's individuality. Ultimately, what is lost is not only the private emotional releases we all need but, most importantly, the creativity that leads to human achievement.
>
> Privacy makes possible individuality, and thus freedom. It allows us to cope with the larger world, knowing there is a place where we can be by ourselves, doing as we please without recrimination."

It is your right to sequester some or all of your assets safely offshore, and it may be your duty, if that is the only way to protect your privacy, and therefore your freedom.

Computers and Privacy

Information about you has become a commodity. Everything from purchases you make to visits to an abortion clinic or where you spent your last vacation, all give information about you. This information becomes part of databases that flow from hand to hand without your knowledge or consent.

Until the advent of the computer age, people took for granted privacy in their personal affairs. But now, through data brokers, information hunters can track you down anywhere. They can get on-line and access parish or county records, they can frequently access telephone logs and other private information, they can easily secure business records, bankruptcy records, lawsuits and property ownership records.

Some of the privacy debate on the Internet relates to tiny files of specific information called "cookies," that allow companies to keep track of what you do when you visit their web sites. In essence, cookies brand your computer so the retailer's site can determine if you visit again and what interests you there. Part of the problem is that companies are collecting, sharing, and selling detailed information on web travelers gained from their cookies. Cookies can contain information such as your age; income, gender, as well as a list of the things that you've purchased online and the other sites you visit regularly. This information is frequently compiled and recombined and may become part of a profiling database accessible by others with less honorable intentions than simply selling you something.

Internet Snooping

In 1998 I received a bulk e-mail from Spies-R-Us, a company that for less than $20 would sell what it called its SNOOP COLLECTION, "300 giant resources to look up people's, credit, social security numbers, current or past employment, mail order purchases, addresses, phone numbers." The promotion said: "The Internet is a powerful mega-source of information, if you only know where to look. I tell you how to find out nearly ANYTHING about anybody, and tell you exactly where to find it." For example, you can "find out a juicy tidbit about a co-worker," or "check out your daughter's new boyfriend."

The promotion advised you to "Research yourself first! You'll be horrified, at how much data has been accumulated about you." And now, for twenty bucks, any yahoo with a computer can find it out as well. That's not even the worst of it. A company called International Intelligence Network conducts "Public Information and Asset Tracking" seminars, through which anyone can learn how to get more than 50 pieces of financial information on anyone through Internet public records search. By 2001 the price of this program had increased to $25 but now includes access to additional databases and a software system designed for private detectives to help one in organizing search information and reports.

On December 26, 2000 I received an email advertisement for *Internet Spy and You* that includes this: "Secrets never intended to reach your eyes, get the facts on anyone! Find out secrets about your relatives, friends, enemies, and everyone else, even your spouse. Get anyone's name and address with just a license plate number, find that girl you met in traffic. Get anyone's driving record, get unlisted phone numbers, discover dirty secrets your in-laws don't want you to know, learn about your mysterious neighbors. Find out what they have to hide."

People are buying and selling information about you, combining it with information from other sources and creating profiles on you. Most of this is for commercial purposes — someone wants to sell you something. But this information is available to anyone who might spend the money to buy it — a former spouse or anyone else seeking leverage over you for any reason. You may find yourself the target of someone who sues others for a living, or a down and dirty competitor, kidnappers, or simply those that deal in the kind of gossip that ruin people's lives.

Other information seekers may be legitimate, although still invaders of privacy. The Marriott Hotel, for example, puts the names of its guests together with records of the vehicles they drive and the property they own to find out who is most likely to respond to their mailings. In 1999 through 2000 the news media carried multiple articles about U.S. Bank after it was discovered they had been collating and selling information about their customer's private financial circumstances. Even as you read this, somebody with $25 worth of software may be ransacking databases gathering information about you — finding out what you have and where you have it. And it may be perfectly legal in the country where you live.

Technology's Continuing Threat

The controversy over privacy is an unwelcome outgrowth of the Space Race and the microchip and computer that were its offspring. With them came a Pandora's Box of electronic devices that have made information about you readily available.

Electronics made it possible, for example, to tap telephone lines — to listen in to private conversations. Other devices made it possible to eavesdrop on things going on inside your home. Radio transmitters are now small enough to be hidden inside cardboard or behind wallpaper. In many countries the judicial systems have made such evidence inadmissible in court, for example in 1967, in Katz v. United States, the Supreme Court broadened this prohibition to make wiretapping and other electronic surveillance illegal without a valid warrant.

The next year saw the Crime Control Act, which set up a system through which courts can approve wiretapping. And the Supreme Court ruled that even in cases involving national security, there must be a court order for wiretapping. But most agencies, competitors, and those that deal in the gray zones of propriety have no intention of telling a court how they got their information. They gather data to seek advantage. Government and private organizations both are in the business of gathering information about you. And by the year 2001 both legal and illegal snooping was rampant in all parts of the globe.

For most of history, it was simply physically impossible to gather, assemble, distribute and update information about everyone. Imagine all the typewriters, mimeographs, manila folders, card files and file cabinets it would take. The sheer cost and volume of work it would take to keep track of you protected most people's privacy. But computers have changed all that — powerful information management tools are within the reach of virtually everyone.

Government agencies such as law enforcement, regulators and taxing authorities, as well as private groups like banks, credit card companies, insurance underwriters, employers, and medical merchandisers all now have reams of information about you. And they share it, and use it in ways over which you have neither knowledge nor control.

What About Rules

There are rules that give you some rights — "fair informational practices" laws. These were enacted in various countries beginning in the 1980s when it became clear the safeguards to protect privacy were not sufficient for the computer age. These rules cover credit, insurance, banking and law enforcement.

Unfortunately in America, the purported champion of individual freedom, one does not have the same protection as those who live in Sweden, France, Germany and several other countries. These countries have national data protection or privacy protection commissions that license computer data banks, receive complaints from citizens and enforce the rules. But if you live in the U.S., you're pretty much on your own.

Big Government and Big Companies

Intel, the world's leader in chip manufacture and design, has been wrestling with the privacy issue for some time. Intel produces about 83% of the world's computer processors, which puts them smack dab in the middle of the raging shift to computer technology by virtually everyone. In 1999 a group of privacy advocates wrote letters to "socially responsible" investment funds who held at least a billion dollars in Intel stock asking them to sell their positions based on Intel's alleged deal with the U.S. government to individualize and reference every computer sold anywhere in the world. On the surface this feature seemed benign but how it could be used to invade a person's right to privacy became a matter of some debate.

Intel found itself trapped between government's pressure for them to collect and provide information verses privacy activists' efforts to block Big Brother's agenda. Evidently Intel assumed the government had greater power and agreed to assist them with their objectives. Directly thereafter Intel found itself the target of a boycott launched by privacy advocates who feared that hackers would access information about individual computer users due to the new personal identification numbers stored in the Pentium III microprocessor. In a clear concession to this pressure Intel finally capitulated allowing computer buyers to turn the internal tracking feature off in order to protect their privacy. (This of course presumes that one knows they can do it and understands why they should.)

The privacy issue is now becoming a very big deal with larger companies who see the proverbial handwriting on the wall. According to an article in USA Today (December 2000):

"Add another seat around the conference table: Chief Privacy Officers are joining the executive ranks at major technology companies across the USA. IBM appointed its first CPO on Wednesday, becoming the latest company to create the high-profile position. No one had heard of a "chief privacy officer" two years ago. Now there are about 75 in the USA, according to James Grady, an analyst at Giga Information Group. The number is expected to grow as large corporations follow the lead of the small Internet companies that started the CPO trend. Companies are finally realizing that privacy will not arise by accident."

Privacy advocates tend to love cash and fear such things as smart cards. Dollar bills are dumb. They don't know where you dine out, whom you call or where you spent your last weekend. Cash allows a certain level of anonymity but as we shall see there is a massive movement by governments to eradicate the use of cash in all but the most incidental of purchases. Once again this puts the individual squarely in jeopardy from bureaucrats and powerful authorities. The bottom line is that when someone is able to access your transaction records they have incredible details about your life. Whereas we generally believe that commercial institutions gather information on us for benign reasons, government's underlying motives may be another matter entirely.

Governments Abuse Privacy

The Federal Communications Commission, at the behest of regulations precipitated by the Federal Bureau of Investigation, has ordered cellular and digital phone companies to install tracking technology. In January of 2000 Internet privacy organizations unsuccessfully sought a reversal of this mandate through the federal appeals court. As it now stands, law enforcement agencies are supposed to be able to triangulate the exact whereabouts of any cellular or digital phone user without oversight, which means without a warrant or court order.

This means that any law enforcement person having access to this technology can track their wife or boyfriend's whereabouts at any time of the day or night and no one will know they've done it. What may be even worse is that cellular service providers must give authorities the packets of information that constitute the calls themselves and provide lists of the phone numbers being called and the numbers from whence inbound calls are coming. George Orwell's famous book *1984* seems to have been incredibly prophetic. It predicted that a future government rife with wiretaps would be referred to as "Big Brother." And today Big Brother is indeed watching and listening in on its citizens.

Governments will have, and in some countries already do have, access to tracking your every whereabouts whenever you're carrying a cellular or digital phone. Law officers are allowed in many countries to obtain the exact location of a cellular telephone customer without a court order and without advance approval. According to FCC rules, the technology must pinpoint within 125 meters any cellular or digital phone that is turned on, whether a call is in progress or not.

Whereas governments seem to be in the business of violating personal privacy rights they are at the same time careful to retain privacy over the information they generate. From *The Great American Bathroom Book III* comes this quote:

"The estimated annual cost to U.S. taxpayers for keeping government documents secret is $20 billion per year. That's $6 billon more than the entire NASA budget."

More on Echelon

In chapter 1 you were introduced to Echelon, the super spy network capable of listening in on virtually anyone's private conversations anywhere on the planet. Originally designed as a tool of military intelligence, it has been expanded to focus inward on domestic traffic. When information first leaked about the incredible power cloak and dagger agencies now held, The New Statesman, an English publication reported:

"In the booming surveillance industry they spy on whom they wish, when they wish, protected by barriers of secrecy, fortified by billions of pounds worth of high, high technology." "...and they don't give a damn about personal privacy or commercial confidence. Project 415 is a top-secret new global surveillance system. It can tap into a billion calls a year in the U.K. alone."

Journalist Duncan Campbell was commissioned by the European Parliament to secure and provide evidence regarding Echelon, whose existence at the time was denied by all those involved with this highly secret project. He presented an indepth report, which included evidence that the National Security Agency, in Fort Mead, Maryland, intercepted a phone call from a French firm bidding on a Brazilian contract and then allegedly passed the information along to an American competitor, which subsequently won the contract. So much for government integrity, but does it really surprise us that anyone who has access to this kind of unbridled power, and the right to snoop without oversight, would find a way to use it to advance their own agenda? Does anyone hear the heavy breathing of Darth Vader in the wings?

Lord Acton's epic warning that "power corrupts, and absolute power corrupts absolutely" is a standard by which we must gauge all government's demands for broader authority to act without careful external oversight.

It bears repeating that the erosion of personal privacy coupled with the alarming increase in citizen control laws has been achieved under the cover of fighting the "war on drugs." The assault on both privacy and personal property rights has been justified with convincing arguments by law enforcement spokespersons and politicians. They claim that the common good demands that they have greater flexibility to surreptitiously invade an individual's privacy so that the state can improve the quality of the protection it provides its citizens. And, yes there is truth in their argument. But almost without exception, upon closer examination one may observe that the common good coincidentally happens to benefit the political concepts of those in power.

European Computer Crime Proposal

In December 2000 a controversial European drive to tighten cybercrime laws came under attack by privacy, civil liberties, and human rights advocates. A 41-nation Council of Europe's latest draft convention "are consistent with the existing framework of U.S. law and procedure" according to an announcement placed on the U.S. Department of Justice website. Those who are opposed claim the pact would stretch the long arm of the police improperly, trample on individual privacy, and erode police enforcement accountability.

In a statement distributed six weeks earlier by privacy groups around the world, critics said information logs based on archived data had been used to track dissidents and persecute minorities. "We urge you not to establish this requirement in a modern communications network," said a 27-group coalition that included such organizations as the Internet Society, Privacy International, and the American Civil Liberties Union. They went on to say "Police agencies and powerful private interests acting outside of the democratic means of accountability have sought to use a closed process to establish rules that will have the effect of binding legislation."

Remote Computer Scanning

In Newark, New Jersey the FBI rigged a suspects computer in late 2000 such that they were able to monitor their target's every keystroke. Not just email messaging or where and what sites he choice to visit on the web, but actually every keystroke of information related to his home financial accounting, personal journal entries, and private correspondence. Normally communications between a lawyer and his client are considered sacrosanct under the concept of solicitor-client privilege, but in this case, the suspect's correspondence with his personal lawyer were retrieved right along with everything else. If this kind of technique becomes commonplace there will be a dramatic increase in the number of quasi-legitimate break-ins to private residences.

The Clipper Chip

The Clipper Chip is a cryptographic device that was designed to permit government agents to obtain "backdoor keys" held by government "escrow" agents that would enable them to defeat encrypted communications and provide them with access to scrambled voice transmissions.

Although the clipper chip was designed to defeat only voice encryption its sister chip, code named "Capstone" was developed to decrypt private data transmissions. Eventually both became referred to as the "Clipper Chip." Newsweek (January 15, 2001) in their cover article entitled "Beating Big Brother" used this analogy:

"What if you had to leave a copy of your front-door key at the police station?" "Even Joe Six-pack, who didn't know encryption from a forward pass would be an anti-Clipper convert."

The article went on to say:

"Opposition came from all quarters. The ACLU found itself agreeing with Rush Limbaugh, who attacked Clipper on his radio show. Digital hippies savored the William Safire column "Sink the Clipper Chip," where he noted that the solution's name was well chosen "as it clips the wings of individual liberty.""

For readers from the international community the above quotation may not mean much. But the American Civil Liberties Union agreeing on anything in public with America's best-known conservative talk show host is rather like a rabbi converting to Islam.

Other than the White House and the FBI, did anyone want this kind of personal invasion technology available to the government? Well, once it became known and moved into the light of public opinion and out of the dark of an agency obsessed with secrecy, the National Institute of Standards, and Technology was required to solicit public comment on Clipper. Notwithstanding a huge public relations campaign launched by the White House, only two of three hundred and twenty individuals and organizations responding agreed with Clipper.

Once again it was the FBI that paid for the design and development of this technology whilst claiming that because encryption programs are increasingly available to the buying public it will interfere with the FBI's ability to conduct wiretapping activities when needed.

No evidence in support of these claims by the FBI has ever been provided. In fact, according to records they themselves released, they conducted fewer than 800 "legal" wiretaps in all of 1992. (The emphasis is on legal!) It is to protect the viability of that small number of wiretaps from an unsubstantiated risk that the FBI and the NSA have repeatedly proposed to compromise the security of billions of electronic transactions and transmissions. Talk about overkill. Do you suppose we might be wise to consider one more time that famous observation about unbridled power?

Privacy and Economics
Most first world countries and many developing nations have made strides in securing economic rights for the individual. According to the 2001 Index of Economic Freedom, a joint publication of the Wall Street Journal and the Heritage Foundation, more countries expanded economic

freedom during the past year than curtailed it. The survey demonstrated that 70 of the 155 countries that were tracked and rated had granted their citizens greater freedom, while 52 imposed new restrictions.

As pointed out earlier, improved privacy rights result in greater freedom, which are closely followed by the prosperity that arrives as the result of individual enterprise. So, it should come as no surprise, that the Heritage Foundation reports that in the year 2000, countries with expanded freedom also had higher rates of economic growth.

The 2001 Index of Economic Freedom reports that the top five nations in the world in economic freedom are now Hong Kong, Singapore, Ireland, New Zealand, and Luxembourg. Not surprising, the least free are North Korea, Libya, Iraq, Cuba, and Iran.

In an effort to promote open markets, the 2001 Index calls for a new Free Trade Association of countries that share a commitment to free trade and free capital movement. This means that government's roles are curtailed and diminished and the private rights of citizens are enhanced, including the rights to privacy.

Membership in the Free Trade Association requires good scores in 50 different economic variables grouped into 10 categories. The first ten countries to qualify may surprise you, in order they are: Chile, Czech Republic, Denmark, Estonia, Hong Kong, Ireland, Luxembourg, New Zealand, Singapore, and the United Kingdom.

Privacy and Government Needs

The U.S. Constitution guarantees many things — such as the right to free speech, freedom of religion and assembly — even the right to keep and bear arms. But the "right to privacy" is not guaranteed in the Constitution. What you have in the States is a tradition of Supreme Court rulings and interpretations of various Amendments to the Constitution — primarily the Fourth and Fourteenth.

The Fourth Amendment shields one from "unreasonable search and seizure" and other law enforcement arrest and pre-arrest techniques. The Fourth Amendment is part of the Bill of Rights — a sacrosanct element of the protection citizens demanded for themselves during the formation of the Republic. Unreasonable search and seizure was abhorrent to the framers of the Constitution because at one time the British used to enter colonial homes, ransack their dwellings and take things without probable cause that a crime had been committed. The British had meaningless, easy-to-get writs and pieces of paper to justify their intrusions. Often enough, these unacceptable violations of privacy came because the Crown wanted to extract more taxes and expand upon their own resources.

The Fourth Amendment is the one that prevents officials from searching a person, their automobile or their home without "probable cause" or a valid search warrant. But this is a Constitutional Amendment protecting one from the government — not from other private citizens. If you are an American someone may be executing an electronic search of your possessions right now with complete immunity.

The gap in protection of the "right to privacy" in the Constitution has been noted and — short of adding an Amendment — the judicial system has gone a long way toward guaranteeing privacy rights. Other Amendments to the Constitution have been broadly interpreted so as to protect the individual, but technology is moving ahead at such a pace that secret governmental projects not open to public scrutiny may have already made these guarantees all but useless except in the direct prosecution of an event.

The Fourteenth Amendment has been used by the U.S. Supreme Court in (Mapp v. Ohio), in effect, to prevent police from using against a defendant evidence they gathered through an illegal search. The Court said one could not be forced to testify against one's self with such evidence — a violation of the Fifth Amendment protection against self-incrimination.

The Fourth Amendment is not enough to protect privacy today because it was written in the Eighteen Century after the American Revolution — long before either the Electronic or Information Revolutions. After all, who could have imagined in the days when information traveled at the speed of a horse or a ship and when it took days or even weeks to find out important news, that information about private citizens would someday be bought and sold in an instant?

In the United States the question might be well posed as to whether or not you have the right to keep your affairs to yourself — the "right to privacy?" The answer is "yes and no." As noted earlier, there is no Constitutional protection of rights to privacy, but the legal system has rallied to interpret many Amendments in a favorable way.

The First Amendment, for example, guarantees the right for a person to associate with whomever they wish. The Third and Fourth protect one from unlawful search and seizures. (These have been significantly weakened as of late) The Fifth defends against self-incrimination. And the Ninth says that the rights enumerated in the Constitution "shall not be construed to deny or disparage others retained by the people." These Amendments have been woven together into a broad tapestry that includes privacy. But what does the term privacy really mean?

There is no single definition of privacy that everyone accepts. According to Justice William O. Douglas, the "right to privacy is older than the Bill of Rights." He made that decision in the case of Griswold v. Connecticut. Douglas said that privacy was protected under the "penumbra" or shadow of other constitutional guarantees.

Earlier, in 1928, Justice Louis Brandeis when referring to privacy said it is the "right to be let alone." A political scientist, Alan Westin, in his book

Privacy and Freedom, said we ought to define privacy as the right of persons to control the distribution of information about themselves. His definition does not have the force of law, but it is a valuable thought. If we use his concept, then privacy is invaded when someone gathers information about you and perhaps makes public what only you should have the right to disclose.

The Crux of the Privacy Problem

The reason "privacy" is such a problematic "right" is that it runs counter to government's interests. An absolute protection of the right to privacy means assassins, criminals, drug dealers, revolutionaries, saboteurs, spies, terrorists and other troublemakers could possibly hatch their plots behind the cover of their right to privacy. As a result the FBI has been pressing the telecommunications industry to help it through the bewildering maze of technological innovations so it can wiretap more easily. The FBI claims to only conduct about 800 wiretaps per year out of 250 million telephone numbers. Of course those are only the "legal" wiretaps. We've recently learned from former U.S. agent's telling tales out of school on a Big-Brother government, that the reported numbers represent only the smallest fraction of the actual wiretaps.

The FBI now claims that their agency, (not to be confused with the National Security Agency (NSA), which spearheads the Echelon satellite eavesdropping project), needs the capacity to intercept 60,000 lines across the country at any given moment in time. According to James X. Dempsey of the Center for National Security Studies, the FBI is actually asking for the ability to tap 1 percent of all the phones in existence. Why? Is this about catching drug-dealers and kidnappers or about citizen control?

Citizen control laws tend to precede significant shifts in dictatorial power, i.e.: Nazi Germany, Soviet Russia, Fundamentalist Iran, etc. The historical list is incredibly long and without exception the people are always worse off after the transition period. This tendency of people to ignore history, and believe that somehow "this time things will be different" brings to mind the famous quotation of Will Durant, co-author with his wife of the eleven volume series *The Story of Civilization,* when he said, "those who ignore history are bound to repeat it." Sobering words we should consider with great gravity.

Barry Steinhardt, associate director of the ACLU, points out that:

> "The problem is that wiretapping is the worst kind of indiscriminate search. The FBI has to intercept thousands of innocent conversations every time they wiretap a suspect. I think it's time for us to reevaluate the use of wiretapping."

The courts will tell you your rights to privacy are not absolute –

governments around the world retain the right to invade it. Each of the 50 states has its own laws on privacy as do the over 200 countries of the world. Well, at least about 25% of them do, the rest still do pretty much as they please. And guess what? Their economies reflect that attitude. The only universal standards of privacy seem to be those inferred from the U.S. Constitution, and those now seem to apply only to government agencies!

The main reason G-7 governments are fighting against rights to privacy is due to their own need for revenue — the blood of their existence. In many places, certainly in America, the government is steadily becoming the adversary to the people. Forty-five federal agencies now have the right to carry guns to enforce their own rules and laws — and we're not talking about state and local police here. Federal fiefdoms are rapidly becoming an enemy to privacy, liberty, and freedom, the very rights the U.S. government was created to protect in the first place.

The problem seems to have begun in 1913 when the U.S. instituted an income tax. Prior to that, excise taxes and other taxes carried the burden. World War I and the huge cash drain it brought to America meant that government needed a greater flow of revenue. The problem with an income tax is how does the government know how much you have earned? It relies for the most part on the honesty of its citizens. But let's face it: people lie, especially when it comes to paying out money they would prefer not to. Knowing that fact about human nature, government took action to pry into the personal financial affairs of its citizens. And pry and pry they did, and pry and pry they do, regardless of whether you are a U.S. person or not. A former Chairman of the Senate Foreign Relations Committee, a U.S. Senator from Idaho sums it up:

> "The marvel of all history is the patience with which men and women submit to burdens unnecessarily laid upon them by their government."

The Dilemma

These are the horns of government's dilemma. On the one point, free governments are instituted to protect citizens and their rights — including the right to privacy. On the other point, governments believe they must violate that privacy in order to get the revenue they need to exist. Given that choice — between your rights and funding your government's expansion — which do you think bureaucrats will choose?

For example, back in the U.S. again, the Fifth Amendment protects against self-incrimination, stating, "No citizen shall be compelled, in any criminal case, to bear witness against himself, nor be deprived of life, liberty or property, without due process of law." But U.S. tax investigators, the U.S. Securities and Exchange Commission and others can seize financial and personal records to be used against one without due process. These vulnerable records include those in the possession of banks, with accountants, investment brokers and others.

Even a person's garbage can be used to testify against an individual. The IRS and other law enforcement agencies are allowed to poke through curbside trash for evidence without a search warrant. The Securities and Exchange Commission can enter your investment advisor's office and rummage through his or her files without a search warrant or the permission of the advisor.

The U.S. government admits to having about 25 files on every American — some have as many as 200. (Some recent authors claim the government has approximately 70 files on every adult in America.) Whatever the number, these files are stored predominantly on computer, and they know a lot about you. It sort-of reminds me of the cold war and the huge efforts the free world put forth so that we would never be subject to the type of information gathering the KGB performed on its citizens.

The Privacy Act of 1974 was intended to protect citizens from federal invasions of privacy. It prohibits agencies from exchanging personal information they have on file. But the Paperwork Reduction Act (1980) had the effect of allowing any agency to have access to personal data any other agency had gathered about you. This makes it possible for their computers to cross check your activities — the IRS checking with banking or the passport office for example. The Computer Safeguards Bill of 1988 set new limits on government's use of computer records, but agencies quickly found new ways to subvert the intentions of this bill. Sorry to say, but if you are an American you are quite simply an easy target.

Violence and Privacy

The world's remaining super power seems to be wasting much of its youth. The U.S. sadly sees too many of its young people destroyed by violence. American children are twelve times more likely to die of violence than children in the rest of the industrialized world. And it is getting worse. From 1950 to 1993, murder rates have tripled and suicide has quadrupled in children younger than 15.

During a three-day anti-money laundering conference I attended in Miami, Florida in 1997, a banking panel from Switzerland was responding to questions from the floor. One of the questions dealt directly with street violence in Europe, a concept virtually unknown to the Swiss. About half of the 400 people in attendance were from U.S. three letter enforcement agencies, the balance of the attendees comprised legal and financial professionals from forty countries. U.S. enforcement spokespersons were disturbed that the Swiss were not enthusiastic about allowing them routine access to the banking records of American's who maintained bank accounts in Switzerland; an act which at that time would cause the Swiss to violate their country's privacy laws. From the Swiss perspective it would seem that whenever the U.S. government wanted confidential financial information from Swiss bankers, they immediately alleged that drug money was involved, whether or not there was any demonstrable evidence of such allegations.

A U.S. law enforcement person speaking from the floor was embarrassingly outspoken in his opinion that citizen rights to privacy were the underpinnings of violent crime. He went on to say that any one who wanted personal privacy had something to hide and it should be assumed that they were conducting some kind of criminal activity. (A sentiment shared by U.S. anti-money laundering trainers sent to all the Caribbean island jurisdictions in late 2000 to teach bank employees about the evils of Americans using offshore banks.) It was quite dramatic when a spokesperson for the Swiss delegation quietly pointed out that there were only five violent crimes that ended in the death of someone in his home city of Geneva, Switzerland during all of 1996. He readily admitted that he did not understand the profusion of violent crime in the U.S. where possibly as many people were killed in the greater Miami area in the past twenty-four hours as for an entire year in Geneva.

You could have heard a pin-drop when he softly made the point that rights to privacy had not spawned violent crime in Switzerland notwithstanding they had supported rights to privacy for the individual for almost 700 years!

Banks Forced to Collaborate

A major invasion of personal and corporate privacy is the enlistment of banks to report on your activities. In my experience you can't open a bank account anywhere in the world any longer without providing extensive information.

Curiously enough, the U.S. is the easiest place in the world to open a bank account notwithstanding U.S. regulator's incredible pressure throughout the year 2000 on offshore jurisdictions forcing them to inaugurate extensive "Know Your Client," "Client Due-Diligence," and "Anti-Money Laundering" policies and procedures. It takes less than fifteen minutes to get a bank account opened in a typical U.S. bank verses about four weeks for a U.S. person to get an account opened offshore.

The "Bank Secrecy Act" of 1970 was actually the U.S. Congress' way to eliminate bank secrecy. Only the government would have the gall to call this a bank secrecy act! Through it, banks are required to store an electronic copy or microfilm reproduction of both the front and back of each check, draft or similar instrument drawn upon it and presented to it for payment. Banks must also keep a record of each check, draft or similar instrument received by it for deposit or collection, together with an identification of the party for whose account it is to be deposited or collected.

Extensive Source of Funds depository information is now required from virtually all world banks and particularly those based in classic tax haven jurisdictions. Although this has not substantially curtailed the use of safe harbours it has made day-to-day operations considerably more difficult for trust companies and private banks.

Transparency laws forced on offshore jurisdictions by G-7 country overlords, that were in turn driven by U.S. regulators and enforcement agencies, have caused incredible problems in many of the traditional safe haven jurisdictions during the year 2000. Some countries such as the Bahamas and Cayman Islands were literally forced by the U.S. to capitulate and pass emergency legislation allowing the U.S. government transparency to their bank's otherwise confidential client information.

Access to bank information in the States was challenged, and wound up in the Supreme Court in U.S. v. Miller. The court upheld the government's right to nose through bank records when it proclaimed, "bank customers whose records are sought by the government — for whatever reason — have no right to (expect) that access is controlled by an existing legal process." That means deposit slips, withdrawal forms and checks are considered to be public domain documents.

So, bank records are routinely subpoenaed — even if they are not directly involved in a case.

If a third party is thought to possess information possibly connected to an investigation, that person's information can be dragged out into the open as well. You can be a completely disinterested and innocent by-stander and have your personal records aired in the open for all to see. The majority of Americans are essentially asleep at the switch on this issue. They do not know, or simply do not understand the implications of these developments, and that their rights to privacy, liberty, and freedom have been gradually slipping away.

Some argue that if they have nothing to hide why does privacy matter. I can assure you that it does matter a great, great deal! My guess is that you close your drapes at night, not because you have anything criminal to hide, but simply because someone looking through your windows may not have honorable intentions. And, to expect that those working for any particular government are somehow more honest than the rest of the world's rank and file is to stick one's head firmly in the sand and deny the truth when it's staring you in the face. Remember, "Power corrupts, absolute power corrupts absolutely."

In theory, even in the U.S. a person has the right to challenge their infamous taxing authority if they attempt to investigate bank records via the authority granted them through the Tax Reform Act of 1976. If you are suspected of a crime, however, you have no right to protest. Now seriously, would the IRS be investigating you if you were not suspected of something? Would you call this cylindrical reasoning? Three years ago the U.S. public was lulled away into complacency when the Congress passed legislation to curb privacy abuses by the IRS, but have these abuses actually stopped? I don't think so...

Private Information Snoops

Governments argue that they have the right to keep tabs on your activities for the sake of domestic security and to prevent tax evasion. But what about commercial snoops, are they entitled to ransack your personal information at will? There are private firms known as "asset locators" whose job it is to find out where your keep your stuff and how much stuff you have. Disgruntled employees or others often employ them with a lawsuit in mind. Crooks, swindlers, competitors, long-lost relatives and others who want what you have can access important confidential information by retaining these investigators.

While waiting in the departure lounge in St. Kitts, West Indies, I met a lawyer who specialized in high profile multi-million dollar divorce cases. He told me that his minimum client retainer was a million dollars. As it turned out we were both flying to San Juan, Puerto Rico, then through Dallas, Texas and then on to our respective destinations. Later, in the Admiral's Club in Puerto Rico, we were to discover that our seat assignment to Dallas was next to one another. So from St Kitts to Puerto Rico, and then on to Dallas we spent many hours together. In the course of conversation, he shared with me that he was presently working on a divorce pre-planning strategy. The husband had no clue that a divorce was pending or that he was the target of a detective agency, which had been collecting the trash every day for almost a year from an entire thirteen-story office building in Los Angeles. All of this effort to find any scrap of paper from one office on one floor that would help lead them to information to use as leverage to put the unsuspecting husband in an indefensible position.

Is that scary or what?

Keeping Confidence

Imagine King Hezekiah's surprise when the prophet Isaiah told him he had cooked his own goose with his tendency to brag. (2 Kings 20:13-17)

King Hezekiah — the Biblical figure who ruled Judah after David and Solomon but before Jesus — committed the cardinal error of revealing his wealth to his enemies. The King of Babylon sent an envoy to visit with Hezekiah because it was common knowledge the old Hebrew king had been ill.

Instead of merely receiving the letters and a gift from the Babylonian king and sending the messenger on his way, Hezekiah "showed him all that was in his storehouses — the silver, the gold, the spices and the fine oil — his armory and everything found among his treasures. There was nothing in his palace or in all his kingdom that Hezekiah did not show them."

When Isaiah the prophet learned that the king had showed this wealth to the envoy from Babylon, he warned Hezekiah: "The time will surely come when everything in your palace, and all that your fathers have stored up until this day, will be carried off to Babylon. Nothing will be left." And that, in fact, is exactly the way it happened.

Wise people from the time of Hezekiah to today have learned from his example: Be careful with whom you share information. Hezekiah's people lost both their wealth and their freedom for the lack of privacy.

Spinello tells us there is a direct link between privacy and freedom: "...those who violate our private space by acquiring confidential information without permission may use it to exercise control over our activities," he warns. "Thus, there is a close relationship between privacy and freedom." We must defend the individual's right to privacy, whether on the battlefield, in the courtroom, or in financial institutions.

Part of the personal defense of freedom-loving people, personal sovereigns if you will, may be to place some or most of their assets outside their home. country, regardless of where they live. Make sure you have something safe, beyond prying eyes and grasping hands. Ultimately, it is the only way to ensure you are able to gain, or retain, a measure of personal privacy and the attendant personal freedom it can provide.

On a personal level there may not be a great deal we can do as individuals to curb government expansion and government abuse, but we would do well to understand the lay of the land and prepare for what inevitably lies ahead, which is the topic of the next chapter.

3

Government Expansion, Government Abuse

"We have from time to time complained about the complexity of our revenue laws and the almost impossible challenge they present to taxpayers or their representatives. Our complaints have obviously fallen upon deaf hears"
Arnold Raum
Senior U.S. Tax Court Judge

Social Planning

Frederic Bastiat, a deep thinking French journalist of the early 1800s warned of the evils of collectivism and the protectionist doctrines forced on legislative bodies by private interest groups. Prior to the publication of the *The Communist Manifesto,* Bastiat was teaching through satire that the requirement of good government was to look far into the future and consider the natural consequences of the special favors, coveted licenses and protectionist policies that virtually all governments provide to an honored few.

Bastiat's most famous work "The Petition" tells the story about candle makers who wanted the government to block out sunlight so consumers would need more candles. Funny, perhaps even silly, but such satire rings true because it illustrates the presumption that all governments ultimately find themselves in the business of selling special privileges. No government is exempt from abuse of power, and in fact, few people vested with political power, and left unto themselves without legitimate oversight, will for long resist the pull to manipulate their position in order to achieve their own personal ends. Another of Bastiat's prophetic pronouncements also has the ring of truth: "Government is the myth whereby half the people try to live off the other half."

Understanding the tendency of human nature to use and abuse power to their own selfish ends, assemblies of American colonists studied in the experiences of history, ultimately put together a document designed to create a government by the people and for the people which should ever maintain careful oversight and authority over those granted limited power under its charter. This work and the dedication of the people committed to it eventually matured into the most powerful political force on earth. Today this amazing document, the Constitution of the United States, has been discarded as a relic of history by many who receive their authority from its law, but all too frequently act as though it places them *above* the law.

This book began with the illustration of a tidal wave and the devastation it can cause and the huge changes it can effect in the lives of those living on the seashore. And yet, were you boating, and out to sea as the tidal wave passed under your hull, you would likely not recognize the life-threatening power moving beneath you. A sea change is sweeping under us today. We are living through the death-throes of over-ripe, and in some cases, corrupted national governments and this has enormous significance in our lives.

No single government is to blame, although some are considerably more guilty than others. There are over 200 countries in the world, half of which do not ensure individual liberty and are sketchy about personal property rights. It is clear why citizens of these countries are quick to access offshore financial services when they have assets at risk. However, the countries we generally think of as free democracies now show serious tendencies towards abuse of the very freedoms they espouse, particularly in the areas of police enforcement, victimless crimes, forfeiture and seizure laws and expanded and abusive taxation schemes. It is in these countries that the great race to offshore financial centers is in full swing.

Victimless Crimes

It may seem foolish, even laughable, but a modern issue that tends to illustrate the power granted to the state is embodied in the question, *"Should police have the power to handcuff and jail people who don't wear seatbelts?"* Stop and think this out to its final conclusion. "If the police have the right to haul you off in handcuffs for not wearing a seatbelt, scan your house at whim with a thermal imaging gun, and set up random roadblocks so dogs can sniff your car for drugs, then victimless crimes will be to blame," says Steve Dasbach, the national director of the American Libertarian Party.

The criminal justice debate going on in many countries is no longer about what is permissible when catching violent criminals like murderers, rapists, and robbers. The debate now is centered on just how far law enforcement can go in violating personal rights to privacy in order to catch people who harm no one but themselves. For example, in order to combat a whole list of personal acts that have no actual victim, police may be entitled to use sting operations, paid informers, anonymous tips, door breaking raids, searches without proper authority, and high-tech surveillance. How far should we go to protect people from themselves? When we act to impose reasonable ideas with police force, have we not destroyed personal liberty? Doesn't freedom encompass the right for a person to be just as wrong as they want to be as long as they are not infringing upon the rights of others?

Law enforcement's inclination is to push the limits of their charter, which in turn puts them in the position of violating citizen's privacy and personal property rights. There are some that say this is the price we pay for an advanced civilization, but this is a false conclusion when viewed in terms of history and in fact almost assures that an enlightened society will be crushed if it allows the "ends to justify the means."

Forfeiture, Another Face of Tyranny

In Roy Timpe's paper on U.S. forfeiture laws entitled *Forfeiture: Another One of the Faces of Tyranny* he begins with the following:

> "What would you say about a set of laws that allowed prosecutors to take the property of innocent people, encouraged law enforcement to act like bounty hunters, and gave public officials control over millions of dollars without requiring a public accounting? That is exactly what we have with our current forfeiture statutes."

There are now so many case studies citing governmental abuse of power that one might logically conclude that this has become a very serious issue, perhaps the most serious political issue now facing civilized people everywhere. Current laws in the United States allow federal and state agencies to seize your assets based only on their opinion of a connection between your property and a crime. Once enforcement agents have probable cause, which can be something so thinly constructed as a statement by someone who holds a grudge against you or a competitor who seeks to destroy your business, government agents can seize your property and you have only 10 days to post a bond equal to 10% of the value of the property seized. If you fail to post the bond the property is gone and you never even get a chance to defend yourself in court.

Assuming you can afford to post a bond in such short order the burden is on you to prove that you didn't know about the purported connection between your property and an alleged crime. In other words, you and your property are deemed guilty immediately and you must then prove your innocence.

The federal government uses seized property to fund expansion of their "War on Drugs" now cleverly renamed the "War on Crime." This quiet renaming of the "War on Drugs" to the "War on Crime" blurs issues and allows for the use of expanded powers granted enforcement agencies to fight the drug trade to now be used in other areas of investigation not intended by initial legislation.

Generating additional funding for policing agencies through seizures generates a huge conflict of interest in law enforcement. Nothing makes this more clear than the U.S. Attorney General's August 1990 memo to all federal prosecutors that cautions that forfeiture income was below budget projections. The memo goes on to say "Every effort must be made to increase forfeiture income during the remaining three months."

The Pittsburgh Press in their investigations of federal forfeitures said that over 80% of the people who loose property to government seizures are never arrested let alone convicted of a crime.

Forfeiture and Seizure Legislation

Police and prosecutors worldwide have been widely reported as describing civil asset forfeiture as the "greatest single weapon in the war against drugs." They claim that it hits criminals where it hurts, "in their pocketbooks." A noble concept if it we could believe it. The theory sounded good on paper and in television sound bites but put in practice the outcome has been something vastly different. What was not considered was the radical restructuring of law enforcement priorities and power. The lure of money and other assets appear to have caused law enforcement agencies to shift their priorities away from apprehending violent criminals and toward the more lucrative pursuits of civil forfeiture.

It has been reported that over 200 forfeiture laws now exist in the U.S. alone whereby enforcement agencies may confiscate private property without having to pay for it, and without even having to arrest anyone, much less prove the property owner guilty of any crime. Those losing property to asset confiscating agencies are rarely the drug lords that forfeiture legislation was designed to combat, rather it is all too often the average citizen that does not have the will or the resources to fight back. Terrified and embarrassed they simply keep their mouth shut rather than endure the social stigma that would inevitably follow were they to aggressively engage a predatory enforcement agency.

The corruption of policing agencies does not stop with the federal government. Under U.S. federal confiscation laws local or state police can seize property even if the seizure is illegal according to state law. If a local police department turns illegally seized assets over to an appropriate federal agency they can then receive back a portion of the seized proceeds even if the forfeiture was in violation of their own state laws. Police departments are able to gain additional funding is this way even if their motivation in going to the feds was only to evade state laws put in place to curb this kind of abuse. The FBI, for example, has set up a commission program to encourage all policing agencies, local, state, federal and international, to seize assets and turn them over to them.

Fifteen years ago civil asset forfeiture was unheard of in the U.S. and in most other countries which respect personal property rights. But many law enforcement agencies fueled with expanded authority to fight the war on drugs have pressed beyond the objectives of protecting their populace and have succumbed to the temptation to literally loot and pillage. The temptation to seize ill-gotten public loot is just too strong. We really should have known this, after all ... "Power corrupts, and absolute power corrupts absolutely."

In a 34-page report released by State Auditor Jim Petro from Ohio, many officers were linked to the disappearance of seized assets. A news clipping summary surrounding this event says: "Actually this is a problem nationwide that so far has received little publicity. It would be hard to estimate how much of the loot obtained through forfeiture and seizure is subject to mysterious disappearance but it is believed to be very large."

According to an Associated Press article, "$145 billion hasn't solved government problems with information systems," and the General Accounting Office ("GAO") is now reporting on massive waste and loss with the seized loot." The GAO has released a 233-page report on government abuse and management ineptness that includes the following: "...significant enhancements to internal controls and property management are still needed...to effectively reduce the vulnerability to theft and misappropriation of seized property..."

In only one of the many federal agencies of the U.S. government, (the Department of Justice), it was discovered that a half billion dollars annually is added to their budgetary income from the proceeds of seized goods taken without due process and without ever having to prove anyone's guilt. It has been estimated that a billion a year is being added to other federal budgets. With untold additional billions coming to rest in state, police, and sheriff department coffers might it be reasonable to assume that some enforcement agencies might be showing dangerous signs of more aggressive behavior in seizing personal property?

The U.S. is now the world's leader in forfeitures and seizures. Like the Mafia and the infamous KGB, some government agents seem to have the will to take what they want, when they want and any intelligent person will think twice before trying to force them to recant.

The Justice department has aggressively exported their seizure activities and spread the process throughout the world in an effort to gain extra funding. Recent reporting on this situation leads us to believe that many asset seizures are not sufficiently accounted for and may be available as almost a slush fund for department heads. How can this be? Simply by offering a portion of the seized funds to the enforcement agency in the country where the assets are taken.

This export process has worked and similar legislation has now been passed in England, Australia, Luxembourg, and numerous other jurisdictions. In fact, the U.S. is insisting that various South American countries must pass forfeiture and seizure legislation or they will not extend to them favorable trading relationships.

Equitable Sharing
In the last few years seizures have become much more commonplace and their appeal may have transformed the criminal justice systems of many

jurisdictions. The major impetus for such a transformation is the enactment of forfeiture laws that allow agencies to keep the lion's share of the assets they confiscate. This financial incentive has caused many agencies to become dependent on seizures to keep budgetary requirements in balance. It also threatens to produce a new kind of police that is self-financing, independent of governmental budgetary oversight and therefore unaccountable.

The concept behind the U.S. Department of Justice's equitable sharing program is that state, local and international law enforcement agencies that assist the United States in securing the forfeiture of assets deserve to share equitably in the fruits of those forfeitures. It has been clearly demonstrated that equitable sharing fosters improved cooperation amongst law enforcement at all levels.

In Australia equitable sharing between the federal government and state governments occurs in very much the same way as the States. In both countries extremes of behavior by police have been encouraged by the incentives created by nefarious freeze order, forfeiture and seizure laws. And, in Canada things may be deteriorating even faster as well meaning Canadians try to keep up with their big brother to the south.

Out of Africa

An Associated Press article in late 2000 dealing with the recent developments in Zimbabwe is exemplary of the expanded seizure laws some countries are proliferating. This particular article told how Zimbabwe was in the process of seizing white-owned farms and giving them to poor blacks.

> "At least 120 white-owned farms will be immediately taken over and given to black peasants who do not own land, the government announced. The farms will be evenly distributed around Zimbabwe, and are part of a government plan to transfer about 1,500 farms, mostly owned by the descendants of British settlers, to landless peasants."

The article goes on: "Critics say President Robert Mugbe is using land seizure to court political support in rural areas at a time when his government is besieged with protests over high taxes and soaring prices."

The Zimbabwe seizures have made international news and the BBC produced a well-documented film on this truly scary scenario but the point may have been lost on most. Whenever a supposedly democratic government starts down the road of seizures in order to generate additional funding or to achieve political gain, the freedom of that people are about to be history.

Probable Cause

Dateline NBC won top honors in the Investigative Reporters and Editors awards a few years back. Dateline received their reward for a television program entitled "Probable Cause," an expose of the misuse of Louisiana's asset forfeiture law. In its investigation, Dateline found evidence of unfair seizures of property and a system that benefited judges overseeing the cases. And though the state has subsequently addressed the problem with new legislation, their exhaustive efforts seem to prove how pervasivethe problem can become if allowed to go unchecked. Dateline can't cover everybody.

In America alone over 200 seizure laws have been passed in the past twenty years, a concept literally unheard of in prior periods. Maybe Justice needs to take her blindfold off, as she seems to be confused over the purpose for seizing private assets. If we could somehow solve our democratic dilemma that she must keep it on, we might make it possible for her to see that rather than becoming the "greatest single weapon in the war against drugs," the real purpose served by these laws is simply profit and the acquisition of goods to support a growing bureaucracy.

A District Attorney Blows the Whistle

David Heilbroner, a former assistant district attorney who now teaches at John Jay College of Criminal Justice in Manhattan, tells of a frightening experience when he was stopped by a forfeiture squad for changing lanes in a rental car without a proper signal. He was carrying $300 in travel money and he knew what they wanted.

> "I have known hundreds of police officers, worked with them daily. Still my hands were trembling and I know that anyone carrying more than a few dollars in cash raises police eyebrows."

In his published works David Heilbroner reports on the corrupting influence forfeiture has on police.

> "Police officers, sheriffs and Drug Enforcement Administration agents have come to rely on asset seizures as a major source of funds. Officials can't directly raise their salaries with forfeited funds, but nothing prevents them from using the money to buy perks and to appropriate seized items for their own use."

In one particular article David Heilbroner closes with a question: "Has the lure of easy gain turned law enforcement officials into dangerous bounty hunters?"

Suffolk County District Attorney Ralph Martin, stated the following to the Boston Globe:

"It is not unusual for us to split the (forfeiture) money at the court house and we take ours and the police take their share with them. That's the way it works."

The Bergen Record, (Hackensack, NJ) printed a front-page story by Michael Moore and Jim Consoli entitled "Seized funds pay for frills - $500,000 for conventions." The story details how New Jersey county prosecutors and the state attorney general spent over $500,000 in seized funds on conventions. Much more money was spent on booze and entertainment than on law enforcement education. The Record reported that less than 1% of a convention tab went for educational programs. It was also reported that golf outings for prosecutors were charged to the tab of Camden Country Democratic Chairman George Norcross. Norcross, who was under investigation by the state attorney general for corruption, was reimbursed out of forfeiture funds that were administered by the prosecutor.

Informants - The FBI

An investigative report released by U.S. Representative John Conyers, Chairman of the House Government Operations Committee in August of 1992 revealed that in the two prior years the U.S. Justice Department spent $28.6 million in finders fees paid to informants for liquidated assets seized as a result of their information. (A similar program, believed to be much larger, is also in play with the U.S. Internal Revenue Service.)

Sixty-five FBI informants were paid more than $100,000 per year for gathering information on assets the agency could seize and sell, about two dozen persons made between $100,000 and $250,000 and eight persons made over $250,000 per year snitching on others. One snitch was paid $780,000 for leads on worthwhile assets to seize.

Justice department informants are rarely typical law-abiding citizen making an honest living. They are frequently criminals with extensive records that bargain their sentences away and get money to boot. Some government agencies routinely trade off convicted sentences in exchange for budget enhancing asset seizures. Stories about agency seizures based on the single testimony of an already known criminal are massive. In many cases no evidence is ever produced other than a single highly questionable statement made by a convicted felon.

Informant testimony may be a necessary evil in order to convict drug traffickers and deal with matters of serious and violent crime. However, even with proper criminal forfeiture procedures, which appear to be thin at best, legitimate corroboration ought be required for paid informants and especially where informants receive reduced sentences in exchange for their testimony.

Informants - The IRS

In conversations with former high-ranking IRS officials it seems that informants, who they refer to as "snitches" routinely receive a 10% commission on seized assets. Unlike FBI informants who are generally out for the money or simply seeking reduced sentencing, IRS snitches generally comprise ex-wives, ex-business associates, or ex-employees. (People who have an ax to grind.)

The IRS informant program is thought to be much larger than the FBI's but no one really knows because the IRS is more cloaked in secrecy than the CIA, according to its former official librarian. Further, in 1998 the U.S. General Accounting Office called the IRS "not auditable for the fourth straight year in a row," so even if we did get information the government accounting office would refuse to validate it. The IRS refuses to reveal their informants in any case for "privacy reasons." Now wouldn't that cause the Founding Fathers to rollover in their graves? The government is supposed to be transparent and responsible to the people, not the other way around.

Informants - The SEC

Informants to the Securities & Exchange Commission are another matter altogether, their informants generally have something to gain much greater than a commission or simple finders fee. For those readers who are familiar with securities markets the term "selling-short" should mean something to you. There are other creative ways to make huge gains by driving a public company's stock down and there are people that have made this their business. This can be a complex and convoluted issue and could easily be a book by itself but suffice it to say that it is my personal belief that the integrity of no agency of the U.S. government is at greater risk of being compromised than that of the SEC. (Yes, even at greater risk than the staff at the Drug Enforcement Agency, whose agents are regularly in the news for playing on both sides of the field.)

The SEC is the defacto controller of the two largest financial markets in the world, The New York Stock Exchange and the Nasdaq Stock Market. If you were to sit down and make a list of all the large companies you know, chances are very high that over 90% of them will be publicly traded companies. The SEC has incredible power to effect individual listed companies and they wield that power with limited external oversight. In fact, most of the hundred or so SEC licensed broker-dealers with whom I've spoken do not believe the SEC has any real oversight whatsoever. SEC oversight is purported to be comprised of five Commissioners, two appointed by the Republican Party, two by the Democrats, and one by the sitting President. However, they may be little more than window-dressing considering they have no authority over SEC staff.

Ever since the SEC was cut-free of direct Congressional authority,

(1933 and 1934), they have steadily moved towards becoming an institution for itself, responsible to itself, whilst assuming ever-greater authority and expanded power so pervasive, and of such magnitude, as to be virtually beyond constraint. Ask any principal of a securities firm and he will whisper that this is so, while carefully looking over his shoulder to make certain no one hears him dare criticize the agency that holds his entire financial livelihood in its hands.

The numbers in the financial markets are huge, certainly much greater than the illicit drug market, and the likelihood that a compromised SEC agent or group of agents might be discovered is minuscule because the SEC protects its personnel from virtually all forms of external examination. Further, the SEC is a steady source of information to the media which keeps them in good stead. Virtually all large media institutions are publicly traded companies anyway and therefore ultimately subject to the SEC. In other words, no reporter would dare attempt to investigate the SEC or the reporter's employer would be toast. A free-lance reporter would be unable to sell an article highly critical of the SEC to a major media house because it would immediately put that media firm in real jeopardy. Add this to the SEC's passion for internal privacy (of course they keep their informant's names confidential) and you have a prescription for massive governmental abuse.

What is to keep an unethical businessperson from suggesting to someone well placed in one of these all-powerful government agencies that they trash his or her competition? One of my colleagues has suggested that if we were in Mexico, the answer is Zorro. Unfortunately, in the U.S. the target of this kind of reprehensible assault has no one who can prevent him from suffering the consequences of an enforcement agency isolating him for investigation.

Forced Settlements

Asset freezes and seizures prior to trial can be accomplished without any actual charges being made against the target. Freeze orders may be used as a bullying tactic to force property owners to settle out of court — even when the government has no case. When a property owner knows that fighting a case all the way to trial will take several years, due to court system backlogs and delaying tactics, a skill well honed by government lawyers, the detention of property pending trial is often enough to force a property owner to strike a deal with the government even if the property owner is absolutely in the right.

Consider the case of the prestigious law firm of Kaye, Sholer, Fierman, Hays & Handler, the firm that defended Lincoln Savings and Loan. When the government sued the firm they simultaneously froze all the firm's assets. Their bank could not honor the check's they had issued, so the law firm could not pay their staff and within one week they were forced to settle without the government ever having to prove anything. Their alternative to settlement was to be immediately forced out of business and lose their entire clientele to scandal.

In British Columbia Canada abuse of power is definitely on the increase. In 1999 the BC Securities Commission, acting at the request of the U.S. Securities & Exchange Commission, froze a private company's funds ostensibly for investigation purposes. The company had never bought or sold a single share of publicly traded securities nor were they in anyway associated with the buying, selling or promoting of securities. The SEC did not file a lawsuit and refused to provide information as to what they were investigating or why they had a need to freeze this company's banking activities. Caught without evidence and having extended themselves beyond their charter, rather than apologize and release the freeze order on the company's account, the BCSC "leaked" completely unsubstantiated and false rumors (provided by the SEC) to the media about the company, thereby frightening away its customers. They then used copies of the news articles they themselves had caused to be printed to justify the need for their freeze order.

Thus we see another company with a perfect credit record and no history of any wrong-doing rendered immediately powerless and forced to watch it's employee's checks bounce, payments for routine bills be returned unpaid, creditors threaten to sue for returned checks, etc. All of this took place without the company or its personnel ever having been officially accused of any wrongdoing. The BCSC destroyed a reputable business and forced them to close their doors all to please agents of the U.S. government who had a grudge against a person they assumed was involved in the Canadian business. Once again we are reminded that, "Power corrupts, absolute power corrupts absolutely."

The belief that any government should be able to seize property prior to trial is reminiscent of the fairy tale "Alice in Wonderland," where the rule you may remember is, "punishment first, trial later."

On April 25, 2000 the Hyde bill became law in the United States, the original version having passed in the House of Representatives with an overwhelming majority of 375 to 48. This compromise bill is designed to contain and limit some forms of seizures, in its current version it is overly weak and legally untried, but it is a start in the right direction.

Abusive Tax Laws

Canada is vying for the top honors in instituting abusive tax laws, but the size and global reach of the U.S. still make it the more frightening of the two. Taxation policies from the U.S. Congress must share the blame for these failings. Because of changes it has made almost every other year for two decades, the tax code is completely out of control. What began in 1913 with a 14-page law and a one-page form, is now so complicated that the nation's 125 million-plus taxpayers spend close to $10 billion a year just to get help preparing their tax returns.

According to Sam Johnson, a U.S. Congressman from Texas:

"The IRS has 480 different tax forms, plus 280 more to explain how to fill out the first 480. The original Tax Code had 11,400 words; today it is 7 million."

The old U.S. tax code is 9,451 pages long, 820 pages of which were added because of 1997's tax legislation. The IRS' simplest form, 1040 EZ, has a 28-page instruction book. Recent changes that took effect in January of 2001 have added hundreds of additional pages to taxation legislation and a whole new host of reporting requirements. One particular bill regarding offshore financial providers entitled "Qualifying Intermediaries" is 244 pages and might as well be written in Sanskrit for all the sense it makes.

According to Fortune Magazine April 13, 1998, "To complete the regular 1040, a taxpayer must spend an average of nearly ten hours. Own a small business? Add another ten hours for the dreaded Schedule C. Have investment income? Get ready for a blizzard of capital gains rates on Schedule D. If you have time to kill, you could settle down with the IRS's roughly 240 other forms."

The Boston Tea Party — one of the first acts of armed opposition to British taxes by the American colonists and the action that ultimately led to outright rebellion against the crown — erupted because of taxation only a tenth as heavy as the tax burden Americans shoulder today. Can it last? Is it even possible to assume that 5,000 years of recorded history to the contrary, the United States will end run the consequences of fiat paper money, bureaucracy bloat, and an exponential growth in the laws and rules that regulate lives?

Those that have watched the explosive growth in seizures under the Clinton Administration are in hopes that the Bush consortium will eventually stop the insanity. It is not likely to come soon. Seizures are entrenched in the bureaucratic system and already have become a mainstay of unregulated, low accountability funding for enforcement agencies of all kinds.

There is plenty of rhetoric to be sure, but government has never, of itself, curbed its own insatiable appetite for spending. Seizures without accountable oversight come dreadfully close to absolute power. Sanity seems to be gone, philosophy takes precedent over reality. Is it any wonder many Canadian, Australians, Europeans and Americans are saying, " Thanks but no thanks!" to big government and are looking for offshore alternatives to protect assets?

Education
With the collapse of Soviet communism, the chances of an all-out

world war have faded dramatically. External violence is receding as a threat throughout most of the developed nations. Of course, internal violence is another matter entirely and seems to be on the increase. Nevertheless, most European countries are cutting back on defense despite the tragedy in the former Yugoslavia. When the Germans closed military bases, they wanted to convert them to schools — the next great battlefield.

Public schools are receiving ever-increasing attention and money in an effort to improve performance. Politicians repeatedly tell us if we'd just give them more money to administer for worthy causes, such as our children's education, that everything will turn out right. Sounds great and wouldn't it be nice if a complex problem were this easy to solve? But taken as a group, politicians are generally inclined to use what I refer to as the Rockefeller solution, "Got a problem, throw money at it." Of course he meant *your* money.

Public education in many countries is now in a shambles partially due to two critical issues consistently ignored and rarely discussed. These twin problems are compulsory attendance and governmental control. Compulsory attendance is the root of many behavioral problems and government control inhibits individual thought and the teaching of truth.

Government schools are designed to support government objectives, which do not necessarily include a well-balanced education. How can a society develop intellectually and assert they are free when everyone is forced to learn the same government approved facts and to conform to the same politically correct thinking? Society would benefit if truth and competitive ideas were taught, and only those who wanted to learn were in the classrooms.

When central governments control the educational process one must expect that school curriculums will be designed to create individuals who support the government's policies and who will conform to its desired behavioral patterns. Throwing more money at institutions that force conformity to central government's policies simply erodes personal liberty that much faster and does little to build clear-thinking individuals. Just imagine what would happen if competitive industry were controlled in this fashion. We know this as communism, and we know it doesn't work.

Most educational systems are so thoroughly controlled and carefully regimented that is it terribly surprising that virtually all the self-made billionaires in the world jumped out of college and hit the bricks before their minds were thoroughly beaten into submission and they had lost the ability to think for themselves? Strange, and maybe even a little weird, but true.

The value and benefits of diversity are great. And who among us has not been carefully instructed in the worth of cultural and ethnic diversity? Then why is it that where diversity is needed most, in the institutions that educate our future leaders, truth is politicized, modified, and all to frequently abandoned, in order to suit the party line and endorse the collectivist agenda of so many educational institutions? Diversity of thought is condemned where that diversity conflicts with those ensconced in the roles of power within the hallowed walls of the educational arena. The ultimate solution is to remove the control of schooling from government agencies and entrenched educational bureaucrats and put it back with a local electorate.

Irrelevant Borders

What we understand as "countries" or "nation states" today are relatively recent in human history — the past 500 years or less. Newcomers as they are, they may already be on their way out the door.

We define a country by its borders and by a single secular authority in charge of the territory and representing it to the rest of the world. National governments have an authority that is superseded by no other body within a given country. But the heart and soul of what makes a country is the power to tax. No matter what you call an area, if it does not have the right to demand money of its citizens and have the power to take it from them if they don't pay, you don't have a country.

For a number of reasons countries are not what they used to be, and that is an important thing to remember when deciding where to put your money. In one of those odd congruities of history, the things that separated countries (communism verses capitalism) largely disappeared at the same time the means to unite them appeared. Contending ideologies that divided the world into hostile camps ceased being an issue in the late 1980s and early 1990s. At that very moment in history, the Internet emerged as a fast, economic way to communicate and do business across borders.

The Internet poses a threat to national governments, as we know them because it facilitates trans-national loyalties and affiliations in a way that governments cannot control. The things that are important these days have a way of ignoring borders. Just ask the Laplanders in northern Scandinavia who could not eat their reindeer meat because a decade after the Chernobyl nuclear power plant meltdowns it was still contaminated with radiation. Or ask the parents of children hooked on cocaine-based drugs imported into the U.S. through any number of holes in the border. Or ask the residents of California, Texas or other border states where illegal aliens have come to roost. The same is true of Germany, the Netherlands, France and England, where immigrants have taken over whole communities.

Yet the main threat to national governments is the loss of their control over money. It is now possible to conduct major transactions across borders using the Internet and offshore banking. And governments are in a weakened position to get a piece of the action with a tax. Taxing is the kind of thing governments are able to do well when goods or people or cash are passing through checkpoints at borders or ports or train stations or airports. But when deals are made for information or for goods already within the jurisdiction, how does government track and tax?

Governments know the handwriting is on the wall. That's why there is so much talk about controlling the exchange of information over the Internet. Of course, when the issue is spun for the public's consumption it will be all about protecting our children and never about the real issue of how to tax and control.

Who Needs It?

Why do we pay taxes? Most people would say because they feel they must. During times of national emergency such as natural disasters or wars, most citizens of any country will acknowledge, if only grudgingly, that a government is necessary to protect them from danger.

But the popularity of Libertarian, Survivalist and other anti-government groups widely considered until very recently at the fringe of society, is merely the tip of the iceberg in the public's apathy toward government. Many mainstream Americans consider themselves "Independent" when it comes to voting because they no longer feel an attachment to the two-party system.

A generation ago, Jimmy Carter called the IRS "a disgrace to the human race." And, the U.S. income tax is held in such low esteem that former Congress' chief tax writer, chairman Bill Archer of the House Ways and Means Committee, believes it should be "torn out by the roots."

By and large, much of what government offers in the way of services are things people can and would just as soon do without — or they would rather have them provided by private industry on a voluntary basis. One reason Europeans have an attitude of indifference toward government is the success they have seen from the recent deregulation of monopoly industries. The telephone companies in particular lost their monopoly status, and notwithstanding the soothsayers, the result has been much lower costs and vastly improved service. Citizens everywhere have made careful note of this result, and many would like to see the same deregulation of other government-provided services, such as Social Insurance and other types of retirement programs, possibly postal systems, prisons and education.

Ever since the U.S. Congress established the withholding tax in the states, the public and some legislators clamored for tax reform. After all federal income tax was instituted to pay for a war and it was supposed to end directly thereafter. From at least one point of view, we have regularly had tax reform, about every four years or so. However, the tax reforms that have survived the legislative quagmire have, without exception, made the system more complex and dramatically increased the costs of compliance. The more complicated the tax structure becomes the more taxpayers complain and seek solutions. And yet complexity is exactly what legislators find so advantageous.

The incredible, almost unknowable intricacy of the U.S. federal tax

system provides a forum upon which professional legislators may pontifi-
cate. They can give speeches about its unfairness and then promise that if
they could just have expanded powers they will provide the needed tax
cuts and make the system more fair. Don't hold your breath. In my experience legislators don't really want to reduce taxes, they only want to talk
about reducing taxes. According to Trent Lott, U.S. Senator:

> "Almost every time we pass a tax bill, we make the code more
> complex, increase the burden on the taxpayer, and make it
> harder to enforce."

In these regards the Washington Post summed up this situation with:

> "The worst thing about (the week before taxes are due) may
> not be the taxes themselves, but the commiserating rhetoric of
> the politicians who, having created the present tax system, will
> spend the next few days deploring it as if it were the handi-
> work of strangers."

On the other hand, President Ronald Reagan did reduce taxes in
fulfillment of his campaign promises. Perhaps George W Bush will follow
through on his campaign commitments and do likewise. If President Bush
is successful it will be good news for the entire world, provided the U.S.
Congress will keep expenses within a reasonable budget — tongue held
firmly in cheek. After all, it isn't taxes that are really the problem it is
government's spending.

Military and Protection

Governments are putting themselves out of business. The main objectives of government should be to implement honorable laws that provide for the protection of each individual's liberty and ensure our personal
property rights. Police and the court systems protect us from criminals at a
local level, and armed forces and the political process are designed to protect us from invasion at a national level. World War is no longer a probable
event. The warfare of the future is emerging in a different form. There is
no Evil Empire likely to stage an all-out attack. But there are a host of
rogue states with the means to develop chemical or germ warfare or to
smuggle a small nuclear device through porous borders. It's still a dangerous world, but dangerous in a different way.

The point is that it is fair for national defense consumers to ask why
money is being spent on multi-billion-dollar, missile-firing nuclear submarines capable of wiping out whole continents, when this particular tool
is inappropriate to meet the threats of the day. Former U.S. president
Dwight D Eisenhower, the famous Commander in Chief of Allied forces
in World War II, warned the populace as he left his presidential office that

they were in constant danger of being manipulated by defense manufacturing industries. A sobering thought. Yes, a strong military held subject to freely elected civil officers is needed, but the billions of dollars spent in black budgets on unknowable and unaccountable projects is a detriment to freedom. How can the government be subject to the people when the people are continually lied to by government agencies, wrapped in the flag, and claiming national security?

Nationality does not have the emotional import it did when there was greater danger of war. There is no moral onus to looking elsewhere, to shopping for the best national domicile. The day is likely coming when governments will compete with each other for their revenue base. Competitive jurisdictions? You bet. The fact that you were born within the territory controlled by one particular country no longer means you must be their lifetime customer. You do have choices.

Shop Around

Computers and the Internet make it possible to do business from practically anywhere in the world. Why, then, operate out of jurisdictions that tax higher than others?

It is possible today for an accounting firm in The Netherlands to handle work for a company in Los Angeles. Through faxes and e-mail and Internet telephony, there may be no particular cost advantage to doing business with the firm down the street. Every professional in the world now has the opportunity to do business from wherever they wish, assuming they have received the coveted licenses from government to represent clients in that area.

Enlightened persons who learn the options and explore the possibilities shop around. Choosing national options is no different than in the U.S. Pacific Northwest where people in Washington State buy goods right across the river in Portland, Oregon to avoid the 8% Washington State sales tax. It's just the marketplace in action. This is why there is already trillions of dollars sequestered in offshore financial centers.

U.S. Taxation

Ironic, is it not, that the United States — which was founded to guarantee freedoms to its citizens — has become an oppressive regime for the sake of gathering taxes.

There was no income tax until 1913, when the government anticipated getting into World War 1 and needed more revenue to pay for the fight. Preparing for war was the rational for the income tax for the rest of the twentieth century. Once government got their grip on the huge sums of money coming in through a federal income tax system, spending spun out of control and over spending became a normal event. In 1916, one man, John D. Rockefeller, could have paid off the entire U.S. national debt.

By 1997, Warren Buffett and Bill Gates combined could not even pay the interest on the U.S. national debt for a period of only two months! The interest on the U.S. national debt for two months approximates $50 billion — yes that's spelled with a "B."

To keep the cash flowing, the U.S. government has chiseled away at the freedom of its own citizens. Huge bureaucracies, like the IRS, FBI, ATF, SEC, NSA, CIA, DEA, and on and on have assumed authority to pry into your personal financial affairs, invade the privacy of your home, record your phone, email and fax communications, seize assets and snoop into every aspect of your lives in the pursuit of money to run a $1.8 trillion dollar government appetite.

A Meeting With The Enemy

It occurs to me off and on that I must be getting paranoid having focused so long on government's abuse of power. After all, good government is critical to us all, and most government employees are just like the rest of us, mostly honest, wanting the best for our families, committed to do what's right, struggling to get ahead. And then a lawyer contacted me for a private offshore consultation. Up until a year prior he had been responsible for prosecuting all the high profile criminal tax evasion cases for a several state area over the preceding fourteen years. My first thought was that perhaps I was not being paranoid enough.

As you might suspect I was understandably apprehensive about his calls. After all, the saying "Trust me I'm from the government and I'm here to help you" is sort of like believing the fox will take good care of the chickens, and I like to think my momma didn't raise no dummies. On the other hand, curiosity finally overcame caution and I agreed to meet on neutral ground in a restaurant where we could visit without interruption. Mr. X, as I will call him, showed up with his former IRS co-worker, a forensic CPA with lots of letters behind her name. We spent several hours exploring one another's experiences and I am pleased to report that this particular tax lawyer and his associate have now come over to the light side of the force. But what I still find remarkable is that after fourteen years of criminal income tax prosecutions he simply had no idea about the real motivations for why people go offshore.

According to these former agents, the IRS teaches staff that the only reason anyone would ever go offshore is for tax evasion. A patently false assumption. Nevertheless the government had such a dismissal record of retrieving assets from offshore in taxation cases that he had sought me out to help him protect his new private practice clientele. (Darth Vader had become Luke Skywalker) I explained to him that hiding assets from the government did not fit my job description after which our visit moved on to telling "war stories" about various business experiences. His stories were truly hair-raising and mine seemed tame in comparison. Both of these former high-level agents confirmed what I had feared for a long time. That the IRS is almost completely arbitrary when deciding against whom they will pursue criminally and against whom they will pursue in a routine civil action.

They shared with me that IRS prosecutors and their staff were carefully trained in bankruptcy law because regardless of whether or not they prevailed in court with a criminal prosecution that in close to 98% of the cases (his quote not mine) their target would be forced into bankruptcy due to the legal expenses and life disruptions forced on the target. He admitted that when the IRS decided to take someone out, the target had little chance of maintaining a reasonable life or financially surviving the government's attack. Perhaps worse is that he readily admitted that many of the people they went after were probably not guilty but that the IRS staff did what they did because they had a job to do and after all they were evaluated on how many people they successfully hammered. Pretty scary!

Social Insurance

In the publication entitled, *Free to Choose* by Milton Freedman (the Nobel Prize-winning economist), he says:

> "Social Security has been promoted through misleading labeling and deceptive advertising. Consider a paragraph that appeared in a Department of Health, Education and Welfare booklet entitled *Your Social Security*: "The basic idea of social security is a simple one: During working years employees, their employers, and self-employed people pay social security contributions which are pooled into special trust funds. When earnings stop or are reduced because the worker retires, becomes disabled, or dies, monthly cash benefits are paid to replace part of the earnings the family has lost." This is Orwellian doublethink. Payroll taxes are labeled 'contributions' or as the Party might have put it in the book 1984, 'Compulsory is Voluntary'."

The bumper sticker craze of the 1980's seems to still be going strong in California, where one popular bumper sticker declares:"I love my country but don't trust my government," which pretty much sums up the feelings of a lot of us, regardless of what country we call home.

Taxes are critical to the smooth operation of government services, however shouldn't there be reduced government and a means of support that does not violate freedom and the individual's right to personal privacy? Why not a point-of-sale modified national sales tax in every country? Paying when you buy would eliminate the need for all those investigative and controlling agencies that want to know all about your private life, your private banking activities, and so forth. Or, perhaps that's the point — citizen control.

By abolishing income tax and disbanding horribly abusive government organizations like the infamous IRS, SEC, EPA, and eviscerating other oppressive secret three-letter agencies, it may be possible to regain our personal liberty. In the meanwhile, it is no surprise that wealth continues to flow to confidential offshore jurisdictions.

4

Free Agency

"We have learned by sad experience that it is the nature and disposition of almost all men, as soon as they get a little authority, as they suppose, they will immediately begin to exercise unrighteous dominion. "

Joseph Smith

The Enemy

Austrian economist Ludwig von Mises (1881-1973) stood in diametric counter position to any and all governments who would restrict the rights of the people. He stated bluntly that civil liberties were impossible under socialism or any other form of collectivist arrangement. Arguing against the intellectuals of his day he presented a persuasive case for free markets and exposed errors in all forms of governmental intrusion on the life's of individuals and the workings of an economy.

Ludwig von Mises observed with stark clarity that:

"... those is charge of the supreme conduct of government affairs, ultimately determine which ideas, teachings, and doctrines can be propagated and which not. Whatever a written and promulgated constitution may say about the freedom of conscience, thought, speech and the press and about neutrality in religious matters must in a socialist leaning country remain a dead letter."

Mises dream for mankind is a powerful statement about how we ought judge the value of any government's contribution to its people:

"The working of the market is not hampered by government interference. There are no trade barriers; men can live and work where they want. Frontiers are drawn on the maps and they do not hinder the migration of men and shipping of commodities. Natives do not enjoy rights that are denied to aliens. Governments and their servants restrict their activities to the protection of life, health, and property against fraudulent or violent aggression. They do not discriminate against foreigners. The courts are independent and effectively protect everybody against the encroachments of officialdom. Everyone is permitted to say, to write, and to print what he likes. Educa-

70

tion is not subject to government interference. Governments are like night watchmen whom the citizens have entrusted with the task of handling the police powers. The men in office are regarded as mortal men, not as superhuman beings or paternal authorities who have the right and duty to hold the people in tutelage."

Free Agency

At its most fundamental level, liberty is about the power of choice. An individual's power to freely choose between outcomes is greater than any right granted by government. It is a fundamental element of life as a human being. This ideal was first broadly set forth in that remarkable document, the Constitution of the United States. Permeating and undergirding its entire framework is the commitment to individual rights and personal liberty. The recognition that every individual has the right to personal liberty is the substance of its core.

One of the most dramatic concepts expressed by ancient prophets and philosophers is the principle of free agency. The ancients argued quite convincingly that "imagination" or "creativity" and its correlative, the "power to choose," was in fact the single thing that separated man from animals. It seems that the incredible ability to imagine an outcome and then to consciously choose that result is only present in humankind. It is the greatest of all our capacities.

The book of Genesis taught that man and woman are God's children. Other parts of the Bible refer to God as "our Father," strongly inferring, or at least conveying the mental image that mankind is literally a part of God's family. (A belief once fervently affirmed, but not much in vogue today.) The extraordinary book of Genesis forms the foundation for both Judaism and Christianity. Contained within its pages is another important notion, a message which suggests that when individuals are able to discern the difference between good and evil and make thoughtful, independent choices between them, they are acting as gods. Sound like heresy?

And God said, Let us make man in our image, after our likeness:"

"So God created man in his own image, in the image of God created he him; male and female created he them."

"For God doth know that in the day ye eat thereof, then your eyes shall be opened, and ye shall be as gods, knowing good and evil."

"And the eyes of them both were opened..."

"And the Lord God said, Behold, the man is become as
one of us, to know good and evil;"

The Power of Choice

Simple observation indicates that we appear to be the only living
things on planet earth that can imagine something clearly in our mind and
then do it. For example, stop reading and look around. If you're indoors
consider that everything in the room in which you now sit was first a
thought in someone's mind. Slow down and rethink that last sentence and
consider this concept through.

Everything created by man is first mentally considered, then a choice
is made, and then it is constructed. What other living creature has imagined and chosen to do something new, something none of their predeces-
sors have done? What has a chipmunk, a whale, a dog, or an ape, done for
this generation of chipmunks, whales, dogs, or apes? They live, and they
have instinctive behavior, but they have been denied the power of true
choice. In order to choose you must be able to imagine the effects of your
choice and actions.

Our ability to imagine multiple outcomes and choose to pursue the
one we feel is best suited to our situation is the basis of true freedom.
There is no greater power on earth. It is the source of all of our accom-
plishment and it is the source of most of our misery. As far back as the
beginning of civilized humankind we observe that thinking man concluded there was no greater gift.

Reviewing the sweep of history, it is fairly clear that personal freedom and true individual rights are a situation found infrequently, anywhere on the globe. The great breakthrough on the subject of personal
liberty was, and still is, the Declaration of Independence and its attendant
document the Constitution of the United States.

The U.S. Constitution

"The U.S. constitution is the most wonderful work ever struck
off at a given time by the brain and purpose of man."
                                                    Gladstone

It does not matter from what country you hail, where you live, or
your particular political persuasion, the fact is that the U.S. Constitution
was a remarkable feat. Those that framed this phenomenal work believed
they had been touched by deity and revered their work with an almost
spiritual awe. The second president of the United States, one who personally participated in the drafting of the Constitution, had this to say about
its construction:

"Our constitution was made only for a moral and religious people. It is wholly inadequate to the government of any other."

Powerful words but today this statement is politically incorrect and at best these words evoke a smug quiet tolerance by the newly enlightened intelligencia. Today a person of education and substance would hardly dare to say such a thing. In the present age many people, perhaps most, no longer seem to believe in the foundational morality they once did. Decisions of law have replaced principles and ethics. But I wonder, do you suppose that the majority of people in the world actually believe that just because something is legal, that it's therefore moral? In our heart of hearts, do we honestly suppose that our ripened and enlightened society is balanced and on the right track?

Evidently the U.S. Congress and the expanding bureaucracy it has spawned no longer deem the Constitution adequate to the government of the people. To see how far the U.S. has traveled from its basic tenants one must look no further than the way Congress itself assesses its value. How much new legislation was passed this year? How many new laws have been enacted which now must be sorted out by litigation to determine what they really mean? How many special concessions have been granted the privileged? How many volumes have been produced on the nuances of any given judge's thinking on legal technicality? How many new rulings, which have the effect of law, have been put in place through essentially secret committees?

Unfortunately these are the details on which the lives of real people hang. The result of incessant tinkering with technicality and favor granting is that there are now approximately fifteen million laws, and rulings that have the effect of law, which have been enacted by Congress and/or the bureaucrats that endeavor to control the lives of both Americans and much of the rest of the world. Oh yes, like it or not, America is now the king of the world, and within the halls of American government they increasingly exercise their influence in exactly the same fashion as any historical potentate.

America is rich and America is powerful and in America one can find anything one wants to buy. But America has lost its way and strayed from the principals upon which it was founded. Simply said, because the first and fundamental principle of the Constitution, and probably human life itself, is the doctrine of free agency — the individual's right to choose.

Each of us ought have the inalienable right to be just as wrong as we want to be, until that right impinges upon the rights of another. Many years ago I recall a teacher telling a classroom of students that "Your rights end where my nose begins." I puzzled over that statement for years to come and still remember the unease with which I grappled with the concept. Rights to personal liberty may be hard to define at times. But like pornography, you know it when you see it.

The great American experiment was based on individual, inalienable rights. It was created from something much finer, and better, than technical debate. James Madison, considered to be the "Father of the Constitution," had this to say:

> "Whatever may be the judgment pronounced on the competency of the architects of the Constitution, or whatever may be the destiny of the edifice prepared by them, I feel it a duty to express my profound and solemn conviction, derived from my intimate opportunity of observing and appreciating the views of the Convention, collectively and individually, that there never was an assembly of men, charged with a great and arduous trust, who were more pure in their motives, or more exclusively or anxiously devoted to the object committed to them, than were the members of the Federal Convention of 1787."

The Constitution of the United States and its predecessor the Declaration of Independence make crystal clear that the most important single function of government is to secure the rights and freedoms of individuals. To think otherwise is to not understand the basic underlying principals on which the framers of this incredible document staked their lives.

Thomas Paine said this:

> "Rights are not gifts from one man to another, nor from one class of men to another.... it is impossible to discover any origin of rights otherwise than in the origin of man; it consequently follows that rights appertain to man in right of his existence, and must therefore be equal to every man."

No conflict should exist between civil order and individual rights. Both concepts are based on the same fundamental principle: that no individual, group, or government should have the right to initiate force against any other individual, group, or government.

Ezra Taft Benson, a fervent constitutionalist and former Secretary of Agriculture to President Eisenhower, made this important observation about personal rights:

> "If we accept the premise that human rights are granted by government, then we must be willing to accept the corollary

that they can be denied by government. The important thing to keep in mind is that the people who have created their government can give to that government only such powers as they, themselves, have in the first place. Obviously, they cannot give that which they do not possess. So the question boils down to this: What powers properly belong to each and every person in the absence of and prior to the establishment of any organized form of government?"

Solid thinking indeed! In the Preamble to the Constitution the great purposes of this inspired document were set out:

"WE THE PEOPLE of the United States, in Order to form a more perfect Union, establish Justice, insure domestic Tranquility, provide for the common defense, promote the general Welfare, and secure the Blessings of Liberty to ourselves and our Posterity, do ordain and establish this CONSTITUTION for the United States of America."

Here the people speak as sovereign. The people declared they were establishing government and that it existed to ensure the blessings of liberty.

J Reuben Clark, Jr., former Under Secretary of State and Ambassador to Mexico, said this about the establishment of the government of the United States:

"Deeply read in history, steeped in the lore of the past in human government, and experienced in the approaches of despotism which they had, themselves, suffered at the hands of George the Third, these patriots, assembled in solemn convention, planned for the establishment of a government that would ensure to them the blessings they described in the Preamble. The people were setting up the government. They were bestowing power. They gave to the government the powers they wished to give. The residuum of power was in them. There was no emperor, no lex regia here."

And in the inspired words of Thomas Jefferson, as found in the Declaration of Independence:

"We hold these truths to be self-evident, that all men are created equal, that they are endowed by their Creator with certain unalienable Rights, that among these are Life, Liberty and the pursuit of Happiness. That to secure these rights, governments are instituted among men, deriving their just powers from the consent of the governed."

A Word About Equality

To say we are born equal does not mean we all come to earth with the same talents and abilities. Such a philosophy flies in the face of prudent observation. We are certainly not born with the same talents. Mozart was born with incredible musical talent. He composed his first symphony at five. Try as I might, and notwithstanding my attempt to appreciate good music, I cannot do likewise. But, the Constitution and the Declaration of Independence did inspire, and endeavor to secure, the equal right for any person to become as unequal as they want to become. This has everything to do with personal self-discipline, a subject much pooh-poohed, by the current intelligencia.

You see, if I really wanted to write a symphony it may not be nearly as good as Mozart's work, but it could be done, were I to make the personal investment in time and goal-directed energy. The decision then is mine, just as it should be. Mature, independent, well-thinking individuals should revel in their personal sovereignty. People are simply superior to governments. People form governments, not the other way around. In the words of Frederic Bastiat:

> "Life, liberty, and property do not exist because men have made laws. On the contrary, it was the fact that life, liberty, and property existed beforehand that caused men to make laws in the first place."

The proper role of government should be restricted to those activities within which any individual citizen has the right to act. Proper government derives its power from the governed. Its responsibility is to protect its citizens from the loss of freedom, physical violence, theft, and other such matters. Ezra T. Benson was right on target when he said:

> "No individual possesses the power to take another's wealth or to force others to do good, so no government has the right to do such things either. The creature cannot exceed the creator."

The German sociologist, Franz Oppenheimer, dramatically presented the ultimate coercive and parasitic nature of the State. He set forth the premise that there were only two means by which man could obtain wealth, and that these two methods were mutually exclusive. The first method was simply production and voluntary exchange. The second method was robbery by the use of violence. He refers to the latter as "political means."

Political means are clearly parasitic, for it requires previous production for the exploiters to confiscate, and it subtracts from, rather than adding to, the total production in society. Oppenheimer goes on to define the State as the "organization of the political means," or "the systematization of the predatory process over a given territorial area."

Is There Meaning?

So what does all this mean? Big governments have decided, and evidently a large number of their citizens agree, that bureaucrats and taxing authorities are better suited to making the majority of our decisions for us. This philosophy requires that the individuals in each political system subjugate their personal rights in exchange for government coddling. No matter how you mask this process, or what you call it, this is collectivism, socialism, or communism, and it always ends with the rights of the individual being usurped by the state. Anyone with an eye to history must know that when we embark upon this road it may look bright in the short run, but just around the corner it will foster suppression and misery.

Are we as individuals encouraging free agency or are we participating in a process that will thwart our futures? If we are not careful we will find ourselves doing exactly what the Germans did prior to World War II and the Russians did immediately after their revolution. Have we not learned that when mankind gives up their rights "for the greater good," it's essentially a lie? Of course it may have some temporary advantages, but in the long run it always ends badly.

The oft-told story of the "frog in the pot" bears repeating because it speaks so loudly of our conditioning. It has been said by those who claim it's true, that if you drop a frog in a pot of boiling water it will immediately bounce out. But, if you place a frog in a pot of cold water and then slowly turn up the heat, the frog will eventually boil to death. Because the heat rose gradually the frog was sapped of the energy to leap from the pot. The rights that many of our forefathers fought to ensure and preserve are rapidly eroding. Are we being gradually conditioned to the point we simply don't have the energy to resist? This seems the right time to use one of my favorite quotes:

> "The freedom and happiness of man...are the sole objects of all legitimate government." "Oppose with manly firmness any invasions on the rights of the people"
>
> Thomas Jefferson

The entire free world seems to be bogged down in legalese and bureaucratic nonsense. In America the Congress has proliferated so many federal agencies that government expansion is exponential. Agency authority continues to grow and a form of totalitarianism is alive and well within the bureaucratic establishment. Although some governmental agencies provide important services they also strip us of our liberty. Most, if not all, of these rapidly expanding fiefdoms encroach on individual rights. Bureaucracy's mission is to regulate and control. And woe be it to the man or woman who stands in their way.

The U.S. federal government has produced forty-five different federal agencies that now have the right to carry guns to enforce their rules and laws — and these numbers do not include such things as state and local police. Federal fiefdoms are rapidly becoming the enemy of the individual, of privacy, liberty, and freedom; the very rights the U.S. government was created to protect in the first place.

There is an ancient prophetic story, said to be written for our day, where a clandestine society of "robbers" organized a network to acquire wealth and to gain control over the people. Eventually they penetrated the highest levels of government, they secured the seat of judges and eventually sealed the fate of freedom. Through their secret societies and covert combinations they gained control because so few were paying any attention. Prosperity was abundant, so why would anyone want to rock the boat?

In the U.S. today, many federal agencies, wielding power the way they do, are simply acting unconstitutionally. The conflict between new legislation and America's foundational document is avoided by the Congress simply refusing to address it.

In what way are some federal agencies unconstitutional? Because they combine powers of the legislative, executive, and judicial branches of government – three branches or segments of the federal government that were designed to always and forever remain independent and equal so as to offset, regulate and act as oversight and balance of the one against the other. This is the essential operational requirement of the Constitution in order to prevent one branch of government from assuming greater control of government and usurping the power of the people. Some agencies:

- Have assumed the power to make rulings, rulings that have the force of law.
- Have assumed the power to enforce their own rulings, a position taken by kings.
- Have assumed the power to penalize when their rulings are violated, a power exercised by dictators.

But no one rocks the boat. To do so would brand one as a radical or as one out of the main stream. Addressing this subject, Ezra Taft Benson states:

"They (federal agencies) are unconstitutional because they represent an assumption of power not delegated to the executive branch by the people. They are also unconstitutional because the people have no power to recall administrative agency personnel by their vote."

"To all who have discerning eyes, it is apparent that the republican form of government established by our noble forefathers cannot long endure once fundamental principles are abandoned. Momentum is gathering for another conflict..."

And again from J. Reuben Clark, Jr:

"... in my opinion, built from observation over the years, when the true history of our detours from constitutional government is written, it will be found that they were largely put in motion...and aided and abetted by certain fellows trying to destroy the right and tradition of the Supreme Court of the United States to declare laws unconstitutional. They are gradually — not too gradually — trying on us all the tricks the Roman Emperors used in order to hold their autocratic power, in an effort to build here a lex regia concept either through a dictator or through a socialized, Sovietized government that will establish the same sort of society."

In the words attributed to John Adams by Daniel Webster, he sums up his commitment to the personal sovereignty of the individual when he says:

"Sink or swim, live or die, survive or perish, I give my hand and my heart to this vote...It is my living sentiment, and by the blessing of God it shall be my dying sentiment. Independence now, and Independence forever."

Ensure your independence. Establish a plan and move some of your resources to safe havens. Assert your self-reliance and defend your liberty.

5

Predatory Litigation

*"...the foundation of the destruction of this people is beginning to be laid by the
unrighteousness of your lawyers and your judges"*

Alma the Younger
Circa 82 BC

For Americans Only

This chapter is directed to residents and citizens of America. Of
course everyone in the western hemisphere is technically an American but
those of you not in the States may just as well skip over this chapter, unless
you live in Puerto Rico, or Guam, (both U.S. territories). Of course Canadians may want to pay attention as recent legislative changes are moving
them closer to the brink of predatory litigation. And there are those in
England and other jurisdictions who are clamoring to copy the dismal
situation that now exists in the U.S. civil judicial system, so you may also
want to pay attention. If you are not American but do business in the
States, or do business with anyone from the States, perhaps you too should
take a moment and read this chapter.

The statistics tell the story:

5% or less of the world's population reside in the U.S.
20% or thereabouts, of the world economy is U.S.
70% of the world's lawyers reside in the U.S.
94% of the world's lawsuits are in the U.S.

Bizarre numbers aren't they? Two questions come to mind: why is
this, and how does it affect us? As to why, I offer two possible answers:
There are too many lawyers, or Americans are simply too greedy. Are there
too many lawyers? Well, in the United States there are over 700,000 practicing lawyers and there are more students in law school than there are in
practice.

What does American greed have to do with lawsuits? In the States
anyone with a gripe can sue anyone else, whether or not there is any real
justification for damages. If the target of a lawsuit just happens to have
easily identifiable wealth, chances are very good the entire litigation process can be pursued on a commission basis. This means that without shell-
ing out any money, a person with a real or imagined gripe against someone *with* money can all to frequently get a law firm to aggressively pursue

litigation for a percentage of the settlement or judgment rendered.

A society with a large quantity of lawyers is oriented towards litigation. Legal confrontation, handled on a contingency or commission basis, is focused on the transferring of wealth through disputes. This is what I call "predatory litigation."

With so many lawyers chasing work, it is no wonder the U.S. is the most litigious society the world has ever seen. All those lawyers seeking revenue means everyone's assets have become a target. Incredibly, in the States if your income is $50,000 per year or greater, you have a one in four chance to be involved in a lawsuit in the coming year.

Q: Why do so many lawyers have broken noses?
A: From running into parked ambulances.

It may be a bad joke, but it illustrates the pressure toward litigation that is natural in a society so professionally weighted toward lawyers. And if it's a bad joke, there are plenty more as bad. Just go on the Internet and search for lawyer jokes. There are thousands listed.

You can pretty much tell where a person — or a society — is conflicted by the object of its jokes. We joke about sex, spouses, money, ethnic groups — and lawyers. I have yet to see a lawyer joke that is not hostile, and perhaps that says more about non-lawyers than it does about lawyers. After all, we're the ones who keep them in business.

Actually it may be a cheap shot to blame lawyers for lawsuits. It could be argued that there would be no prostitutes, for example, were there no johns to patronize them. I agree with Walt Kelly, creator of Pogo Possum, whose cartoon character said: "We have met the enemy and they is us."

Today's society is the problem, lawsuits are the symptom and lawyers are the facilitators. Lawyers are in business because of simple human greed. For a nostalgic treat, rent the 1960's movie "A New Leaf," starring the late Walter Matthau. He plays a spoiled rich guy who squanders his fortune and then can't pay his bills. Matthau's butler advises him to marry, " . . . because marriage is the only way to acquire assets without working." Ah, what naive and simple times those were. Today the quick path to riches is litigation.

Do Americans look for something for nothing more so than other nationalities? Maybe so. After all, most American families originally traveled to the "land of the free and the brave" in search of opportunity — whether it was the chance to operate a hot dog stand in Brooklyn or homestead free farmland in Oklahoma or strike it rich in the gold fields of California — they all went looking for something.

When the free stuff all got taken up with the closing of the American frontier, the get-rich-quick spirit seemed to stay alive through Hollywood, where there was the chance to make it big as a movie star with not much more than a cute figure, good connections, and a flashy smile.

Something-for-nothing is also enshrined in Las Vegas and now dozens of other locations throughout the U.S and the world. In Vegas, even in the airport is the sound of the slot machines plinking out unearned winnings. This city is the Mecca where pilgrims come with hearts full of hope seeking adrenal kick and the fast buck.

I'd like to believe that my mental musings about something-for-nothing is just a negative take on a lousy situation, but a U.S. national survey revealed the following mind-set held by a majority of those supposedly seeking wealth:

A U.S. Belief System?

In 1997 a friend of mine, a Ph.D. in Russian studies with the CIA who now heads up an investment firm, shared with me the results of a U.S. study where those surveyed ranked their opportunities for achieving wealth. The following reveals the unfortunate results:

1. Win the lottery
2. Win a civil lawsuit
3. Receive an inheritance

What does this tell you about the orientation of a growing number of people? What does this say about modern morality, self-reliance, and personal self-discipline?

It takes hard work to develop a business or invest wisely. It takes hard work to build assets and diligently accumulate them into an estate for your own security, your retirement, or as an inheritance for your heirs. Apparently the majority of Americans now believe it's easier to put a buck into a slot, pull the lever and get a cascade of free money. But what's worse is that a majority of people evidently also consider it perfectly acceptable to find a reason to sue someone in order to make their fortune.

Is it really okay to exploit a real or imagined harm, find a lawyer who'll take a suit on commission, and take a shot at getting into the pockets of a successful person who has spent the time to accumulate assets? Unfortunately it is easier and quicker to sue someone than it is to commit oneself to worthwhile goals, hard work, long hours, and ethical conduct.

The Threat To Business

Everyone who has anything is vulnerable. But professionals and business owners, large and small, are prime targets for lawsuits. After all, other than rock stars and athletes, who has more wealth to plunder?

In Africa, Europe, Asia and Latin America, business people are sometimes kidnapped for ransom. The problem is bad and getting worse. International companies with offices in Brazil, Peru, Russia, the Middle East and much of Africa now have visiting executives met by bodyguards to escort them virtually everywhere they go. Multinational companies have discovered that to ignore the hazards of doing business in these areas is to invite problems. But in the U.S. the shakedown comes through lawsuits. Of entrepreneurial companies going public between 1986 and 1993, 62 percent had been sued, according to a survey by the National Venture Capital Association as cited in Investors Business Daily. In that same period of time, 19 of the 30 largest companies in Silicon Valley were hit with lawsuits — totaling half a billion dollars.

"Joint and several liability" or the "deep pockets" approach is an open door for assaults on business assets. Through joint and several liability, if a firm so much as does business with another company that is the target of a lawsuit, it can be dragged in as a defendant to pay damages. It's called the "tort tax," and according to Tillinghast, an insurance consulting unit of Towers Perrin, it cost business owners in America $132.2 billion in 1991 and was estimated to grow by 12 percent per year since 1980.

Some parts of the country are worse than others. Alabama is known to be the best place in the country for plaintiffs seeking damages in product liability cases. Juries there have made some of the highest awards anywhere in the country. The situation is so bad the U.S. Supreme Court in 1996 actually struck down several Alabama laws that required high damage awards and declared them unconstitutional.

Few reasonable people would suggest that companies should not be held liable for defective or dangerous products. But it is also true that product liability lawsuits have stifled entire industries, from breast implants to water slides. For example after paying out billions of dollars in breast implant lawsuits for difficult to define side-effects ranging from mental instability to constantly being tired, medical researchers finally concluded that breast augmentation had no real medical side effects. That hasn't kept lawsuits from being filed or specialized law firms from continuing to gain huge settlements or jury judgments based on the claimant's charge that their lifestyle has been plagued with a whole host of aches and pains.

There have been Congressional efforts to limit punitive damage awards to $250,000 or three times the compensatory damage, whichever is greater. But there are powerful forces at work against such limitations. One obvious reason is that class action lawsuits for product liability amounts to a $250 million per year income for plaintiff's attorneys, plus all the legal fees the defendants must pay their lawyers.

The Future

What's the future of lawsuits in America? There will be a lot more of them if the lawyers have their way. Take California, for example, where practically every tenth person you see is a lawyer. The state has prided itself on being the leader in so many things — and now in lawsuits as well.

Attorneys and their clients have become increasingly creative in their reasons for suing. As a matter of fact, the trial lawyers there were the largest financial backers of a ballot measure that can be seen as a model of what may be in store for the entire country some day.

California lawyers sponsored Prop 211, which did not pass but represents something of a legal "wish list" for the lawyers who specialize litigation on commission.

The ballot measure would have made it even easier for stockholders to sue if they lost money on a stock. "Strike suits" are those that target a company when its stock prices drop. There are people whose sole business directive is to buy stock they think will lose value. Then they sue. And there are law firms who specialize in just this type of lawsuit. One based in San Diego reports that they have secured $22 billion in settlements.

The idea was to protect the savings of retirees by giving them greater power against securities fraud. But the biggest winner would have been the state government and the lawyers. The measure would have allowed "punitive damages" against a defendant found guilty of "willful, outrageous or despicable conduct" in stock manipulation. But the people who lost money in such stock frauds would not benefit, as such awards would have gone to the state! Punitive damages have not been previously allowed as blunder for state or the federal government security suits. If the measure had passed, there is no telling what heights governments may have, or may yet reach with the "punitive damages" concept.

At the federal level the U.S. Securities & Exchange Commission, certainly one of the world's great predators, already has so many ways to seize the assets of anyone unfortunate enough to show up on their radar screen that to give them greater resources to blunder and pillage would be to effectively turn the keys to the economic kingdom over to them. This is an agency, which has become essentially unaccountable to the American people and already has such poor external oversight that even the U.S. Congress can no longer direct its activities. Amazing, as it may seem, I have been legally gagged by this particular federal agency from sharing the story of their complicity in secret combinations, tyranny, and a complete lack of concern for truth.

Numerous government agencies have seized authority not granted or even available to them under the Constitution, and with this power to "catch the guilty," they seize the assets of many innocents, frequently destroying their lives in the process. After all, chasing criminals to add largess to their budgets is hard work, but plundering the naïve is easy pickings.

California also toyed with the idea of allowing plaintiffs to collect 100% of damages from deep-pocket defendants. This means that all expenses of a lawsuit could wind up the liability of someone only marginally involved in any given scenario. Even companies headquartered outside California could be dragged into their lawsuits. Several large accounting firms sponsored a study to learn the consequences of such laws, among their findings:

1. a large increase in legal staffs
2. the huge payoff for frivolous lawsuits would result in the equivalent of a 1.6% increase in California State income tax on business, an estimated $1.5 billion per year from the beginning
3. a large exodus of businesses from California

The estimated job loss was such that almost 300,000 people would lose their employment over the next decade as businesses fled such an oppressive atmosphere. And it's not just companies that would suffer. The loss of business would cost every household in the state as much as $235 per year. Eventually state tax revenues would drop by almost $5 billion over a ten-year period.

The rest of us would be dragged into this lawyer's feast whether we wanted to be or not. The Economic Strategy Institute of Washington, D.C. estimated that such a law in California would cause a drop in U.S. GNP of from $48 billion to $102 billion, and that eventually almost 2 million Americans could lose their jobs.

Whether or not such a law passed in California this time is not the issue; the point is that creative trial lawyers are seeking ever-broadening avenues toward even more lawsuits. And although they may not achieve their goal today or tomorrow, they are going to continue in that direction until they reach the Promised Land of your assets.

More About The Government

The government is into the lawsuit business big-time. Take the experience of James L. Fisher, for example. Since 1972 he had been president of Towson State University and had served on the board of directors of Baltimore Federal Savings & Loan, a solid pillar of the community. But when the S&L failed in 1988, the federal government slapped him with a $32 million lawsuit charging him with gross negligence. He couldn't afford the legal fees of $14,000 per month, so at the age of 61 he spent his time researching his own defense.

"I had read materials, listened to experts, participated in discussions, and attended monthly meetings in good faith," he wrote to the Baltimore Evening Sun. "And so at the age of 61 and after a lifetime laced with volunteer public service, I am disillusioned, my life threatened by an irrational creature of government that may not be checked in time to save me."

For such exposure, most bank directors are paid the princely sum of $2,000 to $6,000 per year — plus a checking account without fees. He's not the only one to suffer under strange, government-sponsored negligence lawsuits.

Lawrence Brown, who appraised real estate for Pacific Savings Bank, was sued for negligence for $28 million by the government. The problem in the case against him was that four of the six alleged negligent appraisals the government claimed were critical to loans made by Pacific were made after the loan proceeds had already been distributed, so they had nothing to do with the decision to lend. Nor was there evidence that Brown had even made the appraisals himself — he died a broken man before he could testify on his own behalf.

I think it is ironic that the government now sues former directors of banks and savings and loans which failed when it was the very same government that created the conditions that undermined their stability. In 1981 the Democratic dominated Congress passed new rules about real estate that made lenders take notice of deals they would have shrugged off in the past. The next year banks were allowed to double the loan size for commercial real estate and to make them on much looser terms.

Savings banks financed considerable new developments across the country in the early 80s. But when Congress overhauled the tax laws in 1986 the real estate market collapsed taking the banks right along with them. The government was always the real culprit.

Facing The Legal Reality

We have a judicial system where a lady spilling coffee on herself after leaving a drive-through restaurant sues because the coffee was hotter than industry standards, and is awarded $2.8 million in damages. Hasn't the American judicial system lost touch with reality? Do you suppose it is safe to assume that much of the judgment was earmarked for the lawyers who dreamed up the suit in the first place?

Typically, a law firm working on a "contingency basis", (the legal term meaning they are working for a cut of the proceeds), collects its expenses directly off the top of settlement or judgment receipts. It then usually takes half of any balance that is left. Contingency resolutions frequently end up with from 75% to 100% of actual receipts, thence comes the conventional wisdom: "In civil litigation, only the lawyers win." The implications of this reality have been so immense that in 1999 and 2000 it was widely reported that individual law firms earned over a billion dollars from legal settlements in those years.

According to U.S. News & World Report, August 24, 1998, in an article entitled "It's a tort world after all," coverage was given to some interesting contingency litigation.

• In a suit over faulty plastic plumbing installed in Sun Belt homes, lawyer George Fleming won a settlement of $170 million in cash, plus costs for reinstalling pipe. From the total award he demanded $108 million in cash, nearly two-thirds of the cash portion of the settlement. (I wonder how that computes on an hourly basis.)

- A Minnesota bank teller, pressed by her employer to take a lie detector test when she was questioned about missing funds, sued for emotional damages and won $60,000.
- A Hindu plaintiff mistakenly bit into a beef burrito and sued claiming he had clearly ordered a bean burrito and suffered emotional damage because beef is forbidden in his religion. (Unearned income from lawsuits evidently is not.)
- A 56 year old Texan got $1.8 million when a dog scared him by darting in front of his bicycle, his wife got another $50,000 for loss of household help, companionship, and sexual affection.
- The New York subways are a prime target for contingency litigation with lawyers winning between $40 to $50 million a year.
- One couple sued for $10 million for injuries received when they were hit by a train while having sex on the tracks of the New York subway.
- In another case, one homeless man on heroin and another who had a bottle of wine for breakfast loitered on the tracks and got $13 million for having got burned by the third rail. (They got another $9,000 for loss of income as squeegee men washing car windshields at corner stop lights.)
- A New York drunk lost an arm when he fell in front of an oncoming train and got $3.6 million.
- An Illinois woman whose late husband, an immigrant from Korea, climbed down onto the New York subway tracks and urinated directly on the third rail, thus electrocuting himself. She was awarded $1.5 million because there were no signs in Korean warning against such behavior.
- A fleeing mugger was shot after trying to rob a 71-year-old man and was awarded $4.3 million.
- Recently a woman sued charging that her dog was killed by a neighbor's secondhand smoke. — What do you think? Is the American judicial system on the right track?

Given an out-of-control tort system where judges bend over backwards to help plaintiff's lawyers reach deep pockets, and in which the plaintiffs' bar is able to frustrate tort reform by purchasing decisive political influence through campaign contributions, what is your recourse?

If you have anything or have accomplished anything or have served anywhere — from a school board to a Little League — you may be the object of a lawsuit and your assets may be seized.

Conclusion

Most lawsuits get settled out of court, but you still have to pay an attorney and often large sums in "walking away money." It's common knowledge among professional "suers" that most people and companies will pay what equates to a "ransom" just to make the suit go away. And you would likely do it too. Because once a case comes before the court, especially if it is submitted to a jury, you have no idea what the outcome will be. Your assets are literally dangling in the wind.

One of life's most unpleasant experiences is receiving legal service. This is especially true if you pride yourself on personal honesty and integrity. You must now live with the stress and uneasiness of having litigation pending against you. It works on you; it disrupts your life, it interrupts your social relationships, it puts a cloud over your activities for the foreseeable future. And, you must deal with this, all the time knowing that the outcome is uncertain. Even if the litigation is frivolous, it will be vexatious. And there is always the chance that the presiding judge or jury might not agree with your view of matters.

U.S. juries tend to give awards to those they consider financially less fortunate, particularly if they are attractive or present themselves well. This appears to have more to do with whom jurors identify as opposed to any form of reasonableness. If a Plaintiff's lawyer were to paint you as one who has "deep pockets" that may be all it takes for you to find yourself with a legal judgment to pay.

In my opinion the U.S. legal system is no longer about discovering truth, it's very much more about who presents the best case and, all too frequently, who the jury feels can afford to lose the most. As a result of this reality, and other pressures that may be unique to your situation, such as your status in the community, the risk of a "finding" of negligence and how that effects your professional career or business, the anticipated trial tactics that may expose your personal history, business secrets or confidential family matters, you will surely find yourself under huge pressure to settle.

Is anyone surprised that it's the upward middle class and the wealthy that get sued? People who do not have readily available resources to seize, or are considered "judgment proof" rarely find themselves a target of predatory litigation, unless they have insurance coverage. It's simple economics. If lawyers don't believe you've got access to a large pool of assets, their primary negotiating leverage is gone. (Not to mention their anticipated paycheck.)

Lawsuits — perhaps the fear of them as much as the reality — are one very good reason to move a portion of your assets to a safe haven.

6

The Offshore Evolution

"Where possible, all business should be domiciled offshore in a tax-haven jurisdiction. This is particularly important for Websites and Internet addresses, where there is virtually no advantage in locating in an on-shore, high-tax jurisdiction."

Lord William Rees-Mogg

The Tax Haven

As long as there has been money, people have wondered how to keep it. The more money, the more urgent seemed the question.

The concept of offshore banking is as old as commerce. The Island of Delos off the coast of Greece was one of the places the wealthy of ancient times stored their treasures. Protected by water, with few natural resources other than a descent harbor, the leaders of the island learned that the rich of the mainland would pay handsomely to know that their valuables were safe and protected.

Delos set the pattern for financial havens. For the most part, they are tiny island nations with limited natural resources located near a major, thriving economic center. But there is more to it than that today. A tax haven or offshore financial center is often within a country — such as the state of Nevada within the U.S. Paradoxically, countries that are insensitive to their own citizens' need for protection and tax shelter sometimes become havens for the over-taxed and under protected of other countries. The United States is a prime example of this oddity.

How It Begins

A good example of how and why a tax haven nation, now known as an offshore financial center (OFC) is developed is the Bahamas Islands. In the early 1960s this string of sandy atolls near Florida still flew the British Union Jack. Centuries ago, many ships plying her waters sported the Jolly Roger. The coves and sheltered beaches were a paradise for pirates, who creamed the flow of wealth from the galleons of the Spanish Main. For centuries these islands have been a sleepy backwater — beautiful to be sure, but primitive and undeveloped.

Despite its beauty and comfort, the Bahamas repelled would-be investors with its high-tax philosophy. The result was a net outflow of capital from the islands. This fledgling country eventually determined that were they to survive and prosper changes must be made. Their leaders realized the Bahamas would never reach their potential unless they reversed the flow of wealth out of the islands. At first they enacted exchange control laws — almost always a bad idea, but the first knee-jerk response of economically unsophisticated politicians. Eventually they looked at other options and decided that if their own laws drove money from their country, might they be able to tap into the out-flow of wealth from other, more prosperous nations if they changed their own laws?

The Bahamas instituted a two-tier tax system. There would be one set of laws for the citizens of their country, and another for foreigners. At the same time, the islands clamped the lid on any information leaking out about the financial dealings of those with money in their country. They introduced bank privacy laws.

The response was almost immediate. Americans and Canadians seized the opportunity to shield assets from prying eyes — and groping hands. The fact that the islands are a beautiful vacation getaway made investing there all the more attractive. A new synergism evolved — the wealthy invested money there and then came to visit their money. Tourism soared as the rank and file clamored to visit the vacation spots of the rich. Progressive banking laws coupled with a penchant for confidentiality earned the Bahamas an excellent reputation as an offshore financial center. Today tourism accounts for well over half the total annual revenues in the Bahamas followed in second place by bank service fees!

A Growth Business

Jealousy is a powerful motivator. Other nations saw the prosperity the Bahamas had earned as an offshore banking center and wanted their share. Like the ancient island-banking center of Delos, these havens tend to be near large economies where citizens' rights are on the decrease and government spending is on the increase. Near the U.S. and Canada, for example, are Antigua, the Bahamas, Belize, Bermuda, British Virgin Islands, the Cayman Islands, Dominica, St. Kitts & Nevis, the Turks and Caicos, Grenada, St Lucia, and others. All of these tax haven nations, which as we've already learned are now called Offshore or International Financial Centers, are of rather recent date.

Frequently bank accounts in offshore jurisdictions are held in the name of a trust or an international business corporation, (IBC), which has been formed and is managed from one of the more tax friendly jurisdictions. The IBC designation in an offshore jurisdiction indicates that the ownership of the corporation is foreign to that country and generally speaking has been granted government guarantees that it may operate tax free so long as it's business revenue does not come from within that country.

Government estimates indicate the formation of approximately 140,000 IBC's during a one-year period (1999) for the Caribbean region alone. In my experience from providing consultation services to a number of trust companies located in offshore jurisdictions, one can estimate that about 80% of these companies immediately opened bank accounts, 11%

tied offshore credit cards to these accounts, and 14% of these new companies opened investment accounts with a brokerage firm from which to manage surplus company funds. As to the average amounts of cash flowing through these companies I could only guess and probably guess badly simply because the information is considered highly confidential. However government estimates for the total funds administered offshore are set forth below.

Near Great Britain are the Channel Islands — Jersey, Guernsey and Sark along with the Isle of Man, all OFCs. Some of the largest financial institutions in the world are located in these smallish, out-of-the-way islands.

Within Europe are the long-time havens of Austria, Switzerland, Liechtenstein, and Luxembourg. And in more recent years Europe has gained Bulgaria, Ireland, and Hungary as new havens for wealth. In the Mediterranean are Gibraltar, (also part of Europe), and Malta. Not to be outdone, the Middle East now have a collection of tax haven jurisdictions of their own. The island nation of Mauritius in the Indian Ocean, along with the Seychelles, serve as havens for Africa and the Indian subcontinent.

In the Far East, Hong Kong built itself into a financial center with its liberal corporate and banking laws. In 1996, over 15,000 new IBC's were formed in Hong Kong alone and pundits to the contrary this business continued to grow right through 2000, notwithstanding this jurisdiction is now under the control of mainland China. The Philippines and Singapore have passed new laws to attract offshore money. These centers tend to serve the citizens of such countries as Japan and Korea.

Australia and New Zealand persons tend to use the Cook Islands, Marshall Islands, Vanuatu, Nauru, Western Samoa, and the Marianas, as their havens of choice although Australians are increasingly accessing services from the Caribbean.

Oddly enough, some of the very countries whose citizens place their wealth offshore are themselves tax havens for citizens of other countries. Both England and the United States draw vast sums of money from foreigners because they offer tax advantages to foreigners that are not available to their own citizens.

Evolution Of The Tax Haven

Walter Diamond could be called the godfather of the offshore world. His offshore career began at the start of World War II when he was asked to help liquidate German, Italian and Japanese banks while serving as National Bank Examiner. It was then that he realized what little information existed for U.S. investors to assess foreign taxes.

Mr. Diamond has not only witnessed the incredible growth of tax havens, he has actively recorded and put them into perspective in a three-volume work entitled *Tax Havens of the World*. He began this labor of love in 1974. Co-authored with his wife Dorothy, the two energetic octogenarians are now responsible for quarterly updates covering more than 70 jurisdictions.

The reason that such knowledge became essential was due in no small measure to the fact that the top U.S. marginal tax rate had risen to 90% between 1930 and World War II, motivating American individuals and businesses alike to seek tax relief offshore.

It wasn't until the early 1960s however, that the U.S. government took serious steps to address tax avoidance. As well as reducing the top marginal tax rate from 90 to 70% during the Kennedy administration, other steps were taken to stem the flow of money moving offshore. The "no holds barred" Gordon Report produced for the Internal Revenue Service posted severe sanctions against offshore centers which "refused to tell all to Uncle Sam," and was the beginning of a long series of attacks against tax havens. This was followed by the Gallagher Report, sponsored by the Bank of England, which made recommendations to the five tax havens, all of which were British Territories, on what must be done to recapture their financial legitimacy.

Something over a decade ago, *Offshore Investment Magazine* described 21 places an international investor should know about. In their latest update of *Tax Havens,* Walter and Dorothy Diamond outline more than 70 OFCs in detail.

While the list of tax havens has tripled in eleven years, so have the products and services available. Vehicles such as the asset protection, purpose, charitable, spendthrift, debenture and protective and unit trust, protected cell company, the offshore mutual fund, international business company and personal foundations are much more prevalent as are free trade, export and processing zones in a number of offshore jurisdictions around the world. There has also been a raft of new products such as limited liability companies, banking units, captive and re-insurance company charters and hybrid companies as well as permutations of existing structures to perform new, more complex duties.

A clear indication of the speed at which the use of offshore jurisdictions has grown is the amount of funds now residing offshore. In 1989 it was estimated that less than $500 billion was deposited in offshore funds compared with $5.2 trillion ten years later. As was noted in the Organization for Economic Cooperation and Development's (OECD) 1998 harmful tax competition report, a five-fold increase was sited between 1985 and 1994 to more than $200 billion flowing to tax havens in the Caribbean and South Pacific alone, "a rate of increase well in excess of the growth of total outbound foreign direct investment."

The $500 billion figure released by the International Monetary Fund in 1989 included $100 billion invested by members of the shipping industry, who were among the original users of offshore jurisdictions. They did it not so much for risk protection, but more to take advantage of lower wages and operating costs. Captive insurance companies accounted for

$50 billion while foreign trusts held approximately $200 billion. The balance resided in direct investment, corporations and offshore bank accounts.

Today the ratios are somewhat different but all sectors have exhibited incredible growth. Of the estimated $5.3 trillion offshore today, more than $2 trillion is retained in trusts, of which the fastest growing segment is asset protection trusts, as high-net worth individuals rush to counter the threat of litigation-happy lawyers and their jack-pot hopeful clients.

U.S. Crime Verses Tax Avoidance

Offshore shipping interests have grown 500% to $500 billion while the industry has been decimated in the United States, with the exception of cruise ships. Captive insurance has also grown five-fold, accounting for $250 billion in premiums and $500 billion in assets. (See Chapter 17 to learn how an independent business owner or professional may utilize this incredible resource.) Bank deposits now sit at $750 billion, although total onshore and offshore bank deposits have exploded to $1.5 trillion. Walter figures that a good portion of the $5.3 trillion invested in offshore funds is invested in an estimated $5 trillion of global mutual funds around the world.

There is little doubt that offshore centers have been the victims of their own success by way of the attention garnered from their high-tax big brothers. Growing offshore use poses a threat to growing onshore tax-happy governments and cuts into tax revenues. As a result there has been increased efforts to stem the free movement of capital out of the clutches of the tax collector. Here is a summary of the attacks against offshore centers by the industrialized nations in the last few years.

In April 1998 the OECD produced a report entitled *Harmful Tax Competition: An Emerging Global Issue*, which crystallized the attack on offshore centers. Previously denounced more or less unofficially by high-tax nations as conduits for money laundering and tax evasion, the report signaled the beginning of a more formal attack on offshore centers. The report laid out a set of 19 recommendations made to stop what it deemed to be harmful tax competition.

The father of the OECD's harmful tax competition initiative, Mario Monte, was also instrumental in developing the Draft Code of Conduct on Business Taxation, which sought to include tax avoidance within tax evasion. In fact, high-tax governments looking for scapegoats have mounted a carefully orchestrated media campaign against offshore centers that combine tax avoidance (which is legal) with tax evasion and money laundering.

Cases involving the use of the Bank of New York and offshore banks by Russian criminals to launder billions of dollars and suspected tax evasion by U.S. citizens facilitated through Guardian Bank and Trust in the Cayman Islands were effectively used by onshore authorities to drive these charges home.

This report made it clear that high-tax nations were changing the rules of international commerce. Now, their goal would be to target nations that offered low tax rates and bank secrecy as ways of attracting investment.

This campaign was in addition to the vast efforts being exerted by the US, G7, EU and OECD to reduce money laundering around the world. Led by the Financial Crimes Enforcement Network (FinCEN) formed as part of the US Treasury and the Financial Action Task Force (FATF) created by the G7, both in 1990, nations were targeted that were considered to have ineffective legislation to battle money laundering. At the top of their list of undesirable practices is bank secrecy.

Little more than a year after publication of the OECD's harmful tax competition initiative, the first shot was fired in the name-to-shame game by rich nations. It came in the form of a report issued in late May by the Financial Stability Forum (FSF), a group of financial regulators established by the G7 after the Asian crisis in 1998 to study methods of reducing global financial volatility.

Offshore financial centers were broken down into three groups based on the their legal infrastructures, levels of financial supervision and cooperation (with the powers that be) to combat the money laundering threat. **Group I** nations were those with supervisory practices and levels of cooperation that placed them in good stead with rich nations. They were Hong Kong, Luxembourg, Singapore, and Switzerland.

Dublin (Ireland), Guernsey, Isle of Man, and Jersey were also included in this category, though continuing efforts to improve the quality of supervision and co-operation were encouraged.

Group II jurisdictions were judged to be in the middle of the pack with regards to legislation and supervision. They were Andorra, Bahrain, Barbados, Bermuda, Gibraltar, Labuan (Malaysia), Macau, Malta, and Monaco.

Group III were the 25 OFCs judged to have the lowest levels of legislation, supervision and cooperation. They were Anguilla, Antigua and Barbuda, Aruba, Belize, British Virgin Islands, Cayman Islands, Cook Islands, Costa Rica, Cyprus, Lebanon, Liechtenstein, Marshall Islands, Mauritius, Nauru, Netherlands Antilles, Niue, Panama, St. Kitts and Nevis, St. Lucia, St. Vincent and the Grenadines, Samoa, Seychelles, The Bahamas, Turks and Caicos, and Vanuatu.

The report, although critical, was nonetheless polite and made no threats of future sanctions against transgressors who did not make attempts at amends. This good will from the G7 was to be short-lived.

The next array was fired with a report published by the Financial Action Task Force (FATF) on June 22, 2000 entitled *Review to Identify Non-Cooperative Countries or Territories: Increasing the Worldwide Effectiveness of Anti-Money Laundering Measures.* The report named a total of 26 jurisdictions that had been examined for money laundering measures of which 15 were determined to be non-cooperative.

They were Bahamas, Cayman Islands, Cook Islands, Dominica, Israel, Lebanon, Liechtenstein, Marshall Islands, Nauru, Niue, Panama, Philippines, Russia, St. Kitts and Nevis and finally St. Vincent and the Grenadines.

According to the report, a number of issues arose during the review process, which "raised questions of interpretation." These included the following items to which the Forum took offence including:

- Practices that allowed intermediaries to introduce business to banks where the obligation to 'know the client' was with the intermediary and not the bank,
- Difficulties in determining beneficial ownership of some legal entities including companies issuing bearer shares and trusts,
- The existence of IBCs that can be formed by intermediaries and subject to fewer verification and disclosure requirements than other companies.

The FATF recommended that financial institutions should give special attention to business relations and transactions with persons, including companies and financial institutions, from the "non-cooperative countries and territories" mentioned.

Then, as promised, the much-awaited OECD report entitled *Towards Global Cooperation - Progress in Identifying and Eliminating Harmful Tax Practices* was published on June 26, 2000. It named those nations engaged in what it believed to be "harmful tax competition" as defined one year earlier in the April treatise. There is no doubt that this document was intended to intimidate tax havens into compliance with the wishes of the high-tax big boys.

It began by naming member nations engaged in "harmful tax practices." Those listed by category were:

Insurance
Australia - Offshore Banking Units
Belgium - Co-ordination Centres
Finland - Åland Captive Insurance Regime
Italy - Trieste Financial Services and Insurance Centre
Ireland - International Financial Services Centre
Portugal - Madeira International Business Centre
Luxembourg - Provisions for Fluctuations in Re-Insurance Companies
Sweden - Foreign Non-life Insurance Companies

Financing and Leasing
Belgium - Co-ordination Centres
Hungary - Venture Capital Companies
Hungary - Preferential Regime for Companies Operating Abroad
Iceland - International Trading Companies

Ireland – International Financial Services Centre
Ireland – Shannon Airport Zone
Italy – Trieste Financial Services and Insurance Centre
Luxembourg – Finance Branch
Netherlands – Risk Reserves for International Group Financing
Netherlands – Intra-group Finance Activities
Netherlands – Finance Branch
Spain – Basque Country and Navarra Co-ordination Centres
Switzerland – Administrative Companies

Fund Managers
Greece – Mutual Funds/Portfolio Investment Companies
Ireland – International Financial Services Centre [Taxation of Fund Managers]
Luxembourg – Management companies [that manage only one mutual fund (1929 holdings)]
Portugal – Madeira International Business Centre [Taxation of Fund Managers]

Banking
Australia – Offshore Banking Units
Canada – International Banking Centres
Ireland – International Financial Services Centre
Italy – Trieste Financial Services and Insurance Centre 8
Korea – Offshore Activities of Foreign Exchange Banks
Portugal – External Branches in the Madeira International Business Centre
Turkey – Istanbul Offshore Banking Regime

Headquarters regimes
Belgium – Co-ordination Centres
France – Headquarters Centres
Germany – Monitoring and Coordinating Offices
Greece – Offices of Foreign Companies
Netherlands – Cost-plus Ruling
Portugal – Madeira International Business Centre
Spain – Basque Country and Navarra Co-ordination Centres
Switzerland – Administrative Companies
Switzerland – Service Companies

Distribution Centre Regimes
Belgium – Distribution Centres
France – Logistics Centres
Netherlands – Cost-plus/Resale Minus Ruling
Turkey – Turkish Free Zones

Service - Centre Regimes
Belgium - Service Centres
Netherlands - Cost-plus Ruling

Shipping
Canada - International Shipping
Germany - International Shipping
Greece - Shipping Offices
Greece - Shipping Regime (Law 27/75)
Italy - International Shipping
Netherlands - International Shipping
Norway - International Shipping
Portugal - International Shipping Register of Madeira

Miscellaneous Activities
Belgium - Ruling on Informal Capital
Belgium - Ruling on Foreign Sales Corporation Activities
Canada - Non-resident Owned Investment Corporations
Netherlands - Ruling on Informal Capital
Netherlands - Ruling on Foreign Sales Corporation Activities
United States - Foreign Sales Corporations.

More importantly, the report went on to name 36 "non-cooperative" tax havens, all of which were non-member nations for engaging in 'harmful tax competition.' The list comprised:

Andorra
Anguilla
Antigua and Barbuda
Aruba
Bahrain
Barbados
Belize
British Virgin Islands
Cook Islands
Dominica
Gibraltar
Grenada
The Channel Islands of Guernsey/
  Sark/Alderney/Isle of Man/Jersey
Liberia
Liechtenstein
Maldives
Marshall Islands

Monaco
Montserrat
Nauru
Netherlands Antilles
Niue
Panama
Samoa
Seychelles
St Lucia
St. Christopher & Nevis
St. Vincent and the Grenadines
Tonga
Turks & Caicos
US Virgin Islands
Vanuatu

In efforts to avoid inclusion, six nations gave advance notice that they would comply with OECD recommendations. They were Bermuda, the Caymans, Cyprus, Mauritius, Malta and San Marino. All six sent basically identical letters to the OECD pledging compliance. Austria also agreed to cancel issuing Sparbuch pass holder accounts (anonymous numbered accounts) to avoid being included. At time of writing, at least four more were expected to tender commitment letters agreeing to 'play ball' with the OECD, with the Bahamas at the top of the list.

These lists have been used by high-tax nations to issue advisories against institutions in non-cooperative nations as a tactic to pressure them into compliance. U.S. Treasury first issued advisories against the 15 nations named in the list issued by the FATF. A similar advisory was placed on Antigua and Barbuda last year, which, from the US Treasury standpoint, rendered the desired result. That nation agreed to enhance money-laundering legislation to the satisfaction of the US.

Other G7 members of Canada and Japan followed with banking advisories and Germany announced similar moves to follow.

This move by the U.S. was only the first in a series of measures designed to pressure offshore centers to comply. Other moves will follow. Under the Clinton-Gore Administration additional legislation was being considered and possibly sanctions, targeting banks and countries that fail to kowtow to the demands of the FATF in the money laundering battle. It is interesting to note how closely together these reports were published. Not only does this strategy have the effect of concentrating pressure, it has served to further blur the line between tax avoidance and money laundering.

It remains to be seen whether the Bush Administration will pursue these measures with the same self-righteous zeal but early indicators are that things may improve. According to Robert Bauman, former U.S. Congressman, he believes that the Bush administration will pull back from the Clinton-Gore's move towards greater central control and the reduction of citizens rights to conduct their affairs as they see fit. A partial quote from Bauman sets forth his opinion quite clearly:

"...probably means the death or major disfigurement of that horrendous Clinton plan to give the U.S. Treasury Secretary power to cut off foreign nations from the American banking system."

A U.S. organization known as the Center for Freedom and Prosperity (www.freedomandprosperity.com) is challenging the OECD by launching the "Coalition for Tax Competition." This group champions competitive international markets including the rights of low tax and no tax haven nations. It will work with governments, financial institutions, multinational businesses and individuals to fight the OECD's phony "harmful tax competition" scheme.

While there has been plenty of warning that wealthy nations were on the warpath against offshore financial centers, OFCs have been painfully slow in mounting a counter-offensive. This is due in part to the competition that exists between them and the vain hope that the threats of action by their rich brethren would not be followed through.

In fact the speed with which first six OFCs gave in to OECD demands demonstrates that there was no plan put in place by tax havens to deal with this eventuality as a group. It would seem clear that they have taken the approach of each fending for itself. This is indeed unfortunate since the opposition is very organized and judging from recent efforts, quite determined. However, they are learning and are now making efforts as a group to counter pressure from high-tax nations.

In the *Jewish World Review* (Dec 27, 2000) Walter Williams, a syndicated columnist and conservative economist who regularly takes the helm of the Rush Limbaugh radio talk show (the number one talk show in the world) was quoted as follows:

> "The Organization for Economic Cooperation & Development (OECD)...released a report...that should worry us all. In OECD's view, harmful tax competition is when a nation has taxes so low that saving and investment is lured away from high-taxed OECD countries. The OECD demands that nations as diverse as Panama, Liberia, and Bahrain — as well as offshore financial centers in the Caribbean and the Pacific end their harmful tax practices. In the OECD's view it is bad when Canadians move to the United States to escape high taxes or when a Frenchman invests his money overseas in order to avoid high taxes. The bottom-line agenda for the OECD is to establish a tax cartel where nations get together and collude on taxes."

Dr. Daniel Mitchell, a senior fellow at the Washington-based Heritage Foundation, along with Andrew Quinlan, a former senior staff member of the Joint Economic Committee of Congress, have co-founded the Center for Freedom and Prosperity. The center's first mission is to publicize and attack OECD's anti-taxpayer agenda. They argue that the "harmful tax competition" lament of OECD is really the welfare state talking.

Walter Williams ends his paper with these chilling words:

> "You don't have to be an economist or rocket scientist to

know that when there are attempts to eliminate competition of any sort, including tax competition, watch out and man the barricades."

The OECD has deferred the publication of an official "blacklist" of tax haven jurisdictions regarded as having harmfully competitive regimes. It is possible that this deferral has been prompted by strong criticism from the powerful Business and Industry Advisory Committee to the OECD. The advisory committee has stated its view that:

1. Tax competition is a healthy phenomenon, and
2. It is unwarranted taxation by governments, rather than competition between them, which is harmful.

For its part, the OECD has indicated that the deferral of the official blacklist is to facilitate the co-operation of the offshore jurisdictions, so that they might avoid being named on the list of uncooperative tax havens.
    According to Quinn Sutton, an offshore consultant with the firm Morgan Carter & Young,

"As traditional financial centers are changing their laws, business is shifting to other jurisdictions. Many of these jurisdictions have been placed on the potential OECD black-list. Interestingly, this blacklist has served as "free advertising" for these jurisdictions and they appear to be experiencing increased business activity as a result."

Let's hope that those in positions of authority in the "tax haven" jurisdictions consider carefully the impact of their decisions. To simply cave-in to a U.S. led effort to destroy offshore financial services will correspondingly destroy the booming business activity spawned in these typically small island jurisdictions and potentially ruin their economies. Being on the "blacklist" is not necessarily a bad thing and countries with courage may end up collecting a huge surge of new business.

The Money Laundering Attack– Victory at Any Price?

According to Walter, the U.S. Treasury Department now estimates that global annual money laundering activities have been cut in half from the original $500 billion estimate put forward in the mid 1990s (although one would never know it judging by recent media attention on the topic.)
    It is interesting to note that the latest official U.S. estimate still puts the amount laundered every year around the world at roughly $500 billion, which is 2.5% of the size of the global economy (GDP). If the U.S. Treasury is claiming to have made progress against money laundering, why

is it keeping the new estimate such a secret?

The vast majority of the money laundered today is alleged to be accomplished through global wire systems and based on the amount of money moving daily. Exactly what portion of the funds wired are laundered funds? According to 1999 figures in *Economist* magazine, more than $1,740 trillion is wired globally every year. There is more than $740 trillion wired through the U.S. alone annually. A figure of $500 billion (using earlier money laundering figures) represents less than 1% of the money wired around the world annually. And, if Walter Diamond is correct in his quote from the U.S. Treasury, the amount is only half that or less than one half of 1%.

According to Robert Bauman only 932 people were convicted of money laundering in the U.S. in 1998, despite the cost to the private and public sectors estimated to exceed $10 billion. This works out to an average of more than $10 million per conviction! One has to wonder if the high price we all pay for this shotgun approach is worth it, especially when one considers that the dollar cost does not take into account the assault on the financial privacy of all citizens.

Offshore Investor – What Does It Mean?

High-tax nations have made it clear that they will not sit idly by while tax havens attract investment through generous tax incentives.

Bearer shares, IBCs, trusts, limited liability companies, foundations and the myriad of other entities granting preferential tax treatment to income earned internationally by non-resident individuals and companies are at some risk. So is any arrangement that depends on secrecy. From the point of view of the offshore investor, those who utilize these structures directly should be actively looking for alternatives, as there is an increased chance of scrutiny by onshore authorities.

Now, more than ever, arrangements need to have economic purpose other than simply saving taxes to survive scrutiny and even this may not protect those conducting business in nations that remain blacklisted.

As one commentator noted, this attack is not about going after the single investor or millionaire who moves offshore in an attempt to avoid paying taxes, although this practice will be rendered more difficult. It is an attempt by the U.S. and other nations to curtail the activity of multinationals in reducing tax burdens by shifting income to lower tax jurisdictions also known as tax sheltering. Advisories and sanctions against nations offering such benefits will make it more costly and time consuming for companies to accomplish this feat, albeit at the expense of third world economies.

It is no secret that the U.S. Treasury is on the war path against corporate tax shelters and will go to extreme measures to stop them. It and government spin doctors have cleverly used recent money laundering cases as the catalyst to attack bank secrecy in foreign jurisdictions and initiate money laundering legislation. They have put increasing pressure on offshore centers, even though far more money laundering is accomplished through Miami, London, New York or Los Angeles than probably all of the offshore island jurisdictions combined. But then that would cause legislators to admit to their own internal problems, and it is much easier and politically astute to "blame" the problem on smaller island nations that have no real way to defend themselves in the U.S. media.

The U.S. Money Laundering Act of 1999 made it illegal in the States to launder criminally derived proceeds through foreign banks. It granted additional authority to U.S. agencies to investigate and prosecute foreigners laundering funds through U.S. And it provides U.S. district courts with jurisdiction over foreign banks that violate U.S. laws and American federal prosecutors greater access to foreign business records located in jurisdictions that maintain bank secrecy laws.

What does this accomplish? It provides U.S. courts with greater powers to go after those breaking U.S. laws and chase taxes abroad. It also challenges the ability of anyone deemed to be a lawbreaker to protection under foreign secrecy laws. This is an important step in breaking down corporate tax shelters, many of which rely on subsidiaries or arms-length entities located offshore. Under existing money laundering legislation, actual or suspected tax evasion is a money laundering offense.

It is estimated by the U.S. Congress that by abolishing a broad range of corporate tax shelters, Treasury would raise more than $7 billion in taxes over the next five years. To put this in perspective, using Robert Bauman's calculations, this means that it will cost the public and private sectors $50 billion to collect $7 billion over the same time frame.

One of the troublesome shelters to Congress is the avoidance of taxes enjoyed by insurance companies legally offering "offshore captives" through low or no tax havens such as Bermuda, the British Virgin Islands, Turks & Caicos, Caymans, and Grenada. But for the present this is a viable option and the insurance lobby in the U.S. Congress is very strong, so I do not expect to see this option closed out in the near future.

How else will offshore centers compete if they cannot offer tax advantages to foreigners? This seems to be of little concern to the rich economies that have their own problems coping with the costs of aging populations and burgeoning bureaucracies with armies of civil servants and politicians awaiting generous taxpayer-supported pensions.

The fact that pressuring OFCs to change taxation policy is not legal under international law is of little consequence if the courts are presided over by judges predominantly from OECD nations.

The good news is that the left-leaning Democrats who were fond of using the wealthy as scapegoats have been replaced in Washington along with Clinton appointee, Lawrence Summers, Secretary of the U.S. Treasury.

Summer's replacement, Paul O'Neill, along with George W. Bush and his Republican administration do not share the Democrats zeal for supporting the also left-leaning OECD in its campaign to eliminate tax competition. If anything the Bush administration is expected to support tax competition, which is good news for the offshore investor and businessperson.

Challenges to Implementing Initiatives by High Tax Nations

It is one thing to make a wish list of practices that the OECD and other agencies of the industrialized nations would like abolished but it is quite another matter having that list fulfilled. Without the support of the U.S., this high-tax crusade is made even more difficult.

The OECD has named more than 60 practices utilized by member nations, which it would like abolished. Many are important to attracting new investment to these nations. Each will be defended vigorously by the nation offering them. It is difficult to imagine how these nations will ever agree to abolish a significant number of these incentives. How can they expect OFCs to do what they are unable or unwilling do themselves?

Another major challenge facing these initiatives is the fact that most of the jurisdictions named are poor compared to the U.S. and have relied on tax incentives to attract investment to their shores. In many cases this has been done with the support and blessing of high tax nations.

For example, during the Thatcher and Major regimes in the U.K., British dependencies were encouraged to diversify and enlarge their offshore industries to reduce the need for assistance from the home country. As recently as the mid 1990s, the U.K. contributed more than US$3 million to help Anguilla develop its ACORN computer system to allow online registration of offshore companies. This system has now been identified as a point of concern with the OECD.

Information technology not only encourages the money to flow more quickly and easily to jurisdictions with the least resistance, it is an absolute necessity. In this new economic spirit Robert Mundell was elected the Nobel laureate in economics in 1999, and thereby rewarded for his time-proven theory that high taxes and big governments only contribute to economic malaise. Governments responding positively to this challenge will emerge the winners in the new economy while those who insist on draconian tactics to intimidate and threaten will ultimately be left behind. Nations with oppressive regulatory and tax regimes continue to experience an exodus of capital to more friendly domiciles. The harmful tax competition initiative will not magically reverse this tendency.

The proposed unification of international taxation also proved troublesome. Even the EU nations have found it difficult to agree on taxes. The Directive on Taxation and Savings introducing a 20% withholding tax for European nations has hit a roadblock as the U.K. fights to resist, lest London lose its enviable status in the Eurobond market. Such a tax would surely cause a mass exodus of funds to the very nations the OECD seeks to reprimand. It appears that the best these nations will be able to agree on is greater transparency regarding bank deposits. While the matter has yet to be finally settled, the U.K. remains resolute in its opposition to the tax.

It also appears likely that the OECD harmful tax competition initiative may violate international law. Under the UN Economic, Social and Cultural Rights Covenant.

> "All peoples have the right to self-determination. By virtue of that right they freely determine their political status and freely pursue their economic, social and cultural development."

States cannot unilaterally impose their tax policies on third states. The authors of the OECD tax initiative have simply substituted the word "competitive" for the word "harmful." Competition in international business is deemed to be necessary and healthy. In the recent anti-trust case against Microsoft in the U.S., the court ruled that the company could no longer engage in tactics designed to eliminate the competition. Is the OECD harmful tax initiative not simply attempting to accomplish exactly what the U.S. condemned Microsoft for doing?

The UN is concerned that by targeting money laundering and tax avoidance together and by tarring all offshore centers with the same brush they risk drastically reducing the effectiveness of anti-money laundering initiatives. Nations that have adopted effective anti-money laundering legislation are being lumped together with those that have done nothing, effectively punishing them for the positive steps they have taken. Such an approach endangers the effectiveness of efforts directed at international crime, which is why the UN wants to separate the two, preferring to deal with tax issues separately.

However, the heavy-handed approach of the European Union (EU) and OECD has also been challenged by the UN, which proposed instead to develop a "white list" to encourage nations to comply. But more importantly, it aimed to segregate serious money laundering crimes from tax issues, concerned that lumping the two together will make the already onerous task of reducing crime impossible.

The Pot Calling the Kettle Black

While OECD member nations claim foul play against small island jurisdictions because they are havens from punitive high tax locales, many of these same nations have serious tax haven characteristics themselves. For example, U.S. banks have been paying tax-free interest to non U.S. persons and legal entities since 1921. U.S. laws providing for this kind of tax shelter cannot be changed without dramatic consequences to the entire U.S. economy.

In 1966 a regulatory change was attempted for ultimate implementation in 1972. However, it was twice postponed. Eventually the exemption was made a permanent feature of the revenue code. Exemption from U.S. capital gains tax (other than on real estate transactions) is also afforded non-U.S. persons or legal entities.

The impact of these tax shelter options for non-US persons is such that the U.S. is almost certainly the largest tax shelter nation in the world.

Another inherent problem with both EU and OECD initiatives is the glaring biased and unilateral nature of the attack. Other than Luxembourg and Switzerland, offshore centers are not represented in either group. The approach is patently unjust and will surely be challenged in international courts. A UN initiative separating the widely diverse issues of money laundering and taxes at least provides offshore centers an equitable international forum, as opposed to one dominated by wealthy industrial nations.

The Privacy Defense

Arguments that citizens have a right to privacy in financial affairs will fall on deaf ears of governments where tax avoidance is involved. Yes, citizens do have a right to privacy but that right ends where taxes are concerned, at least with cooperating OECD nations. However, as long as criminal acts including tax evasion are not being committed, rights to financial privacy and confidentiality are increasingly in demand, but not being provided onshore.

The recent adoption of legislation mandating tax evasion a crime in Bermuda is clear indication of this trend. The nation is somewhat unique in this regard in that it possesses a vibrant insurance industry and is aggressively promoting e-commerce. This is evidenced by the new e-commerce legislation and construction of the new multimillion-dollar Cable and Wireless telecommunications hub to attract global companies doing business on the web.

Other Overseas Dependent Territories such as Cayman, the British Virgin Islands, Turks and Caicos and Anguilla will not be so eager to adopt tax-evasion legislation, as they have much more to lose. The same holds true for the Netherlands Antilles. However, at the end of the day they may be forced to choose between maintaining a link with the mother country and independence. In this regard, at least, independent countries such as the Antigua, the Bahamas, St. Kitts and Nevis, Dominica, Grenada, St. Vincent and the new offshore haven of St. Lucia have the advantage. They can be more resistant to cooperating with foreign tax authorities if they agree to do their parts to reduce non-tax-related money laundering offenses.

Tax fraud is also being addressed by the offshore centers. The trend to cooperation with foreign tax authorities will continue to increase if recent negotiations between the U.S. and the Caymans, the Bahamas and Bermuda are any indication. For example, the US relies on taxation for 92% of government revenues. The remaining 8% is the result of administration fees. Cayman relies on indirect taxes for 87% of its revenue with the remaining 13% coming from administration fees. Both countries lose if their respective economies are reduced through tax fraud and are equally motivated to cooperate on reducing it. This explains why Cayman recently agreed to drop the fiscal exemption clause in its Proceeds of Criminal Conduct Law, which effectively allows such cooperation. However, the Caymans have not gone so far as to declare tax evasion a crime as is the case in Bermuda but this move may not be very far away. Tax avoidance in one country may be tax evasion in another due to a difference in tax laws. There is no short-term solution to this problem. Allowing a free exchange of tax information between high and low-tax nations would surely under-mine the economies of the latter and there is no easy solution to this challenge. However, with unrelenting pressure from the U.S. and OECD, such an exchange may one day be a fact.

The matter of financial privacy is also a long way from being re-solved. Citizens in the U.S. and elsewhere are realizing that they have no right to privacy in financial affairs. This is one strong motivator for utiliz-ing banks and corporations offshore. Nations promising to protect this precious commodity will reap the benefits of private and corporate invest-ments from those who do not require tax treaties to conduct business. For this reason, complete transparency between independent offshore jurisdic-tions and OECD nations is unrealistic, certainly in the near-term.

Multinational corporations require confidentiality for many of the same reasons as do individuals and a valid reason for operating offshore is to reduce tax compliance and reporting costs. They are still required to report to the IRS, Inland Revenue, or their counterpart for international operations that touch high-tax shores. Those headquartered offshore how-ever, limit this exposure to onshore subsidiaries.

Of equal importance is the protection of commercial confidentiality in such areas as proprietary software, intellectual property and technical data from the competition. This danger has steadily increased onshore with the growth of predatory legislation in the US whereby a company simply has to charge another with theft of intellectual property to be given free access to such technology in the courts. A free exchange of information between offshore operations and onshore creditors is of little interest to these companies.

The rapid acceptance of Mutual Legal Assistance Treaties by Canada, the United Kingdom and the United States with many offshore jurisdic-tions, particularly in the British Isles and Caribbean providing an exchange of information on money-laundering, fraud and criminal activities have so far avoided tax matters. An agreement among nations to abolish what they deem harmful tax competition is also a long way off, based on the failure of negotiations among European Union members for a 20% withholding tax.

Another surprising turn of events has been the entry of five Ameri-can states (Montana, Colorado, Delaware, Alaska and South Dakota) into the offshore arena offering services such as trusts and offshore banking to foreign investors.

It is extremely unrealistic for rich nations to pull the financial rug out from under offshore financial centers without offering them viable alternatives to replace those industries that it has sentenced to purgatory. So far no alternatives have been announced or even suggested.

Are wealthy nations prepared to reinstate aid to these nations to replace the income lost by the reduction of offshore services industries? Believe it or not the answer may be a qualified yes, at least for the first year; that is, if we're to believe the offer rumored to have been made to the Bahamas as inducement for them to comply with U.S. driven objectives. Let's hope that other jurisdictions are not enamored with this poisoned-bait as the net result will almost certainly destroy their foreign investment, international trade, cripple tourism, and ultimately their future potential for economic growth.

Emerging evidence suggests that a carefully orchestrated campaign linking money laundering and tax issues together could ultimately backfire on the U.S. led OECD.

Onshore high-tax nations have two choices in the competition for investment with offshore centers. They can reduce spending and the size of government, thereby reducing taxes to keep investment dollars at home, or they can resist this movement and instead adopt draconian legislation and attack the competition. It is obvious which tack they have decided to take. Dracula is alive and well.

Bloated unresponsive bureaucracies slowed by labor protectionist policies prevalent in many onshore nations are an anachronism to the emergence of the new e-commerce model. In the new millennium, businesses and governments alike will be compelled to adapt quickly and efficiently if they are to survive. As top-heavy pyramid corporate styles are besieged by new efficient computer savvy management team paradigms, inefficient, expensive and ponderous governments will find it increasingly more difficult to find acceptance with tax-weary voters who themselves are being forced to change with the times.

Global Commerce

Walter Diamond is cautiously optimistic about the future of offshore centers. His comments at a recent conference of The Offshore Institute say it all:

"As an economist accustomed to tracking capital outflows for nearly 50 years, it is my firm conclusion that as goes the world economy, so goes the offshore world, no matter whether direct or indirect investment, which includes servicing income, money or other assets transferred."

An examination of projected world growth for the next decade reveals much about the potential future of offshore jurisdictions. While there are challenges facing all nations and issues to be settled between high and low tax governments, no one can deny the benefits that all will enjoy as goods and materials move across continents and oceans with greater ease and speed. The Internet is allowing such transactions to occur more simply and inexpensively.

It is expected that the funds residing offshore will surpass the $6 trillion mark towards 2010. This assessment underestimates the growth of international investment and stock trading made possible electronically from anywhere in the world, including offshore. It is challenging indeed to estimate the effect in dollar value that this will have on capital flows, even in the face of efforts by various governments to stifle this activity. Short of erecting physical and electronic walls to curtail this movement, it will continue to expand.

Success enjoyed by offshore centers will increasingly depend on the extent that they are able to participate in the electronic revolution sweeping the globe. The Internet is freeing investors, businesspeople and entrepreneurs to conduct business from anywhere they wish, and doing so offshore offers many benefits.

Efforts by industrialized bureaucracies to tighten the tax net have been viewed by many libertarians as a last gasp attempt to assert their punitive political will on capital flows. But ultimately, top-heavy governments are doomed to fall in line and become more efficient and customer friendly.

Offshore financial centers, like the rest of the world, are undergoing tremendous change. The recent attacks from high-tax governments are not new and will continue as long as they are seen as a threat to tax revenues. Tax collectors would have us believe that investing or conducting business offshore is illegal, but nothing could be further from the truth. Granted, OFCs have been used by the unscrupulous for illegal activity, but no more so than in the industrialized nations.

A Russian Experiment

Sometimes becoming a tax haven is a tool of manipulation and control. Take the Russian republic of Ingushetia, for example. This tiny area is adjacent to the breakaway republic of Chechnya, which for years has been the scene of a bloody war of independence. Fearful that rebellion could spread to other Muslim-populated areas such as Ingushetia, Moscow took a bold step.

In 1994, Russia granted the tiny republic "offshore" status within the Russian Federation. And according to *The Economist* (March 1996), it shall become a tax haven to the rest of the world. The benefits are obvious. The new Hotel Assa, in the capital Nazran, is sumptuous, looking over an artificial lake. Germans have built a new airport. And a new capital named

"Sun City" is under construction. It's the old concept of the carrot and the stick. The Russians have battered their Chechnyan minority to force them into submission and keep them within the fold. But more effective in pacifying the natives has been the wealth that has come to Ingushetia as a new tax haven.

Why England

England has become the mother country to a host of tax havens, and for very good reasons. Remember the Falklands War? Argentina invaded and occupied a barren and insignificant string of British islands off its own coast in 1982.

Many other countries might have decided it was not worth fighting over and negotiated some face-saving way to exit the scene. But not the Brits. They dispatched an entire fleet — complete with nuclear weapons — and were prepared to obliterate Argentina if need be to defend their sovereignty.

Why is any of this important? Because it demonstrates that any British possession or protectorate is going to remain British until hell freezes over. And that determination breeds a great deal of confidence. That's why many of the countries offering the best asset protection are former British colonies. These Commonwealth countries have enough independence to form their own business and tax laws, yet retain an aura of security through their affiliation with Great Britain.

The Sovereign Individual

In January 1997 a book entitled *The Sovereign Individual* was released. Written by Lord William Rees-Mogg and James Dale Davidson, it forecasts the pending collapse of the dominant systems in our society. They seem dead serious in their conclusions and amazingly lucid with their arguments. Lord William Rees-Mogg is a financial adviser to some of the world's wealthiest investors. He is a director of J Rothschild Investments, General Electric, PLC, and the M&G Group, the largest unit trust (mutual fund) in the U.K. He was formerly the editor of the Times London and vice chairman of the British Broadcasting Corporation. Davidson has equally impressive credentials. He comments:

"Citizenship is obsolete. To optimize your lifetime earnings and become a Sovereign Individual, you will need to become a customer of a government or protection service rather than a citizen. Instead of paying whatever tax burden is imposed upon you by grasping politicians, you must place yourself in a position to negotiate a private tax treaty that obliges you to pay no more for services of government than they are actually worth to you."

In Conclusion

The offshore business is so lucrative that countries compete with each other for it. Like any other competition, newcomers must offer advantages the old guard does not. New IBC, privacy, trust, and banking laws are being passed in nation states all around the globe, as jurisdictions line up to serve the citizenry of those disgusted with the bloat of bureaucracy, evidenced particularly in the U.S., Canada, Italy, and other European countries.

Two decades ago there were few offshore financial centers and their use was surrounded by myths of drug money and other illicit activities. There were few professionals specialized in offshore practice and these were generally focused on only one or two jurisdictions. Today the offshore industry has developed into a major global business, spanning all quarters of the world, involving, in one way or another, approximately half of the world's financial transactions by value.

Forty-seven of the world's top fifty banks are either located or have substantial business presence offshore. So are most of the world's largest companies. To ignore the benefits the offshore world has to offer would be financial suicide for these corporations.

By the same token it is essential that the offshore investor, entrepreneur and businessperson develop a thorough understanding of the strengths and weaknesses of various offshore centers as places to conduct their business. For serious offshore investors it may be preferable to utilize a number of jurisdictions each for various purposes. For example, one legal structure could be used for international banking, one for domiciling the business, and one for investing capital.

Those who take the time to research the incentives and benefits offshore centers have to offer will be rewarded with an international business strategy that will pay handsome dividends well into the future while insulating participants from regional market upheavals and economic malaise.

About Money

III

7

The Origins of Money

"All substance is energy in motion. It lives and flows. Money is symbolically a golden, flowing stream of concretized vital energy."

The Artist's Way
Julia Cameron and Mark Bryan

Introduction

The next three chapters deal specifically with money, where it came from, what it is based upon, and how it made the transition from commodities to paper, and eventually, on to numbers stored in computer systems. The reader might rationally ask the question as to why this information is important to one who is interested in moving business activities or other assets offshore. And the simple answer is that you may want to skip the next two or three chapters and move on, particularly if you are the impatient type.

However, if you will take the time to work through this summary of pertinent historical lore, I believe strongly that by the time you finish chapters 7, 8, and 9, which comprise all of Section III, you will be amazed at how much you've learned. I'm also convinced that you'll be shocked at how little you really knew about these important subjects and glad you've gained new insights that may be applied in your life. If you decide to skip ahead at least take the time to read the third chapter in this section, Chapter 9, entitled "Money & The Fed." I guarantee it will be worth your time.

Mysterious Origins

The very origins of money remain clouded in mystery and controversy. How did it come to be? The commonly held position is that money arose as a system to replace barter. While barter is a straightforward way to do business, it is problematic in its purest form. How many fish should my ax be worth, and how do I divide my ax into smaller denominations in exchange for a small fish? But did the cumbersome nature of early barter lead directly to currency, or did the whole process come about for some other, more subtle reason?

Glyn Davies, the Welsh author of *A History of Money From Ancient Times to the Present Day,* takes the position that economic factors were not the most important in the development of money. He writes:

"Archeological, literary and linguistic evidence of the ancient world and the tangible evidence of actual types of primitive money ... demonstrate that barter was not the main factor in the origins and earliest development of money."

Instead of money for commerce, Davies theorizes that an organized money form developed out of a need for some form of compensation for the victims of crimes of violence. He suggests that payment with a currency seemed preferable to "an eye for an eye, and a tooth for a tooth." (Would you call this blood money?)

He goes on to say that the verb *to pay* stems from the Latin *pacare,* which means to pacify, appease or make peace with, by means of the appropriate unit of value customarily accepted by both sides. He also theorizes that money came about to pay for a wife. The head of the family had to be compensated, Davies speculates, for the loss of services performed by the daughter.

The use of money seems to have evolved out of deeply rooted customs. The clumsiness of barter provided an economic impulse but that does not seem to have been the primary factor. If it is true, that money arises from impulses far removed from the mere desire to do business, then perhaps there are other motives fueling the development of money, motives that are crucial to understanding its future.

Money appears to be anything that is widely used for making payments, and accounting for debts and credits. Tradition and current definition tell us that money is a unit of accounting, a common measure of value, a medium of exchange, a means of making payment, a standard for deferred payments, and a store of value.

In a larger sense, though, money has an even greater function.

Money Is Power

Regardless of the initial motive for its development, money is an instrument of national prestige and power. The nation with the most highly respected and efficient monetary system will likely be the dominant force of its day.

This was true from the most ancient times, and coins were the best propaganda weapon available for advertising Greek, Roman or any other civilization before mechanical printing was invented. An example might be the coin issued by Philip of Macedonia, on which he celebrates his triumphant chariot race in the Olympic games of 356 BC.

But prestige is merely the fragrance of power. Money was and continues to be a weapon of national domination. In coinage as in other matters, the Greek city-states strived desperately for predominance, as did their archrivals, the Persian emperors.

When Philip's son, Alexander the Great, succeeded in vanquishing the Persians, he quickly put an end to one aspect of that rivalry by eliminating Persian currency and establishing uniformity over much of the known world with Greek money. In so doing, he followed the example set a century earlier among the Greek city-states. Athens, in B.C. 456, forced the city Aegina to take Athenian "owls" as their currency and to stop minting their own "turtle" coins. A few years later, in B.C. 449, Athens issued an edict ordering all foreign coins to be handed in to the Athenian mint and forced all her allies to adopt the Athens standard of weights, measures and money.

In the many wars through the 20th century, it was common practice for conquerors to displace the currency of the vanquished with their own. After goose-stepping into a country, the Nazis, for example, shoved aside the local money and substituted the Reichsmark. Then they rigged the rate of exchange in their own favor. That, according to William L. Shirer in his *Rise and Fall of the Third Reich,* was how Germans were able to buy up factories and other assets in Austria and elsewhere.

From earliest times money has been both a symbol and a method of control. With that in mind, it should surprise no one to learn that in the aftermath of the Cold War there is more American cash in Russia than in any other country outside the United States, and that the people of that nation prefer it to their own currency.

It should also not surprise anyone to learn that U.S. currency is the target of economic terrorists and counterfeiters, simply because the dollar is also America's Achilles' heel. Yet as the predominant power of the day, America is also the source of newer, more efficient electronic money and a new, electronic marketplace.

The Revolution of Money

The marriage of money and power found no more graphic expression than in ancient Britain. The early Brits used sword blades as coins — a practice Julius Caesar regarded as backward. Backward or not, they got the connection right. As a rule, the more highly evolved a nation's system of exchange, the more powerful that nation is likely to be.

The Mayan Indians of pre-Columbian Central America, for example, developed a high civilization with an elaborate system of barter as their means of commerce. Their cities often included vast market areas full of bright colors and wonderful smells, similar to the Indian markets of Guatemala and Mexico today. The lowland Mayans put together three- and four-way trades so that the person with beeswax could trade for blankets and eventually wind up with pottery. The Mayans enjoyed this form of commerce because it was also a way for them to socialize.

The Quiche Mayans of the northern Yucatan Peninsula lost their independence when they were conquered by the invading warrior Toltecs of central Mexico. The Toltecs emphasized both human sacrifice and currency—cacao beans (chocolate), gold and jade. The Mayans' highly social way of doing business was overwhelmed by the more aggressive one, but t'was ever thus. One reason the Toltecs prevailed was that they were more efficient — they spent less time and energy conducting business and they had more time to produce goods and to fight. Use of currency was a causative factor in the Toltecs' potential for war.

Commodity Currencies and Banking

The Toltecs' chocolate was a commodity currency, a currency based on a substance that was so broadly desired that it was accepted as payment by almost anyone in the domestic marketplace. The ancient Greeks, for example, used iron nails as currency The Romans used salt because it was always needed for preserving food and was widely desirable. In fact, they often paid their soldiers with sacks of salt, which is where the word *salary* comes from. Cattle, was relatively easy to transport locally and was in nearly in universal demand, so the Romans used livestock as a form of cash until the fourth century B.C. The word *pecuniary,* or pertaining to money, comes from *pecus,* the Latin word for cattle. And in English, the words *capital, chattel* and *cattle* all have a common root.

Animals continue to be a medium of exchange in some locales through the present day. The Kirghiz of the Russian Steppes, for example, use horses as their main monetary unit. Sheep are secondary, so sheepskins are used only for small transactions. And in parts of Africa wealth is measured by the size of one's herd of cattle. The problem with cattle as cash is that wealthy people find themselves spending too much time feeding and watering their money, which is why a dead commodity currency makes more sense than a living one.

Other commodities used as money at one time or another include amber, beads, drums, eggs, feathers, gongs, hoes, ivory, jade, kettles, leather, mats, oxen, pigs, quartz, rice, vodka, tobacco and yarns.

Banking is more nearly an outgrowth of barter than it is of currency. In the Greek world the basic unit of weight was the drachma, which means "a handful of grain." Grain was the basis of trade in ancient Mesopotamia and Egypt. Unlike a commodity currency such as beads or feathers, here it was the actual commodity itself that was transferred.

Grain and other commodities were stored in royal palaces and temples for safekeeping. Because grain is so bulky, receipts for it came to be used for transfers not only to the original depositors but also to third parties. Eventually, private houses in Mesopotamia also became involved in these banking operations and laws regulating them were included in the Code of Hammurabi.

In Egypt, banking was the result of centralizing grain harvests in government warehouses. Written orders for the withdrawal of portions of grain became used as a way to pay debts to others, including the tax collector and contributions to the religious establishment as well as other traders.

When the Greeks under Alexander conquered Egypt and set up the Ptolemy dynasty (from B.C. 323 to B.C. 30), warehouse banking became even more sophisticated. The scattered government granaries became a network of grain banks with a central bank in Alexandria where the main accounts from all the state banks were recorded. Payments were transferred from one account to another without grain changing hands. The warehouse receipts callable for grain were in fact money, or a mechanism for exchange, and were not unlike the commodity-backed currencies of the recent past such as the British pound sterling, redeemable for silver, and the U.S. one dollar silver certificate, also redeemable for a like amount in silver.

The Egyptians continued to use the granary warehouse system of banking even after they introduced coins into their economy. Internal commerce could be conducted with receipts for grain, while precious metals were reserved for foreign purchases. This arrangement was a precursor to the way international commerce is conducted today, with paper money serving internal commerce and bullion being reserved for transactions between nations.

Banking that centers on currency rather than commodities arose because of the many coins in circulation. Moneychangers carried around a table on which they exchanged coins of different nations, taking a profit for the transaction. The word *bank* comes from the Italian *banca,* which means "bench" or "counter." These business tables often got set up around temples or other public buildings. It was evidently one of these early bankers whose table Christ overturned when he used a whip to drive the moneychangers from the Temple of Jerusalem.

From ancient times banking was an industry that appealed to enterprising souls in isolated places with few natural resources. As we've already reviewed, in the second and third centuries B.C. the barren island of Delos off the Greek mainland became the ancestor of today's Bahamas, Caymans and other island banking centers. Delos had only two assets — a good harbor and the Temple of Apollo, around which trading and financial activities developed. Coinage was king in Athens, but on Delos financial transactions became very sophisticated. Real credit receipts replaced coins; accounts were set up and maintained for clients. On simple instructions of a debtor, a payment was made to a creditor.

Delos prospered and survived because it was not a threat to the major powers of the day Carthage and Corinth. Both of these banking centers were eventually destroyed by Rome. As a result, when Roman commerce needed to become more complex, it adopted from the model of Delos. However, the Romans remained stubbornly attached to coins instead of progressing to a system of payments on account.

The art and science of banking was practically forgotten with the fall of the Roman Empire and had to be reinvented many centuries later. Not until the Crusades was banking as an institution resurrected, and then only because the urgency of warfare demanded a system to transfer huge sums of money to pay for supplies, equipment, soldiers and ransom funds.

A piece from the Portland *Oregonian* shared this tidbit of interesting historical trivia about the recording of ancient transactions:

First-Degree Writer's Cramp

Any Roman who tried to multiply in his head CCLXV by XLIV had his work cut out for him. But imagine what the ancient Egyptians were up against with their system of symbols, described in a recent article from the *Journal of Economic Education:*

- The symbol for 100 was a coiled rope, for 1,000 a lotus blossom, for 10,000, a pointed finger, for 100,000 a tadpole, and for 1 million, a man stretching his arms to the heavens in astonishment.
- For the Egyptians, 3,456,789 would appear as three amazed men, four tadpoles, five pointed fingers, six lotus blossoms, seven coiled ropes, eight circles and nine vertical lines.
- An economist analyzing the U.S. budget deficit would begin by drawing some 400,000 pictures of amazed men. (Probably not so far fetched a visual)

Money and Sex

"Money it turned out is exactly like sex, you thought of nothing else if you didn't have it and thought of other things if you did."

James Baldwin

Warfare is not the only impulse behind the development of money. Sexuality played a major role as well. Objects that can be invested with a high degree of emotional value because of their use as adornment or jewelry can have a dual life as currency. In the tropical Fiji Islands, the natives used whale teeth especially as bride money, serving the same purpose as an engagement ring in Western society. Whales' teeth are called *tambua,* meaning they had a religious significance — from whence we get the word *taboo.*

In North America the natives used *wampum,* or seashells, as currency not only because they are easily transportable, but they could also be used as jewelry The earliest countable metallic money or coins were the Chinese *cowrie* made of bronze or copper and named after the cowrie shell of the Indian Ocean. A pictograph of the cowrie was adopted into Chinese as the written symbol for money.

In Western Africa the natives wear *manillas,* which are metallic objects that served as both jewelry and currency as recently as 1949. They have been described as an "ostentatious form of ornamentation, their value in that role being a prime reason for their acceptability as money." In many other cultures even to this day women wear gold coins as jewelry.

It is precisely because gold and silver make good jewelry and because they are generally expensive to come by and somewhat rare that they have been universally acceptable as mediums of exchange.

All That Glitters

The ancient Lydians (who once lived in the area occupied by modern Turkey), stamped small round pieces of metal into coins as early as B.C. 2500. Because their metals were so common, however, they were extremely easy to counterfeit. As a result, people did not have enough faith in these early coins to use them for large purchases.

Then the Lydians found that the rarer and prettier the metals used, the better the coins served as a medium of exchange. As early as B.C. 700 they minted coins of a pale yellow, gold and silver alloy called electrum. Concerned about counterfeiting, the Lydians stamped weight and intricate seals on their coins to make them harder to duplicate. Thus they endeavored to guarantee purity and value. Coins worked and their use spread from Lydia to both Greece and Persia.

As a means of exchange, the Romans began using raw chunks of copper. Each pound of such copper was called an "*as.*" In fact, the word *estimate* comes from *aes tumare,* which means "to value copper." Selling objects in exchange for pounds of copper was a form of commodity currency. Goods were exchanged for goods.

A major leap in money production came when government got into the picture by issuing currency — objects symbolic of goods rather than being the goods themselves. Rome began issuing copper coins in B.C. 338. To convey a sense of value, these often bore the image of an ox, a sheep or a hog. Similarly, some 3,000 years ago, the Chinese began stamping their coins with images of useful items, such as spades, hoes and knives.

In B.C. 269 the Romans also issued coins of silver, such as the denarius, equal to 10 asses, and the sestertius, or 2 1/2 asses. Then in B.C. 217 came Rome's first gold coins, the *aurei*, with values of 20, 40 and 60 sesterces. The talent, which was equal to 6,000 denarii, was also a unit of weight, varying from Rome to Greece to the Middle East, but generally being the equivalent of around 58 pounds.

The words *spend, expenditure* and *pound* all came from the Latin *expendere,* which means "to weigh." The currency of some countries still implies a unit of weight. Consider the British pound sterling and the Italian lira, which comes from the Latin word for pound. The peso of many Spanish-speaking countries is also a unit of weight. But the names are strictly symbolic. If the Italian lira indeed weighed a pound, it would take a three-quarter-ton pickup to haul around enough of them to equal one British pound.

One of the benefits of coins is that they can be counted out rather than weighed. Coins are also relatively easy to transport — certainly easier than a herd of cattle — and they can be stored without having to clean up after them. Coins can be minted in small or large denominations, so goods can be priced more precisely.

Coins were practically perfect as a medium of exchange … except for one thing.

The Vulnerability of Money

From the earliest times, nations at war have known that the best way to cripple an enemy is to strike at its currency. When the Spartans captured the Athenian silver mines at Laurion, they released the 20,000 slaves who kept the supply of precious metal flowing. With the mines closed, the Athenians faced a shortage of money and, in B.C. 406, issued bronze coins with a thin coating of silver.

The result was that the coin shortage became even worse. The good, pure silver coins disappeared from circulation because people hung onto them while spending the new ones to get rid of them. Aristophenes commented on this situation in his play *The Frogs,* produced in B.C. 405. He wrote, "The ancient coins are excellent … yet we make no use of them, and prefer those bad copper pieces quite recently issued and so wretchedly struck." The Athenians took the bad coins out of circulation as soon as they could—in B.C. 393.

It wasn't long after the Roman government got into the currency business that it made a discovery. In B.C. 264, in the first of Rome's three wars against its main rival, Carthage, the Romans found they did not have enough copper to pay their war debts. However, through experimentation they learned they could reduce the *as* from one pound to two ounces of copper. By cutting the value of the currency by five sixths, they liquidated their war debt almost immediately. Pretty clever sleight of hand, the example of which is still followed by governments the world round.

By B.C. 202, the Roman government had reduced the metal content of the *as* coin to one ounce, and by B.C. 87 to half an ounce. Now, as then, the problem with government-issued currency is that too often it is debased in order to pay for what government could not otherwise afford — most often its wars for power and dominion. Many governments that came into being to protect people from one another became themselves the thieves of the people

Post-World War I Germany is a prime example of theft through inflation. To pay its war debts, the German government simply issued currency until it lost all value. The hard work and savings of the people evaporated and the Allies were left holding a bag of worthless paper money. In the five years following the war, the German mark had so depreciated that it took 726 million of them to buy what one mark formerly bought in 1918. By 1923, according to the *Wall Street Journal Guide to Money & Investing,* it was actually cheaper in Germany at that time to burn money than to use it to buy firewood.

Profit in Money

Burning money instead of firewood is the exception. Because money is so useful, it's perceived worth generally far exceeds its actual cost of production. This is certainly true of paper money, and was almost always true with coins.

Coins commonly carried a substantial premium over the value of their metallic content, more than high enough to cover the cost of minting and kings, dictators, and even free governments could turn this premium into profit. This profit on the production of currency is called seigniorage, and amounts to hundreds of millions of dollars annually for the U.S. Treasury alone. (More about this later.)

Profits from the production of money opens it to abuse. In times past, currency was regularly recalled and replaced — in ancient capitals every six years, then every three years and eventually every other year. Existing coins were brought in to maximize profit as well as to prevent counterfeiting of earlier issues. New coins were struck with new images, yet they had to be made clearly distinguishable by authorities and be readily acceptable to the public.

Issuing money is historically such a lucrative business it is really no surprise that governments insist on a local monopoly. The profits from minting supplemented the revenue English monarchs raised from taxes. Such profit from reissuing currency may also explain why Britain redesigns its money so often—and may be one hidden reason for the new U.S. currency. And, of course there is the issue of over-issue. Lord William Rees-Moog sums this up with his pithy statement:

"There never will be a shortage of politicians willing to spend where they have not taxed, nor is there any shortage of economists wishing to advise them of the wisdom of supporting trade and employment by issuing more money.   No money whose issue is controlled by a politician is ever better than the needs the next election will allow."

In God We Trust

There has been a credibility problem ever since government got into the money business, which is why heads of state do everything possible to build confidence in their currency. The images of the ox, sheep and hog of early, more innocent times, gave way in time to profiles of the Roman emperor himself. Jesus Christ, when questioned about the justification for paying taxes, pointed to a denarius and asked whose portrait was on it. When the people said it was Julius Caesar's portrait, Christ instructed them to give to Caesar that which was Caesar's and to God that which is God's.

Certainly money has always belonged to Caesar. When Caesar died, the Roman treasury contained 700 million sesterces, and his own private treasury, 100 million. This looting of the public funds by the one in power has been endemic in societies even to our own day. It is a serious reason to question government's monopoly control over the money supply.

To gain credibility with the people, the Roman government stored its treasure in strongly built temples to the gods. Perhaps the rulers thought religious scruples would discourage thieves. More likely those managing the money simply wanted to imply that the gods were behind the currency

As a matter of fact, the word *money* comes from the Latin word *moneta,* which was another name for the goddess Juno, wife of Jupiter, king of the Roman pantheon of gods. When the Romans established a mint at the temple of Juno Moneta, the word *moneta* became a generic term for a place where money is made.

Putting "In God We Trust" on the U.S. dollar may not be much more than America's way of saying "me too" to an old tradition.

8

Paper Money

"The most important thing I have learned is that we don't spend money as much as we consume it. Money is food. We consume it and convert it into things — the feelings, associations, symbols, and statutes we believe in. To some, money is converted into power. To others, money is converted into security. To others money is converted into getting by the best way they can. To others money is converted into self-esteem. To others money is converted into survival. To others money is converted into magic. To others, sex. To still others, beauty. To many, money is converted into sin. And to still others money is converted into evil. The fact is that money does not exist without people. Money has no meaning without people. Money is simply an idea we have agreed upon. An idea, which represents to every one of us our net worth in the world."

Michael E. Gerber

When Marco Polo returned to Venice after traveling to the throne of Kubla Khan, the great Mongol emperor of China, he told stories of wealth so fabulous his fellow Italians assumed he must have made them up.

A Great Discovery

One of the most farfetched of these stories was about money made of paper, stamped with the emperor's seal — a red token in the middle of the note—and signed by his treasurer. Polo reported that the Chinese did not use gold or even silver in their transactions, but notes printed on a cotton paper about the size of the palm of a hand. This was totally incredible to his fellow Italians, who, like their Roman forebears, thought of money as coins and nothing else.

Polo actually saw this paper money being minted. He was amazed at the flimsiness of the paper it was printed on. Although the money wore out quickly, it could be returned to the government and traded in for new bills and for every 100 bills the Chinese turned in, they received 97 in return. This three percent is the profit from making money —*seigniorage.*

The lure of profit from seigniorage was so powerful that the Chinese government suppressed the notes issued by the banking guilds of Szechuan Province, and Kublai Khan himself prohibited use of Chinese metal coins— that bore images of spades and hoes—in order to give his paper money a better market share.

The Mongols did not introduce paper money. About the year *650,* the Chinese Imperial Treasury issued the earliest paper cash. The Chinese learned to accept paper for their goods, and they were still accepting it a century after Khan, during the Ming dynasty, when the emperor issued the Kwan—currency the size of a piece of typing paper—which is the oldest surviving paper money. The Chinese paper money was originally guaranteed by metal reserves, but when these were exhausted, the emperor printed more notes nonetheless. As a result, the notes depreciated in value.

The Need for Paper Money

Earlier forms of currency did not disappear with the introduction of paper money. Goods have continued to be used as a form of currency from ancient times until today. At the end of the 14th century in Europe, for example, when imported spices were rare and precious, people could buy a plow horse for a pound of saffron, or a sheep for a pound of ginger. Coins did not disappear when paper money made its appearance.

But as the value of commerce increases, traders need more flexibility in making exchanges than giving either goods or coins. This is especially true in frontier areas. When government money is rare, private paper currency has often been the fuel for growth. Frontier New Zealand makes the point. When Scottish farmers arrived in 1848, there was no local bank, nor even a bank branch from elsewhere. On the opposite side of the world from Great Britain, these hardy adventurers had no way to issue currency that would represent the goods and services they created.

James Macandrew arrived in 1851 with some bank notes he had brought along. With the hope of starting a bank, he set up a store, then wrote to the local newspaper about the "effect which would be produced by the circulation of *5,000* or *10,000* pound notes, judiciously distributed among the honest and industrious tradesmen and agriculturalists of the colony. It was to be to industry and labor what fuel is to the steam engine — setting all its wheels and parts in motion."

Unfortunately, because the would-be banker failed to do his paperwork properly, he could not get a charter from the colonial administrators. His bank was not able to circulate bank notes. By the next year the settlers were clamoring for money. Forty of them sent him a letter pleading for promissory notes, no matter how small the amount.

Stepping into the void, Macandrew issued his own paper money, backing it up with the goods being offered for sale at his store. Soon, the settlers were using Macandrew's scrip to pay their debts. Some of his competitors objected, but the local newspaper said it was of no concern to anyone except Macandrew and the people who could either use or refuse his money as they saw fit. In only 10 months, his private currency accounted for a third of all the money in the area. Macandrew's paper money worked because people trusted that it was backed by goods from his store, because they were on the other side of the world from the mother country and needed a medium of exchange, and because government had not stepped forward to satisfy the need.

Sweden introduced paper bank notes to Europe in 1661. Picking up on the idea, the British issued paper promissory notes to their soldiers from Massachusetts in *1690.* The colonies also paid their fighting men with promissory notes. This early paper money promised an eventual payment of "hard currency," which, in those days, meant gold or silver. But precious metals were in short supply, and all commerce with the mother country had to be in hard currency.

The early settlers in New England saw that the Indians traded among each other for seashells, or wampum, and quickly figured out how to turn that to their own profit. They originally used the shells to buy beaver pelts, which could he sold to the mother country. But once the settlers generally developed confidence that the wampum would always be worth a pelt, they used the shells as currency among themselves. According to Peter Wayner, author of *Digital Cash,* the practice was so widespread that in 1641 the government of Massachusetts officially recognized wampum as currency.

The benefit of wampum was, that unlike beaver pelts, the shells would not rot. The disadvantage of wampum was that black shells were twice as valuable as white ones, and in short order counterfeiters were using small drops of dye to change colors. The "shell game" lasted until the beavers were killed off and the natives could no longer produce pelts. With nothing else of value behind the shells, they became worthless.

A year after Massachusetts recognized wampum as money, Virginia made tobacco leaves its currency. By 1727, its colonial government recognized paper currency backed by tobacco as legal tender that could be used to settle debts. The government set up tobacco warehouses that graded the quality of the tobacco and issued paper that could be redeemed for specific grades. Like the wampum that could he exchanged for beaver pelts, the tobacco was sold mostly to Europe in exchange for hard goods. Tobacco continued to be used as a currency until 1787, when the Constitution banned the states from having their own currency and reserved that right for the federal government.

England wanted the colonists to pay taxes to the mother country in gold. The colonists wanted to pay in paper money similar to that which England was circulating in America. The notes England was paying its soldiers had no value in England, and the colonies' scrip was considered worthless. To put an end to the problem, in 1751 the crown forbade New England from issuing any paper money and, in 1764, banned printing of money in the rest of the colonies as well. This heavy-handed suppression of domestic policy helped bring about the Revolution. The colonials decided not to pay for the rebellion through taxation. Instead, they issued paper money and used it to pay the troops. Early on it was deemed an act of patriotism for a shopkeeper to accept paper currency.

Private Money

Through the Coinage Act of 1792, the dollar became the basic unit of money in the United States. It was copied after the Spanish dollar then circulating widely in the fledgling nation.

The word *dollar* actually comes from the German name for a silver coin minted in a valley in Bohemia in the 16th century— Joachimsthaler. The coin was popular throughout Europe, and was called the *daalder* in Holland and the dollar in Britain. At least a dozen other countries besides the U.S. call their currency dollars— countries from the Bahamas to Zimbabwe.

Not long after independence, in 1791, the First Bank of the United States was chartered. Modeled after the Bank of England, it was able to enforce discipline among the many other banks by requiring them to redeem their paper currency for gold or silver — an action that spawned enemies by restricting the supply of money. Adding to the antagonism, the First Bank of the United States was a private bank that competed against the others for loans and deposits.

Eventually the First Bank of the United States became so unpopular that the Senate voted it out of existence in 1810. The immediate result was monetary chaos. Banks filled the void with private paper money called scrip, which was supposed to be backed by gold or silver, although all too frequently neither of these was actually available. When it came to working with bank notes, "buyer beware" was the watchword. Picture a gentleman from Philadelphia traveling to Baltimore to make a purchase without knowing what his money was worth there or which local bank currencies he could trust.

Some banks acted with integrity and issued currency only in proportion to deposits. Others issued more — debasing the value of their money. When banks failed, the private money became worthless. Because of these troubles, bank-issued money sometimes had to be exchanged for a fraction of its face value, especially if the notes were issued by a bank in a distant state. The War of 1812 led to creation of the Second Bank of the United States in 1816. To build faith in the value of the bank's notes, each piece of currency had to be personally signed by both the president of the bank and the cashier. People were still suspicious of the power of a central bank, and it too went out of business.

There was not the same credibility problem with privately minted coins and, as a matter of fact, many of them were more highly regarded than those produced by the government. One of the first private coiners was John Higley, a blacksmith in Granby, Connecticut, who minted copper coins in 1737 and 1738. He let the market determine the value of his coins, according to Brian Summers, senior editor of *Readers Digest* in his paper "Private Coinage in America." The coins said nothing about trusting in God—merely: "I am good copper value me as you please." These coins were in general use until the U.S. Mint opened in 1792.

In 1783 Chalmers of Annapolis, Maryland, minted silver shillings that people of the day considered very good quality Reporting on privately coined gold, Joseph Coffin wrote that between 1830 and 1861 many private gold coins were struck in various sections of the country. The first was in 1830 by Templeton Reid, an assayer at the gold mines of Lumpkin County, Georgia, the same county in which the Dahlonega Federal Mint was located. His coins were in denominations of *$2.50, $5* and $10. Many were later melted because they were worth more as bullion than their face value.

Christopher Bechtler of Rutherfordton, North Carolina, arrived in the U.S. along with his sons and nephew from the grand duchy of Baden in 1830. Getting into the money business, between 1831 and 1847 they produced gold coins in denominations of $1, *$2.50* and *$5*— and they prospered despite competition from the federal mint established in 1837 in Charlotte.

Bechtler's coins were accepted and passed at face value in all of western North Carolina, South Carolina, western Tennessee, Kentucky and parts of Virginia. One person of that time said he was 16 years old before he ever saw a coin other than that produced by the Bechtler mint. These coins filled a need and continued to circulate after the mint closed in 1847. The Bechtler coins had neither national emblem nor official guarantee of purity, but were accepted by all. When owners turned them in to be reminted into federal currency, there was enough extra weight in them to pay the government the cost of reminting—seigniorage—, which is the profit from making money.

Bechtler made his profit by keeping some of the gold people brought in to be minted into coins. He weighted it out in their presence. A visitor to his mint at the time said, "Christopher Bechtler's maxim was that honesty was the best policy, and the maxim appeared to govern his conduct." The visitor observed that Bechtler's "transactions were conducted with quite as much simplicity as those at a country grist mill, where the miller deducts the toll for the grist he has manufactured." Bechtler minted more than 3 million coins, which continued to have an important role in the War Between the States.

Today, new money comes into being as the commercial banks expand the money supply through the "fractional reserve system." They are empowered by government to lend out more than they have on deposit. In effect, they have made "new money" by extending credit to businesses and others, letting them borrow money that does not exist, to accommodate new value they have created by making new goods and services. (More about this in the next chapter)

There never is as much currency in existence as the sum total of all money that bank records would indicate. In the U.S. it is the Department of Treasury's Bureau of Engraving who prints money. In 1993 the total was 10.6 billion currency notes. The government's fee for producing this new money—seigniorage—is the $400 million extra dollars it retained to pay its own bills. Bechtler's was not the only private mint. As a matter of fact, these sprang up in a number of places, especially in the West, when there was not enough government money to handle the flow of commerce. After gold was discovered in California in 1848, at least 15 mints sprang up between 1849 and 1855. The bullion content of some of these coins was less than their face value, so the coins were rejected by the marketplace and passed out of circulation.

Some private mints in the Gold Rush days held to principle and produced high-quality coins. The specie of Moffatt & Co., Kellogg & Co. and Wass, Molitor & Co. were widely accepted in the Old West. The *San Francisco Herald* (Jan. 8, 1852, as cited by Brian Summers) had especially high praise for the coins of Wass, Molitor & Co., because the company "had stepped forward in this emergency, and are now issuing a coin of the value of $5 to supply the necessities of trade."

Their coin was actually worth $5.04 because it was heavier than the U.S. *$5* gold piece. "The high reputation for honor and integrity enjoyed by Wass and his associates in this enterprise is an additional guarantee that every representation made by them will be strictly complied with. The public will be glad to have a coin in which they can feel confidence, and which can't depreciate in their hands," the newspaper commented.

Another private Western mint of high reputation was the one in Denver, operated by Clark, Gruber & Co. Between 1860 and 1862 they minted coins to satisfy the demand for a circulating medium, something the central government had not accomplished. The Clark, Gruber coins either met or exceeded the gold bullion value of similar U.S. pieces, and in less than two years they issued $3 million in coins. They did such a good job the federal government bought them out and closed one of the last private mints.

The United States backed its currency with both gold and silver—a practice referred to as bimetallism. The U.S. mint valued one ounce of gold as worth 15 ounces of silver. But since the supply and demand of these metals varied, their market prices changed. If gold was in short supply, it became worth more than 15 ounces of silver. Like the ancient Greeks of Athens who held onto their silver coins when copper ones were introduced, Americans stopped circulating their gold when it became more valuable than silver.

In this young country, the value of the metals fluctuated against each other as new discoveries brought new sources of supply into production. The U.S. government shifted the relative weights of the coins to bring their market value into line. Wayner observes, "This realignment process often brought much debate as people would choose sides based upon their interests. The debtors would endorse whatever metal was growing cheaper, hoping that they would be able to pay off their debts with less work. The lenders would push for 'hard' money that was contracting so as to force people to pay off their debts with more metal."

The Civil War

Once again, warfare was the impetus to vast changes in the monetary system. When the U.S. Civil War broke out in 1861, few people could have envisioned its huge costs. Abraham Lincoln was correct when he said that less than one-half day's expense for fighting could have purchased the freedom of all the slaves in Delaware. The *Wall Street Journal* reports (Feb. 13, 1996) that the Civil War cost the two sides a total of $6.6 billion in 1860 dollars, which was enough to buy the freedom of all the slaves at their 1860 market value, give each slave family 40 acres and a mule and $3.5 billion in reparations to former slaves in lieu of 100 years of back wages.

No sooner did blood begin to flow than the money followed, and there were runs on the banks as people brought in their paper money and demanded gold bullion. By the end of the first year of the Civil War, neither the banks nor the U.S. Treasury would honor redeemable paper currency. Paper dollars did, however, become the standard in the U.S. during the Civil War. To pay its war debts, the federal government first issued paper money in February 1862. Salmon P. Chase, Secretary of the Treasury, replaced the gold-backed money with notes that were theoretically redeemable at some unspecified time. This money was called "greenbacks" because the bills were printed in green ink to avoid confusion with the gold certificates also in circulation. The greenbacks quickly fell in value relative to gold coins and bullion still in circulation. The government issued new notes in June of 1862 and again in January 1863.

War made for drastic actions. Nevada was brought into the Union as a state during the Civil War because of its booming silver mines. By the time the war actually broke out, one report holds that as many as 10,000 brands of private paper money were circulating and perhaps a third of it was no good. The National Banking Act of 1864 established a uniform currency and in the process drove out of business the competing private money. The Act allowed holders of these notes to turn them in for legal U.S. currency. Thereafter, no one besides the U.S. government has been empowered to mint currency. While the war was underway, the value of paper money seesawed back and forth along with the fortunes of the Union. When the Union was losing, their paper money lost value. When it was winning, greenbacks were almost on par with gold.

In the Confederacy, people came to view their own paper money with suspicion. The South did not issue specie, according to Summers. Instead, people hoarded their Bechtler coins and many contracts and agreements during the war specified Bechtler gold as compensation rather than the Confederate states paper money or the scant supply of federal coins still in use.

Following the war in 1873, the U.S. temporarily stopped minting silver dollars, which had the effect of ending bimetallism. In 1879 the federal government began issuing paper money redeemable for gold. (The first U.S. silver dollars were minted in 1794, and almost 900 million of them have been minted since. Although the Treasury stopped routine production of silver dollars in 1935, it has occasionally produced limited editions, such as the rather famous Eisenhower silver dollar.)

In the late 1800's and on into the early 1900's, America was in an uproar about which metals should back their currency. The supply of gold was not increasing as fast as the economy, which meant money became harder to get and bought more goods and services than previously—classic deflation. This was good for lenders, because it meant their debts would be repaid with more valuable money, but it was bad for debtors—many of whom were farmers.

The bullion controversy divided the nation. The farmers of the prairie states wanted money backed by silver, which was abundantly streaming out of the Nevada mines. But the bankers of the East, like their forebears the English overlords, wanted "hard money," which meant gold. Silver-tongued orator and politician William Jennings Bryan was a supporter of the prairie populists. While seeking the Presidential nomination of the Democratic party in 1896, he delivered his famous speech, in which he said: "We will answer their demands for a gold standard by saying to them: 'You shall not press down upon the brow of labor this crown of thorns, you shall not crucify mankind upon a cross of gold.'"

Bryan was defeated by William McKinley, and the Free Silver movement disappeared when the bimetallism problem righted itself as more gold discoveries brought the monetary expansion the populists wanted. But the struggle left its imprint on the American psyche.

The Wizard of Oz

It seems that the famous play which became a Hollywood film *The Wizard of Oz* was actually a metaphor of its era. Hugh Rockoff of Rutgers University maintains that the children's classic by L. Frank Baum was a Jonathan Swift-style literary treatment of the controversy of the day — one that would have been immediately recognized by people living at the time. He points out that the controversy about bimetallism was as heated a subject in their time as abortion issues are in ours. Everyone had an opinion, and everyone felt strongly about it.

Mr. Rockoff points out some recognizable symbols:

* The Wizard of Oz. Oz is the abbreviation for ounce—as in an ounce of gold or silver.

- The Silver Slippers. The movie has Dorothy wearing ruby slippers, but in the book they were silver. She had to fight the Wicked Witch of the West for control of them.
- Dorothy. She was swept away from the prairie states by a tornado. Dorothy represented the goodness and innocence of the American people. The evil forces are always trying to keep her and her silver slippers from returning home.
- Toto. Rockoff says the dog's name represents the teetotaling party, which stood for Free Silver and against free alcohol.
- The Wicked Witch of the East. Represents the Eastern bankers and their demand for gold.
- The Wicked Witch of the West. Represents McKinley because he dominated the West and subjugated its people by keeping America on the gold standard.
- The Yellow Brick Road. Gold is customarily stored in ingots or bricks.
- The Cowardly Lion. William Jennings Bryan, who roared about silver during the election of 1896 but after his defeat by William McKinley dropped the issue.

Curiouser, and curiouser, as Alice said in Wonderland.

Making Money

It wasn't until 1963 that the U.S. government ceased issuing silver certificates that could actually be exchanged for silver. Today, what the Department of Treasury prints is called "federal reserve notes," and they are backed only by the full faith and credit of the government. This is a "fiat currency." As a creation of the government, it has no intrinsic value and can't be redeemed for anything. Consequently, U.S. government money is now totally symbolic and like it or not, it is the basis for the rest of the world's monetary systems.

The value of world currency has been abstracted from commodities, meaning that it is not redeemable for anything but another bill of the same denomination. For example, the value of a U.S. dollar is now strictly a function of the credibility of the American government, its military, and the greater economy.

As "legal tender," the currency circulated by the U.S. government must be accepted as payment of debt. Checks, credit cards and trade dollars are not legal tender, because the issuers are private organizations and not the government. That's why U.S. merchants can refuse to accept your check or credit card, but not U.S. cash. Although, as a practical matter, it's difficult to rent a car, let alone travel, without a major credit card.

The dollar has now reached an exalted position of usefulness and has many sterling qualities, no joke intended. It is fungible, which means that if a person loses a $20 bill, any other $20 bill will replace it. It is anonymous, which means a person can spend it without having to show identification or give a signature. It's almost as if cash were just made to be spent. But we don't have to sell anyone on the desirability of money, do we really? Just how sought after the U.S. dollar has become is the next order of business.

The Almighty Dollar

- As many as half the residents of the former Soviet Union keep their savings in American currency, most in $100 bills.
- The people of Russia hold more U.S. dollars than rubles.
- American cash accounts for one fifth of the world's currency supply.
- The U.S. dollar makes up 60 percent of the world foreign exchange reserves.
- Of the total U.S. currency now in existence approximately two thirds is in circulation in other countries.

The Coin of the Realm

In Latin America, Africa, Asia and across the whole span of the former Soviet Union and its former Eastern European satellites, people who have anything of value also have a cache of U.S. money in the household, tucked away in a safe or under the mattress.

While staying in the home of friends in Vera Cruz, Mexico many years ago I had a powerful illustration of how important U.S. dollars had become in the eyes of those outside the States. It was a weekend and I needed to change some U.S. currency into pesos and mentioned this to Rubien, the 14-year-old son of the family with whom I was staying. He got very excited about his being able to exchange Pesos for dollars and he charged off to a secret hiding place in his home where he kept a cache of money. I was shocked when he returned and proceeded to exchange a thousand U.S. dollars for me into pesos at the current exchange rate. Like so many others in the world, he had already learned that stockpiling American dollars was the thing to do.

His father, who was part of the ruling family of the area, explained the reality of life today: "Terry," he said, "If you speak English and have U.S. dollars, you can go anywhere and do anything in the world." The reality of this statement has been proven to me again and again in perhaps a hundred countries around the world. The U.S. dollar has become the coin of the realm, as perhaps no other currency has since the denarius of Roman times.

Why would the average Russian prefer dollars to rubles? Let's take the example of a typical Russian veteran of World War II who had served his country faithfully in the war, and then went on to work the rest of his days within the Communist system. If he had been frugal and had managed to amass a savings of 50,000 rubles when he retired in 1990, his nest egg would have been worth $87,500 U.S. dollars at the official exchange rate (one ruble in 1990 was worth $1.75).

Within six years, however, as the Soviet system crumbled and the ruble had to duke it out unprotected against stronger currencies, Soviet money plunged to its market value: 5,290 rubles to the dollar. That means that the Russian retiree saw a life savings evaporate: The 50,000 rubles in 1996 was worth $9.40—scarcely enough for a meal at McDonald's.

A Major Export

Currency is quite possibly America's most important export, but it is much more than that. The real value to America is that the flow of currency does not come back into the U.S. economy. If all of the U.S. money were returned to the States and circulated there the country would be awash in surplus cash prompting runaway inflation.

It works like this: Cash is printed and pays for the goods and services purchased by the U.S. government. Instead of circulating in only the U.S. economy and driving up prices the money is siphoned off and does not return. Because the U.S. Treasury pays no interest on the dollars held overseas that don't make their way into American interest-bearing accounts, it saves an estimated $15 billion per year, according to *Time* magazine. The *New Yorker* maintains that every bill in circulation is in effect an interest-free loan. An equivalent amount in government securities would cost the United States more than $25 billion in annual interest payments.

The U.S. Treasury makes a profit on money. Like the ancient Mongol emperors of China and the German coinmakers of the Old South, the U.S. government charges a few points for the value added by producing the currency. This seigniorage amounts to about $400 million per year. William Safire, columnist for the *New York Times,* adds:

> "The Treasury borrows … money for nothing and lends it at about 6 percent—which means we make nearly $25 billion every year on the cash 'float,' mostly from abroad. No wonder Treasury and the Federal Reserve are so eager to protect the faith of dollar holders in the dollar; cash is their cash cow."

It is a good export for U.S. banks, too. In effect, they "buy" cash from the Federal Reserve, pack it up, fly it abroad in the original U.S. government packaging, and receive fees for such transactions. In 1994 alone, a small number of American banks shipped more than $20 billion in new $100 bills to about 50 Moscow banks, accepting in return gold bullion, diamonds, and other currencies.

Money is such a good business that the Feds produce loads of it. Somewhere in the world there exists for every single American the equivalent of about $1,400 in bills, which is a curiously large quantity. So much cash per person could lead to ruinous inflation, except for the exodus of money. The Federal Reserve may not have a solid grasp of how much cash is flowing abroad — but they have a good idea that two thirds of all U.S. currency has left the country.

Adding to the control issue, a *Wall Street Journal* article (June 3, 1996) contained the following:

"The San Francisco Fed's Los Angeles branch is being investigated for doctoring numbers in the cash handling reports it compiles for Washington. Monthly discrepancies sometimes totaled tens of millions of dollars."

"Estimates of currency held abroad are subject to considerable error," Federal Reserve Chairman Alan Greenspan was quoted in *Time* magazine. "We are looking at this issue in considerable detail." But it is bound to continue. According to Theodore F. Allison, assistant to the Board of Governors of the Federal Reserve, "Issuing currency is about the best racket there is for a government."

Why the Dollar

What makes one currency more valuable than another? Quite simply, it is the political, economic and military strength of the country. The U.S. dollar is sought after because the U.S. government, for the most part, has a history of respecting its value. Even if the dollar were devalued, it is not likely to be steamrolled, as regularly happens to the peso of Mexico. If money is a store of value, those who have crystallized their efforts into currency don't like to have all that work go up in smoke through hyperinflation or sudden devaluation. That's why a stable currency is a desired currency.

Political upheaval leads to money problems. Fascist dictators take the money and send it to their own private bank accounts. Revolutionaries start social programs they can't pay for and wind up bankrupting the country in their own way.

Most people in the world believe American democracy assures there will be no drastic swings to the left or to the right. Observes William Safire:
"Despite all the grumping here about unresponsive government; and despite the tut-tutting abroad about American hegemonism and cultural decay — the eager acceptance of the new U.S. C-note proves that people everywhere have faith in the stability that flows from freedom in the United States of America."

Let's hope he's right for all of our sakes. America remains the largest economy in the world with technology and productivity that are among the best. The country's natural and human resources and her political and economic systems have given more prosperity to more people than anywhere else on earth. All the activity of conducting much of the world's business in dollars helps keep the U.S. dollar in high demand.

Wealth Through Strength

In my opinion, the virtually undiscussed true strength of U.S. money is its military. U.S. cash is the coin of the realm because America is perceived as the greatest power in the world. Because America is viewed as impregnable, people all around the world feel safe with savings in U.S. money, and safer yet if they hold U.S. dollars in banks not located within the States.

Much of the world's gold supply is stored underground, 14 floors below the Federal Reserve Bank in New York. Foreign governments maintain as much as 10,000 tons of gold there, more than anywhere else in the world, and by far more than in Fort Knox. With gold considered the currency of last resort, government banks trust the Federal Reserve to transfer it among themselves — from holding area to holding area deep below the hustle of New York City.

Seen in this light, Americans have been feasting for decades on the victories won in World War II. But the real banquet was served as a direct result of the defeat of Communism in the Cold War. The U.S. basically bankrupted the competition—ran them flat out of business. There now is no viable alternative to the economic system America has evolved; capitalism is the only game in town. The frosting on the cake was the Persian Gulf War. It showed how technologically superior U.S. armaments are to anything else on the market and, by extension, how safe the U.S. is from major threats.

Everyone wants to associate with a winner, and this is why, despite occasional perturbations and fluctuations, the German mark and the Japanese yen were never a real threat to the U.S. dollar. However, the unity now being shown by the European Community may change all this, and although the Euro has yet to be any real threat to the dollar, things may change. There are those who argue, as did Linda Himelstein of *Business Week,* that fund managers who control as much as $2 trillion in assets will demand higher interest rates in the U.S. or they will take their money elsewhere.

A universal currency must grow from a strong economy and a strong military to protect that economy. The former Soviet Union once had a strong military but a weak economy. Germany and Japan have recently had strong economies but weak militaries. At this particular point in time, the U.S. is the only country with both.

Looking Hard for Hard Money

Even before the USSR collapsed, the U.S. dollar was well received everywhere in the world. Now, throughout Russia, China, Cuba and Eastern Europe, dollars are indispensable. Taxi drivers in Kazakhstan want to be paid in dollars, as do many restaurants in Kiev and Moscow. A major museum in St. Petersburg won't take rubles — only dollars. A Russian importer of IBM computers flashed his wad of American $50 bills to a *Time* magazine reporter and said: "What do I need rubles for? I want real money."

What is "real money"? In the island nation of Western Samoa, the tala is real money, but that is the only place on earth where it is changeable. If you leave the country with tala in your pockets instead of dollars, the Samoans have trapped hard currency in their country and you have something you can't spend. As to the question what is real money and where does it come from we move to the next chapter where your "eyes may be opened" and you may learn truly vital information about money you simply never knew.

9

Money & The Fed

"To emit an unfunded paper as the sign of value ought not to continue a formal part of the Constitution, nor ever hereafter to be employed; being, in its nature, repugnant with abuses and liable to be made the engine of imposition and fraud."

Alexander Hamilton

Money

Money, we all need it, we all want it, and we all use it. It impacts much of what we do throughout the majority of our lives, it shapes a considerable amount of our thinking, and it sparks much of our action. But, oddly enough very few people really know how money is created and what that actually means to them. We tend to leave such weighty matters to those who seem to know more about these issues than do we. History teaches us that this is a very big mistake. When the people are not informed the privileged few have control. Study this chapter carefully. Your improved understanding of the way things really are will better prepare you for the choices you'll want to make to secure your financial future.

Overview

It's like watching the weather during tornado season. Economists worldwide view actions of the Federal Reserve Board with a mixture of fear and wonder, because the Federal Reserve has the power to raise or lower interest rates, and therefore wield enormous power over the world economy.

How much power? Consider this: Every time the Federal Reserve raises rates one quarter of a percentage point, about 50,000 home buyers in the U.S. are priced out of the market, according to economist David Lereah of the Mortgage Bankers Association. But the implications go way beyond the borders of the United States. The whole world holds its breath each time the Federal Reserve Board or its chairman has anything to say about anything.

Stock prices rise or fall according to how heavily dependent companies are perceived to be on borrowings. In theory when rates are high, many investors may switch from buying stocks in business to bonds from government.

Higher interest rates cause the dollar to rise against other currencies. A stronger dollar makes U.S. goods relatively more expensive in the international marketplace, and imports more accessible – thus potentially idling

U.S. factories and accelerating an imbalance of payments. The ripple effect of all these changes acts as a brake on economies – companies slow down and lay off workers, who are then unable buy, which if not remedied in time will cause recessions or worse. And so the Fed steps back in and lowers rates to head off disaster. And so the cycle goes. There is an expression offensive to many but that contains some truth, which says that when the U.S. sneezes Canada catches cold, Europe gets a fever and Australia and much of the rest of the world gets pneumonia.

That's an enormous amount of power. What is this Federal Reserve institution and who are the people who have such control over our lives? And, just how far does their power actually go?

The Federal Reserve System

The Federal Reserve System sometimes referred to as the "Fed," is not federal, and there are no reserves, at least not in any traditional sense of the term. The Fed is a quasi-private company controlled by a select few.

Stock shares in the private company called the Federal Reserve are issued to federally chartered commercial banks. However, the stock does not represent incremental ownership, the shares cannot be sold or pledged, and shares in the Federal Reserve do not provide for ordinary voting rights, as they normally do with other private corporations.

The U.S. government does not own any stock in the Federal Reserve System, but the Fed has a TOTAL monopoly over government banking activities, and its decisions literally affect the lives of virtually everyone on the planet.

The decisions made by the Fed are rendered in secret meetings, weeks prior to the release of any information to public sources. All notes and transcripts of such meetings are destroyed prior to public announcements, so that no information will be available under the Freedom of Information Act. Neither the FBI nor the CIA enjoys such secrecy.

The Fed exists to ensure profits to a select few along with maintaining general economic stability, and it is the single most important board piece in the game of world domination; not by the United States, as you might logically presume, but by influential bankers and power brokers.

The Federal Reserve System is the beating heart of a legalized cartel. It is the epitome of a secret combination designed to get gain at the ultimate expense of the uninformed public. This institution is the source from which fiat money flows, money backed by nothing. In its truest form, this is counterfeit money, which the U.S. government requires that every American accept or suffer the consequences of the use by government of overwhelming force. In this, citizens are stripped of their fundamental rights and liberty.

The U.S. Constitution actually requires that money be only gold or silver or certificates redeemable in gold or silver. The founding fathers were historically informed. Gold and silver are the ONLY money that has stood the test of 5,000 years of recorded history. This requirement has been overruled by a compromised legislature, although a Constitutional amendment to validate this action has never been passed.

The Federal Reserve is the third resurrection of the centralized monopoly originally chartered by the Continental Congress in 1781. The same men, who initially chartered the private business that would gain an absolute monopoly over money, eventually realized the error of their ways and refused its renewal. When the Constitution was first drafted it included the language from the former "Articles of Confederation" which said:

> "The legislature of the United States shall have the power to borrow money and emit bills of credit."

This is the process by which fiat money begins, i.e., emitting bills of credit. However, the framers of the Constitution were collectively so appalled by the inflation and inherent corruption this process bred, that an overwhelming majority of the Constitutional Convention — amounting to a four to one vote — removed the words "emit bills of credit," from the Constitutional language. Alexander Hamilton spoke for this majority when he said:

> "To emit an unfunded paper as the sign of value ought not to continue a formal part of the Constitution, nor ever hereafter to be employed; being, in its nature, repugnant with abuses and liable to be made the engine of imposition and fraud."

The fathers of the Constitution had experienced first hand the results of fiat currency. Fiat bills were then widely referred to as simply paper money, meaning it was paper only with no guarantees of redemption of anything of underlying value.

Paper money, or fiat currency, is not to be confused with the paper bills, which are actually receipts, or claim checks, which may be redeemed for whatever backs it, normally gold or silver. For example, U.S. dollars up until the 1960's were actually "silver certificates," meaning they could be redeemed at any government mint for their value in silver.

Early American patriots saw clearly that the government should NEVER again be granted the right to issue paper money without legitimate backing and without a complete check and balance system. Thomas Paine summed up these feelings when he said:

> "The punishment of a member (of Congress) who should

move for such a law ought to be death."

Even a corrupt government bureaucracy cannot inflate a fully backed commodity currency, provided of course, someone is minding the vault. London Times editor William Rees-Moog had this to say:

"Neither a state nor a bank ever have had the unrestricted power of issuing paper money without abusing that power."

He went on to point out that:

"There never will be a shortage of politicians willing to spend where they have not taxed, nor is there any shortage of economists wishing to advise them of the wisdom of supporting trade and employment by issuing more money. No money whose issue is controlled by a politician is ever better than the needs the next election will allow."

Article 1, Sections 8 & 10 of the Constitution of the United States say that "Congress shall have the power..."

"To borrow money ... to coin money, regulate the value thereof, ... and fix the standard of weights and measures ... to provide for the punishment of counterfeiting..."

"No state shall ... coin money; emit bills of credit, ... (or) make anything but gold and silver coin a tender in payment of debts."

There is no question that those responsible for drafting the Constitution were careful and precise with their words. The American colonies had previously been flooded with paper fiat money to the incredible detriment of its citizens. Inflation always follows the circulation of fiat money and to the best of my knowledge there has never been an exception in the history of the world. Some of the original colonies had experienced inflation of over 1000%, the results of which wiped out the lifetime savings of the majority of the colonists. Those that framed the Constitution understood plainly the danger that lurks where government is allowed to grant to itself, or anyone else, a monopoly to create paper fiat money.

Banking

Throughout much of history goldsmiths handled the business of banking. Merchants and citizens brought their gold and silver, usually in the form of coins, to a goldsmith. The goldsmith's job was to store and protect these valuables in their vault. For this they charged a fee. The goldsmith-banker issued paper receipts, which represented claim checks for the coins deposited with them. These paper bills were generally in a standard and recognized form and were therefore widely accepted as money based on the reputation of the goldsmith, his family and fortune.

Banking was the act of storing coins and bullion and making loans. Loans were made from the assets of the banker's themselves, not the stored assets of others. If a person storing their coins with a banker wished to earn interest by allowing their gold to be loaned to third parties, they understood clearly that the money was not readily available for use until the borrowing party had paid back the loan and interest. Most borrowers wanted paper money, not bulky coins, so when they received their loans of coin they typically would leave them in the vault and instead take paper bills representing the gold or silver coin actually on deposit.

All legitimate paper money was historically 100% backed by gold, silver, or whatever commodity was identified on the face of the bill. Paper bills were "receipt money," because they were simply receipts for an equal amount of gold or silver held on deposit at the bank which had issued them. Any banker that created paper bills, for which they did not have gold or silver in the vault, was guilty of fraud. Paper money without backing, where people have been forced to accept it by government, is called "fiat money."

A Central Bank

The Federal Reserve is the central bank of the United States. It was established in 1913. The U.S. had tried such a system in the past and it was abused. Because of this, Americans viewed with suspicion the centralization of power and authority in banking — especially when it is an imported system, one concocted by the banking families of Germany, England, and France.

The central system gained a foothold after the financial panic in 1907 — one it would appear, that was prompted by certain monopolistically inclined eastern and foreign banks. The pressure was on Congress to do something. The answer was a national bank — the Federal Reserve — one that was supposed to become a lender of last resort to the private banking system. The theory was that private banks could turn to the Federal Reserve for loans when other banks were unable to provide them. The Federal Reserve was to pool the resources of participating banks to create an "as-needed" fund for these last-resort loans to provide liquidity in times of uncertainty.

Banks were then making money by lending out the large majority of their customer's deposits, rather than simply their own holdings. So, if a number of depositors became insecure about the health of their bank and all tried to withdraw deposits at the same time, there was rarely sufficent liquidity to accommodate such a "run on the bank." When this sort of thing began it typically caused financial panic.

The initial argument for the Fed was convincing, but it evolved into something far more powerful than simply a lender of last resort. The Federal Reserve became the entity that controls all banking activities, which in turn controls most business activities and deeply influences the business cycle itself. The Federal Reserve is also the creator of new money out of nothing.

The seven-member Board of Governors of the Federal Reserve Bank, including the chairman and directors, have become the most potent force in existence controlling our financial lives. And yet they are unelected and unaccountable to the lives of the very people they control. Though they are more influential than even the highest elected officials, they are appointed by the sitting President and confirmed by the U.S. Senate to serve 14-year terms, with no direct accountability to the voters.

The Federal Reserve is not an agency of the U.S. government, although it is a government creation. It is a corporation owned by banks that are members that hold stock in it. Every bank that has a Federal charter is required to buy stock in the Federal Reserve and to be members of the system. Banks with state charters have the option of whether or not they wish to become members, but all banks, no matter what their membership status is, are under the control and influence of the Fed.

The chairman of the board of directors testifies before Congress twice per year about how the Fed is handling the nation's money supply and what can be expected in the economy. The media, with great interest, covers these appearances, but most people are simply unaware of their import.

Cross Purposes
The Federal Reserve operates under what has been called the "dual mandate" — two directives from the federal government that many say are contradictory. Congress passed the Employment Act of 1946 and the Humphrey-Hawkins Act of 1978, which is the Full Employment and Balanced Growth Act. These acts call on the Fed to "promote effectively the goals of maximum employment, stable prices and moderate long-term interest rates."

What this means is the Fed has been directed to create economic growth with low inflation. Inflation yes, but hopefully low inflation. Rapid business growth has historically come when the Fed creates more money, lowering interest rates to banks and lending money that had not existed previously. Yet this new money — with nothing backing it — always creates inflation.

Inflation is the "hidden" tax. It is the result of government's over issue of money and it robs the poor and middle class of their hard-earned equity.

Only if the economy has grown in terms of productivity and if a substance of widely perceived value backs the new money, can new money be issued without causing inflation.

How much money is created is a decision made by the seven members of the Fed who form the majority of the 12-member Federal Open Market Committee (FOMC). This group has the final say on the cost and availability of money and credit in the economy.

When an American sends in his or her taxes, the money eventually winds up passing through the Federal Reserve System, which operates for the government the way your bank operates for you. Checks are issued from the Fed for everything from submarines to Social Security checks.

Show Me The Money

"Where is most of the money in the banking system today?" asks Bruce J. Summers, the Fed's system-wide director for automated services. "Not in the vault. It's on computer records. We protect the value of the information." They also protect the currency by gleaning out counterfeit and worn bills, which add up to several million dollars each day.

One of the more intriguing things about the Federal Reserve is how it creates money. The picture that comes to mind is of a printing press, churning out sheet after sheet of dollar bills. And, while that indeed happens, the real creation of money is silent and invisible. The Federal government issues securities, which are debt obligation instruments such as bonds. The Federal Reserve buys these on the open market. It buys these securities in a kind of shell game by issuing credit to the government, which then writes checks against it, and presto — new money is put into circulation.

Let's say you held a U.S. Treasury bond and decided to sell it. The Federal Reserve, using power granted to it by the Congress, would pay you money that did not exist before — whatever the face amount of the security. (It's not the same as when you or I write a check on our bank accounts and the money is then withdrawn. When the Fed does it the banking reserves are added to, not subtracted from.)

Once you've received payment for your security you make the deposit to your bank account. Through the "fractional reserve system," your commercial bank must keep a certain amount of your deposit on reserve – perhaps 10 percent. But it can lend out the rest – what they call the "excess reserves." The person who borrows that money spends it and the business where he or she has spent it can now deposit it in their bank. That bank now has new money it can lend out. And, so it goes, until the original purchase of the Treasury security could now have multiplied the amount of money in circulation up to nine times the sum of the new money government created out of nothing to begin with.

When you add the original government debt to the bank created fiat money, the total is approximately ten times more currency put into circulation than the amount of the underlying government debt. The banking system, underwritten by the FDIC, has therefore expanded the amount of money multiple times for every dollar the Federal Reserve has created out of nothing to begin with.

To the degree that this newly created money floods into the economy in surplus of goods and services, it causes the purchasing power of all money, both new and old, to decline. Prices go up because the relative value of the money has gone down. The result is the same as if that purchasing power had been taken in taxes.

The reality of this process is a hidden tax of up to 10 times the national debt. Americans have paid over the years, in addition to their federal, state, and excise taxes, a completely hidden tax equal to many times the national debt. Of course, the Federal Reserve can also shrink the money supply by selling securities in its portfolio. The money paid for these securities is absorbed, like a sponge, and taken out of the economy — not actually put into any bank account.

Shell Game

If this all seems like a shell game, it's small wonder. A currency with nothing behind it is not only fictitious and dangerous it is simply illegal. Or at least it would be, if you or I or anyone else were to embark upon such an unscrupulous scheme.

It's often said that those who do not know history are doomed to repeat it. We are neither the first generation nor is the U.S. the first nation to try to do business with an artificial currency. But the ultimate consequences in terms of inflation and subsequent creditability have been so disastrous in the past that the founding fathers strove to prevent this kind of corruption in the United States for all future generations.

The U.S. Constitution (Article 1, Sections 8 and 10) already quoted earlier bears repeating, as it stipulated that:

> "Congress shall have the power ... to borrow money ... to coin money, regulate the value thereof, and of foreign coin, and fix the standard of weights and measures; ... No state shall ... coin money; emit bills of credit; [or] make anything but gold and silver a tender in payment of debts."

The drafters of the Constitution were clear in their intent: "coin" money means to stamp pieces of metal. The young country already had its belly full of paper currency. Many states issued their own paper money from 1690 to 1764. It was so much easier to simply print money than risk the ire of citizens by exacting taxes. The result was run-away inflation — as high as 2300 percent in Rhode Island before the Revolution.

Experience with inflation is why the Constitution clearly prohibits states from issuing "bills of credit" or paper money. The flaw, however, is that the drafters did not also directly prohibit the federal government from doing so. In the course of fighting off the British, the Revolutionaries resorted to paper money in order to pay for the staggering cost of providing for men and supplies. At the beginning of the war in 1775, the federated colonies had a total money supply of $12 million. But the Continental Congress issued another $2 million by June, and authorized another $4 million soon thereafter. The presses churned out the money year after year as the war dragged on, until the original $12 million had another $227 million added to it —plus $200 million in money-like certificates issued by the Continental Army — in addition to the money issued by the states. It amounted to an increase of 5000 percent in five years.

The result of all that money chasing goods was runaway inflation. Thomas Jefferson saw what happened and called it by its right name — taxation — which he called "the most oppressive of all because [it is] the most unequal of all."

When the country returned to money backed by precious metals, the country also returned to a stable currency and to prosperity. This is a lesson that evidently must be relearned by future generations.

Origins of the Fed

It was ironic that the very country from which the Revolutionaries sought to free themselves — England — gave them their example of a financial institution that again controls them. Yet that is exactly what happened. Following the example of the Bank of England, the Continentals organized the Bank of North America in 1781. The ambitious name was because they hoped Canada would join them in a continent-wide nation free of British rule. That was not to be their only disappointment.

The Bank of North America – a private bank that functioned as a central bank — was not given the power to directly issue the nation's money, but it could produce bank notes the government would accept. The bank was the depository for Federal funds, and immediately created out of nothing more than a million dollars, which it loaned to the government. Other sleights of hand with gold loaned from France, money created out of nothing and loaned to bank officers, brought the bank to low esteem. It was yet another casualty of the Revolutionary War and the bank's charter was not renewed.

The entire concept of a central bank had been discredited. Yet the prospect of the power to create money from nothing is so appealing that the U.S. Congress again succumbed. Congress may have been empowered only to "coin" money, but it desperately wanted to "print" it. And so, Congress pulled a fast one by delegating the right to print money to a separate entity, and then "borrowed" this printed money and spent it. The kicker is that the entity that "lends" this money is actually creating it out of thin air.

Today the IOUs the government creates are the bonds and T-bills you and I buy — with the money the bank has created. Congress has gotten around the Constitutional proscription against creating bills of credit by having the Federal Reserve Bank perform this job.

Thus was born America's second central bank in 1791 — the Bank of the United States. Like the previous bank, the new one was made the official depository of federal funds and was given the monopoly of issuing bank notes. These notes were not forced on the public for private debts, but the government would take them for taxes and duties. The bank was required to redeem its notes in gold or silver. The purpose of the bank was to create money for the federal government, and like its predecessor, issued so much that the result was inflation. In five years wholesale prices rose by 72 percent, which was tantamount to a hidden tax on the citizens. And, as always, it was the fundamental backbone of society that was hurt the worst. Those that faithfully saved money for investment and their retirement saw those savings evaporate through government fraud. The Bank of the United States became a hot political issue in its day, and its charter was not renewed.

By 1811, it went the way of its predecessor and was out of business. The War of 1812 again put Washington in the position of wanting more money than it had. The war was so unpopular that Congress feared levying taxes to pay for it. Yet the past method of conjuring up money out of a central bank was denied to them. Instead, the U.S. government encouraged the proliferation of private banks, from which it borrowed, and then relieved them of the obligation to redeem their notes with gold or silver.

Banks loaned out in paper money much more than they actually had on deposit in hard currency. By 1814, when people wanted their silver and gold and the banks were unable to deliver, many of these banks failed, leaving note holders ready to riot.

The chaos in banking gave support to arguments for yet another national bank. In 1816, Congress gave a 20 year charter to the Second Bank of the United States — it was actually the third central bank by that time. In a great irony, this bank refused to accept any notes from other banks unless the notes were redeemable by gold or silver on demand. But when the other banks made the same demand back, the Second Bank of the United States recanted on the issue of hard money.

This bank was more efficient in extending its reach across the young and growing country, so its acts of expanding and contracting the money supply had dramatic impact in the national economy. Once again, the American public wanted a sounder currency. So strong was the sentiment that Martin Van Buren and Andrew Jackson worked within the new Democratic Party to abolish the national bank. When Jackson was elected in 1828, that's exactly what he set about doing. The bank's existence became the central issue facing the nation, until it, too, was finally put to rest by 1837.

Jackson was successful in instituting several monetary reforms — such as requiring the use of hard currency or coin for transactions under $5. But times were changing. People began using checks instead of bank notes for their major transactions. This left bankers the opportunity to once again lend out much more than was on deposit. Money in circulation almost doubled in four years. When the contraction in the money supply came, as it inevitably did, banks failed and depositors were the losers.

To protect depositors, states such as New York devised a "safety fund," as early as 1829. New York banks were required to contribute from one half of one percent up to a total of three percent of their total capital stock to this fund. When the crash came in 1837 the banks were swamped with depositor demands for their money. The only thing that saved the system was that the State of New York agreed to accept the now worthless bank notes as payment for canal fees. In other words, the taxpayers picked up the burden, as they have ever since. This system is the precursor to the Federal Deposit Insurance Corporation, or FDIC.

The Civil War, like the Revolutionary War, encouraged the government to create more money. During fiscal year 1861, expenses for the Federal Government had been only $67 million. After the first year of war, expenses rose to $475 million. By war's end they were $1,300 millions. Taxes covered only 11 percent of that total. The national deficit swelled to $2.61 billion.

There was no central, national bank at the time and smaller, state banks were not in a position to create enough receipt money to pay for the war. The North issued bonds to be paid at the end of the war in gold, but that was not enough to pay the bill. An income tax was tried, but it was extremely unpopular. The only option was to print money not backed by precious metals. The $432 million of them printed during the war became known as "greenbacks." In effect, the government became its own Federal Reserve Bank by issuing money from nothing as a wartime expedient.

The pressure of war led to other creative efforts. The National Banking Act of 1863 established a system of nationally chartered banks — not one central bank. But control was firmly held in the East. It was a wartime emergency tool to create a market for government bonds which were transformed into money, a process that later became the model for the Federal Reserve Systems' money creation machine.

What happened is that the Federal government issued government bonds, which the bank purchased. The bank immediately turned them back to the Treasury, which exchanged them for an equal amount of "United States Bank Notes" with the bank's name engraved on them. These notes were legal tender for taxes and duties, and therefore most people accepted them as cash. Money was created from nothing — government debt was transformed from bonds into cash.

The money so created during the Civil War was not considered legal tender for all debts — just what was owed to the government. The official money was government issued coins and greenbacks. (Ironically, the South never did issue its own coins — U.S. and private coinage remained legal tender throughout the South during the war.)

Money created in this shell game fashion did become the legal tender of the nation with creation of the Federal Reserve Bank half a century later. With the Federal Reserve System, the government creates money by converting debt into legal tender through loaning to a system of its own creation. The original intention of the Founding Fathers, that America's money be backed by precious metals, was completely thwarted. It was sacrificed as an expedient in waging war. Now that the wars are over, there is no incentive to return to safer ground.

Problems

What would you do if you had the power to create money out of nothing? Would your area of temptation be toward pleasure and sensual thrills? That's the temptation of young people. The old, gray heads running the show at the Federal Reserve lean toward the weakness of older men — toward power.

With the ability to create money, the Federal Reserve is a player in the game of co-opting and controlling the world. The Fed has become so effective in manufacturing money out of nothing that it has become the model for the IMF (International Monetary Fund). In fact, this organization could not exist without the flow of American dollars created by the Federal Reserve. Central Banks of industrialized nations, just like the Federal Reserve — guarantee loans to developing countries. This means that if the borrower defaults, the taxpayers of the lending nations pick up the debt themselves. This money props up cooperative heads of state by giving them access to vast wealth.

The game that is being played now involves co-opting the heads of state of less developed countries. The world's largest and most influential banks make loans to these governments. These countries are frequently unable to repay the loans. They then offer to pay the interest only or default altogether. To keep these loans out of the default column, Fed supported major banks make ever-larger loans so the interest payments can stay current on their books. In this way, the largest U.S. banks are assured of not suffering defaults whilst booking huge interest income, and eventually will have the taxpayers to bail them out when the debts simply become to overwhelming to refinance.

Former enemies now find themselves beholden to the IMF. Russia and her former satellites now grovel for the dollars that only the Federal Reserve-backed world economy can provide. Thus, entire countries are brought into vassalage to the international fund, to the machine that churns out money from nothing. This system is accountable to no one government and is beyond almost everyone's control, yet has as its base of power, the ability to saddle you and me with repaying the obligations it makes.

It bears repeating that when the founders of the U.S. Constitution spoke of paper money, they were actually referring to fiat currency, or a form of paper money that has no backing and is nothing more than a bill of credit representing increased government debt. This is completely different from a paper currency that represents, in effect, a claim check on something considered of universal value, such as gold, silver, grain, or some other sought after commodity.

George Mason, a delegate from Virginia to the original Constitutional Convention stated he had a "mortal hatred of paper (fiat) money." He is quoted as saying, "Paper money is founded upon fraud and knavery."

Oliver Ellsworth, the third Chief Justice of the Supreme Court, said:

"This is a favorable moment to shut and bar the door against paper money. The mischief of the various experiments which have been made are now fresh in the public mind and have excited the disgust of all the respectable parts of America."

George Reed, a Delaware representative to the Constitutional Convention, declared that a provision in the Constitution granting the new government the right to issue fiat money "would be as alarming as the mark of the beast in Revelations." And, John Langdon from New Hampshire warned that he would rather reject the whole plan of federation than to grant the new government the right to issue fiat money. George Washington was of a similar opinion as were the vast majority of those assembled to produce, as Gladstone put it: "The ....most wonderful work ever struck off ... by the brain and purpose of man."

So what happened? How did this heroic beginning slide into a situation so wanton that it strips us of our liberty and deprives us of our property?

In G. Edward Griffin's wonderful book entitled *The Creature from Jekyll Island*, which I highly recommend, he says:

"The accepted version of history is that the Federal Reserve was created to stabilize our economy. Even the most naïve student must sense a grave contradiction between this cherished view and the System's actual performance. Since its inception, it has presided over the crashes of 1921 and 1929; the Great Depression of '29 to '39; recessions in '53, '57, '69, '75, '81, a stock market "Black Monday" in 1987, and a 1000%

inflation which has destroyed 90% of the dollar's purchasing power."

It takes well over $10,000 to buy now what it took only $1,000 to acquire when the Federal Reserve was formed to "stabilize our economy." This incredible loss in value was quietly transferred to the federal government in the form of hidden taxation, and the Federal Reserve System was the mechanism by which it was accomplished. The details of the creation of the Fed have now largely come to light — it was the brainchild of Paul Warburg, working in concert with the authors of the most famous monopolies of all times, the Rothchilds, Morgans, Rockefellers, and other extremely wealthy influential world players. Daddy Warbucks of Little Orphan Annie fame was patterned after the life and character of Paul Warburg.

Anthony Sutton, former Research Fellow at the Hoover Institution for War, Revolution and Peace, and also Professor of Economics at California State University at Los Angles provides unique insight:

"Warburg's revolutionary plan to get American Society to go to work for Wall Street was astonishingly simple. Even today, academic theoreticians cover their blackboards with meaningless equations, and the general public struggles in bewildered confusion with inflation and the coming credit collapse, while the quite simple explanation of the problem goes undiscussed and almost entirely uncomprehended. The Federal Reserve System is a legal private monopoly of the money supply operated for the benefit of the few under the guise of protecting and promoting the public interest."

The United States government has succumbed to the attraction of spending whatever it will, without the bureaucracy actually having the funds to pay for its excesses. Taxes, always an unpopular issue, can now be reduced while government spending goes unchecked, merely by government waiving their magic wand and "emitting bills of credit" to the Federal Reserve who in turn creates more fiat money to put in circulation.

History will not be forever robbed of its lessons. Inflation ALWAYS follows the circulation of fiat money. Inflation is the hidden tax paid by every one of us as we are robbed of real equity.

I urge you to implement strategies to protect your privacy, to develop real asset protection and to substantially reduce your taxes where possible. Given the precarious state of an interdependent economy it is also a good idea to set something aside that has historical value as money, just in case the worst happens in our lifetime, and we see a temporary collapse of the economic system due to irresponsible government and fiat money.

Decisive Information

10

Frequently Asked Questions

"Out of intense complexities, intense simplicities emerge."

Winston Churchill

The Preamble

To the uninitiated, the whole idea of going offshore with some portion of your business activities or estate planning can be intimidating. How do I do it? Is it legal? Will I lose my money? There is much room for misunderstanding and misinformation on these issues. Compounding the problem is the shortage of places to go for straight answers. There are those with a vested interest in planting seeds of doubt regarding the entire offshore experience. By that I refer to the taxing authorities, bankers, and others who seek some form of control over others. The more of your assets that are safely offshore, the less is within their grasp. In Dr. Arnold Goldstein's excellent book entitled, *Offshore Havens*, comes this quote:

"You may be one of the millions of Americans who are completely hoodwinked by the IRS...our bankers...and countless others who, for their own self-serving reasons, perpetuate the myth and lies about offshore banking. Doesn't everyone believe that offshore havens are evil, dangerous or illegal?"

"The fact is that most of America has been duped and deceived by this deliberate avalanche of distortions — even outright lies — about offshore havens. Consequently, most Americans have absolutely no idea what offshore banking is all about. Instead, they believe what they read or hear from a controlled media that paints offshore havens as a hangout for tax evaders, money launders and assorted crooks, and scofflaws. Uninformed lawyers, accountants and financial planners still advise their clients that offshore havens are illegal, too risky, or otherwise unworthy of consideration. They should know better — but don't!"

As with anything else new, there is a learning curve and there are Frequently Asked Questions — FAQ's. The questions I am most often asked have to do with the legality and appropriateness of investing off-

152

shore. Direct answers to specific questions should aid in clearing up misconceptions right up front.

It is a well known reality that the use of international financial centers (offshore jurisdictions) is considered by sophisticated global money managers to be a safe and reasonable way to conduct business. And, they should know, considering hundreds of billions of U.S. dollar equivalents are invested in offshore funds.

Standard & Poor's is the best known and most highly regarded information resource on publicly traded companies. The S&P 500 Index, for example, is reported on daily around the world. Their voluminous publications on everything from penny-stocks to government bonds are respected worldwide. The company publishes *The Standard & Poor's Guide to Offshore Investment Funds*, which you can purchase from their website at www.intl-offshore.com, for $149.95 USD, plus shipping and handling.

Excerpts from this guide:
- Those artificial barriers we call nation states are constantly being broken down by technology and the commerce that springs from it.
- Nation-states – and more particularly the revenue-seeking governments of nation states – have not caught up with this increasingly international world of individuals.
- Social and demographic changes have led to pressure on government expenditure, while at the same time the need to be re-elected has put downward pressure on taxation.
- This squeeze has led governments to give up on providing adequate retirement pensions and encourage their citizens to provide for themselves.
- Those with an international outlook are beginning to wonder why they should be limited by a particular government's controls on how and where they may save and invest – and be taxed heavily for this dubious privilege.
- Indeed, internationally minded individuals are questioning why a particular nation state should be able to demand an interest in how they organize their personal financial security when the very same government admits that it will be able to do little to support them in the future.
- It is for this reason that many investors are turning to offshore funds, which provide freedom and control for individuals to plan for their financial security without being regulated by tax-hungry governments.
- Going offshore provides wealth protection whether from punitive taxes or from creditors and excessive charges due to legal damages, something which professionals in the US will understand well.
- As well as protection, offshore investors gain the freedom to invest in

pretty well whatever they want.

- This is not to say there is no consumer protection with offshore funds. Indeed, most offshore financial centers are very keen to uphold a good reputation and therefore only allow in reputable investment managers and keep a close eye on their activities.

On the whole, offshore funds do have greater freedoms, not the least being the freedom from the costly process of reporting to such regulatory bodies as the U.S. Securities & Exchange Commission.

What follows are specific questions frequently encountered with clear answers in simple English.

What is an "offshore haven?"

An offshore haven is a country, or jurisdiction other than that where the investor lives. Offshore also refers to jurisdictions with carefully crafted legislation designed to encourage investors from outside their country. Typically there are specific tax-holidays outlined in such legislation or, as is the case of numerous island jurisdictions, there is a guarantee of no taxes at all for certain types of qualifying companies or trusts based from within their legal jurisdiction.

In the past going offshore also conveyed the concept of more flexible regulatory requirements related to company formations, banking, insurance and mutual fund formation and management. However, in the past two years this situation has been reversed in many jurisdictions where perhaps most offshore locations now actually require greater due-diligence regarding company formations and the opening of banking relationships than do countries such as Canada or the U.S. Many offshore jurisdictions also provide much higher standards of personal and financial privacy, than may be available in your home country.

What is offshore banking?

There are at least three distinctly different meanings to the term offshore banking. The first means merely that you are using a bank based and operating from a country other than the one where you reside. For example, an American is banking "offshore" if he or she opens an account with the Royal Bank of Canada in Toronto, which, by the way, a lot of Americans did until the first quarter of 2001. (A senior officer with that bank confided that he expected they would lose 90% of their American depositors during 2001 because they, along with many other major world banks, were being forced by the U.S. government to automatically report on the banking activities of U.S. citizens — Orwell was right.) So to clarify the first interpretation, anyone using a bank based anywhere outside their own country is technically involved in offshore banking.

The second meaning to the term offshore bank is a legal one that denotes that a bank license has been granted to a corporation in one country or legal jurisdiction such that it may only do business with customers in another jurisdiction. In other words, the clients of the bank are not allowed to be citizens or residents of the country where the bank is based. Offshore banks are licensed in such a way as to be as attractive as possible to depositors from other countries thereby benefiting the country that licensed the bank by generating licensing fees, generating a demand for local professional services, and by creating greater employment. Many countries promote and license offshore banks, including the U.S., which uses the term "international banking facilities," rather than "offshore banking."

The third meaning for offshore banking is an inference to using a financial services provider in a country that does not have income tax and does not have a mutual legal assistance treaty with your home country. Without a specific treaty one country will rarely enforce or investigate a crime that is not also a crime in their country. For example, income tax evasion is a crime in the U.S. (income tax deferral and avoidance is not) but a number of countries do not have income tax and therefore cannot recognize it as a crime and certainly have no interest in helping the IRS prosecute depositors in their jurisdiction.

Why use an offshore bank?

Privacy and Asset Protection. One of the most important aspects of offshore banking is personal or corporate privacy and banking confidentiality. Funds and other assets are significantly better protected from creditors, and/or any other form of lien or confiscation action, in an offshore jurisdiction that in your country of residence. Keeping assets offshore considerably reduces the likelihood of litigation from lawyers working on a contingency basis, a serious problem in some countries. Legal predators look for deep pockets and will generally not pursue someone who has taken the time to protect themselves from frivolous claims.

Is it legal to have an offshore bank account?

Absolutely! In most Western countries it is perfectly legal to have offshore banking relationships. Questions surrounding offshore banking legalities usually are related to when a person fails to report offshore income to his or her country of domicile at tax time. In other words, income earned from certificates of deposit or other forms of investment in conjunction with an offshore bank may be tax-free in the country where the bank is located but your country of residence may require that you report it. It is not illegal for Europeans, Latinos, (with some exceptions) Canadians or Americans to invest offshore, maintain bank accounts, and/ or investment accounts.

Is it legal to send money offshore?

Few first world countries have restrictions on the amounts you may send offshore. South Africa and New Zealand used to have heavy restrictions on outflows but both have lightened these restrictions. The U.S. does not, nor can it ever, have a law forbidding the movement of funds offshore. In fact, no country that depends upon international commerce can invoke such a law without ruining its own economy.

Every country that has passed legislation restricting the movement of money outside their own jurisdiction has virtually destroyed their international trade. When that happens they are unable to sell their products offshore or import others, which means their currency loses value quickly. Contrary to popular myth, if you are a U.S. citizen there is no restriction on the amount of money you may move, or when you may move it and there is virtually no restriction on where you move it, with the possible exception of Cuba and North Korea. And in both of these cases restrictions have recently been reduced.

Is it easier to circumvent taxation offshore?

Yes, it is. With the exception of U.S. persons, beginning in 2001, offshore banks do not report earned income to taxing authorities, or anyone else, even though these earnings may be reportable and taxable under the laws of your homeland. Europeans have greater flexibility in these regards, however U.S. persons are taxed on income regardless of where it is earned or received. There are certain deductions available, specific to your homeland and citizenship, when one lives and works offshore.

Offshore investors are essentially considered to be on the "honor system." This is changing for Americans as a result of the new Qualified Intermediary legislation that went into effect January 1, 2001 that forces many of the largest offshore financial institutions to report directly to the IRS on the activities of Americans abroad. The IRS estimates that about one third of all the earned income within America goes unreported. What percentage of offshore earnings goes unreported is anyone's guess. There are generally stiff penalties for failure to report income to your home country. However, it should be understood that ownership of an offshore bank account does not constitute a presumption of tax evasion.

Do I have to pay taxes on money earned abroad?

In some countries the answer to this question is that you do not. However, increasingly these options are being limited as the legislatures of virtually all countries seek to increase revenues. If you're an U.S. citizen the money you earn anywhere must be reported. However, if you're living abroad and working for a non-U.S. company, you may be entitled to a $76,000 tax fee exemption per year. And if you're married and you're both working offshore that number is twice that much. You are also entitled to housing, transportation and some other expenses, which can be paid by your employer and not be considered taxable income. This is a good deal if you can swing it.

Properly organized offshore corporations may provide certain tax timing benefits, and in some cases even tax reduction mechanisms, particularly if the offshore corporation is properly "de-controlled." However, just because you open a bank account in a country that has passed bank secrecy laws does not excuse you from the responsibility to report income earned to the taxing authorities in your home country.

What are the primary reasons for having wealth placed offshore?

1. Privacy. Your rights to privacy are all but gone in several nations, particularly if you reside in or are a citizen of the United States.
2. Asset Protection. To secure yourself against future predatory litigation. If you earn $50,000 a year or more and live in the U.S. you will be sued an average of seven times in your life. And this number is growing.
3. Tax Planning. Advantageous use of foreign jurisdictions and their tax rules for reduction of tax liability can be extremely valuable.
4. Estate Planning. Family and asset protection trusts, possibly as an alternative to a will, for accumulation of investment income and long-term benefits for beneficiaries on a favorable tax basis. However, although an offshore trust is still one of the best asset protection strategies around, one must consider it tax-neutral because taken by itself it has no tax advantages.

What constitutes a favorable jurisdiction?

A desirable jurisdiction should be politically neutral, follow a policy of free trade, not interfere with the commercial activities of corporations established there, and provide reasonable assurances of personal and corporate privacy.

Language, the quality of telecommunications, convenient time zones, availability of professional infrastructure, and other issues are also important.

Most popular jurisdictions have a legal system derived from a western country and greatly favor corporations that are non-resident in nature. There must be a solid commitment to the protection of private property and the promotion of international trade.

Will my money be safe offshore?

As safe as you want it to be. In an age when major Japanese and English banks have closed and U.S. banks have failed right and left, you may wonder if your money is safe anywhere. But historically the safest banks are located in the jurisdictions that have had the longest standing history of private banking. For example, I have been told that Switzerland has never had a bank failure. But this falls under the category of a faith-promoting rumor. Russian banks have about the worst record and should be avoided.

In the U.S. the number of banks defined as "problem banks" by the Federal Deposit Insurance Corporation increased 750 percent from 1980 to 1988. The FDIC is currently reporting that approximately 1,500 banks in the U.S. are unstable. Even on a per-capita basis this is a dismal record.

Do offshore banks make riskier investments than other banks?

Not if you look at the relative track records. The Savings and Loan debacle and the hoard of U.S. banks — that together have run up a tab of over $500 billion, an amount paid directly by the taxpayers — hardly seems like a record to brag about. Add to this the procession of bank executives marching off to prison or being fined. No other industrial country can top this miserable record of mismanagement, ineptitude and corruption. Although the Japanese seem to be vying for second place and of course England has recently had its problem banks on a huge international scale.

By contrast, banks in countries that do not have a depository insurance program to bail them out seem to be more careful as to how they do business. They realize that their greatest asset is their own success. There are many countries that have their own deposit insurance program. But most often the insurance is through private industry rather than the government. Often enough this insurance can be for the entire balance of an account, rather than only for $100,000 which is the case in the U.S. The U.S. Federal Deposit Insurance Corporation does not cover most people with surplus funds anyway. Why? Simply because most of people seek earnings higher than the small amount paid in passbook savings and instead opt for short-term money market accounts, or similar higher interest products. And these types of investment vehicles, although liquid and secure, are rarely insured by government.

Will I earn more or less interest offshore?

Chances are good that you will earn more offshore than in the U.S. Typically, international banks pay higher rates. If you are a U.S. person you may be interested to compare the daily U.S. T-Bill rates with the Euro-Dollar Bond rates. The Euro is almost always paying a rate of 20% more than that of the U.S. T-Bill rate. International banks based in an OFC often operate with lower overhead and greater tax concessions than do U.S. banks. It is the recognition of this fact that has led to so many American bank mergers and subsequent reduction of overhead — largely through layoffs and closing of redundant branches.

Interest rates in the eastern Caribbean (the West Indies) are regulated by the Central Bank in St Kitts and those rates tend to be lower than available in the U.S. One should take an international view to these options, which may mean living in one country, having a corporate structure in another, have banking based in a third country, and so forth.

What about offshore scams?

In addition to the normal business risks associated with any endeavor, con artists ply their trade almost as easily offshore as they do domestically. Actually, and contrary to public opinion, it is almost always more difficult for anyone, including criminals, to set up bank accounts, brokerage accounts and secure other financial services offshore. Banking standards and "Know Your Client" procedures are considerably more stringent offshore than onshore. But there are still bad offshore deals promoted by good people and real scams promoted by bad people, just as there are domestically.

There is a con I hear of all too frequently, which is supposedly an offshore deal but is really a presentation made in your home country and usually by someone you have reason to trust, who actually believes what they are pitching. The swindle is usually a story about an "insiders deal" based on a concept variously referred to as "offshore high-yield investments," "bank debenture trading," "bank roll-over programs," "fractional trading," etc." These programs are typically introduced to potential investors through relatively naïve, domestic network marketing people or via the Internet. This particular scam is very alarming and seems to reinvent itself under slightly different names and stories again and again. On a single day a couple of years ago I received three separate contacts from apparently true believers who were pitching the benefits of the bank-trading program with which they were involved.

Most, if not all, of the bank debenture type trading programs circulating in Australia, Canada, and the U.S. appear to be a new aberration of the age old Ponzi scheme. In a Ponzi scheme, sometimes referred to as a "pyramid scheme," the first people into the deal may receive significant yields but their return is paid from new investors entering the program rather than an actual return on invested funds. In this way there are legitimate people in the deal that actually make money and are therefore true believers. But eventually the demand for payout exceeds new investor deposits and the program shuts down with the last people in the door loosing their entire investment. The reason each of these programs seem to work so long is that people in the deal are so enamored by the money they think they are making that they allow their initial investment, plus the return they believe they have earned, to be continually reinvested. So many people actually believe in these deals that in one particular year two close friends were visibly upset when I dared to question the veracity of the bank-trading program with which they had become involved. In the end, both lost their investment.

New versions of the bank trading scam seem to resurface every few months and in my opinion this is a very serious problem that just will not seem to go away. I strongly suggest that anyone contacted by bank trading program promoters refuse to explore this kind of investment scheme.

Isn't it extremely difficult to do banking offshore?

It doesn't have to be. Banking offshore can be relatively pain free. New accounts are opened in offshore centers on a daily basis and millions of legitimate dollars flow through them annually, all without the slightest problem. After all, international finance is the lifeblood of these centers. They frequently have no other source of income, and they truly want your business. It is true, that to open a bank account internationally takes more time and requires more effort than opening an account at the corner branch of a domestic bank.

Many international banks will allow you to have your money held in the currency of your choice or in several currencies, as a hedge. Secured credit cards are the norm with international banks because they do not typically ask for taxpayer identification information nor do they generally require that you complete a credit application or check on your finances. However, once you've received an offshore card you can charge on it the same way you would a domestic credit card. Conversions are made at your offshore bank if you hold balances in a currency other than where you are using the credit card.

What do I look for in an offshore bank?

- Is the bank well established and reputable?
- Do the bank employees speak English?
- Does the bank have experience in handling customer from countries other than those in which they are located?
- Can you manage your accounts by phone and fax?
- Will you have a personal account manager and will he or she complete wire transfers the same day requested?
- Are the fees for personal attention reasonable?
- Does the bank offer benefits to nonresident customers?
- Does the bank routinely handle multi-currency transactions?

Daily administration of an offshore company, if provided by professional corporate managers or a fiduciary such as a licensed trust company, will resolve most of your concerns. A good administrator will know the precise requirements of each bank and the most efficient way to fulfill them. In turn, the banks will know from past experience that accounts opened and operated by that administrator are well managed, monitored and maintained. The benefits of this good relationship are passed on to the client.

How do offshore havens get started?

Certain countries, or legal jurisdictions within countries, seek to make it attractive for you to incorporate and carry on financial activities within their jurisdiction. There are so many tax efficient jurisdictions competing on the world market for your business that it can be somewhat overwhelming just trying to sort through all the positive options.

What's an IBC?

IBC stands for "international business corporation." IBC is the term most often used when referring to a corporation formed in an offshore jurisdiction where the purpose of the business is to do business in a place or places other than the jurisdiction itself. For example, a person in England causes an IBC to be formed in Grenada in order to handle business for anywhere in the world EXCEPT Grenada.

What maintenance requirements are there for an IBC?

All jurisdictions have at least two requirements:
1. Maintaining a registered agent or office; and
2. Paying an annual registration, franchise fee, or flat tax fee

Do I have to travel abroad to invest offshore?

No. Offshore investing does not mean that you have to live abroad, or even travel abroad. Offshore investing can be done from your own home through qualified professionals who will function on your behalf with reputable offshore banks and professional firms. Investments within your country of residence can generally be purchased on your behalf from an offshore location.

Don't you have to be a millionaire to invest offshore?

Let's define a millionaire. If you mean that a person needs to have a million dollars in cash the answer is definitely not! You can start a bank account offshore with as little as $1,500 or so. But it is true that some offshore banks will not open and manage accounts for less than $500,000. These are generally larger private banks based in Switzerland, Austria, or England. If you're going to simply explore overseas investment, you may want to start with a few thousand and learn as you go. Perhaps $50,000 is a good level to begin serious offshore investing.

What will my accountant think?

As discussed at the end of chapter one, accountants from all over the world are now becoming more familiar with why and how their clients can successfully enjoy the benefits of offshore jurisdictions. A periodical of the American Institute of Certified Public Accountants has endorsed offshore planning as evidenced by a bulletin in late 1999 and again in early 2000, which includes this statement:

"To prepare for the 21st century, CPA's must be aware of the hottest, most important tax-savings and asset protection devices. Once thought of as reserved for the very rich, offshore planning is available for virtually all clients, and should be part of overall planning."

Solicitors, tax lawyers, financial advisors and accountants from all over the globe are now specialized in working through offshore jurisdictions. Referrals for qualified professionals are available from the Sovereign Crest Alliance (www.sovereigncrest.com) and/or the International Tax Planners Association, (www.itpa.org). Referrals are also usually available through local chapters of the Chartered Accountants association, BAR association, the AICPA, and so forth.

You now know about the whys and the wherefores of taking your money offshore. But before you take the plunge, learn how a tax haven within the borders of the U.S. — the state of Nevada — can fit into you plan of asset protection.

11

Offshore in Nevada

"The freedom and happiness of man...are the sole objects of all legitimate govern-
ment." "Oppose with manly firmness any invasions on the rights of the people"

Thomas Jefferson

Nevada

Nevada is the jurisdiction of choice for many Canadians, Europeans and Latinos. It is also a great place to start offshore for an American. What? Offshore for an American? Yes, actually if you are a U.S. person and you live and operate a business from any of the other 49 states, Nevada is considered offshore or "foreign" insofar as your jurisdiction is concerned. Nevada is truly an excellent option for many folks, regardless of where they may live.

If you've ever been to Nevada, you quickly sense something in the air. It isn't necessarily the sound of coins jingling into the pan of a slot machine. It isn't the sound of buccaneers fighting it out on pirate ships in front of a casino. It isn't the sound of people on street corners handing out advertising for prostitutes.

What's in the air is the freedom that makes all these things possible. Nevada is perhaps unique in the United States as a place where the frontier spirit of freedom still holds full sway. That spirit of freedom carries through to personal economics as well. And you can enjoy the economic freedom Nevada offers — and never even go there.

Nevada, among other pluses, has no state income tax. The state doesn't need income tax because the revenues from the gaming industry carry half the tax load. Many taxes you find common elsewhere in the U.S. do not exist in Nevada. There is also the mentality that what a person earns a person ought to be able to keep. It's a mindset that I share and I suspect you do, too. Nevada also respects privacy — more about that later.

The Nevada option is really quite simple. In some respects it is easier for a European, Australian or someone from South American to grasp the values inherent in a Nevada strategy than it is for a U.S. person. For the average American the concept usually comes as a surprise, as they tend to think of the U.S. as one cohesive whole without considering the benefits of using another U.S. state as a business strategy in itself. The following example assumes one is from the U.S. But if you're not from the States, you'll still benefit by reading it because much of the information may apply directly to you.

What follows is a legal, ethical business strategy. Although when you first hear how it works it seems as though something must be wrong. Let me assure you, the only thing wrong about what you are about to read is that you probably haven't yet done it yourself and reaped the benefits.

The Secret

This is the principle in a nutshell: you transfer profits from a high-tax jurisdiction to a jurisdiction where the taxes are lower or non-existent. The Nevada option works like this: first we will assume that you have a business that generates income in the state where you currently reside, and that your home state has some form of state income tax. The Nevada strategy calls for you to form a corporation in Nevada.

With the help of a skilled professional, you so arrange your finances that the business in your home state continually owes money to your Nevada Company — so much so that the business in your home state shows little or no profit. The profits show up in your Nevada Corporation where there is no state income tax and where no one knows you own the company. This is called profit upstreaming. The IRS calls this kind of strategy income stripping and they don't generally like it. But in the case of a state-to-state strategy like this one, it may not have any effect on federal taxes, just state income tax, so they really don't care. Do I have you confused? Read on, things will clear up.

Put in other words, by owning two companies, one in your home state that conducts your business and the other in Nevada that simply is a creditor of your operating business, you have the capacity to shift funds out of your home state and to Nevada, thus reducing net earnings in your home state company. Why is this valuable? You have just saved an amount equal to the state income tax that would have been due from your home state business earnings, minus the costs of maintaining the Nevada Company. You have also gained a significant measure of privacy because Nevada does not provide for shareholder information in any public record.

This conceptual process has been simplified for the sake of explanation. But doing it right, so that your "corporate veil" cannot be pierced, usually takes the input and assistance of someone knowledgeable in these matters. Is this a valid business approach? Tens of thousands of people throughout the United States have enacted this simple strategy, and folks from all over the world use Nevada as a base of operations for their U.S. activities.

Why Nevada

The Nevada Option is a consequence of decisions made by the Founding Fathers of the United States. They decided that individual states should have the right of taxation. In other words, the citizens of each state have the right to tax themselves as they see fit. And different states tend to see things differently.

Nevada has chosen to permit gambling. The result is an "industry without smokestacks" that attracts billions of dollars into the state. Nevada gets half its revenue from taxing casino income.

This means there is no need for personal or corporate income taxes. Nor are there taxes that are common elsewhere, such as franchise taxes, franchise on income, special intangible taxes, capital stock taxes, chain store taxes, admissions taxes, stock transfer taxes, state inheritance taxes, and gift taxes.

The variety of taxation methods between states is part of what makes life interesting in the U.S. For example, on the West Coast of the U.S., (what Easterners call the left coast) Oregon has a long-standing taboo against sales taxes. Every now and then some politician gets the bright idea of asking the voters to approve a sales tax. Not only does it never pass, it is also usually the kiss of death for that politician.

Neighboring states like Washington on Oregon's north border, and California directly to the south, both have high sales taxes — well over 8 percent in some parts of Washington on almost everything you purchase. Not surprisingly, residents of border communities in Washington State (not to be confused with Washington DC which is on the East Coast of the United States) do much of their retail shopping in Oregon, and skip paying the tax. Supposedly it is wrong to do this without paying a "use tax" to the state of Washington, but state revenue officers glumly throw up their hands and acknowledge the problem.

Oregon benefits with one of the hottest retail markets in the country as wealth crosses state lines from all directions in the quest to avoid paying sales tax. It may seem like Oregon has an unfair advantage over its neighbors, but the price of forgoing a sales tax is a high state income tax – 9.2 percent — as well as some of the highest property taxes in the country.

Oregon's high state income tax is surpassed by California's personal income tax of 9.8 percent. The beneficiary is Nevada, where there is none. If people will cross state lines to avoid paying 8 percent on the purchase of a television, how much more will they cross state lines to incorporate and save 10 percent of their company's net earnings?

A Simple Example

A firm I once consulted helped an individual from California who liquidated an asset with no underlying cost basis and received about $1.5 million. Had she paid state income taxes in California it would have cost her about $150,000 right off the top before dealing with federal taxes. With her Nevada Corporation in place, all of that wealth remained in her own hands. That is to say, in the hands of her Nevada Company which she owned. Pardon me a small digression; all this talk of saving state income tax reminds me of Libertarian Jeff Daiell's pithy comment:

"When Barbary Pirates demand a fee for allowing you to do business, it's called "tribute money." When the Mafia demands a fee for allowing you to do business, it's called "the protection racket." When the state demands a fee for allowing you to do business, it's called "income tax."

Nevada is not the first domestic corporate shelter. Delaware has been the home to scores of major corporations — mainly because corporate directors had more control there than the shareholders. But Nevada and Wyoming both improved on Delaware's laws, and made the rules more favorable to both large and small corporations. The most recent incorporation rush started in Nevada on March 13, 1987, when legislation was approved protecting corporate directors and officers from personal liability for acts committed on behalf of the corporation or by the corporation. These laws along with more flexible capitalization and maintenance requirements have made Nevada the "incorporation capital of the America," upstaging Delaware, which had previously held this honor. Anyone from outside the U.S. seeking to do business in the U.S. should look to Nevada first.

Privacy
For some, the most appealing aspect of incorporating in Nevada is the respect for privacy. Nevada does not keep the identity of shareholders in the public record. In other words, who owns a corporation is no one's business but the owner. If someone is pursuing your assets and they suspect you might own a related Nevada corporation, they're going to have more hurdles in discovery than in most states. A record search, for example, generally ends up at a dead end.

Nevada requires that corporations have at least one officer and one director – but it can be the same individual or, in the case of an LLC, the managing member can be another corporation. There are professionals in Nevada who will function as the officer and director of your company. They are essentially a nominee and will do as instructed, provided that their instructions do not violate the laws under which they operate. These services should be used in conjunction with a corporate headquarters package, which in effect provides a virtual office for the company, that includes a telephone number, someone to answer the phone, a fax number, a mailing address, a bank account, and a trained individual who acts as the director/officer of your corporation.

Nevada nominee officers and directors are frequently lawyers or skilled trust officers who specialize in such matters. A nominee officer is not required to know the shareholders or even know their names. The nominee need only know from whom he or she is to take instructions, and where the list of shareholders is kept — not necessarily who is listed on the shareholder ledger. Only under court order is the whereabouts of a shareholders list required to be made available. And the shareholder list can be maintained in another country altogether. Can you imagine how frustrated some predatory lawyer in your home state is going to be when trying to connect you with your Nevada Corporation? Not only can you save income tax levied from your home state, you can also build a firewall of privacy to protect assets.

In addition to the full service corporate headquarters providers, there are companies that offer only resident agents and mail forwarding services. The total annual costs for these services range from a low of about $85 per year. Corporate headquarters providers charge from around $2,000 to a maximum of about $3,500 per annum; which includes such things an on site office for use when you are visiting Nevada, a local city business license, Nevada corporate bank account, listed phone number and operator, office address (as opposed to a PO Box), and other validations for a legitimate presence in Nevada.

Other Advantages

Nevada has other advantages over Delaware and all the other U.S. states. Delaware has been too quick to share information with the federal government that Nevada considers private. Delaware also charges a franchise tax in addition to a state income tax. Nevada, on the other hand, has no state income tax (there is a constitutional ban on such a thing), and no corporate income tax, and there is no franchise tax either. Even though the franchise tax in Delaware is slight, it still means annual disclosures, including dates of stockholder meetings, places of business outside the state, and revelation of the number and value of shares issued. Nevada asks for none of this information.

In fact, as a matter of policy, the state of Nevada involves itself as little as possible in business and corporate transactions. Shares in a corporation can be sold or transferred with no state taxes. Unlike some states that tax a corporation according to the number of shares issued, Nevada has no tax on corporate shares. Neither is there a succession tax, which is a type of inheritance tax some states require. And stockholders and directors need neither live in Nevada nor hold their meetings in the state. You can hold corporate meetings in your own home or take a tax-deductible trip to Hawaii to do so. Your corporate records can be kept anywhere — your home, India — you decide.

Nevada has nothing to say about what kinds of stock your corporation issues — preferred, common or whatever. Nevada and Wyoming also allow "bearer shares." This means shares of corporations can change hands with no names attached to them. Share transactions can be anonymous. Neither does Nevada have an inventory tax, a unitary tax, a state inheritance tax or personal income tax. The lack of inventory tax alone has made Reno, Nevada one of the warehouse and distributions centers of the West

Coast. At one time inventory taxes in California drove scores of distribution businesses across their east border to Nevada for financial shelter.

Other advantages to Nevada are that directors can change the bylaws of the corporation without interference from the state. And, there is no initial or minimum capital required to start a corporation. A Nevada corporation can buy shares of its own stock and hold them, transfer them, or sell them. The corporation can use the stock to buy or lease real estate or acquire options for them. Stock can be used to pay for labor or services, and whatever the directors decide these things are worth is essentially beyond anyone's question. (With the exception of the IRS, which tends to question anything they do not immediately understand.)

Nevada does not require tax reports, and it does not share the information it does gather with any of the other states or the federal government. Nevada is the only state that does not share information with the IRS, and it makes them mad. As a matter of fact, the last reported effort of the IRS to get such information from the state was in 1991. The fed tried to get information from Nevada's Department of Taxation, Department of Motor Vehicles, Employment Security, Gaming and Control Board, as well as the Secretary of State's office. They soon learned that for them in Nevada, it's "no dice." If the IRS wants information, the burden of proof is on them to prove they need it on a case by case basis. They simply can't go on a fishing expedition ransacking state records trying to find people to harass. Nevada has even backed off joining a consortium of states to share information with one another because it could be a way for the IRS to gain access to information about Nevada corporate shareholders indirectly.

A Sobering Story

The state of Nevada has denied sharing information with outside government agencies, which evidently prompted an IRS raid on a major and reputable Nevada resident agent firm in 1997. Laughlin & Associates has formed and managed an estimated 30,000 Nevada companies over the past twenty-eight years. Laughlin earned a good reputation and regularly teaches seminars in Reno to non–Nevada residents demonstrating the value of using Nevada companies as part of a business strategy.

The IRS suspecting some of the Nevada companies might be used to under report federal taxes had been trying to get lists of company owners from Nevada resident agents for years, unsuccessfully. In defiance of state authorities the IRS got a federal court judge to sign a sealed warrant for them to access the files of Laughlin, the oldest and best known of the resident agent companies. In a message of incredible intimidation, and without any advance notice, early one morning an estimated forty federal revenue agents bearing arms sealed off the building of Laughlin & Associates in Carson City, Nevada (Carson City is the State capital of Nevada.) Ten more agents brandishing automatic weapons and flak jackets went to the home of the founder of the company, who had actually passed away some months earlier. They held at gunpoint the founder's 70 year old widow, who was in her nightgown, while they ransacked the place looking for who knows what. They even broke her front door because she was slow in answering, a result of her still being asleep when they arrived.

The son of the founder, Lewis Laughlin, was then running the company. He was a skilled presenter and capable businessman in his early thirties who had engendered broad based acceptance in both the local and national business communities. As coincidence would have it I spoke with Lewis the afternoon of the raid. He told me that, quite understandably, his mother was completely terrorized to wake up finding armed agents crawling all over her home and private property. (She was to die not long thereafter and it was his strong conviction that the government was to blame.)

Lewis went on to say that neither his mother nor he had any idea what the IRS was looking for because they simply refused to tell him. Evidently a federal marshal presented a sealed subpoena at their office and then IRS agents proceeded to haul off 70 four-drawer file cabinets and the contents of every drawer of every desk in the facility. No explanation was given for the search and seizure other than a commitment that the records would be returned in ten days.

As of the time of this writing, several years later, all the files have still not been returned and the IRS has never given any explanation for their conduct.

Things at the business eventually returned to normal, but the incredible stress placed on Lewis by this horrible experience and the lack of any conclusion regarding this critical matter, took a heavy impact. Lewis died in 2000, in his early thirties, at his home of stress related causes leaving a young wife and four-year old child.

No charges were brought against Laughlin & Associates, or to the company's legal counsel's knowledge, had any of their clients been targeted as a result of the infamous raid. Technically, any information gained in the raid that was not specific to the individual or company cited in the sealed subpoena cannot be used against any one else in a subsequent proceeding under the legal doctrine "fruit of the poisoned tree." This entire incident is another disgusting example of an abusive federal agency circumventing state laws by simply breaking them. It seems rather clear that the IRS was sending a message that they could do anything they wanted, whenever they wanted, and state laws be damned. As a testimony to a well-run business Laughlin & Associates continues to thrive and aid thousands of new clients each year. But two, and possibly three family members are now gone as a likely result of a violent government agency.

Subsequent to the initial IRS raid on Laughlin, the Republican majority in Congress commenced an investigation of the IRS for abusive tactics. Not as a result of the Laughlin incident particularly but because so many similar stories were being repeated around the country. Shocking stories were told in Congressional hearings, which angered and mobilized a normally docile populace when some of the testimony was aired on television, giving Congressional leaders sufficient stroke to rein the IRS enforcement section in strongly. Eventually a number of enforcement agents left the IRS, and Congressional authority over this run-amok federal agency has been enhanced.

Frankly, I doubt seriously if the IRS will dare pull this stunt anytime in the near future and certainly not at Laughlin & Associates.

Caution

If you decide to do business in Nevada and you intend to use a nominee officer and/or directors, select them wisely because Nevada protects nominees better than those that may fill a similar function in any other state. For example, Delaware has a longer statute of limitations to sue a person acting in this capacity when improper dividends have been paid.

It is important that one be alert that articles of incorporation in Nevada may eliminate or limit the personal liability of a nominee officer/director regarding claims resulting from breach of their fiduciary duty. This is true in just about all cases other than those involving the improper payment of dividends.

In Nevada, director indemnification is an absolute right. While in Delaware it is at the discretion of the court, the same as virtually all the other states. Of course as the controlling stockholder, you can fire a nominee any time you want — but an unethical operator might be able to do damage before you find out about it. What it all means is, be careful to whom you trust your assets, just as you should anywhere else in the world. This is where the help of an experienced expert in choosing the corporate nominee director/officer is important. Contracts can be written in such away that the officer/director can make no move without your approval. But it takes knowledge to gain this fail-safe protection.

On the plus side, if you choose to serve your own corporation in some capacity and you are in a position to incur liability, there are creative ways you may indemnify yourself. You can issue yourself insurance in the form of trust funds, self-insurance or give yourself a security interest or lien on assets the corporation holds. Be aware that unless prevented, a nominee corporate officer could indemnify him or herself by placing a lien on the assets of your corporation, and the authority to do this is absolute. In most other states this is illegal, but not in Nevada. So unless there is fraud, the decision of the board of directors regarding money is final, and is neither void nor voidable.

This is why the nominee services contract with your corporate officer/director must contain key provisions; giving you power to preempt or void any such decision, and here again is where expert counsel is important.

How it works

It really is quite simple. It is so simple in fact that as stated earlier, literally tens of thousands of people do it. To review: you have a corporation in your home state that generates, say, $250,000 per year in profits annually. If you paid taxes in a high rate jurisdiction like California, $25,000 of that would go to the state every year.

Instead, you spend $85 for a corporate charter in Nevada, $695 prevailing rate on a one-time basis to get set up with your Nevada corporation, and about $2,400 per year (on average) for your Nevada headquarters package. Then, you arrange to have your high-tax corporation forever in debt to your low-tax Nevada Corporation. Your Nevada Corporation could buy shares in your local corporation, or could lend it money. Your local corporation never need pay off the debt, and it accrues a high interest rate on the balance.

The Nevada Corporation could take a mortgage on your home, your car, your boat or airplane, such that you no longer appear to have any equity in them. You can keep title, but drain out the equity of an asset, so that it is not attractive to someone seeking to sue you. You can encumber property with trust deeds transferring the equity to your Nevada corporation. You can have a public filing, typically a UCC-1, that shows the equity in the property in your home state has been pledged to the Nevada corporation to secure a previous loan. You have thus restructured ownership of both possessions and cash flow such that they are held by the Nevada entity.

Assets encumbered in this way are relatively judgment proof — at least from any judgment rendered for litigation with your home state corporation. And, of course, you've saved almost 10 percent on your company profits. In this example you're spend about $2,500 per year and you come ahead about $22,500. But the real advantage is not the taxes saved, it is privacy and the security you've gained. All kinds of potential problems might crop up in your home state downstream. But if your Nevada structure is organized correctly, you will have constructed a neat little fortress to protect those assets.

In order for your Nevada corporation to avoid being dragged into court in your home state — let alone submitting itself to its laws and taxes — it must avoid conducting business in your home state. There are a number of criteria that must be met for your Nevada corporation to give you improved protection. You need to have a bank account for your corporation, through which you conduct your major business, such as buying and selling and paying for contract services. Having the bank account allows you to conduct the rest of the activities that legitimize your Nevada corporate shield.

You should have an actual business office address in Nevada, which is provided by your corporate office package. One excellent proof of this is a canceled check from your Nevada Corporation for rent. This is why there are services to provide such addresses — a post office box does not demonstrate the same level of substance. You also need a telephone listing at that address. You can prove that with a monthly telephone bill and canceled checks paying for it. You should plan on securing a business license in the city where your address is located. You also need someone at the office to answer the phone and take messages. All of these services are provided with an appropriate headquarters package for one annual fee.

Nevada requires that you file a one-page list of officers and directors each year on the anniversary date of your incorporation. This list must include their name(s), address and the name and address of your resident agent. Nevada requires a fee of $85 to file this list every year — but that is the extent of the state's fees and the state's reports. Which makes it just about the most hassle free location for a corporate charter anywhere in the world.

Too Good To Be True?

Does all this sound too good to be true? Well, it is true. And it is because of the nature of corporate law. It is so true that many celebrities, such as Michael Jackson, Madonna, Chevy Chase, etc., funnel their earnings through Nevada. Corporations are considered legal, although artificial "persons" with most of the same rights as a natural person. Corporations can buy, own, and sell property. They can sue other corporations or natural persons or be sued by either. A corporation is an entity in itself with its own identity, separate from yours. When it enters into contracts, the corporate officers or shareholders are not obliged by the terms, only the corporation.

If a corporation is sued, the corporate shareholders are not personally responsible for the liability. It is a thing that is apart from you — it is not you — even though you may control it and enjoy great benefits from it. For example, the corporation could accumulate debts that benefit you, and then go bankrupt, leaving your estate out of the settlement. (Please don't misunderstand. I'm not suggesting this as a strategy — just pointing out the implications.)

A Nevada corporation can help you in dealing with a failing business situation. Say, for example, you have several businesses that are generally doing very well, but you have one company that is doing so poorly it is dragging down the rest. You can incorporate that company separately, wait to see if it improves and then if need be file bankruptcy for it, leaving the rest of your operations intact. If it is an income property, the lender will be restrained from foreclosure until you have the opportunity to sell or refinance the property, or come up with a reorganization plan to handle the loan.

If you have a Nevada corporation, you can push a bankruptcy procedure far away from your solvent operations. A Nevada company can become the holding company for the stock of your other troubled corporation. Since the holding company is headquartered in Nevada, the subsidiary can file bankruptcy there. It won't be as embarrassing in your home state, and your lender — if the bankruptcy is a property — will have a harder time contesting the procedure.

An example of applying this principle is a New York City taxi company that has 100 cabs. It has filed 50 corporations in Nevada - one for every two cabs. If they ever get sued, two cabs is the limit of assets that can be taken. An Alaska oil company did the same thing with each of its oil wells, and a ski lodge the same with each of its chair lifts. If anything goes wrong on any part of these operations, the financial consequences are limited.

These protections are what are known as the "corporate veil." Those who benefit from the corporation are protected by it. As I mentioned earlier, the keys to preserving the corporate veil are maintaining the bank account, business address, business license, telephone number and personnel, and not to co-mingle funds between you and your corporation. If these standards are upheld, the corporation is entitled to the benefits and advantages due a corporation.

Offshore Asset Protection

The ultimate in security for assets is to take the principles used in Nevada and apply them overseas. That is, move equity from your domestic holdings and place them in a carefully selected foreign country, through the vehicle of an offshore asset protection trust or international business corporation (IBC). Business entities such as these can separate legal ownership from beneficial value. In other words, although you benefit from the assets, you no longer legally own them. Rockefeller wisdom is said to be: "Own nothing, control everything."

If organized correctly and you are forced into court, you can state with a clear conscience that the de-controlled corporation is not owned by you. To do this, you shift assets of your Nevada Corporation through a lien or mortgage. Or, you simply issue all the stock in your Nevada Corporation to an offshore trust, corporation, or LLC. This places ownership of sensitive assets farther and farther away from grasping hands and predatory lawyers. Your separation from the offshore legal structure may be guaranteed by a variety of international agreements, such as the Hague Convention, laws regarding the sovereignty of nations and trust laws.

The Summary

By now it should be clear to you that if you are an American and you HAVE anything, or you have more than one income source, you should have at least one Nevada entity and perhaps several. The cost to purchase a pre-formed Nevada corporation is relatively modest. You can fax, mail, or phone-in, or email a purchase request.

There are several qualified sources for Nevada companies. If you want to reach someone directly you may want to call 775-324-7676 in Reno, Nevada, (www.nevcorp.com) or contact Laughlin & Associates at 775-883-4874 (www.laughlinassociates.com) or Nevada Corporate Headquarters at 702-873-3488 (www.nchinc@nchinc.com). If you seeking help in developing a strategy, want legal or accounting assistance, or are thinking through the right jurisdiction for a business strategy, call the Sovereign Crest Alliance at 869-466-3794 (www.sovereigncrest.com) for a qualified professional based in your country, state or province.

After you've purchased a Nevada corporation, you must activate it with the IRS by securing a tax identification number. Be certain to declare a fiscal year date different from that of the calendar year. This action will allow you future flexibility in shifting income between your corporation and yourself for any given year. (Discuss this concept with your accountant, legal or financial advisor. There are a number of additional benefits that may present themselves.) A good date you may want to consider is having the fiscal year end January 31st.

Why is the date of the fiscal year so important? Well, as you likely know, a U.S. person filing a joint return can earn up to $40,100 and still only be subject to 15% federal income tax. Your personal corporation is only assessed 15% up to the first $50,000 of net income annually. This means, with some planning you and your corporation can earn up to $90,000 collectively and only be subject to a maximum of 15% federal income tax. And, by keeping your company qualified in Nevada you eliminate state income tax altogether. Further, many normal purchases you might want to make, such as computers, etc., may not be tax deductible to you as an individual, whereas if purchased through your corporation the entire amount may come right off the top of your taxable income.

Using additional Nevada corporations correctly, you can shift income progressively forward into different fiscal periods delaying tax due dates for sometimes years into the future and then settling up by spreading earned income over several corporations, thereby not exceeding the lowest federal tax bracket of 15%. However, because of sister company rules, this latter strategy is becoming more tedious to accomplish correctly. So if this is your plan, make sure you are working with a tax lawyer or accountant that understands your objectives clearly at the beginning. Oh, and by the way, during those years of LEGAL tax settlement DELAYS, you could be earning interest or investment income ON all that money. Of course if you don't mind paying a punitive 39.6% federal income tax, PLUS FICA taxes, PLUS Medicare, PLUS State income taxes, the aggregate which generally exceeds more than half your earned income, then you're still going to want to invoke privacy and asset protection strategies if you intend to protect what's left.

Both Nevada and Wyoming have excellent LLC legislation. To learn more of this hybrid legal structure see the Nevis LLC in Chapter 14. The principals are basically the same. Now, before you move boldly ahead with a plan to transfer assets, make sure you're not violating fraudulent transfers laws, the subject of the next chapter.

12

Unlawful Transfers

"There are many legal and ethical devices that can and should be used to protect the assets of those in every income bracket. If you have a home, a bank account, investments, corporate securities, valuable family heirlooms, or you feel that you just cannot afford to start all over again, then your assets are at risk in today's litigious and over taxed society and should be protected."

The Author

Concepts

Any transfer of assets a debtor makes with the actual or constructive intent to hinder, delay, or defraud a creditor is fraudulent. Likewise, transfers by a debtor for less than a fair and reasonable consideration, where the debtor thereby becomes insolvent and incurs debts beyond a reasonable ability to pay, is generally considered fraudulent under law. In these situations, a creditor will likely have protection afforded by fraudulent conveyance statutes and gain relief from the court thereby voiding prior transfers to satisfy an outstanding judgment.

The subject material included in this chapter reviews what constitutes a fraudulent transfer and how to avoid making them. The treatment and application of this information may determine just how quickly or how completely you may be able to transfer assets into estate planning structures. Part of your overall plan may be to protect your estate from possible future creditors whilst ensuring that taxes are minimized. Or, for those living in highly litigious jurisdictions, namely the United States and its territories, protection from predatory litigation may be your highest priority. But regardless of why you have decided to move assets, the laws related to fraudulent transfers, which exist in most countries, should be carefully considered before proceeding.

Laws have been around for centuries that provide protection for those who are forward thinking and avail themselves of mechanisms that legally protect an estate for heirs. In 1998 I attended a lecture in Puerto Rico where a British solicitor presented a workshop on English trust law providing precedents that were 800 years old. The concept of taking assets offshore to be held in trust is as old as commerce and as we shall have seen in earlier chapters, the isle of Delos off the coast of Greece was one of the places the wealthy of ancient times stored their treasures under a type of trust agreement with the leaders of that island.

There are laws and legal precedents that have serious consequences for those who transfer assets in an effort to defraud creditors. Fraudulent conveyance laws are generally created to protect creditors from debtors who attempt to hide assets to which a creditor might turn for satisfaction of an outstanding but unpaid obligation.

In many jurisdictions a creditor pursuing a legal claim must first initiate and then win a lawsuit against the debtor before going after assets to satisfy a judgment. However, in some cases after receipt of an enforceable judgment, a creditor may find that the debtor has previously transferred assets. In theory, this transfer may now hinder, delay, or preclude the creditor from satisfying their judgment. The creditor's approach might be to go back to court in an attempt to take advantage of various remedies under the fraudulent conveyance statutes.

If a judgment creditor is able to prove to the Court that a debtor's transfer was fraudulent, the creditor may attach or levy directly upon the property or the assets in the hands of the grantee of the debtor. As an alternative, the creditor may endeavor to have the Court void a given transfer rather than proceed against the grantee. The latter is the way counsel might traditionally proceed against a debtor's assets on behalf of their client.

Fraudulent conveyance statutes provide for provisional remedies to protect creditors' rights, who have not reduced their claim to a civil judgment. Likewise, a potential claimant who does not know the extent of their damages or who merely has a potential conditional claim may legally benefit from these provisions.

When a creditor or claimant discovers or believes that you might have transferred assets in a way that will hinder, delay, or frustrate the collection in satisfaction of a judgment, that creditor may among other remedies, ask the court for provisional relief including injunctive relief, restraining orders, attachments, and third party receivership for the assets in dispute.

Intent May Not Be Necessary

There are many circumstances where the unlawful actual intent to defraud is not apparent, may not be easily provable, or is in fact not present. There are instances where a debtor may simply gift an asset to a relative, a friend or a person in need for purely charitable purposes. Under the most recent economic times, situations have arisen where a debtor might transfer assets for an amount below fair market value to relieve his or her immediate needs for cash. These examples may be challenged in court as fraudulent transfers without regard to the debtor's subjective or actual intent.

The Statute of Elizabeth (www.blupete.com/Law/Commentaries/ F/Elizabeth.htm) was meant to make certain types of transfers voidable. The creditor may ask the Court to void the transfer and put the parties back in the position they were in prior to the transfer.

Statute of Elizabeth Jurisdictions

The law regarding fraudulent conveyances is considered to have begun in England in the year 1570, with the Statute 13 Elizabeth, c.5, referred to as the "Statute of Elizabeth." This statute provided:

- For the avoiding and abolishing of feigned, conveyor and fraudulent gifts, grants, alienations (and) conveyances ... which ... are devised and contrived of malice, fraud, collusion, or guile to the end purpose and intent, to delay, hinder or defraud creditors...
- Provided that this Act ... shall not extend to any interest ... conveyance ... upon good consideration and bona fide law fully conveyed or assured to any person...not having at the time of such conveyance or assurances to them made, any manner of notice or knowledge of such, fraud, or collision...

However, early on, the Courts allowed a creditor to proceed directly against the transferred property.

An example of a court's use of the Statute of Elizabeth drawn from a 1980's case in Nova Scotia, Canada which begins with Justice Hallett setting out the often quoted threefold test necessary to set aside a conveyance:

1. The conveyance was without valuable consideration. It may not be sufficient if the plaintiff proves only that the consideration was somewhat inadequate ... The consideration must be 'good consideration'; so-called meritorious consideration, that is, love and affection, is not valuable consideration and therefore not consideration within the meaning of the *Statute of Elizabeth* ...

2. The grantor had the intention to delay or defeat his creditors. It is not necessary that the creditor exist at the time of the conveyance ... However, the court will impute the intention if the creditors exist at the time of the conveyance provided the conveyance is without consideration and denudes the grantor debtor of substantially all his property that would otherwise be available to satisfy the debt ... Apart from that situation, intention to delay or defeat creditors is a question of fact. The court must look at all the circumstances surrounding the conveyance. The court is entitled to draw reasonable inference from the proven facts to ascertain the intention of the grantor in making the conveyance. Suspicious circumstances surrounding the conveyance require an explanation by the grantor.

3. That the conveyance had the effect of delaying or defeating the creditors. This too is a question of fact. The plaintiff must first obtain a judgment against the debtor prior to commencement of proceedings to set aside the conveyance under the *Statute of Elizabeth* and must on the application to set aside adduce sufficient evidence to enable the

court to make a finding that the conveyance had the effect of delaying or defeating the creditors."

Jurisdictions that have not adopted a Uniform Fraudulent Conveyances Act, the Statute of Elizabeth, or its derivative, are few. Regardless of your home country, chances are good that either the Statute of Elizabeth is the active fraudulent transfer legislation or some derivative thereof. The statute states clearly that any conveyance made with the intent to "hinder, delay, or defraud creditors" is prohibited.

The language of these statutes suggests a debtor's actual intent must be affirmatively proven. Despite the actual language of the statute, Courts have developed case law supporting areas of constructive fraud, which have been labeled Badges of Fraud. A creditor uses these in proving the debtor's actual intent to defraud.

U.S. courts have recognized that fraud may be established without actual intent to defraud. For example, a debtor who makes an outright gift or sells at below market price to a relative and by doing so does not have enough assets to satisfy debt is in jeopardy. This kind of conveyance would almost assuredly be presumed to be with the intent to defraud even though the debtor had no real intentions of doing so. In some jurisdictions, if a debtor retains use or control of transferred property, a transfer is presumed fraudulent.

Other jurisdictions require proof of actual fraudulent intent, even if under case law the "Badges of Fraud" may be used to prove the intent to defraud. (Badges of Fraud are reviewed later in this section.)

Under traditional statutes, a creditor may ignore the transfer and go directly after the transferred asset in the hands of the transferee. In order to do this, the creditor must be absolutely sure the transfer was a fraudulent conveyance. If the creditor is incorrect, he or she may face a lawsuit from the transferee. More typically, a creditor will have the Court void the transfer and then levy upon the asset.

Uniform Fraudulent Conveyance

In the late 1920's, the Uniform Fraudulent Conveyances Act (UFCA) was drafted and circulated among the U.S. states for adoption. Approximately one half of the jurisdictions in the United States have adopted the Uniform Fraudulent Conveyances Act. These include: Arizona, California, Delaware, Idaho, Maryland, Massachusetts, Michigan, Minnesota, Montana, Nevada, New Hampshire, New Mexico, New York, North Dakota, Ohio, Oklahoma, Pennsylvania, South Dakota, Tennessee, Utah, the United States Virgin Islands, Washington, Wisconsin, and Wyoming.

In the above states the Uniform Fraudulent Conveyances Act is the primary statutory law on fraudulent conveyances. In 1984, there was a new draft promulgated called the Uniform Fraudulent Transfer Act (UFTA).

It was intended to repeal and replace the Uniform Fraudulent Conveyances Act.

However, only a few states have adopted this new draft, namely Hawaii, North Dakota and Oregon. Due to the prevailing use of the Uniform Fraudulent Conveyances Act over the UFTA, and its similarity to legislation enacted in other countries of like manner, the discussion that follows will reference the Uniform Fraudulent Conveyances Act, rather than the UFTA. In most cases the outcome will be the same under either statute.

There are two principal sections of the Uniform Fraudulent Conveyances Act that enable creditors to avoid fraudulent conveyances: (1) avoiding transfers due to actual fraud, and (2) avoiding transfers based on what is called "constructive fraud." This approach is consistent with similar legislation around the globe.

Actual Intent

Actual intent fraudulent conveyances are instances in which a creditor has clear proof demonstrating the debtor consciously intended to hinder, delay, or defraud their creditor. Section 7 of the Uniform Fraudulent Conveyance Act addresses actual or intentional fraud in pertinent part as follows:

> "Every conveyance made and every obligation incurred with the actual intent, as distinguished from intent presumed in law to hinder, delay or defraud either present or future creditors, is fraudulent as to both present and future creditors."

The Uniform Fraudulent Conveyances Act uses language already set forth under the Statute of Elizabeth. Both require actual intent. It is pertinent that present and future creditors may avoid a transfer as fraudulent under Section 7. Therefore, if a transfer is made with the intent to defraud someone who is not yet a true creditor, that transfer is still deemed fraudulent. This has been taken further under case law, Masomi Sasaki v. Yana Kai, 56 C.C. 2nd 406, and its progeny, wherein there seems to be precedent for those who become creditors after a transfer, not needing to demonstrate the debtor specifically intended to defraud subsequent creditors or to defraud a particular subsequent creditor, i.e. An actual intent to defraud either a present or future creditor will give rights under this statute to both.

Evidence of actual intent is rarely readily available to creditors. Difficult or nearly impossible to produce, creditors must rely instead on the "circumstantial evidence" of fraud that developed under the Statute of Elizabeth and frequently referred to as the Badges of Fraud. These are incidental or collateral circumstances that usually accompany a fraudulent transfer, such as an uncharacteristic transfer of assets, transfers to relatives for less than fair market value, unreasonable or insufficient transfer consideration, or transfers still leaving the transferor in possession or control, etc.

Badges of Fraud are not conclusive evidence, but are often considered by the courts to be "circumstantial evidence" of fraud.

Badges of Fraud
1. Insolvency by the transfer.
2. Lack or inadequacy of consideration.
3. Family, friendship, or other close "insider" relationship among the parties.
4. The retention of possession, benefit, or use of the property in question.
5. The existence or threat of litigation.
6. The financial condition of the debtor both before and after the transfer.
7. The existence or cumulative effect of a pattern of transactions or a course of conduct after the onset of financial difficulties.
8. The general chronology of events.
9. The secrecy of the transaction in question.
10. Deviation from the usual method or course of business.

Constructive Fraud
1. A transfer of most or all of a debtor's assets, leaving the transferor with nothing to their name, has been held as a sign of fraudulent intent.
2. Transfers where the transferor has retained possession in the absence of any commercial or business purpose.
3. Transfers for unreasonably low consideration or purport to be more than what the asset is worth.
4. Some courts have held transfer documents that contain the very language "this is a legitimate transaction" would only do so if it were done in contemplation of fraud.
5. The Uniform Fraudulent Conveyances Act has set forth factors under Section 4(b), which should be given consideration in determining whether actual fraud exists. Under current law the factors in Uniform Fraudulent Conveyances Act Section 4(b) are the types of acts considered to be Badges of Fraud.
6. Section 4(b) of the Uniform Fraudulent Conveyances Act reads in pertinent part as follows:

> "In determining the actual intent under subsection (a)(1), consideration may be given, among other factors, to the fact that:
> • the relationship between the transferor and the transferee was a close one;

- the transferor retained possession or dominion after the transfer;
- the transfer was concealed;
- prior to the transfer a creditor had sued, or was threatening to sue the transferor;
- the transfer was of substantially all the debtor's assets;
- the debtor has absconded or has removed or has changed the form of the assets remaining in his possession so as to make the assets less subject to creditor process;
- the value of the consideration received by the debtor was not reasonably the equivalent to the value of the assets transferred or the amount of the obligation incurred;
- the debtor was insolvent or heavily in debt or reasonably should have expected to become so indebted;
- the transfer occurred shortly before or after a substantial debt was incurred."

Proof of the existence of any one of the factors listed above does not in itself constitute prima facie proof that the debtor has made a fraudulent transfer or incurred a fraudulent obligation.

As can be easily seen, these represent "circumstantial evidence," or "badges" of a fraudulent intent. They are not conclusive, nor does any one or combination mean there is actual fraud. It does however; give the Court, and the creditor's attorney, a rational to attempt to convince the Court that the transfers were fraudulent, rather than a family, commercial, or business transaction.

It is generally difficult to prove actual fraud. There is rarely a "smoking gun" type of evidence, and the Badges of Fraud require an extreme amount of research on the part of the creditor. Due to this difficulty, the law has allowed several methods of establishing fraud without any actual intent to defraud. Therefore, the law can determine a transfer was fraudulent irrespective of the actual intent of the transferor.

The Uniform Fraudulent Conveyances Act at Section 4 also contains the principal provisions regarding "constructive fraud."

Section 4 reads in pertinent part as follows:

"Every conveyance made and every obligation incurred by a person who is or will be thereby rendered insolvent is fraudulent as to creditors without regard to his actual intent, if the conveyance is made or the obligation is incurred without a fair consideration."

The legal theory behind the idea of "constructive fraud," or allowing a transfer to be deemed fraudulent irrespective the proven intent of the transferor, is someone who knows they have no money, has or will be incurring new debt, yet transfers assets out of their ownership, "should" know the transferred asset is the only thing of value the creditor would be able to attach if the debt, was not paid. Since the transferor "should" have known that result of their action, the law therefore will deem the transfer was a constructive fraud.

An Example

The law would probably deem as fraudulent, the gifts or transfers of property of an insolvent person to their child, while not receiving any or adequate consideration in exchange. Therefore, if a debtor transfers away property without receiving a reasonably adequate commercial exchange in return, it would be determined that it is so prejudicial to the creditor, who under equitable law owns the property. The law will avoid the transfer in order to give the creditor a remedy, irrespective of the actual intent or thoughtfulness of the debtor.

The Uniform Fraudulent Conveyances Act presents three "presumed-in-law" or "constructive fraud" transfers. All three address a person who is insolvent, will soon become insolvent due to the transfer of the extent of the transfer, or is near insolvent, while not receiving reasonable or adequate consideration for the asset transferred.

The three categories of constructive fraudulent transfers under the Uniform Fraudulent Conveyances Act are:

1. Transfers by an insolvent for less than fair consideration, or for less than a reasonably equivalent exchange.
2. Transfers for less than fair consideration by a businessperson without retaining sufficient capital to meet the likely future needs of that business.
3. Transfers for less than fair consideration by anyone, businessperson or consumer, without retaining enough property to meet his likely future debts as they become due.

The majority of litigation by creditors or by a bankruptcy trustee regarding fraudulent transfer involves one of these three "presumed-in-law" or "constructive fraud" premises for the transfers similar to as set forth in the above court excerpt from Nova Scotia.

Fair Consideration

The law regarding "constructive fraudulent transfers" determines the standard of fair consideration or reasonably equivalent exchange. Under this standard however, the transferor need not receive the exact market value of the property. The law usually allows for something less than fair market value. The law has allowed a certain amount of flexibility due to actual market conditions. People often sell property for less than fair market value, due to the necessity of quick cash, or because they have incorrectly valued the property, or have sold to a buyer who has out negotiated them. Due to these realities of a free-market society, the standard is still a debatable point.

Under several notable court cases, the bench mark for "fair consideration or reasonably equivalent exchange" has been determined to be at least 70% or more of the fair market value. The court is likely to determine that fair consideration was not had and would rule a constructive fraud had taken place.

This 70% rule is merely a guideline. There are instances that may make it "reasonable," under specific circumstances, to sell a property for less than the 70%, and the courts have so held.

Affirmative Defenses

Both the Uniform Fraudulent Conveyances Act and the Federal Bankruptcy Code provide a defense for good faith transferees who give value.

The Bankruptcy Code at Section 548 (c) provides as follows:

"Except to the extent that a transfer or obligation voidable under this section is voidable under Sections 544, 545, or 547 of this title, a transferee or obligee of such a transfer or obligation that takes place for value and in good faith has a lien on or may retain any interest transferred or may enforce any obligation incurred, as the case may be, to the extent that such transferee or obligee gave value to the debtor in exchange for such transfer or obligation."

The Uniform Fraudulent Conveyances Act considers a conveyance made for "fair consideration" when either (1) in exchange for the debtor's conveyance, "as a fair equivalent therefore, and in good faith, property is conveyed or an antecedent debt is satisfied" or (2) the debtor's conveyance is received in good faith to secure a present advance or antecedent debt in amount not disproportionately small as compared with the value of the property, or obligations obtained.

Good Faith Buyer

To successfully avoid a transfer as fraudulent and obtain the transferred asset to satisfy their judgment, a creditor must prove the debtor's fraudulent intent (whether actual or constructive), and that the person acquiring the asset purchased in "bad faith," and attempted to avoid their obligations to their creditor.

Under the Uniform Fraudulent Conveyances Act at Section 9, a person acquiring an asset has total protection under the law if they acted in good faith and pay reasonable or equivalent value. If the debtor had actual fraud as the bases for the transfer and it was easily proven, the creditor or the bankruptcy trustee will not be able to avoid or take the transferred asset from the person who has purchased in "good faith." They would be protected from attack.

The Uniform Fraudulent Conveyances Act at Section 9, requires the "good faith purchaser" to meet the following three requirements:

1. He or she takes the property in good faith.
2. He or she takes the property without knowledge of the fraud that the creditor is seeking to perpetrate.
3. He or she is given fair consideration - that is, a reasonable equivalent exchange for the property received.

If any of the above three elements in the test of the bona fide purchaser is not met, they will not have the protection of the Uniform Fraudulent Conveyances Act. Under this rule a person purchasing for fair market value, having knowledge the transfer of the asset would delay, hinder, frustrate or preclude a creditor of the transferor, then the transferee will not be deemed a good faith or "bona fide" purchaser. The transferred asset would be attachable by the creditor or bankruptcy trustee.

Inadequate Consideration

What if the opposite of the above situation exists, where the person acquiring the asset does so in total good faith and with no knowledge of any creditors, they negotiate paying significantly less that the fair market value, even below the 70% test mark? The principal cases in this area show the law requires the asset to be delivered to the creditor. It is only delivered pursuant to a lien in the purchaser's favor in the amount of the actual consideration the purchaser gave for the asset. This is not fair market value or its replacement value. In essence, the law will protect the purchaser's out of pocket expense of the purchase. The courts consider total protection of one who negotiates to the exclusion of a creditor's rights essentially unfair. Therefore, at the sale of the property for fair market value, the Courts would deliver the purchase amount to the transferee. The remainder would go toward satisfying the creditor's judgment.

Issues Checklist

1. Act when your "legal seas are calm." Whether or not a transfer was in contemplation of a creditor's claim against you is the main focus of a fraudulent transfer claim. It is therefore paramount to "judgment

proof" your assets in advance of legal or financial difficulties.

2. If possible, avoid dealing with close family members, as such transactions are naturally vulnerable to attack. Transfers to trusted advisors or business associates are less likely to be challenged.

3. Maintain paper trails to support your transaction. As you know with corporations, to keep that entity legally formed the "formalities" must be maintained. This habit should be kept up in all your asset structures. In areas subject to an inquiry it is wise to have supporting documentation, showing capitalization or consideration exchanges.

4. If you owe monies to a friend or relative, have the debt formalized in writing or a promissory note. No matter how bonafide the transaction, reconstruction is difficult and time consuming, with pertinent facts being forgotten.

5. To gain maximum protection in forming asset protect structures, have reasons other than asset protection for the transaction. If the asset protection structure is being set up at the same time as the rest of your estate plan, it is estate planning. If it is being set up when you start to do investing overseas, it is global positioning for better access to your investments. If gifts are made to relatives at special occasions, the gift is for other reasons than merely sheltering assets. Timing is important.

6. Seek advice from professional counselors. Advice from your attorney to transfer your assets to your spouse for estate planning purposes or for tax purposes can help negate the inference of fraudulent intent on your part.

7. Numerous transfers are less likely to be challenged. The Courts are less likely to overturn transfers of different assets, to different persons, that are made at different times, for different reasons. Likewise, regular or consistent transfers will support the most recent transfer as normal and not intended to defraud the recent creditor.

8. Never attempt to conceal assets from known creditors or while in a bankruptcy proceeding. Such activity is dealt with harshly and may "unravel" what you have done prior to such activity, and had done legally. There is a subtle, yet distinct difference between lawful asset protection and privacy, and unlawful asset concealment. Follow your attorney's advice to be able to defend the actions you take.

9. State statutes of limitations for fraudulent conveyances are usually from three to six years. In Federal bankruptcy Court, the Court's trustee is limited under Section 548 of the Bankruptcy Code from setting aside transfers "made or incurred on or within one year" from filing the bankruptcy petition. The trustee does have the option of proceeding under State law to gain the benefit of a longer statute of limitation.

10. Don't wait. Even if your legal circumstances are not as calm as you

might like, you can do some planning and asset transfers. And, although a legal structure put in place now may not protect you entirely from a potential creditor you are faced with currently, getting started could protect you against future and yet unknown creditors.

11. Do not rely on the "economic sense" of your creditor. Creditors generally pursue cost-effective means of collecting debts, which is good from an asset protection perspective. However, it would be unwise to believe that a fraudulent transfer will protect your assets simply because it will not make economic sense for your creditor to continue. Whereas it is true that to pursue this type of claim is typically expensive and time consuming, the penalties of fraudulent conveyance are a risk you should not be willing to take.

13

The Offshore Directory

"Nothing is more familiar in taxation than the imposition of a tax upon a class or upon individuals who enjoy no direct benefit from its expenditure, and who are not responsible for the condition to be remedied."

> Harlan F. Stone
> Former Chief Justice
> U.S. Supreme Court

Introduction

This issue of The Offshore Directory is an updated and revised version from the prior edition written in 1998. It offers amendments and updates to the previously listed jurisdictions listing 44 jurisdictions. Unlike the first directory, this compilation of information profiles the majority of corporate domiciles available. This Directory is not intended to represent the author's opinion of these jurisdictions as valid options for the kind of strategies referred to in this book.[1] I have specifically included less known and often criticized countries as locations for incorporation simply because it is important for the reader to be aware of the activities in different jurisdictions, the things that can go wrong in a jurisdiction and the volatility in the offshore realm.

Countries such as Austria, Luxembourg, Liberia, The Netherlands, and Switzerland provide excellent banking facilities and trust management services, but are not recommended areas for incorporation or individual tax planning. There are many other jurisdictions not listed in this Directory. Those jurisdictions were not included for any other reason then space limitations. Here is a partial list of jurisdictions not listed: Macoa (SAR), Nauru, Montserrat, Guam, Japan, Marianas, Puerto Rico, Montana, Micronesia, Philippines, Tahiti, Thailand, Campione, Bahrain, Israel, Lebanon, Alderney, Anjouan, Canary Islands, Hungary, New Zealand, Ingushetiya (Russia), Latvia, US Virgin Islands, Iceland, Monaco, Costa Rica, Uruguay, Denmark, Tonga, New Caledonia, Austria, South Korea, Tunesia and Taiwan.

---

[1] Due to the rapid nature of changes in the offshore industry, the information is this Directory cannot be guaranteed. As with all legal matters, research and consultation with a professional is advised before taking any action or making any legal decisions. This Directory is not intended or designed to be used as an exclusive and expert source of information and is only intended to give some insight into the great many offshore jurisdictions in the world. It does not cover all entities offered in any given jurisdiction and does not list every available offshore locale. Many jurisdictions have a choice of entities and may include: limited liability companies, trusts, banks, exempt companies, partnerships, foreign sales corporations, limited duration, limited life or limited years companies, limited life partnerships, protected cell companies, companies limited by shares, companies limited by guarantees, segregated portfolio companies, dormant companies and many more.

Background

There are a significant number of tax havens available around the world depending largely upon where you are now resident and the particular attributes you require. New jurisdictions are entering the offshore realm every year offering new and creative legislation. An analysis of a jurisdiction may well be based on your location. For example, within the USA the states of Nevada, Delaware, Wyoming etc. are frequently referred to as "tax havens" for U.S. Citizens simply because they are more private with incorporation information and they have no state income tax. There are agent companies in these states that provide interesting legal techniques for residents of other states to significantly reduce future state income taxes. Some of these are worthy of serious consideration, such as the "Daddy Warbucks verses Red Ink" incorporation strategy proposed by Laughlin & Associates of Carson City, Nevada. These same states are considered offshore financial centres for non-nationals of the U.S. In fact, they are competitive in the market for their solid legislation, privacy and low costs.

As to my recommendation regarding the "best" offshore jurisdiction, this is a question that should be posed on a relative basis. To attempt such an answer requires one to understand the individual needs of the person(s) asking the question. Each offshore jurisdiction has something to offer or it would not be successful in developing itself as an offshore financial service center. Some jurisdictions have laws that are better crafted for various legal structures. Others have better infrastructure and a larger number of offshore financial professionals. For example, Luxembourg is the premier offshore location from which to base a mutual fund and 57% of the offshore funds tracked and reported on by Standard & Poors are based in this single location.

Clearly Switzerland, Holland, and the Caymans are much better at handling large sums of money expeditiously than say, the British Virgin Islands, Grenada, or Nevis. However, the latter three — all Caribbean locations — are a good deal more flexible, confidential, and less expensive for filing and maintaining corporations, international exempt trusts, and the like.

Holland (The Netherlands) no longer provides near the quality of privacy it once did. And Switzerland, Caymans and Bermuda have all made considerable concessions in this area. All things considered, Nevis, Grenada, and the British Virgins, would be my first choice from which to domicile an offshore company. And for that reason, entire chapters were dedicated to Nevis and Grenada, and a more lengthy description of the British Virgin Islands is included in this directory.

It should be pointed out that Canadians have a wonderful option in Barbados, where they may pay a very low income tax rate on global business done through a corporation from that jurisdiction and then repatriate funds to their home country. And, Singapore offers great legislation for trading companies based in or marketing to the Far East.

A word of caution — if you're seeking an offshore subsidiary to a public company, there are a host of other considerations that require careful review.

It is important to note that in choosing a jurisdiction you should, at a minimum, look into its reputation, privacy and confidentiality, location, regulation/legislation, ties to other countries, entry requirements, continuing requirements, stability, infrastructure, taxation, mutual legal assistance treaties, benefits and costs. Please do not use the below directory as an absolute measure in your decision. It is easy to have errors creep into this type of work and not all jurisdictions are particularly helpful in providing the information required to compile this type of comparative listing. You should always consult a professional(s) in the field before making any decision.

Offshore Havens (with page number locations)

Africa
Liberia 191
Mauritius 192
Seychelles 195

Asia and Pacific
Cook Islands 197
Hong Kong 199
Labuan, Malaysia 202
Marshall Islands 204
Niue 205
Singapore 207
Vanuatu 209
Western Samoa 211

Europe
Andorra 213
Cyprus 215
(Dublin) Ireland 217
Gibraltar 219
Guernsey (Channel Islands) 221
Isle of Man 223
Jersey (Channel Islands) 225
Liechtenstein 227
(London) United Kingdom 229
Luxembourg 231
Madeira 233

Malta 234
Netherlands 236
Switzerland 237
Western Hemisphere
Anguilla 239
Antigua and Barbuda 241
Aruba 242
Bahamas 243
Barbados 245
Belize 247
Bermuda 249
British Virgin Islands 250
Cayman Islands 254
Dominica 256
Grenada 257
Netherlands Antilles 259
Nevis 261
Panama 263
St. Kitts & Nevis 265
   (Nevis is separate)
St. Lucia 267
St. Vincent and the Grenadines 269
Turks and Caicos Islands 271
United States
   Delaware 273
   Nevada (see chapt. 11, p. 163)
   Wyoming 275

< < < < < AFRICA > > > > >

LIBERIA

Location

Liberia is a small African state situated on the west coast of Africa with Ghana to the east and adjacent to Guinea and Sierra Leone. Its total size is 100,067 km.

Overview

Liberia is a Republic, founded in 1847, with a population of 3,000,000 with many Liberian refugees in neighboring countries. It's legal system, although in upheaval at the present time, is based on English and American common law. . Monrovia is the beautiful capital of Liberia. The official language is English. The official currency is the Liberian Dollar, however the United States Dollar is also widely used. Liberia is known for its shipping registration system, which is second largest in the world to Panama.

Advantages

- Low annual registration fee (US $150)
- Shelf companies are available
- No disclosure of beneficial owner to the government
- No exchange controls
- There is an active shipping registry

Disadvantages

- Liberia is currently experiencing political instability. Liberia finished a civil war in 1996 that had been ongoing since 1989. This has left the country with high tensions and a poor image.
- No public register
- Internal difficulties due to the civil war and political instability

Company Status

Non-resident company

Corporate Legislation Source

Liberian Business Corporation Act, 1976

Company Name

Certain words are prohibited except in specific circumstances, e.g. "Assurance," "Bank," "Building Society."

Must end with an appropriate word or suffix indicating limited liability, such as "Incorporated," "Corporation," "Limited," etc.

Minimum Shareholders

One

Are bearer shares available?

Yes

Minimum Directors

One. The director(s) may be located anywhere in the word and may be corporations with no restriction. If the number of shareholders is less than three there may be the same number of directors. If the number of shareholders is three or more, there must be at least three directors.

Minimum Officers

One secretary required. The officer(s) may be located anywhere in the world without restriction, but may not be a corporation.

Is a registered office and/or a registered agent required?

Yes/Yes

What information is available on the public file?

Registered Agents, Subscriber Shareholders and Articles of Association

What documents must be kept at the Registered Office?

None

Is an annual return required?

No

• Annual administrative meetings are required
• Annual fee payable to government: $150 USD

Taxation

Trading companies and shipping companies whose main business is conducted entirely abroad are completely exempt from taxes.

Taxation Treaties

Double taxation agreements with Germany and Sweden

MAURITIUS

Location

Mauritius is an Island located next to Reunion Island in the Indian Ocean, about 700 km East of Madagascar. Mauritius has a land area of approximately 2,040 km.

Overview

Mauritius is a Parliamentary Republic (Independent Member Country of the British Commonwealth since 1968) with a population of 1,200,000. The capital of Mauritius is Port Louis. Both English and French are the spoken languages. The Mauritian Rupee (MR) is the official currency. Mauritius is known for its high population concentration.

Advantages

- No political instability
- Mostly bilingual work force
- Positioned between European and Asian markets
- Good double tax treaty network for offshore companies
- Particular attractive to French speaking investors
- Shelf companies available for international companies, but not for offshore companies
- Great for India investors
- There is a "Limited Life Company" option where the life of the company may not exceed 50 years. This option is used extensively in individual estate planning strategies.
- Law guarantees privacy and confidentiality and a breach is punishable.

Disadvantages

- Listed in Group III of The Financial Stability Forum's list of 42 jurisdictions that it considers to have significant offshore activities; "May 26th, 2000 press release, "Financial Stability Forum Releases Grouping of Offshore Financial Centers (OFC's) to Assist in Setting Priorities for Assessment".[2]
- Flight connections only through European centers
- All foreigners who work for an offshore company are subject to income tax at a maximum of 15% limited to 22.500 MR.
- International companies must disclose their accounts at the end of the year.
- Mauritius stated it would begin levying taxes on all offshore corporations at a rate of 15% after the first ten years. This is slated to begin on July 1st, 2003.
- Expensive annual government fee

---

[2] The FSF's list is organized in Groups ranging from 1 to 3: Group 1 jurisdictions are jurisdictions the FSF generally, "views as cooperative, with a high quality of supervision, which largely adhere to international standards". Group II jurisdictions are jurisdictions the FSF generally views, "as having procedures for supervision and co-operation in place, but where actual performance falls below international standards, and there is substantial room for improvement". Group III jurisdictions are jurisdictions the FSF generally views, "as having a low quality of supervision and/or being non co-operative with onshore supervisors, and with little or no attempt being made to adhere to international standards". Quoted from "Offshore Financial Centers IMF Background Paper: Prepared by the Monetary and Exchange Affairs Department June 23, 2000. Source: www.imf.org

- Disclosure of beneficial owners to government is required

Company Status
- International company
- Offshore company

Corporate Legislation Source
- Mauritius Offshore Authority
- International Companies Act 1994 as amended, 2000
- International Companies (Fees) Regulations, 1994 (as amended, 2000)
- MOBA Act (Mauritius Offshore Business Activities Act), 1992 incorporating Regulations as amended, 2000.

Company Name
The word "Limited", "Corporation", "Incorporated", "Public Limited Company", "Société Anonyme", "Société Anonyme à Responsabilité Limitée", or "Sociedad Anonima", "Berhad", "Proprietary", "Namloze Vennootschap", "Besloten Vennootschap", "Aktiengesellschaft" or the abbreviation "Ltd", "Corp", "Inc" "Plc" "S.A.", "S.A.R.L.", "Bhd", "Pty", "N.V.", "B.V.", "A.G." or "LLC." may, either in full or in abbreviated form, be part of the name. Except with approval, certain words may not be used, i.e., "Assurance", "Bank", "Building Society", "Chamber of Commerce", "Chartered", "Cooperative", "Government:"Imperial", "Insurance", "Municipal", "Royal", "State", "Trust", or a word conveying a similar meaning.

Minimum Shareholders
- One for an international company. The shareholder(s) may be corporations.
- Two for an offshore company. The shareholder(s) may be corporations.

Are bearer shares available?
- Yes for an international company
- No for an offshore company
- In the next five years Mauritius states it may do away with all bearer shares.

Minimum Directors
- One for an international company. The director(s) may be corporations and may be located anywhere in the world.
- Two for an offshore company. The director(s) **may not** be corporations, but may be located anywhere in the world.

Minimum Officers

- Secretary required for an international company. The secretary(s) may be corporations and may be located anywhere in the world.
- Secretary required for an offshore company. The secretary(s) may be corporations, but must be resident in Mauritius.

Is a registered office and/ or a registered agent required?

Yes/Yes

What information is available on the public file?

Memorandum and Articles of Association, Subscriber Shareholders and the Registered Office and Agent

What documents must be kept at the Registered Office?

Copies of Minute books, records, share register and seal.

Is an annual return required?

- Yes for an international company
- No for an offshore company, but audited accounts are required.
- Annual government fee of $1,500 USD required for an offshore company
- Annual government fee of $100 USD required for an international company (subject to capitalization)

Taxation

There are taxes on offshore profits for offshore companies, but rates vary.

Taxation Treaties

- No double tax treaties for an international company
- Numerous double tax treaties for offshore companies including treaties with Belgium, Botswana, China, Cyprus, France, Germany, India, Indonesia, Italy, Kuwait, Luxembourg, and more.

SEYCHELLES

Location

Seychelles is an Archipelago of over 100 islands located in the western Indian Ocean to the northeast of Madagascar. Only 20 to 25 of the islands are inhabited. The main island of Mahe is the largest island with a land area of approximately 455 km. Most of the island chain is a few degrees south of the equator.

Overview

Seychelles is a Republic (Independent Country within the British

Commonwealth) and is a member of the United Nations, with a population of 79,000. The spoken languages are English, French and Creole, a mix of English and French. The official currency is the Seychelles Rupee (SR). Victoria on Make is the capital. Seychelles economy is now based on tourism with the offshore sector growing in importance.

Advantages
- Seychelles is a well-established jurisdiction with legislation dating back to 1978.
- Incorporation in one day-often within hours.
- Migration of companies permitted
- Excellent location for Europe and the Far East
- Multilingual population
- Shelf companies available
- No disclosure of beneficial owner required

Disadvantages
- Listed in Group III of The Financial Stability Forum's list of 42 jurisdictions that it considers to have significant offshore activities; "May 26th, 2000 press release, "Financial Stability Forum Releases Grouping of Offshore Financial Centers (OFC's) to Assist in Setting Priorities for Assessment". (Please see footnote 2)
- $1,000 USD yearly renewal fee plus a $400 USD Domicile Contribution
- Lack of public registry

Company Status
International business company

Corporate Legislation Source
International Business Companies Act, 1994 (Act 24 of 1994)
Company Name
May not use GmbH. May not use words suggesting the patronage of any government or country. Any other ending besides GmbH should be accepted.

Minimum Shareholders
One. The shareholder(s) may be a corporation.

Are bearer shares available?
Yes

Minimum Directors
One. The director(s) may be a corporation and may be located any-

where in the world without restriction.

Minimum Officers
Secretary. The officer(s) may be a corporation and many be located anywhere in the world without restriction.

Is a registered office and/or a registered agent required?
Yes/Yes
- For European investors the Office may be registered in Zurich.

What information is available on the public file?
Memorandum and Articles of Association, Subscriber Shareholders and Registered Office and Agent

What documents must be kept at the Registered Office?
- Copies of Register of Members and Register of Director
- For European investors the Consul of the Seychelles in Zurich has the keeper of registers and maintains all company records in Zurich.

Is an annual return required?
- No
- There is an annual Fee that is based on share capital

Taxation
International business companies and foundations are exempt. There is also a reduction of duties on raw materials.

Taxation Treaties
Tax treaties with South Africa, Indonesia and The People's Republic of China.

< < < ASIA AND PACIFIC > > >

COOK ISLANDS

Location
The Cook Islands are a group of 15 islands located in the south Pacific Ocean. Tahiti is east of the Cooks and the Samoa's and Tonga are to the west. The main island is Rarotonga. Avarua, on Rarotonga, is the commercial and administrative center of the islands.

Overview

New Zealand is the dominant influence in the Cook Islands. New Zealand dollars comprise the primary currency and there are no exchange controls. The government has firmly continued its support for making the Cook Islands into a true financial center. The population is 19,000, with approximately half living on the main Island of Rarotanga, the islands' business center. The official language is English. Although small in population and on the other side of the world from a U.S. point of view, the Cooks boast good courier and telecommunications and direct dialing is available from most countries. The legal system is based on English common law. The islands were ceded by Britain to New Zealand in 1901. They became fully self-governing in 1965.

Advantages

- Very flexible share holding and debt structuring methods are available here.
- No taxes of any kind are a part of the offshore company.
- There appears to be a high level of confidentiality. Laws that impose penal sanctions on any person who discloses information derived from an inspection of the records of an international company guarantee anonymity in the Cook Islands.
- Convenient for European and Asian markets
- The government is encouraging the growth of the Offshore Center and thus offers few restrictions on the movement of funds.
- No disclosure of beneficial owner(s) required.
- Shelf companies are available

Disadvantages

- Still suffering from bad publicity surrounding the Island's default on loans from Nauru and the rescheduling of loans from other banks over four years ago.
- The location presents slight time zone problems for those in the eastern United States.
- Little Infrastructure, but growing.
- Listed in Group III of The Financial Stability Forum's list of 42 jurisdictions that it considers to have significant offshore activities; "May 26th, 2000 press release, "Financial Stability Forum Releases Grouping of Offshore Financial Centers (OFC's) to Assist in Setting Priorities for Assessment". (See footnote 2)

Company Status
International company
Corporate Legislation Source
International Companies Act 1981–82 as amended 1998

Company Name

Approval required. The words "Bank," "Trust," or "Insurance," are restricted to special license holders. Company name must end in "Limited" or "Ltd.".

Minimum Shareholders

One

Are bearer shares available?

Yes

Minimum Directors

One. The director(s) may be a corporation and may be located anywhere in the world with no restriction.

Minimum Officers

One. At least one joint secretary must be resident in the Cook Islands.

Is a registered office and/or a registered agent required?

Yes / No (No registered agent required, but a resident secretary is required)

What information is available on the public file?

Name and registered office

What documents must be kept at the Registered Office?

Copies of the Register of Members and Register of Directors, secretary, and Charges.

Is an annual return required?

Yes
- Annual government fee: $500 USD

Taxation

No taxes of any kind.

HONG KONG

Location

Hong Kong is a large island chain situated between the East China and South China Seas on the southeast coast of China. Hong Kong Island, the New Territories and Kowloon (1,078 km. Land area) are the primary islands with a population of around 6.75 million making Hong Kong one of the most densely populated areas in the world.

Overview

Hong Kong is a Special Administrative Region (SAR) of The People's Republic of China. Hong Kong was handed back to China on July 1st, 1997. Arrangements were made for the financial district to remain secure for fifty years. Hong Kong is known for it's long term involvement as a trading center. Its population is 6,300,000. The capital and business center of Hong Kong is Victoria on Hong Kong Island. The official languages are Chinese and English. The official currency is the Hong Kong Dollar (HK$)

Advantages

- Very good communications
- Excellent banking infrastructure
- A company may conduct business in and out of Hong Kong
- Great location for all European markets
- Shelf companies available
- Hong Kong is one of the largest financial banking centers in the world, ranking third.
- Listed in Group I of The Financial Stability Forum's list of 42 jurisdictions that it considers to have significant offshore activities; "May 26th, 2000 press release, "Financial Stability Forum Releases Grouping of Offshore Financial Centers (OFC's) to Assist in Setting Priorities for Assessment". (See footnote 2)
- No disclosure of beneficial owner required

Disadvantages

- Recent (1997) changes in government may lead to political instability in the future, especially in 50 years when financial sector begins to see major changes.
- Banking Confidentiality not required by law and is currently questioned and highly suspect
- Tax on income source in Hong Kong
- Time Zone issues for those in North America
- Stiff penalties for non compliance with filing requirements
- Takes two to three weeks to incorporate

Company Status

Private limited company

Corporate Legislation Source

The Companies Ordinance, as amended, 1997

Company Name

The name must end with the word "Limited" either in full or in abbreviated form except for in specific circumstances. Certain words may not be used, i.e., "Assurance", "Bank", "Imperial", "Royal" or a word conveying a similar meaning.

Minimum Shareholders

Two. The shareholder(s) may be corporations.

Are bearer shares available?

No

Minimum Directors

Two. The director(s) may be a corporation and may be located anywhere in the world without restriction.

Minimum Officers

Secretary The secretary(s) may be a corporation, but must be resident in Hong Kong.

Is a registered office and/or a registered agent required?

Yes/No

What information is available on the public file?

Memorandum and Articles of Association, Subscriber Shareholders, Shareholders, Registered Office, Directors, Secretary, Annual returns, Mortgages and Charges.

No need to disclose beneficial owner to government

What documents must be kept at the Registered office?

Register of members, register of secretaries and Directors (may be kept anywhere in Hong Kong), mortgages and charges, minute book, corporate books and seal.

Is an annual return required?

Yes

• Annual government return filing fee and business Registration fee of HK $2,250

Taxation

• No taxes on non-Hong Kong source income. If Hong Kong source income, then pay tax on assessable profits at 16.5%.
• Capital duty of 0.6%

Taxation Treaties

None

LABUAN Malaysia

Location

Labuan of Malaysia comprises a series of small islands and is 50 Kilometers off the coast of Malaysia. Pulau Labuan is the largest of these islands. It is around 92,500 km in size. Labuan is off the northwest coast of Borneo and Sabah.

Overview

Malaysia was formed in 1963 through the unification of the former British Crown Colonies of Malaya, the provinces of Borneo and Singapore. Singapore broke away in 1965 and is now an independent city-state. Labuan is a Parliamentary Monarchy. Labuan has a population of around 50,000. The capital is Kuala Lumpur. Malay, English and Chinese are all common languages in Malaysia and Labuan Island. The official currency is the Malay Ringgit (RM).

Advantages

- Strict confidentiality
- Good political stability
- Currency restrictions enforce in Malaysia are not in force on Labuan Island
- Cheap labour force
- Incorporation in one to three days
- Migration of domicile permitted
- No disclosure of beneficial owner to government required

Disadvantages

- Listed in Group II of The Financial Stability Forum's list of 42 jurisdictions that it considers to have significant offshore activities; "May 26th, 2000 press release, "Financial Stability Forum Releases Grouping of Offshore Financial Centers (OFC's) to Assist in Setting Priorities for Assessment".
- Lacks the developed transport infrastructure to link it to the international financial centers of Singapore and Tokyo.
- No shelf companies

Company Status

Trading and non-trading companies

Corporate Legislation Source

- Offshore Companies Act, 1990, as amended 1997
- Labuan Offshore Business Activity Tax Act, 1990, as amended 1997

Company Name

Words requiring approval: "Finance", "Bank", "Trust", "Royal", "Insurance", "Security", etc. Must have "Corporation", "Incorporate", "Limited", Ltd. Pkc, Societe Anonyme, Sociedad Anonima (S.A.), Aktiengesellschaft (A.G.), Naamloze Vennootschap (N.V.), Perseroan Terbatas (P.T.), or other wording indicating limited liability, as part of the name. A roman character language may be used for the name.

Minimum Shareholders

One

Are bearer shares available?

No

Minimum Directors

One. The director(s) may be a corporation and may be located anywhere in the world without restriction.

Minimum Officers

Secretary. The officer(s) may be a corporation, but must be resident in Labuan.

Is a registered office and/or a registered agent required?

Yes/ Yes

What information is available on the public file?

None

What documents must be kept at the Registered office?

Register of Directors, Register of Secretaries, Register of Members, corporate books, seal and Register of Charges

Is an annual return required?

Yes
* Annual tax/Licence fee of RM 2,600
* Annual return filing fee is RM 100

Taxation

* May repatriate the profits from invested capital
* Special discount rates for industrial sites
* Trading companies pay 3% income tax.
* All non-trading companies, which hold only securities and immovable, are entirely free of tax.

Taxation Treaties
There are at least 50 double taxation agreements with Labuan Island (Malaysia)

MARSHALL ISLANDS

Location
The Republic of the Marshall Islands is located about 2,200 miles southwest of Hawaii in the Pacific Ocean. From 1947 to 1990 the islands were part of the U.S. administered Trust Territory of the Pacific Islands. The Marshall Islands are divided into two parallel chains separated by about 125 miles. The capital is Dalap–Uliga–Darritt on Majuro Atoll.

Overview
The Marshall Islands are heavily dependent on aid from the United States. The islands have a serious balance of trade deficit and have embraced international banking as a mechanism to improve their economy. Tourism and banking are of primary economic importance. The Marshall Islands became internally self-governing in 1979 and signed a free association agreement with the U.S. in 1983, which was approved by Congress in 1986. The Marshall Islands became a member of the UN in 1991.

Advantages
- Corporate law based on New York and Delaware statutes
- Allows for British or US corporate management structures.
- Corporate Law is some of the most modern in the world.
- Corporate redomicilation into and out of jurisdiction

Disadvantages
- A relatively new offshore jurisdiction with little experience and slight infrastructure
- Heavily dependent on U.S. government
- Time zone difficulties
- Listed in Group III of The Financial Stability Forum's list of 42 jurisdictions that it considers to have significant offshore activities; "May 26th, 2000 press release, "Financial Stability Forum Releases Grouping of Offshore Financial Centers (OFC's) to Assist in Setting Priorities for Assessment". (See footnote 2)

Company Status
Non Resident Corporation
Corporate Legislation Source
Marshall Islands Business Corporation Act 1990

Company Name

Any name not already being used by another corporation. May use any suffix except the following: "Bank," "Foundation," "Chartered," "Partnership," "Establishment," "Insurance," and "Trust."

Minimum Shareholders

One

Are bearer shares available?

Yes

Minimum Directors

One. The director(s) may be located anywhere in the world with no restriction.

Minimum Officers

One. The officer(s) may be located anywhere in the world.

Is a registered office and/or a registered agent required?

No / Yes

What information is available on the public file?

Registered agents address, Articles of Incorporation, Amendments, Voluntary filings, Dissolution

What documents must be kept at the Registered Office?

None

Is an annual return required?

No

Taxation

Non-resident corporations are exempt from tax.

Taxation Treaties

None

NIUE

Location

Niue is an island in the south Pacific Ocean. It covers an area of approximately 255 square kilometers and is considered one of the world's largest coral islands.

Overview

Niue is a self-governing territory in free Association with New Zealand. Niue regulates internal affairs and New Zealand regulates and controls external affairs. Niue is a member of the British Commonwealth. The population of Niue is 20,000. The currency is the New Zealand Dollar and the official languages are English and Polynesian.

Advantages

• Incorporation documents in any language if together with a translation into English.

- Shelf companies are available.
- No exchange controls
- No disclosure of beneficial owners to government is required

Disadvantages
- Listed in Group III of The Financial Stability Forum's list of 42 jurisdictions that it considers to have significant offshore activities; "May 26th, 2000 press release, "Financial Stability Forum Releases Grouping of Offshore Financial Centers (OFC's) to Assist in Setting Priorities for Assessment". (See footnote 2)
- Relatively new jurisdiction

Company Status
International business company

Corporate Legislation Source
International Business Companies Act 1994, as amended 1997

Company Name
Company Name must end in: "Limited", "Ltd.", "Corporation", "Corp.", "SA", "Inc.", "Incorporated", "A/S", "AG", "NV", "BV", "GmbH", "Aktiengesellschaft" or any other words signifying limited liability. May be in Cyrillic script, Chinese characters and other accepted language forms with English translation. Certain words cannot be used i.e., "Assurance", "Bank", "Building Society", "Chamber of Commerce", "Chartered", "Imperial", "Insurance", "Royal", etc.

Minimum Shareholders
One. Shareholder(s) may be corporations.

Are Bearer shares available?
Yes

Minimum Directors
One. The director(s) may be located anywhere in the world without restriction.

Minimum Officers
Secretary. The officer(s) may be a corporation and may be located anywhere in the world without restriction.

Is a registered office and/ or a registered agent required?
Yes/Yes

What information is available on the public file?
Memorandum and Articles of Association, Subscriber Shareholders, Registered office and Agent.

What documents must be kept at the Registered Office?
None

Is an annual return required?
No
  - Annual government fees of $150 USD to $1,000 USD subject to capitalization

Taxation
No taxes on offshore profits

Taxation Treaties
None

SINGAPORE

Location
Singapore consists of over 50 islands with the main island of Singapore. Singapore is located in the southeastern tip of Asia, between Malaysia and Indonesia. This area is often referred to as the West Malaysian Peninsula. . Singapore is approximately 627 km in size.

Overview
In 1965 Singapore broke away from the States of Malaysia and is now an independent city-state republic. It has a population of 3,000,000. The official currency is the Singapore Dollar. The capital, Singapore, is a main trading center. Main industries are petroleum refining, electronics, oil drilling equipment, rubber processing and rubber products, Singapore has a long history as a trading nation. Both English and Malay are spoken widely throughout Singapore.

Advantages
- Listed in Group I of The Financial Stability Forum's list of 42 jurisdictions that it considers to have significant offshore activities; "May 26th, 2000 press release, "Financial Stability Forum Releases Grouping of Offshore Financial Centers (OFC's) to Assist in Setting Priorities for Assessment". (See footnote 2)
- Very good telecommunication
- Skilled workforce
- Prime location

- Great infrastructure
- Good legislation for trading companies
- Shelf companies available
- Great for trading structures based in or marketing to the Far East

Disadvantages
- Restricted democracy due to single party and single chamber political system.
- High wage and salary structure
- Local resident director, shareholder and secretary required
- Long incorporation time: Three weeks
- Annual return with audit accounts required yearly

Company Status
- Republic limited company
- Resident limited company

Corporate Legislation Source
Based on British Legal System

Company Name
The company name must end with the words "Private Company" or their abbreviation

Minimum Shareholders
Two. Shareholders must be natural persons and one shareholder must be a resident.

One shareholder is permitted if the company is a wholly owner subsidiary.

Are Bearer shares available?
No

Minimum Directors
Two. The director(s) may not be a corporation and may be located anywhere in the world with the restriction that one director must be ordinarily resident in Singapore.

Minimum Officers

Secretary. The secretary may not be a corporation and must be ordinarily resident in Singapore.

Is a registered office and/ or a registered agent required?
Yes/No

What information is available on the public file?
Memorandum and Articles of Association, Subscriber Shareholders, Directors, Secretary, Registered office, Annual Returns, Mortgages and Charges

What documents must be kept at the Registered Office?
Statutory Registers, Records of the proceedings of directors and shareholders meetings, corporate books and a corporate seal

Is an annual return required?
Yes, must be submitted with audited accounts
• Annual return filing fee S $20

Taxation
Taxes levied when profits are remitted to Singapore

Taxation Treaties
Numerous double tax treaties

VANUATU

Location
Vanuatu (formerly New Hebrides) is a group of about 12 islands and 60 islets extending for about 500 miles in the southwestern Pacific. Vanuatu is located about 1,000 miles northeast of Australia. The capital is Vila, located on the island of Efate.

Overview
Vanuatu's economy is based on agriculture and tourism. Vanuatu has no taxation and is developing an international banking center. The independent republic government is a parliamentary democracy with a judicial, legislative and executive branch headed by an elected president. Vanuatu was the first south Pacific island nation to establish diplomatic relations with Libya and the former Soviet Union. The population of Vanuatu is 140,000. The official languages are English and French and the official currency is the Vatu (VT). The laws in Vanuatu are based on English common law.

Advantages
• Modern, flexible International Companies Act
• Good time zone for the Far East
• Suitable distancing from both Europe and the States, which is considered beneficial by some
• No income or corporate taxes or estate duties

- Twenty-year guarantee of no taxes for international companies
- Despite all the past problems with this jurisdiction, it does offer good legislation for offshore investing

Disadvantages

- A small "telephone window" for needed contact due to the time differentials with North America.
- Tax exempt for only the first twenty years
- Infrastructure is slight, but growing.
- The costs are slightly expensive.
- Past problems with slack Money Laundering/Due Diligence Legislation
- Listed in Group III of The Financial Stability Forum's list of 42 jurisdictions that it considers to have significant offshore activities; "May 26th, 2000 press release, "Financial Stability Forum Releases Grouping of Offshore Financial Centers (OFC's) to Assist in Setting Priorities for Assessment". (See footnote 2)

Company Status

Private companies
Exempt companies

Corporate Legislation Source

- UK common law
- Companies Act 1986 (Cap. 191)
- International Companies Act 1992

Company Name

Can be in any language, any script, with any common ending. May not use the words co-operative or building society.

Minimum Shareholders

One

Are bearer shares available?

Yes

Minimum Directors

One. The director(s) may be located anywhere in the world with no restriction, unless it is a private company in which he must be a resident of Vanuatu.

Two directors are required for some forms of companies in Vanuatu.

Minimum Officers

Secretary. The secretary(s) may be located anywhere in the world.

Is a registered office and/or a registered agent required?
Yes / Yes

What information is available on the public file?
Memorandum & Articles of Association, Registered Office & Registered Agent and Register of Charges

What documents must be kept at the Registered Office?
Company name, Registered Office, Registered Agent, Share capital, Restrictions, Incorporator, Register of Charges and accounts

Is an annual return required?
No
- An Annual Return is required for some company forms in Vanuatu
- Yearly general meeting required

Taxation
No tax on offshore profits

WESTERN SAMOA

Location
Western Samoa is comprised of two large islands and seven smaller ones. Western Samoa along with nearby American Samoa comprises the Polynesian Samoa Archipelago about 1,700 miles northeast of New Zealand located near Honolulu and Sydney. Having a total landmass of approximately 2,728 sq. km, Western Samoa boasts some of the most beautiful coastal cliffs and cays. The capital is Apia, located on Upola

Overview
Western Samoa is very well known for its many beautiful white sandy beaches protected by the coral reefs surrounding the island. The official language is Samoan Polynesian although English is widely spoken and it is taught in all schools. The official currency is the Samoan Dollar (Tala). Western Samoa is a Parliamentary Government based on English common law. Western Samoa has a long history of political, social, and economic stability. Western Samoa has been a fully independent nation since 1962. Parliamentary elections are held every three years.

Advantages
- Western Samoa is an ease of use jurisdiction that requires little maintenance on structures. The current offshore legislation has been around since 1987 and thus provides experience. They have also

demonstrated themselves as a stable and confidential jurisdiction.
- Anonymity and privacy is guaranteed by law
- Corporations may be directors
- No international offshore company pays taxes
- There is no obligation to appoint a resident director
- May transfer companies from other jurisdictions.

Disadvantages
- Very distant from European and American time zones
- Very basic infrastructure
- Listed in Group III of The Financial Stability Forum's list of 42 jurisdictions that it considers to have significant offshore activities; "May 26th, 2000 press release, "Financial Stability Forum Releases Grouping of Offshore Financial Centers (OFC's) to Assist in Setting Priorities for Assessment". (See footnote 2)
- A little of the beaten track. Travel to and from Western Samoa requires a series of flight transfers.

Company Status
International company

Corporate legislation source
International Companies Act 1987, as amended, 1998
International Companies Amendment Act 1991

Company name
Prior approval required. Names can be in any language.

The word "Limited", "Corporation", "Incorporated "Société Anonyme", or "Sociedad Anonima", "Berhad", "Namloze Vennootschap", "Besloten Vennootschap", "Aktiengesellschaft" or the abbreviation "Ltd", "Corp", "Inc" "Plc" "S.A.", "Bhd", "N.V.", "B.V." or "A.G." must be part of the name.

Minimum number of shareholders:
One The Shareholder(s) may be a corporation.

Are bearer shares available?
Yes

Minimum Directors:
One. The director(s) may be a corporation and may be located anywhere in the world with no restriction.

Minimum Officers:
Secretary. The secretary(s) may be a corporation and may be located anywhere in the world.

Is a registered office and/or a registered agent required?
Yes / Yes, if no resident secretary

What information is available on the public file?
Memorandum & Articles of Association, Registered Office & Registered Agent, Subscriber Shareholders, Certificate of Incorporation and other voluntary filings

What documents must be kept at the Registered Office?
Copies of the Register of Members, Register of Directors and Register of Secretaries

Is an annual return required?
No
• $300 USD annual government fee

Taxation
No taxes on offshore profits

Taxation Treaties
No double tax treaties

< < < < < EUROPE > > > > >

ANDORRA

Location
Andorra lies high in the Pyrenees Mountains on the French-Spanish border in the heart of the Pyrenees. It has a landmass of 463 km and is drained by the Valirya River, which splits Andorra into four distinct valleys. Andorra offers an alpine climate with a full range of winter activities available.

Overview
Andorra is a parliamentary principality (democracy) often traveled when going between Barcelona and France. It has a population of 65,500.

The capital of Andorra is Andorra la Vella. Catalan, Spanish and French are all well spoken in Andorra. The official currencies are the French Franc (FE) and the Spanish Peseta (pta). The economy is 80% based on Tourism.

Advantages
- Good telecommunications
- High standard of living
- Confidentiality and secrecy laws are very strict
- Good banking infrastructure

Disadvantages
- Listed in Group II of The Financial Stability Forum's list of 42 jurisdictions that it considers to have significant offshore activities; "May 26th, 2000 press release, "Financial Stability Forum Releases Grouping of Offshore Financial Centers (OFC's) to Assist in Setting Priorities for Assessment". (See footnote 2)
- Formation is subject to the condition that a company have some legitimate local significance
- Must have Andorran shareholders
- If personal capital amounts to less than 5 million Pesetas it must be deposited in full, otherwise a deposit of 25% is sufficient as long as it amounts to at least 5 million Pesetas.
- Disclosure of beneficial owners to government is required

Company Status
Exempt company

Corporate Legislation Source
Andorra Corporations Act, 1983

Company Name
Prior approval is required.

Minimum Shareholders
One

Are bearer shares available?
Yes

Minimum Directors
One. The director(s) may be a corporation and may be located anywhere in the world without restriction.

Minimum Officers
    Secretary

Is a registered office and/or a registered agent required?
    Yes/Yes

Is an annual return required?
    Yes
    • Minimum annual tax fee of $225 required
    • Annual return filing fee of $50 required

Taxation
    No tax on offshore profits

Taxation Treaties
    The EU Treaty is not in force in Andorra.

CYPRUS

Location
    Cyprus is an island in the eastern Mediterranean Sea between Asia, Africa and Europe just south of Turkey, west of Syria and northwest of Lebanon. It is approximately 9,010 square kilometers in size with a population of 700,000.

Overview
    Cyprus is a country situated in the eastern Mediterranean making it very popular with Europeans. The official languages are Greek and Turkish and the official currency is the Cyprus Pound. Cyprus is a member of the United Nations, Commonwealth and the Council of Europe. Cyprus based its Western-type democratic government on the United States model.

Advantages
• Cyprus is a well-established jurisdiction with an excellent history and top of the line infrastructure. Due to its size, it can offer many services.
• Good for Middle Eastern, Central and Eastern European investors
• Extensive double tax treaty network
• Shelf companies available

Disadvantages
• There is a slight taxation on net taxable profit.
• There are no bearer shares
• The language is Greek and Turkish.

- Disclosure of beneficial owner to government authorities required
- Listed in Group III of The Financial Stability Forum's list of 42 jurisdictions that it considers to have significant offshore activities; "May 26th, 2000 press release, "Financial Stability Forum Releases Grouping of Offshore Financial Centers (OFC's) to Assist in Setting Priorities for Assessment". (See footnote 2)
- May join the EU
- Documentation present at the Companies Registry must be in Greek

Company Status
Offshore company

Corporate Legislation Source
- Company Law, Chapter 113, as amended
- Income tax law, 1961 as amended, 1997

Company Name
Certain words may not be used without approval, i.e., " "Bank", "Building Society", "Chamber of Commerce", "Cooperative", "Government:"Imperial"," "Royal", "State", "Trust", or a word conveying a similar meaning. The Company name must end in Limited except in specific circumstances.

Minimum Shareholders
7 for company and 2 for a private company, The Shareholders may be corporations.

Are Bearer Shares Available?
Share Warrant to Bearer are available

Minimum Directors
One for private company, two for regular companies. The director(s) may be a corporation and may be located anywhere in the world without restriction.

Minimum Officers
Secretary. The secretary(s) may be a corporation and may be located anywhere in the world without restriction. The secretary cannot also be a director if there is only one director.

Is a registered office and/or a registered agent required?
Yes/No
What information is available on the public file?
Memorandum and Articles of Association, Shareholders, Registered

Office and Agent, Directors, Secretary, Share capital, Mortgages and Charges

What Documents must be kept with the Registered Agent?
Corporate Books, Seal, Register of Charges and Register of Mortgages

Is an annual return required?
Yes
• Annual government fee of CL7 is required
• Annual general meeting is required

Taxation
4.25% net taxable profit tax in some circumstances. There is no capital gains tax and no estate tax.

Taxation Treaties
Comprehensive tax treaty network

IRELAND

Location
Ireland is located to the west of Great Britain and is separated from Great Britain by the Irish Sea. It comprises most of the land of the Island of Ireland with Northern Ireland at the northern tip. It has a population of around 350,100. The climate is cool, rainy and damp. The capital and primary commercial center is Dublin.

Overview
The Republic of Ireland is a member of the EC. The Republic of Ireland is a common-law jurisdiction. The legal system is similar to the United States, Australia, and England. The Republic of Ireland is a parliamentary democracy with a written constitution. Ireland is not a pure tax haven. However, where an Irish corporation is 100% foreign owned and does all of its business outside of Ireland, there are no taxes.

Advantages
• Full EC membership gives the Irish company a high international status.
• Listed in Group I of The Financial Stability Forum's list of 42 jurisdictions that it considers to have significant offshore activities; "May 26th, 2000 press release, "Financial Stability Forum Releases Grouping of Offshore Financial Centers (OFC's) to Assist in Setting Priorities for Assessment". (See footnote 2)

Disadvantages
• Audited accounts must be filed annually.

- Disclosure of beneficial ownership to the authorities is required unless the shares are held in trust.
- As an EC member pressure may be brought to bear on Ireland to change their taxation system to eliminate this type of company at some stage.

Company Status
Non-Resident Corporation not subject to tax in the Irish Republic on profits, but liable to stamp duty on transfer of shares.

Corporate Legislation Source
Common Law - Companies Act 1963 to 1990

Company Name
Certain words are prohibited, i.e.: "Bank," "Trust," "Insurance," etc. Names must end with "Limited," or "Teoranta."

Minimum Shareholders
One. The Shareholder(s) may be a corporation.

Are bearer shares available?
No

Minimum Directors
Two. The director(s) may not be corporation but may be located anywhere in the world except in Ireland.

Minimum Officers
Secretary. The officer(s) may be a corporation and may be located anywhere in the world.

Is a registered office and/or a registered agent required?
Yes / No

What information is available on the public file?
Memorandum & Articles of Association, Registered Office, list of Directors, Secretary, Shareholders list, Annual Return, Annual Accounts, Mortgages, Charges and share capital

What documents must be kept at the Registered Office?
Register of Directors, Register of Members, Secretaries, Mortgages and Charges
Is an annual return required?
Yes

- Annual return filing fee of L26
- Annual government fee of L225

Taxation

No taxes on offshore profits

Taxation Treaties

No double taxation treaties applicable

GIBRALTAR

Location

Gibraltar is a peninsula located in Europe on the southern tip of Spain. It is directly across the mouth of the Mediterranean from Morocco, Africa. Gibraltar is geographically part of Europe, but only a short jet-boat ride away from Africa.

Overview

Gibraltar is a British Dependent Territory with an elected House of Assembly with laws based on English common law. The official language is English and the official currency is Pound Sterling. It has a population of approximately 30,000. Gibraltar enjoys special status within the European Community. It is exempted from customs tariff, the value-added tax, and the common agricultural policy. Gibraltar is politically stable. The government actively promotes Gibraltar as a first-class international financial center. There is an abundance of professional and banking services.

Advantages

- The first European jurisdiction to provide exempt company status, which allows a business to be controlled and managed from Gibraltar, and still enjoy preferential tax status.
- Probably the most cost effective European jurisdiction.
- The exempt certificate gives a 25-year guarantee of exemption from all Gibraltarian taxes.
- Convenient for European and Asian markets.
- There is a high level of infrastructure including the latest in technology and communication.
- Shelf companies available

Disadvantages

- As a full member of the EC, pressure will likely be applied at some future date to coerce Gibraltar into changing their tax structure.
- Listed in Group II of The Financial Stability Forum's list of 42 jurisdictions that it considers to have significant offshore activities; "May 26th, 2000 press release, "Financial Stability Forum Releases

Grouping of Offshore Financial Centers (OFC's) to Assist in Setting Priorities for Assessment". (See footnote 2)
- Disclosure of Beneficial Owner to Government Authorities
- Slight time zone problems for those in the US
- Mutual Legal Assistance Treaty with US.
- Complex legislation dating far back

Company Status
Non-resident Exempt company

Corporate Legislation Source
- UK common law 1929 Act introduced locally as "The Companies Ordinance."
- Business Names Registration Ordinance, as amended, 1999
- Companies (Accounts) Ordinance, 1999
- Companies (Taxation & Concessions) Ordinance

Company Name
Prior approval not required. Some words are sensitive such as "Bank," "Trust,""Royal,""Holdings,""International,""Insurance," etc. Names must end with "Limited."

Minimum Shareholders
One. The shareholder(s) may be a corporation.

Are bearer shares available?
Technically yes, but under Gibraltar law they are impractical.

Minimum Directors
One. The director(s) may be a corporation and may be located anywhere in the world without restriction.

Minimum Officers
Secretary. The officer(s) may be a corporation, but must be resident in Gibraltar.

Is a registered office and/or a registered agent required?
Yes / No

What information is available on the public file?
Memorandum & Articles of Association, Registered Office, Directors, Shareholders, Annual Return, Mortgages, and Charges, share capital and Certificate of Registration.

What documents must be kept at the Registered Office?

Copies of the Register of Members, Register of Directors, Mortgages and Charges and Certificate of Registration

Is an annual return required?

Yes
- Annual government fee for Exempt company is L225
- Annual return filing fee is L26

Taxation

taxation on Exempt companies
- Capital duty of 0.5%
- The exempt certificate gives a 25-year guarantee of exemption from all Gibraltarian taxes.

Taxation Treaties

None

GUERNSEY (Channel Islands)

Location

Located in the English Channel off the northwest coast of France, Guernsey is the second largest of these British Islands. Guernsey was part of the territory of the Cuchy of Normandy until 1204 when Normandy was freed from English rule and the islands remained allied with England. The capital is St. Peter Port. Guernsey consists of Guernsey Island and the Lihou, Herm and Jethou Islands. The Bailiwick of Guernsey consists of the island of Guernsey, Alderney and the Fief of Sark. The climate is warmer than that of the south coast of England.

Overview

The economy of Guernsey is based on tourism, agriculture, and financial services. Farming is in some decline; the financial service sector is becoming increasingly important. The majority of Guernsey legislation is derived from English common law but there are significant differences, especially as it relates to inheritance and company law.

Advantages

- Guernsey offers stability, a comparatively free economic climate, a penchant for confidentiality, and favorable tax laws for companies.
- Many of the world's most respected financial institutions and international Corporations are based here.
- Guernsey enjoys a high degree of respectability in the world's financial circles.

- Great offshore fund market
- Listed in Group I of The Financial Stability Forum's list of 42 jurisdictions that it considers to have significant offshore activities; "May 26th, 2000 press release, "Financial Stability Forum Releases Grouping of Offshore Financial Centers (OFC's) to Assist in Setting Priorities for Assessment". (See footnote 2)

Disadvantages
- Higher costs
- Relatively slow incorporation process
- Beneficial ownership must be disclosed to the authorities, together with intended trading activities of the company prior to incorporation.
- Public disclosure of shareholders and directors is required.

Company Status
Exempt company
Exempt companies are only incorporated at court sessions, twice weekly.
Corporate Legislation Source
- Companies (Guernsey) Law 1994, as amended 1996
- Companies (Purchase of Own Shares) Ordinance, 1998

Company Name
Prior approval is required. Certain words, i.e.: "Insurance," "Assurance," "Bank," "Trust," etc., require further approval. Names must end with the word "Limited."

Minimum Shareholders
Two

Are bearer shares available?
No

Minimum Directors
One. The director(s) may be located anywhere in the world with no restriction.

Minimum Officers
One. The officer(s) may be located anywhere in the world.

Is a registered office and/or a registered agent required?
Yes / No

What information is available on the public file?
Memorandum & Articles of Association, Registered Office, Share

capital, Shareholders, and Directors

What documents must be kept at the Registered Office?

Copies of the Register of Members and Register of Directors, Board and Shareholder Minutes

Is an annual return required?

Yes

Taxation

No taxes on offshore profits
* Capital duty o.5% (Minimum L50)
* Annual government fee of L500 required
* Annual return filing fee of L100 required

Taxation Treaties

Treaties with the United Kingdom and Jersey

ISLE OF MAN

Location

The Isle of Man is located on the Irish Sea, close to England, Scotland and Ireland. It has a total landmass of approximately 590 square kilometers. The capital is Douglas. The population is approximately 72,500.

Overview

The Isle of Man is a British Crown Colony. It is in the perfect location to provide services to most of Europe. The government of the Isle of Man has actively solicited this European relationship. The economy deals mainly with Agriculture and tourism, but the financial sector is rising. The official and spoken language is English and the official currency is the Manx Pound. The Government is based under English common law. The Isle of Man's economy has until most recently been based on agriculture and tourism. More emphasis is now placed on industrial investment and its financial center activities. The Isle of Man is the only low-tax financial center in Europe that actively encourages new residents. There are over 50 banks, many international that provide discreet effective service. The Isle of Man boasts an excellent compliment of professionals including lawyers, accountants, top flight banking services, insurance, and brokers of all kinds.

Advantages

* Different tax statuses allow clients to obtain the correct corporate structure dependent on their needs.

- Sophisticated infrastructure and high respectability
- No stamp duty, estate duty or capital gains tax
- A stable jurisdiction conveniently located for the European and English investor, the Isle of Man offers multiple structures to meet investor needs, an excellent infrastructure and ease of use options.
- Listed in Group I of The Financial Stability Forum's list of 42 jurisdictions that it considers to have significant offshore activities; "May 26th, 2000 press release, "Financial Stability Forum Releases Grouping of Offshore Financial Centers (OFC's) to Assist in Setting Priorities for Assessment". (See footnote 2)
- No disclosure of beneficial owner to government required

Disadvantages
- Can be expensive for non-trading operations
- Annual fees are twice that of other flexible jurisdictions such as Bahamas, BVI's, Nevis, or Anguilla.
- Some corporate taxes may be assessed.

Company Status
International or Exempt company
Non-Resident companies and LLC's are not discussed in this Directory

Corporate Legislation Source
The Companies Acts of 1931 to 1992, as amended

Company Name
Prior approval of names are required.   Certain words are restricted, i.e., "International," "Bank," "Trust," "Holdings," "Group," "Royal." Names must end with "Limited," or "Public Limited Company." Unless receive special approval

Minimum Shareholders
One - but two are usual. The Shareholder(s) may be a corporation. One member for LLC

Are bearer shares available?
Yes
Minimum Directors
Two. The director(s) may not be a corporation and must be resident in Isle of Man.

Minimum Officers
Secretary. The officer(s) may not be a corporation and must be a

resident of the Isle of Man that is qualified to be an officer.

Is a registered office and/or a registered agent required?
Yes / No

What information is available on the public file?
Memorandum & Articles of Association, Registered Office, list of Directors, list of Shareholders, Annual Returns, Mortgages, Charges and share capital

What documents must be kept at the Registered Office?
Copies of the Register of Members and Register of Directors, Secretaries, Mortgages, Charges, and the Corporate Seal

Is an annual return required?
Yes
- Annual government fee of L300 and annual return filing fee of L45 for tax exempt company
- Yearly general meeting required

Taxation
No taxes on offshore profits

Taxation Treaty
Double taxation treaty with UK

JERSEY
(Channel Islands)

Location
Jersey is located off the northwest coast of France near the Cherbourg peninsula. Jersey is the largest of the Channel Islands. Jersey is approximately 100 miles south of England and 14 miles from France. The capital is St. Helier. The population is approximately 89,000.

Overview
The financial services sector is the primary source of income for this island nation, followed by tourism. Jersey considers itself a tax haven and amendments to the income tax law effective 1989 add to Jersey's overall appeal. There are no laws on bank secrecy or privacy of information, however Jersey banks will restrict the identification of an account holder to senior bank officers and will provide numbered banks accounts upon request.

Advantages

- A highly respected offshore financial center. Jersey has a reputation for seeking elite offshore business.
- Highly sophisticated infrastructure of trust companies, banking services, accountants, lawyers, and other financial related services.
- used as a base of operation for major international corporations and banks
- great offshore fund market
- Listed in Group I of The Financial Stability Forum's list of 42 jurisdictions that it considers to have significant offshore activities; "May 26th, 2000 press release, "Financial Stability Forum Releases Grouping of Offshore Financial Centers (OFC's) to Assist in Setting Priorities for Assessment". (See footnote 2)

Disadvantages

- Relatively expensive jurisdiction as compared with other more convenient jurisdictions. Disclosure of beneficial ownership to the authorities, but not to the public.
- References may be required prior to incorporation.
- Must have standard authorized share capital of L10,000
- Disclosure of beneficial owner to government authorities
- Confidentiality not guaranteed by law

Company Status

Exempt company

Corporate Legislation Source

Companies (Jersey) Law 1991 as amended 1998

Company Name

Names must be approved in advance. Certain words are considered sensitive: "Royal," "International," "Bank," etc. Names must end with "Limited," or "Ltd."

Minimum Shareholders

Two. The shareholder(s) may be a corporation.

Are bearer shares available?

No

Minimum Directors

One. The director(s) may not be a corporation, but may be located anywhere in the world with no restriction.

Minimum Officers
Secretary. The officer(s) may be located anywhere in the world. Secretary may be a corporation in only certain circumstances.

Is a registered office and/or a registered agent required?
Yes / No

What information is available on the public file?
Registered Office, Shareholders, Annual Return, Memorandum and Articles of Incorporation, Directors, Secretary and share capital

What documents must be kept at the Registered Office?
Copies of the Register of Members, Register of Directors, list of Secretaries Minutes of General Meetings of the Directors — available to shareholder/members only

Is an annual return required?
Yes
• Annual government fee of L500
• Annual return filing fee of L120 or 20% rate of income tax.

Taxation
No taxes on offshore profits
Dividends paid to non-residents by local companies are taxed at rate of 20%.

Taxation Treaties
Double tax treaties with UK and Guernsey

LIECHTENSTEIN

Location
Liechtenstein is located between Switzerland and Austria in the region of the upper Rhine. The capital is Vaduz. The population is approximately 30,000. Liechtenstein is 96 square miles in size.

Overview
Liechtenstein is a highly developed, industrialized nation with a healthy economy. Liechtenstein has a firm belief in the free enterprise system and the concepts of personal privacy. Its banks are considered very confidential and tax matters are believed to be a private matter.

Advantages
• Liechtenstein levies no income taxes against any company that is

domiciled there if the corporation does not earn income from within the country.

- Flexible and liberal company law with its own trust law.
- Political stability and bank secrecy laws
- It is possible to not disclose the beneficial ownership of an account to the bank.
- Very strict secrecy laws

Disadvantages
- Can be expensive for non-trading businesses or ones with small assets.
- Listed in Group III of The Financial Stability Forum's list of 42 jurisdictions that it considers to have significant offshore activities; "May 26th, 2000 press release, "Financial Stability Forum Releases Grouping of Offshore Financial Centers (OFC's) to Assist in Setting Priorities for Assessment". (See footnote 2)

Company Status
    Exempt company (taxed at flat minimum)

Corporate Legislation Source
    • Liechtenstein Company Law as amended 1999.
    With the inclusion of EEA regulations, company law has been modified. There is little to no effect on offshore companies as to bookkeeping.

Company Name
    Certain words are prohibited: "Bank," "Insurance," "Liechtenstein," etc. Names must end with "Aktiengesellschaft," "Limited," or "Anstalt."

Minimum Shareholders
    One. The shareholder(s) may be a corporation.

Are bearer shares available?
    Yes –usually bearer shares

Minimum Directors
    One. At least one director must meet professional standards. Currently only Liechtenstein residents qualify. Other director(s) may be corporations and may be located anywhere in the world with no restriction.
Minimum Officers
    One. The officer(s) may be located anywhere in the world.
Is a registered office and/or a registered agent required?
    Yes/Yes.
    Stock Corporation, Foundation and Establishment Corporation: Yes/ No

What information is available on the public file?

Corporate name, domicile, corporate body, date of registration, board members, signatory rights of board members, purpose of the company, legal representation, share capital, modifications of public information, Deed of Incorporation, Articles of Association and Registered Office

What documents must be kept at the Registered Office?

Memorandum and Article of Association, correspondence necessary for registration, confirmation that the minimum capital for formation is deposited with a bank, company limited by shares, and subscription forms

Is an annual return required?

Not for exempt companies.

- Trusts are also exempt, however there are requirements for some reporting on trading activities and a 4% tax applied on dividends.
- Annual return required for Stock Corporation, Establishment Corporation and Foundation
- Balance sheets are required with a few exceptions

Taxation

Companies domiciled, but not active, in Liechtenstein are exempt from all income, fortune or revenue taxes.

Taxation Treaties

Numerous tax treaties for stock corporations

UNITED KINGDOM

Location

The United Kingdom is at the far northwest corner of the Atlantic Ocean with its east side at the North Sea. France is to the southeast; Spain is to the south and Germany to the east. It consists of England, Scotland, Wales and Northern Ireland.

Overview

The United Kingdom is the second largest tax haven in the world next to the United States. It has a population of 58 million. The United Kingdom is a Hereditary Monarchy with a bicameral legislature consisting of the House of Lords and the House of Commons. It is one of the words great trading powers and financial centers. The official currency is the UK pound. The official language is English and the law is based on English common law.

Advantages

- Centralized registration

- Shelf companies available
- Very good tax treaty network
- Good reputation
- Excellent investment center
- No minimum capital
- No disclosure of beneficial owners required

Disadvantages
- Audited accounts filed each year
- Tax payable on profits
- 7 to 10 days incorporation

Company Status
Private company limited by shares

Corporate Legislation Source
- Companies Act 1985, as amended
- The Income and Corporations Taxes Act, 1988

Company Name
Except with the approval certain words may not be used, i.e., "Bank", "Chamber of Commerce", "Imperial", "Municipal", "Royal", "International", or a word conveying a similar meaning. The company name must end in "Limited".

Minimum Shareholders
One, but two are usually used

Are Bearer shares available?
No

Minimum Directors
One. The director(s) may be a corporation and may be located anywhere in the world with no restriction.

Minimum Officers
Secretary The officer(s) may be a corporation, and may be located anywhere in the world with no restriction.

Is a registered office and/ or a registered agent required?
Yes/No

What information is available on the public file?
Memorandum and Articles of Association, Directors, Shareholders,

Registered office, Charges, accounts and Secretary

What documents must be kept at the Registered Office?
Registers of Members, Directors, Directors' Interests, Secretaries and Charges

Is an annual return required?
Yes
* Annual return filing fee L15

Taxation
Corporate tax based on audited accounts and is 21% or higher

Taxation Treaties
Numerous double tax treaties

LUXEMBOURG

Location
Luxembourg is located in Western Europe between France, Belgium and Germany. It encompasses 2,510 square kilometers and has a population 0f 400,000.

Overview
Luxembourg is a constitutional monarchy, gaining independence from Germany in 1867, with a democratically elected Parliament. The legal system is based on Napoleonic Code. Luxembourg is a member of the OECD. The official currency is the Luxembourg Franc. Luxembourgisch, German and French are all commonly spoken.

Advantages
* Highly respected jurisdiction
* Listed in Group I of The Financial Stability Forum's list of 42 jurisdictions that it considers to have significant offshore activities; "May 26th, 2000 press release, "Financial Stability Forum Releases Grouping of Offshore Financial Centers (OFC's) to Assist in Setting Priorities for Assessment". (See footnote 2)
* Shelf companies are available for 1929 Holding Companies

Disadvantages
* Annual government fee of 0.2% per annum on share capital paid quarterly for 1929 Holding Company
* No shelf companies for SOPARFI

Company Status
- 1929 Holding Company
- SOPARFI

Corporate Legislation Source
- Companies Act of August 10, 1915, as amended.
- Code de Commerce

Company Name
Restrictions on sensitive names

Minimum Shareholders
Two. The Shareholder(s) may be a corporation.

Are Bearer shares available?
Yes

Minimum Directors
Three. The director(s) may not be a corporation, but may be located anywhere in the world with no restriction.

For SOPARFI, in order for the company to utilize the Luxembourg Tax Treaty Network, a majority of the Board is required to be ordinary resident in Luxembourg.

Minimum Officers
Secretary. The officer(s) may be a corporation and may be located anywhere in the world without restriction.

Is a registered office and/ or a registered agent required?
Yes/No

What information is available on the public file?
Deed of Incorporation, Articles of Association, Shareholders, Registered Office, Directors and Capital Structure

What documents must be kept at the Registered Office?
Shareholders Register and certain financial books

s an annual return required?
Yes
- Annual government fee of 0.2% per annum on share capital, which is paid quarterly for 1929 Holding CO.
- No annual government fees for SOPARFI

Taxation
- No local taxation on taxes on offshore profits for 1929 Holding Companies
- SOPARFI's are taxed at the rate of 39%, but subject to certain conditions (dividends and capital gains are exempt from taxation)

Taxation Treaties
- 1929 Holding Companies are unable to utilize the provision of the Tax Treaty Network
- Numerous tax treaties for SOPARFI companies including Austria, Japan, Spain and the United States among others

MADEIRA

Location
Madeira is an island to the west of Morocco, to the southwest of Spain and Portugal and to the north of the Canary Islands. Madeira has been an autonomous region since 1976, but still legally and politically a part of Portugal and a full member of the EU.

Overview
Portuguese and English are the two spoken languages of Madeira.

Advantages
- Migration of companies permitted
- VAT number assigned

Disadvantages
- Meetings must be held at registered office
- Tax exempt only to 2011
- Expensive
- 4 to 6 weeks to incorporate

Company Status
Limited (LDA) Private Limited Liability company
Sociadade Anonima (SA, Stock Corporation)

Corporate Legislation Source
Portuguese Company Law

Company Name
Main activity of company must be included in name. May use foreign names. The company name must end in "Limited" or "Lda."

Minimum Shareholders

One for LDA

Five for SA

The shareholder(s) for the LDA and the SA may be a corporation.

Are Bearer shares available?

No for LDA

Yes for SA

Minimum Directors

One. The director(s) may not be a corporation, but may be located anywhere in the world with no restriction.

One. The director(s) may be a corporation and may be located anywhere in the world with no restriction.

Minimum Officers

Not required

Is a registered office and/ or a registered agent required?

Yes/Yes

What information is available on the public file?

Shareholders, Registered Office, Directors, Annual Returns, Objects, Capital Base, Mortgages, Charges and Form of Binding

What documents must be kept at the Registered Office?

Legal documents, accounting books, records and Share Register

Is an annual return required?

Yes

- Annual company tax: $1,000 USD
- Quarterly VAT Accounts
- Tax return must be filed
- Yearly audited accounts

Taxation

Tax exempt until 2011

Taxation Treaties

Numerous double tax treaties

MALTA

Location

Malta is an archipelago of three islands: Malta, Gozo and Comino located in the Mediterranean Sea to the south of Sicily and Italy and to the east of Tunisia.

Overview

The Republic of Malta won Independence from British rule in 1964. It is a sovereign independent state with Parliamentary Democracy. Malta has a population of 360,000. The official languages are Maltese and English with most Maltase speaking Italian also. The official currency is the Maltese Lira. Malta is a member of the United Nations and the Council of Europe. Tourism is Maltese prime source of income. The official language of Malta is English.

Advantages

- Good telecommunications
- Prime location for the European and Asian markets
- No disclosure of beneficial owners required
- Political stability
- Multilingual work force

Disadvantages

- Plans to join the EU
- Must disclose beneficial owner
- Listed in Group II of The Financial Stability Forum's list of 42 jurisdictions that it considers to have significant offshore activities; "May 26th, 2000 press release, "Financial Stability Forum Releases Grouping of Offshore Financial Centers (OFC's) to Assist in Setting Priorities for Assessment". (See footnote 2)

Company Status

- International Trading company
- International Holding company

Corporate Legislation Source

- Companies Act, 1995 (as amended 1998)
- Malta Financial Services Act Centre 1994

Company Name

The company name must end with Limited or Ltd.

Minimum Shareholders

One

Are Bearer shares available?

No

Minimum Directors

One. The director(s) may not be a corporation, but may be located anywhere in the world with no restriction.

Minimum Officers

Secretary. The secretary(s) may be a corporation, but must be a Maltese Nominee Company.

Is a registered office and/ or a registered agent required?

Yes/Yes, must be a Maltese Nominee Company

What information is available on the public file?

Memorandum and Articles of Association

What documents must be kept at the Registered Office?
Share Register
Is an annual return required?
Yes, along with a declaration that the company still satisfies the regulations
- A tax return must be filed annually where applicable
- Annual fees: Trading company: Lm1000 plus 5% tax
    Non-trading company: Lm500 (no tax)
    Shipping company: Lm100 (no tax)

Taxation
Minimum rate of tax would remain at 5%.
Taxation Treaties
Numerous tax treaties, but must make specific request to make them applicable to offshore companies.

NETHERLANDS

Location
The Netherlands is located in Western Europe on the coast of the North Sea. The Netherlands is adjacent to Belgium and Germany. The Netherlands has a total mass of 37,330 square kilometers. It is located at the mouth of three European Rivers: The Rhine, Maas and Schelde.
Advantages
- Long tradition of good service
- Good network of double taxation treaties
- Good infrastructure

Disadvantages
- Shareholder meetings must be within Netherlands
- Long time to incorporate (4 to 10 weeks)
- Incorporation and compliance procedures arborous

Company Status
Besloten Vennootschap: Private limited liability company
Corporate Legislation Source
Dutch Civil Code Book Two
Company Name
Words prohibited: "Bank", "Royal", "Queen", Etc. The company name must be preceded or end with B.V. or N.V.
Minimum Shareholders
One. The shareholder(s) may be a corporation.
Are Bearer shares available?
No
Minimum Directors
One. The director(s) may be a corporation and there are no residence requirements, but in order for the company to utilize the Netherlands Tax Treaty Network, a majority of the directors are ordinarily required to be

residents in the Netherlands.
Minimum Officers
Not required
Is a registered office and/ or a registered agent required?
Yes/No
What information is available on the public file?
Articles of Association, Capital Base, Purpose Clause, Details of Incorporator, Registered Office, Details of Supervisory Directors, Details of Managing Directors, Details of Attorney in Fact and Details of Shareholders
What documents must be kept at the Registered Office?
Share Register, minutes and resolutions, Share Transfer Documents, and administrative and bookkeeping records
Is an annual return required?
Yes
• There is an annual contribution payable to the Chamber of Commerce.
• The annual return filing fee is variable, depending upon capitalization
Taxation
Taxes on offshore profits: 40% on the first NLG 250,000 and 35% thereafter. However, an advance ruling for four years may be obtained from the Dutch Tax Authorities-these depend upon the activity of the company
Taxation Treaties
Numerous double tax treaties

SWITZERLAND

Location
Switzerland is located in central Europe between France and Austria. It total land area is around 41,290 square kilometers.
Overview
Switzerland is a Federal Republic with a civil law system. The population of Switzerland is 7,040,600. . It is one of the most prosperous and stable economies in the world. Main industries are machinery, chemicals, watches, textiles and precision instruments. The Swiss Franc is the official currency (SwF). Known for tourism German, Italian and Romansch are widely spoken. There are excellent domestic and international telecommunications. While treaties with the United States might make it an uncertain bet for US investors, it is worth investigating the various corporate structures available.
Advantages
• Infrastructure

- Extensive double taxation treaty network
- Multi-lingual country making business for most foreigners less difficult
- Listed in Group I of The Financial Stability Forum's list of 42 jurisdictions that it considers to have significant offshore activities; "May 26th, 2000 press release, "Financial Stability Forum Releases Grouping of Offshore Financial Centers (OFC's) to Assist in Setting Priorities for Assessment". (See footnote 2)

Disadvantages

- Expensive
- Many treaties with US
- Requires Swiss directors
- 35% withholding tax
- Incorporation takes three weeks
- No shelf companies
- CHF50,000 paid in capital
- Heavy due diligence requirements under Swiss Money Laundering Act
- Require notice of all Beneficial and Economic Owners

Company Status

Societe Anonyme

Corporate Legislation Source

- Swiss Civil Code
- Swiss Money Laundering Act

Company Name

No restrictions

Minimum Shareholders

Three

Are Bearer shares available?

Yes

Minimum Directors

One. The majority of Directors must be Swiss national and resident in Switzerland. The director(s) may not be a corporation.

Minimum Officers

Not required

Is a registered office and/ or a registered agent required?

Yes/No

The registered office and agent must be in canton of formation.

What information is available on the public file?

Board of directors, any other officials signing, auditors, shareholders and capital

What documents must be kept at the Registered Office?

Share Register

Is an annual return required?

No
Taxation
Annual income tax required
Taxation Treaties
Extensive double tax treaty network

< < < WESTERN HEMISPHERE > > >

ANGUILLA

Location
Anguilla is located about 150 miles east of Puerto Rico and is close to the Virgin Islands. It is a mere six miles north of St Martin. It is the northernmost of the Leeward Islands. Anguilla is 16 miles long and three miles wide and contains some of the best beaches in the Caribbean.

Overview
Anguilla was formerly part of the Federation of St. Kitts and Nevis, but separated from the alliance in 1981. Today it remains a British territory with a democratically elected House of Assembly and with a similar constitutional status to Bermuda, the Cayman Islands, and the British Virgin Islands. The population of Anguilla is 10,000. In April 1993, the Mokoro Report identified the financial services sector as a principal adjunct to Anguilla's tourist-based economy. Adopting that Report, the Anguilla and British governments embarked upon a thorough review and rewriting of the islands financial services legislation. The extensive legislation enacted in January of 1995 was the result. Historically, Anquilla's economy was based on salt production and farming. Tourism is now the primary source of revenue for Anguilla. Fish and lobster are the country's major exports. Anguilla has carefully crafted an image of a "high end" tourist destination. The capital is known as "The Valley," the official language is English, the official currency is the Eastern Caribbean Dollar and the adult literacy rate is 92%.

Advantages
- Ease of formation
- Limited reporting requirements.
- Recently amended, cutting edge legislation offering flexible corporate, partnership and LLC structures
- Adequate confidentiality guarantees with confidentiality governed by the Confidential Relationships Ordinance of 1981
- Zero tax jurisdiction
- No foreign exchange restrictions.

Disadvantages
- Fairly recent entry to the offshore financial services sector

- Mutual Legal Assistance Treaty with the U.S. and Great Britain
- Anguilla is currently experiencing what some say is a government is a state of chaos.
- Slight infrastructure due to population of around 10,000 residents
- Listed in Group III of The Financial Stability Forum's list of 42 jurisdictions that it considers to have significant offshore activities; "May 26th, 2000 press release, "Financial Stability Forum Releases Grouping of Offshore Financial Centers (OFC's) to Assist in Setting Priorities for Assessment". (See footnote 2)

Company Status

International business company
Corporate Legislation Source
- The Companies Ordinance 1994 as amended, 1998
International Business Companies Ordinance 1995, as amended, 1998

Company Name

Prior approval required. Some restrictions apply, such as "Bank," "Insurance," "Trust," etc. Must end in "Limited", "Corporation", "Incorporated", "Sendirian Berhad", "Société à Responsabilité Limitée", "Sociedad Anonima", "Besloten Vennootschap", "Gesellschaft mit beschrankter Haftung", "Naamloze Vennootschapone" or an abbreviation thereof.

Minimum Shareholders

One

Are Bearer Shares Available?

No

Minimum Directors

One. The director(s) may be a corporation and may be located anywhere in the world with no restriction.

Minimum Shareholders

One

Minimum Officers

None

Is a registered office and/or a registered agent required?

Yes/Yes

What information is available on the public file?

Articles of Incorporation, Registered Office and Registered Agent

What Documents must be kept with the Registered Agent?

Articles, By-laws and amendments, imprint of seal and knowledge of where the list of shareholders and other information is kept

Is an annual return required?

No

Taxation

Anguilla is a zero tax jurisdiction. There is a statutory exemption from all forms of income, capital gains, estate profit, corporate, income

withholding or other like taxes.
Taxation Treaties
   None

ANTIGUA AND BARBUDA

Location
   Antigua and Barbuda are located in the eastern Caribbean Sea about 425 kilometers east-southeast o Puerto Rico. Antigua and Barbuda have a total area of approximately 440 square kilometers
Overview
   Antigua and Barbuda is a Parliamentary democracy that has its economy based on tourism with the financial sector a hopeful second. The population is 65,500. The official language is English and the official currency is the Eastern Caribbean Dollar (ECD).
Advantages
* No exchange of information agreements except for with the United Kingdom
* Confidentiality is strict
* Only one director and one shareholder are required
* Minimal reporting requirements
Disadvantages
* Listed in Group III of The Financial Stability Forum's list of 42 jurisdictions that it considers to have significant offshore activities; "May 26th, 2000 press release, "Financial Stability Forum Releases Grouping of Offshore Financial Centers (OFC's) to Assist in Setting Priorities for Assessment". (See footnote 2)
* Criticized for lacking discrimination about its customs
* Annual Directors Meeting (must be held in Antigua and Barbuda)
* Annual Shareholders Meeting (must be held in Antigua and Barbuda)
Company Status
   International business company
   Corporate Legislation Source
   * International Business Companies (Exemption from Income Tax) Act
   * International Business Corporations Act, 1982 (as amended 2000)
Company Name
   The name must contain "Limited", "Incorporated", "Corporation" or the appropriate suffix or other language indicating limited liability.
Minimum Shareholders
   One
Are Bearer shares available?
   Yes, but holder must be a citizen and resident of Antigua and Barbuda
Minimum Directors
   One. The director(s) may be a corporation and may be located any-

where in the world with no restriction.

Minimum Officers

None required

Is a registered office and/ or a registered agent required?

Yes/No

What documents must be kept at the Registered Office?

Articles, By-Laws, Amendments, Copies of unanimous Shareholder Agreement, minutes and resolutions, notices, Register of Shareholders, Register of Debenture holders and Accounting Records

Is an annual return required?

Yes

- Annual Directors Meeting (must be held in Antigua and Barbuda)
- Annual Shareholders Meeting (must be held in Antigua and Barbuda)

Taxation

No tax for 50 years

Taxation Treaties

Treaty with United Kingdom only

ARUBA

Location

Aruba is located off the northwest coast of Venezuela in the southern Caribbean Sea and is close to the northern tip of Colombia. It sustains a population of 70,000.

Overview

Aruba has been under Netherlands rule since the 17th century achieving independence in 1986. The offshore sector in Aruba started in 1995. Dutch, English and Spanish are all widely spoken in Aruba.

Advantages

- Zero tax liability
- No resident office
- Multi lingual jurisdiction: Dutch, English and Spanish
- Strict anti-money laundering laws
- Shelf companies

Disadvantages

- Listed in Group III of The Financial Stability Forum's list of 42 jurisdictions that it considers to have significant offshore activities; "May 26th, 2000 press release, "Financial Stability Forum Releases Grouping of Offshore Financial Centers (OFC's) to Assist in Setting Priorities for Assessment". (See footnote 2)

Company Status

Aruba Exempt company

Corporate Legislation Source

The Companies Ordinance 1994

Company Name

The company name must end in "Ltd.", "Corp.", "Inc.", "SA", "NV", "BV", "GmBH" or the appropriate corresponding word. Cannot use words such as "Bank", "Trust" "Investment" or other words suggesting patronage of Royal Family.

Minimum Shareholders

One. The shareholder(s) may be a corporation.

Are Bearer shares available?

Yes

Minimum Directors

One. The director(s) may be a corporation and may be located anywhere in the world with no restriction.

Minimum Officers

Not required, but officer(s) may be a corporation and may be located anywhere in the world with no restriction.

Is a registered office and/ or a registered agent required?

Yes/Yes

What information is available on the public file?

Articles of Association, Subscriber Shareholders, Registered Office and Agent, details of supervisory directors, managing directors and attorneys in fact, restrictions, share capital and incorporator

What documents must be kept at the Registered Office?

Minute Book, consented resolutions, common seal, Shareholder Register and corporate books

Is an annual return required?

Yes

• Annual government fee of AF500, plus a small annual contribution payable to the Chamber of Commerce (related to the Corporation's issued share capital)

Taxation

No taxes on offshore profits

Taxation Treaties

No double tax treaties applicable

BAHAMAS

Location

The Bahamas comprise approximately 700 islands and some 2,000 cays spread over 100,000 square miles of ocean. Nassau, the capital, is located about 90 miles from Miami, Florida, on New Providence Island. The city of Freeport is located on Grand Bahamas Island only about 50 miles offshore of Florida.

Overview

The Bahamas primary source of gross revenue is tourism, which represents about 52% of the economy. It is considered by some as one of the most beautiful international banking centers in the world. The second largest source of revenue comes from trust and bank service fees on the approximately 250 billion in Eurodollars held by Bahamian banks and corporations. The Bahamas has an excellent legal system based on British common law. The Bahamas has been an independent country within the British Commonwealth since 1973. There is an abundance of bankers, lawyers, accountants, and investment related corporations

Advantages

- One of the newest Caribbean jurisdictions that, as a result, has benefited from mistakes that others have made by implementing highly flexible legislation which allows operation of the company's affairs in the way most desired by the beneficial owner. The Bahamas is a cost-effective option. Once incorporated, a Bahamian IBC is guaranteed exemption from Bahamian taxes for twenty years.
- The Bahamas has proved itself a top notch Jurisdiction with a history of secrecy, confidentiality and good government control.
- There is an excellent infrastructure offering ease of use.

Disadvantages

- Only twenty years of tax exemption
- Because of lack of public registers, ownership can be difficult to prove and thus not recommended for high profile trading operations.
- The Bahamas seems to be under extra scrutiny by IRS.
- Recent signing of a mutual legal assistance treaty with the United States and Great Britain.
- Listed in Group III of The Financial Stability Forum's list of 42 Jurisdictions that it considers to have significant offshore activities; "May 26th, 2000 press release, "Financial Stability Forum Releases Grouping of Offshore Financial Centers (OFC's) to Assist in Setting Priorities for Assessment". (See footnote 2)

Company Status

International business company

Corporate Legislation Source

- Common law
- International Business Companies Act 1989 (No2 of 1990), as amended 1998

Company Name

Certain words are prohibited, e.g., "Assurance," "Bank," "Building Society," etc. Names must end with an appropriate suffix, such as "Incorporated,", "corporation", "Societe Anonyme," "Limited," etc.

Minimum Shareholders

One. The shareholder(s) may be a corporation.

Are bearer shares available?

Yes

Minimum Directors

One. The director(s) may be a corporation and may be located anywhere in the world with no restriction.

Minimum Officers

Secretary. The officer(s) may be located anywhere in the world.

Is a registered office and/or a registered agent required?

Yes / Yes

What information is available on the public file?

Memorandum & Articles of Association, Registered Office & Registered Agent and subscriber shareholders

What documents must be kept at the Registered Office?

Copies of the Register of Members and Register of Directors (if maintained) together with an impression of the seal.

Is an annual return required?

No

$100 USD annual government fee required (amount due dependent on capitalization)

Taxation

No taxes on offshore profits

Taxation Treaties

No Taxation Treaties

BARBADOS

Location

Barbados is an eastern Caribbean island located in the Lesser Antilles in the Atlantic Ocean about 260 miles off the South American Coast. It is the easternmost island in the West Indies Chain. Barbados rates tops for beauty, resources, and infrastructure. It is located near Jamaica, Haiti, and the South American coast. The weather ranges from 78 to 80 degrees F. Barbados is one of the world's most densely populated countries. It's capital and port city are Bridgetown.

Overview

Barbados is a politically stable, economically diversified country. Its primary industries are agriculture, tourism, offshore financial services and manufacturing. This island nation is home to the second oldest parliament outside of England. Barbados gained its independence as a self-governing state within the British Commonwealth in 1966. The British monarch appoints the governor general. The house of assembly consists of 27 locally elected members. The official language is English.

Advantages

- A stable, well-managed, democratic jurisdiction with a well developed legal system
- Low tax rate
- Growing double tax treaty network
- Limited filing requirements

Disadvantages

- Details of shareholders are submitted to the Ministry of Finance when applying for an IBC license.
- Audited accounts are required where total assets or revenue exceed US$500,000.
- One meeting of the directors and one of the shareholders is required within the first eighteen months of incorporation and thereafter within any fifteen-month period.
- Listed in Group II of The Financial Stability Forum's list of 42 Jurisdictions that it considers to have significant offshore activities; "May 26th, 2000 press release, "Financial Stability Forum Releases Grouping of Offshore Financial Centers (OFC's) to Assist in Setting Priorities for Assessment". (See footnote 2)

Company Status

International business company

Corporate Legislation Source

The Companies Act 1982 (based on Canada Business Corporations Act) International Business Companies Act 1991, as amended 1998

Company Name

Certain words are prohibited, e.g. "Assurance," "Bank," "Building Society," etc. Names must end with an appropriate suffix such as "Incorporated," "Societe Anonyme," "Limited," etc. Additional consent or approval is required for the use of certain words, e.g. "Bank," "Insurance," etc. There is also a decided preference by the Registrar of Companies for not approving names using words such as "International," "Global," etc.

Minimum Shareholders

One. The shareholder(s) may be a corporation.

Are bearer shares available?

No

Minimum Directors

One. The director(s) may be a corporation and may be located anywhere in the world with no restriction.

Minimum Officers

Secretary. The officer(s) may be a corporation and may be located anywhere in the world.

Is a registered office and/or a registered agent required?

Yes / Yes

What information is available on the public file?

Memorandum & Articles of Association, Registered Office & Registered Agent and Subscriber Shareholders

What documents must be kept at the Registered Office?

Statutory records and Registers

Is an annual return required?

No

- Annual fee of US $100
- Audited accounts are required where the company's assets exceed US $500,000

Taxation

- 2.5% on all profits and gains up to BDS $10,000,000
- 2% on all profits and gains exceeding that but not exceeding BDS $20,000,000
- 1.5% on all exceeding $20,000,000, but not $30,000000
- 1% on all profits exceeding BDS $30,000,000

Taxation Treaties

Growing Double Taxation Treaty Network

BELIZE

Location

Belize is located on the Caribbean seaboard of Central America. It is located approximately 150 miles due south of Cancun, Mexico, directly east of Guatemala, and north of Honduras. It has pleasant weather much of the year but summers can be very hot. Belize is the starting point of the second largest barrier reef in the world which runs parallel to the Yucatan Peninsula due north to the island of Cozumel.

Overview

Belize has a long history of democracy, peace, and stability. It is a member of the British Commonwealth, the United Nations and the Non-Aligned Movement. Belize boasts a two party system that occasionally trade power without significant incident. Both political parties encourage overseas investment.

Belize has a population of approximately 205,000. The official language is English. Tourism has become a priority. Mayan ecological tours have become numerous. The sugar industry is in decline. The government has aggressively passed laws to attract offshore financial activity. Belizean commercial law is based on the English law model. The court system is similar to that in England.

Advantages

- It is one of the newer Caribbean jurisdictions, benefiting from mistakes other jurisdictions have made.
- They have implemented highly flexible legislation, which allows operation of the company's affairs in the way most desired by a beneficial owner.
- Excellent infrastructure offering an array of high-level professionals, communication devices and an international airport.
- New banking regulations in the last few years have enhanced the already strong regulatory environment and have begun to offer predictable privacy and confidentiality.

Disadvantages

- Because of the lack of public registers, ownership can be difficult to prove. (This may also be considered an advantage.)
- Although the country does have privacy and confidentiality legislation in place, there are those within the financial services sector who do not seem to take it seriously. This attitude seems to be changing and Belize may eventually come of age in this regard.
- Listed in Group III of The Financial Stability Forum's list of 42 Jurisdictions that it considers to have significant offshore activities; "May 26th, 2000 press release, "Financial Stability Forum Releases Grouping of Offshore Financial Centers (OFC's) to Assist in Setting Priorities for Assessment". (See footnote 2)

Company Status
International business company

Corporate Legislation Source
The International Business Companies Act of 1990, as amended 1999

Company Name
Certain words are prohibited, i.e.: "Royal," "Imperial," "Bank," "Insurance," etc.

Minimum Shareholders
One. The shareholder(s) may be a corporation.

Are bearer shares available?
Yes

Minimum Directors
One. The director(s) may be located anywhere in the world with no restriction.

Minimum Officers
One. The officer(s) may be a corporation and may be located anywhere in the world.

Is a registered office and/or a registered agent required?
Yes / Yes

What information is available on the public file?
Memorandum & Articles of Association, Registered Office & Registered Agent and Subscriber Shareholders

What documents must be kept at the Registered Office?
Copies of the Register of Members and Register of Directors (if maintained) together with an impression of the seal

Is an annual return required?
No
$100 USD annual government fee subject to capitalization

Taxation
No taxes on offshore profits

Taxation Treaties
No double tax treaties

BERMUDA

Location

Bermuda and island chain of over 100 islands is located approximately 600 miles off the east coast of the United States roughly due east of North Carolina in the North Atlantic Ocean. There are seven main islands, all connected by bridges. Bermuda enjoys semi-tropical temperatures.

Overview

Bermuda is the reinsurance capital of the world with something over 4,400 captive insurance companies chartered here. Bermuda is a prestigious offshore business hub with an upscale clientele. Bermuda law is based on British common law. It is a fully independent British Commonwealth member. The Queen of England appoints the governor. An appointed Upper House and an elected Lower House administer the country. The governor heads up the cabinet. It has a population of 60,000. The official language is English and the official currency is the Bermuda dollar. Bermuda is known for its luxurious tourists facilities and offshore sector. The only natural resource is limestone. However, tourism and the offshore sector make up the bulk of the economy today.

Advantages

- Highly respected jurisdiction
- Well-known captive insurance jurisdiction
- Excellent professional infrastructure of lawyers, accountants, brokers, and financial advisors
- Extremely cautious and very scrupulous jurisdiction
- One of the most successful and oldest offshore jurisdiction
- Relaxed regulatory environment

Disadvantages

- Expensive
- Incorporation period takes weeks rather than days or hours.
- Minimum capital requirements
- Annual fees to the government are twice to three times higher than it's Caribbean counterparts.
- A board majority must be present in Bermuda.
- Listed in Group II of The Financial Stability Forum's list of 42 Jurisdictions that it considers to have significant offshore activities; "May 26th, 2000 press release, "Financial Stability Forum Releases Grouping of Offshore Financial Centers (OFC's) to Assist in Setting Priorities for Assessment". (See footnote 2)
- Mutual Legal Assistance Treaty with the U.S.
- Complex incorporation procedure requiring disclosure of information.

Company Status

Exempt company

Corporate Legislation Source

Companies Act of 1981, as amended 2000

Company Name

Certain words are prohibited: "Bank," "Insurance," etc.. Names should end with an appropriate suffix such as "Incorporated," "Limited'," and "Ltd."

Minimum Shareholders

One

Are bearer shares available?

No

Minimum Directors

Two. The director(s) may be located anywhere in the world, but a quorum must be present in Bermuda.

Minimum Officers

Secretary. The officer(s) may be located anywhere in the world.

Is a registered office and/or a registered agent required?

Yes / No

What information is available on the public file?

Share Register

What documents must be kept at the Registered Office?

Copies of the Register of Members and Register of Directors, Minutes of Board of Directors and Shareholders Meetings

Is an annual return required?

No

Annual members meeting is required

Taxation

No taxes on exempt companies.

Taxation Treaties

Bermuda is not party to any double taxation treaty

BRITISH VIRGIN ISLANDS

Location

The British Virgin Islands are an archipelago of islands in a horizontal chain 50 miles (80 Km)) northeast of the American Virgin Islands, a US territory. The distance between St. Thomas (American Virgins) and its nearest British counterpart is less than twelve miles. Puerto Rico is 60 miles to the west. This dazzling little country consists of 60 small islands and cays having a total landmass of 59 square miles. The capital is Road Town, Tortola Island.

Overview

The British Virgin Islands are commonly referred to as the BVI's, and they comprise a group of four major and thirty-two minor islands in the eastern Caribbean. Together with the United States Virgin Islands, they form a part of the Greater Antilles rising up from the Puerto Rican shelf about 200 feet below the sea surface. Best known as a common US tourist, boating and diving spot, the BVI's boast beautiful beaches, cays and unparalleled coral reefs. The climate is subtropical with daytime temperatures ranging from 85F to 93F. The official language is English and the official currency is the United States Dollar and the population is around 19,000.

Most Virgin Islanders are the descendants of slaves who worked colonial plantations. More recent immigrants to the islands have come from Puerto Rico, the United States, Venezuela, and the Lesser Antilles. Education and health standards are among the highest in the Caribbean. Christopher Columbus landed in this area in 1493. The British took over the islands they now hold in 1666, and in the same year the Danes occupied Saint Thomas, which is the largest town in the U.S. Virgin Islands. At the closest point, the U.S. Virgins and the British Virgins are only about 3 miles apart.

The climate is subtropical with daytime temperatures ranging from 85F to 93F. The population hovers around 18,000, 34% live in the vicinity of Road Town, which is the capital and primary commercial center. The BVI coastal zone consists of a number of beautiful beaches, cliffs, coral reefs, and sea grass beds, and serves as the primary tourist attraction.

The BVI has a typical British ministerial system of government headed by a governor and an executive council of ministers. They are a self-governing crown colony of the United Kingdom under the 1967 constitution. The governor and the attorney general make up the executive branch of government, a legislative council makes the laws and is democratically elected every four years. BVI boasts a high literacy rate of 98.7%. The U.S. dollar is the local currency, and there are no exchange controls.

In 1984 BVI passed the International Business Corporation ACT of 1984 and launched itself into the financial services industry. This legislation proved extremely beneficial to government revenues and the Banks & Trust Company's Act of 1990, The Company Management Act of 1990, the Trustee Ordinance Amendment Act of 1993, the Insurance Act of 1994, and the Mutual Funds Act of 1996 followed it. Clearly this jurisdiction is dead set on being a competitive force in the growing offshore financial services marketplace.

The BVI has become world renowned for the simple and rapid formation of international business corporations, commonly known as IBC's. This particular financial service product produces eighty million in annual revenues. Over the few years since its inception, the international financial services sector has grown dramatically. By the close of 1984 there were only 235 IBC's formed. By the end of 1996 that number had increased to over 200,000. Citizens from all over the world are deeply committed to

BVI corporations.

Financials services have continued to grow, with fifteen hundred BVI mutual funds representing investments in excess of US $55 Billion developed in an eighteen-month period since the formation of mutual fund legislation. By the close of 1996 there were something over 180 insurance companies based in BVI.

The BVI strategy is to diversify its services by continuing to develop new products. limited liability companies (LLCs) have become a popular vehicle in many parts of the world — beginning in the state of Wyoming and spreading like wild fire — and now BVI is bringing this product on line. It is likely that as complicated tax environments of countries like the U.S. become even more Draconian, two- and three-tiered corporate structures will accelerate the demand for these kinds of products.

Not to be caught resting on their laurels, the BVI government has opened up an office in Hong Kong as a step towards expanding their business activities. They are now expanding copyright and trademark legislation and upgrading their shipping registry. The offshore sector provides significant revenue to the BVI government and is the single largest contributor to its revenue base carrying 45% of the entire government overhead.

According to the BVI government, the IBC came about as a consequence of the disappearance of the double taxation agreement between the U.S., UK, and BVI. The flexibility of the IBC makes it attractive to residents of countries throughout the world. And, interestingly enough, more buyers of the ubiquitous IBC come from Europe than the States. However, recent legislation involving limited liability companies and partnerships are clearly aimed at the upward mobile U.S. middle class.

The BVI has a fully automated Companies Registry that permits Trust companies registered with the country to check company names and pay annual license fees via modem remotely. Granting direct access to the entire registry system to competent trust companies has allowed the jurisdiction to keep up with the pace of accelerating demand.

The BVI Trademark Act has provided another venue for generating revenue streams for government. Currently there appears to be a strong demand for the Registration of Trademarks in order that companies may protect global business activities. The constant threat of piracy of intellectual properties and the need for authors to protect their international copyrights have given impetus to BVI providing a suitable place for registering marks and copyrights. Registration in BVI provides recognition by the International Trademark Standards as well as in the Caribbean territory and the United Kingdom. There have been several thousand trademark registrations filed with the BVI Trademark Registry.

Confidentiality is considered very important. This is a rapidly growing financial center with over 100 Billion Eurodollars under management.

Advantages
- The flexibility of the legislation allows a company incorporated in the BVI's to operate with the absolute minimum of government interference.
- This is a highly popular domicile with over 200,000 IBC corporations having been filed since 1984.
- Annual fees are relatively low.
- The offshore sector in the BVI's has been around since the early 80's and thus the BVI's are one of the largest, most popular and competitive jurisdictions in the Caribbean.
- IT offers quick company formation and inexpensive fees.
- Extensive Tax Treaty Network

Disadvantages
- The lack of public registers can make proof of ownership difficult.
- Banking infrastructure is light but growing.
- Recently BVI has reduced customer anonymity.
- In a series of recent initiatives, the BVI launched a major program to introduce far reaching anticrime legislation. The introduction of a new Code of Conduct marked the launch of this program. The Code sets out general guidelines for the conduct of offshore practitioners and is designed to enhance regulatory vigilance. It was ratified by the Government and the Association of Registered Agents. Under the Code, BVI-licensed service providers are required to ensure that all business referred to them by overseas professionals has been subject to a rigorous "due diligence" and "know your client" principals.
- The BVI Government is introducing due diligence audit requirements to reinforce the Code of Conduct. And, the BVI Government is in the final stages of implementing the Proceeds of Criminal Conduct Bill which criminalizes ALL acts of money laundering, going beyond the Criminal Justice (International Cooperation) Act and the Mutual legal Assistance Treaty signed with the U.S. Government.
- Listed in Group III of The Financial Stability Forum's list of 42 Jurisdictions that it considers to have significant offshore activities; "May 26th, 2000 press release, "Financial Stability Forum Releases Grouping of Offshore Financial Centers (OFC's) to Assist in Setting Priorities for Assessment". (See footnote 2)
- Mutual Legal Assistance Treat with the US and The Criminal Justice Act (International Cooperation)

Company Status
  International Business company (IBC)

Corporate Legislation Source
  Common Law - International Business Companies Act 1984 - as amended

Company Name

Certain words are prohibited, i.e.: "Bank," "Insurance," "Trust." Names must end with an appropriate suffix such as "Incorporated," "Limited," "Ltd," etc..

Minimum Shareholders

One. The shareholder(s) may be a corporation.

Are bearer shares available?

Yes

Minimum Directors

One. The director(s) may be a corporation and may be located anywhere in the world with no restriction.

Minimum Officers

Secretary. The officer(s) may be corporations and may be located anywhere in the world.

Is a registered office and/or a registered agent required?

Yes / Yes

What information is available on the public file?

Memorandum & Articles of Association, Registered Office & Registered Agent and Subscriber Shareholders

What documents must be kept at the Registered Office?

Copies of the Register of Members and Register of Directors (if maintained) together with an impression of the seal.

Is an annual return required?

No

$300   USD annual government fee subject to capitalization

Taxation

No taxes on offshore profits

Taxation Treaties

Good Taxation Treaty network

CAYMAN ISLANDS

Location

The Cayman Islands are situated approximately 450 miles south of Florida. They are south of Jamaica, east of Cozumel and Cancun, Mexico, and west of the majority of the Caribbean islands. The Caymans are tropical with comfortable dry winters and moderately hot summers. They are a popular American tourist spot and offer some of the best scuba diving in the Caribbean. The three islands that comprise the Cayman's total 102 square miles of land. The capital is George Town, Grand Cayman.

Overview

The Caymans are a traditional British tax haven. The government is very supportive of the tax haven industry because it is a major factor in its economic development. Known world round for its phenomenal scuba diving, it is even better known for its tax shelter status. Cayman law is based on English common law. The Caymans are a pure tax haven with no direct taxation being levied on either residents, domestic corporations, or IBC corporations. There is no capital gains, inheritance or gift tax. However, the Caymans have signed an exchange of information agreement with the United States. Law is based on English common law. The official language is English and the official currency is the Caymanian Dollar.

Advantages
- One of the best established of the Caribbean jurisdictions with legislation dating back to 1960.
- Sophisticated legal and banking infrastructures
- Excellent legislation with flexible approaches and options offering investors a high quality jurisdiction.

Disadvantages
- Relatively expensive compared to other Caribbean jurisdictions
- Recently signed mutual legal assistance treaty
- Listed in Group III of The Financial Stability Forum's list of 42 Jurisdictions that it considers to have significant offshore activities; "May 26th, 2000 press release, "Financial Stability Forum Releases Grouping of Offshore Financial Centers (OFC's) to Assist in Setting Priorities for Assessment". (See footnote 2)

Company Status
Non-Resident or Exempt company
Corporate legislation source
- The Companies Law 1960, as amended 2000
- Tax Concessions Law–1999 revision

Company Name
Certain words are prohibited, i.e., "Bank," "Insurance,", "Chartered", "Royal", "Imperial", "Building Society", "Chamber of Commerce", "Trust." Names must end with an appropriate suffix, such as "Incorporated," "Ltd." "Limited," etc.

Minimum Shareholders
One

Are bearer shares available?
Yes, but if authorized the company may not hold lands in the Islands.

Minimum Directors
One. The director(s) may be located anywhere in the world with no restriction.

Minimum Officers
One. The officer(s) may be located anywhere in the world.

Is a registered office and/or a registered agent required?
Yes / No

What information is available on the public file?
Memorandum & Articles of Association, Registered Office & Registered Agent

What documents must be kept at the Registered Office?
Copies of the Register of Members and Register of Directors, mortgages and charges
Is an annual return required?
Yes (Annual list of members and return of capital, shares, calls, etc.)
• Annual general meeting required
Taxation
No tax on offshore profits
Taxation Treaties
None

DOMINICA

Location
The Commonwealth of Dominica is an independent republic island located 30 miles from Guadeloupe to the north and 30 miles from Martinique to the south in the eastern Caribbean Sea. It is 290 square miles of rugged volcanoes, beaches, lush rainforests and coastline. In the eastern Caribbean chain, it has the highest rainfall, rushing rivers, lovely waterfalls, and large banana plantations.
Overview
Dominica was fought over by the British and French before its independence and thus has retained cultural aspects from both. The population is 80,000. The official language is English and the official currency is the Eastern Caribbean Dollar. The economy is based on agriculture. The capital of Dominica is Rosseau.
Advantages
• The 1996 legislation for international business companies, trusts and banks is well grounded and may prove to be the legislation of the future.
• Very simple corporation operations
• Independent Republic
• Good infrastructure
Disadvantages
• Located in the heart of the hurricane belt, Dominica seems to get hit by hurricanes frequently.
• Low level of infrastructure.
• Dominica is relatively new to the offshore sector
• Expensive administrative costs
• Lack of public registers
• No double tax treaties
• Exempt from taxes for only 20 years
Company Status
International business company
Corporate Legislation Source

International Business Companies Act 1996 (as amended, 1997

Company Name

Sensitive words i.e., "Royal", "Imperial", "Trust", "Bank", "Assurance", "Queen", etc. Must end with "Limited", "Corporation", "Incorporated", "Societe Anonyme" or equivalent suffix.

Minimum Shareholders

One

Minimum Directors

One. The director(s) may be a corporation and may be located anywhere in the world with no restriction.

Are Bearer Shares Available?

Yes

Minimum Officers

Secretary. The officer(s) may be a corporation and may be located anywhere in the world with no restriction.

Is a registered office and/or registered agent required?

Yes/Yes

What information is available on the public file?

Copy of Certificate of Incorporation and Good Standing, Memorandum & Articles of Association, Registered Office and Registered Agent

What documents must be kept at the Registered Office?

Copy of Register of Directors and copy incorporation documents

Is an annual return required?

No

$500 USD Annual Fees

Taxation

Free from all taxes for a period of 20 years

Taxation Treaties

No double tax treaties

GRENADA[3]

Location

Grenada is a British Commonwealth located in the lower Antilles of the Caribbean 15,000 miles southeast of Miami and 200 miles from the south tip of South America. Grenada is below the hurricane belt and has not experienced a hard hurricane since 1954. The state of Grenada is made up of the large island of Grenada and two smaller islands, Carriacou and Petite Martinique, which are located to the north of Grenada. Grenada, with a population of around 100,000, forms the southern most of the Windward Islands. It is called the Spice Isle due to the abundance of spices and flowers on the island. The island has beautiful beaches, clear

---

[3] For more information about Grenada, please see Chapter 15, which is devoted completely to the Grenada offshore sector.

blue sea, lowland forest and inland mountain rainforest. Grenada offers great snorkelling, diving, hiking and many waterfalls. The highest point of Grenada is Mount St. Catherine, which rises over 2,740 feet above the sea.

Overview

Grenada is the largest exporter of nutmeg in the world. The official language is English and the official currency is the Eastern Caribbean Dollar. However, the US dollar is used widely. The law in Grenada is based on English common law. The population is around 100,000. The economy is based on tourism, offshore services, banana and spice export.

Grenada is a leading jurisdiction for international business, offshore banking and economic citizenships with an impeccable reputation and unparalleled level of integrity. The variety of services offered in Grenada allows the astute investor many opportunities for integrated financial planning.

Grenada has a commitment to a clean, respectable zone in keeping with a desire to attract legitimate businesses from the international community, the offshore sector in Grenada has developed a level of respectability as a result of striking a balance between the legitimate rights of investors and the need for international cooperation.

Advantages

- Located below the hurricane belt, Grenada offers stability and ease of use.
- It has very liberal offshore legislation and has proven to be a good jurisdiction.
- Grenada legislation is flexible with little reporting requirements and fewer regulations
- Personnel and Office costs are extremely low in Grenada
- Recent amendments to legislation to farther enhance the sector
- New online Name Registry service offering name reservation, Copy requests and the like
- Good transportation infrastructure
- Concessions on imports when setting up an offshore entity
- Confidentiality guaranteed by law
- A flood of companies and banks from other jurisdictions has made Grenada one of the hottest offshore sectors in the Caribbean
- Grenada is currently the least expensive jurisdiction for economic citizenships
- First class worldwide Communications services including fiber optic cable and satellite access.
- Full size airport offering flights on American Airlines, British Airways, Canadian Airways, British Caledonian, BWIA and LIAT among other smaller airlines.
- IBM AS400 System: a newly instituted computerized IBC registry system allows 24-hour access to GIFSA and a variety of automated

services.
- Ongoing commitment to graining for a high industry standard. Training includes seminars, meetings, newsletters, articles and papers.

Disadvantages
- The infrastructure is slight, but is growing.
- The costs are also expensive for some of the entities such as banks.
- Tax exempt for only 20 years
- USA-Grenada Taxes (Exchange of Information) Act
- Recently in the spot light due to a Grenada bank that went into receivership

Company Status
International business company

Corporate Legislation Source
International Companies Act, 1990 as amended, 1996

Company Name
The company name must end in "Limited", "Corporation", "Incorporation" or the equivalent suffix. Sensitive words require approval of the Minister of Finance: i.e. "Royal", "Imperial", "Bank", Assurance", Chamber of Commerce", "Chartered", "Trust", etc.

Minimum Shareholders
One

Are bearer shares available?
Yes

Minimum Directors
One. The director(s) may be a corporation and may be located anywhere in the world with no restriction.

Minimum Officers
None required

Is a registered office and/or a registered agent required?
Yes/Yes

What documents must be kept at the Registered Office?
Articles & Memorandum of Association, Certificate of Incorporation and Share register

Annual Return
No
- Annual licensing fee of $700 ECD is required

Taxation
No taxes on offshore profits for 20 years

NETHERLANDS ANTILLES

Location
The Antilles is part of the Caribbean Leeward Islands and the Windward Islands. These two sets of islands are approximately 500 miles apart. The Windward Islands are east of Puerto Rico and the Leeward Islands are

north of Venezuela. The capital is Willemstad. The population is approximately 195,000.

Overview

The Antilles has a legal system based on the Dutch system of the Netherlands. Although Dutch is the official language, English is widely used and prevalent in business activities. Over the past three decades offshore banking has become a booming business in the Antilles. No tax is paid on the income of companies that collect capital gains, royalties, and dividends. Holding companies pay up to a 3 percent tax on net income. An income tax exemption may be given for as many as 11 years if the new company can demonstrate how it will contribute to economy of the Antilles.

Advantages

- The Netherlands Antilles offers a zero tax rate on net profits arising from offshore business activities.
- No withholding tax on dividends and benefits payable by offshore entities.
- No estate, duty, or inheritance tax is payable on the inheritance of shares in an offshore entity.
- No capital gains tax.

Disadvantages

- No double taxation agreements
- Dutch is the primary language
- Confidentiality is suspect
- High standard authorized share capital requirements
- Listed in Group III of The Financial Stability Forum's list of 42 Jurisdictions that it considers to have significant offshore activities; "May 26th, 2000 press release, "Financial Stability Forum Releases Grouping of Offshore Financial Centers (OFC's) to Assist in Setting Priorities for Assessment". (See footnote 2)
- Must hold shareholder meetings in Netherlands Antilles

Company Status

Non-Resident for tax purposes

Corporate Legislation Source

International Companies Act 1994

Company Name

Prior approval required. Many words are sensitive, i.e.: "Assurance," "Bank," "Insurance," "Chartered," etc. Must end with "N.V."

Minimum Shareholders

One. The shareholder(s) may be a corporation.

Are bearer shares available?

Yes

Minimum Directors

One. The director(s) may be a corporation and depending on the type of structure, may be located anywhere in the world or may be required to be resident in Netherlands Antilles.

Minimum Officers

None Required

Is a registered office and/or a registered agent required?

Yes / Yes

What information is available on the public file?

None

What documents must be kept at the Registered Office?

Copies of the Register of Members, Register of Shareholders, Minutes and resolutions, share transfer documents and administrative and bookkeeping records and Register of Directors and other documents as seem reasonable. All documents can be kept at the "agent's" office rather than the "registered" office.

Is an annual return required?

Yes

- A small annual contribution payable to the Chamber of Commerce is required.

Taxation

2.4%–6%, depending on structure and activity

Taxation Treaty

Numerous double tax treaties

NEVIS

Location

Nevis and its sister country St. Kitts form a single national federation, but have entirely separate corporate legislation. These two Caribbean islands are only two miles a part at the closest point and are located in the Leeward Islands approximately 1,200 miles southeast of Miami. The climate is nearly perfect and the island itself is a natural garden of tropical vegetation. The capital of the federation is Basseterre located on St. Kitts. The commercial center of Nevis is Charlestown. The population of Nevis is 10,000 and St. Kitts 38,000.

Overview

Nevis and St. Kitts form one nation but their incorporation and trust laws are quite different. Nevis has successfully positioned itself as a notable OFC with arguably the most attractive IBC legislation and composition of corporate and trust services found anywhere in the world. For the formation of companies and trust agreements Nevis is far superior from a business persons point of view, for the formation of other financial service companies. St. Kitts has insurance, brokerage, and banking licensing options that Nevis does not.

It is helpful to think of Nevis and St. Kitts as two different states, something like Nevada and California. The Government of the Federation wishes to promote both St. Kitts and Nevis as a regional and international financial center. Accordingly, it vigorously encourages financial activities and is making a deliberate effort to maintain the Federation's attractiveness. Nevis offers a very attractive program for offshore investors. There are no taxes levied in Nevis on income or the distribution of dividends for revenue earned off island. The legal system of the island is based upon English common law. The St. Kitts-Nevis federation is an active member of the British Commonwealth. It is not necessary to file the names of directors, shareholders, or officers with the public register.

Excellent communications facilities offer direct dialing from the U.S., Canada, and Europe. English is the official and commercial language of the island. Nevis enjoys a literacy rate of 96%, greater than the U.S. and one of the highest in the Western Hemisphere. An independent study has ranked the Federation of St. Kitts and Nevis as one of the ten freest nations in the world for seven years running.

Advantages
- Strong political stability
- Total tax exemption is provided by law for IBC companies. Legislation is based on U.S. Delaware law, with English conventions permitted. There are no reporting requirements, no filing requirements, and extremely flexible structures.
- A 98% literacy rate, the highest in the region
- Stable currency
- Economic citizenship options
- Confidentiality

Disadvantages
- Proof of beneficial ownership or management is difficult for lack of public disclosure requirement, however the law does provide for the voluntary disclosure of information.
- Listed in Group III of The Financial Stability Forum's list of 42 Jurisdictions that it considers to have significant offshore activities; "May 26th, 2000 press release, "Financial Stability Forum Releases Grouping of Offshore Financial Centers (OFC's) to Assist in Setting Priorities for Assessment". (See footnote 2)

Company Status
Non-resident domestic companies

Corporate legislation source
- The Companies Act 1996, which has effect in both St. Kitts & Nevis
- The Trusts Act 1996, which has effect in both St. Kitts & Nevis
- The Limited Partnership Act 1996, which has effect in both St. Kitts & Nevis
- The Nevis Business Corporation Ordinance 1984, as amended in May 1995, which has effect in Nevis only.
- Nevis International Exempt Trust Ordinance as amended 1994, which has effect in Nevis only.

- Nevis Limited Liability Company Ordinance 1995, which has effect in Nevis only.

Company name

Name cannot be in conflict with a Nevis pre-existing company. The words "Bank" and "Insurance," or derivatives are prohibited. Corporate suffix required, ie: "Limited," "Ltd," "Inc.," "Corp.," "Corporation."

Minimum number of shareholders

One

Are bearer shares available?

Yes

Minimum Directors

One. The director(s) may be located anywhere in the world with no restriction. There must be a director for each shareholder to a maximum required directors of three.

Minimum Officers

One. The officer(s) may be located anywhere in the world.

Is a registered office and/or a registered agent required?

No / Yes

What information is available on the public file?

Registered Agent's address, and Articles of Incorporation

What documents must be kept at the Registered Office?

Discretionary - documents may be kept anywhere in the world.

Is an annual return required?

No

PANAMA

Location

The Republic of Panama is located between Costa Rica on the north and Colombia on the south. Panama forms the narrowest and lowest portion of the isthmus that links North and South America; Central America. The capital is Panama City. Although the official language is Spanish, most professionals also speak English. The climate is characterized by humidity and heavy rains.

Overview

Panama is notable for its tax and business advantages, notwithstanding the U.S. invasion in 1991. Panama claims to have formed over 600,000 "foreign corporations." Privacy is guaranteed with both bearer shares and numbered bank accounts held in the currency of the depositor's choice. Since the United States invasion the democracy process seems to be working. Although most professionals speak English, their official language is Spanish.

Advantages

- Panama is a very well established jurisdiction that has developed a good reputation over a number of years.

- No exchange controls, no taxes, and no required financial or other annual reports by corporations doing business exclusively outside Panama.
- The legal infrastructure is well developed and the professionals within Panama have marketed the jurisdiction aggressively and actively over an extended period.
- Very strict secrecy laws.

Disadvantages

- One of the few non-English offshore jurisdictions.
- Some concern over political stability.
- There are more directors and shareholders required then in many jurisdictions.
- Listed in Group III of The Financial Stability Forum's list of 42 Jurisdictions that it considers to have significant offshore activities; "May 26th, 2000 press release, "Financial Stability Forum Releases Grouping of Offshore Financial Centers (OFC's) to Assist in Setting Priorities for Assessment". (See footnote 2)

Company Status

Exempt non-resident corporation

Corporate Legislation Source

Civil Law; Law Number 32 of 1927 on Corporations and others

Company Name

The name of the corporation may be in any language and must end with an appropriate suffix, i.e. "Corporation," "SA, " "Inc.," etc.

Minimum Shareholders

Two subscribers, but after incorporation one shareholder is acceptable.

Are bearer shares available?

Yes

Minimum Directors

Three. The directors are not restricted to location.

Minimum Officers

One. The officer(s) may be located anywhere in the world.

Is a registered office and/or a registered agent required?

No / Yes

What information is available on the public file?

Deed of Incorporation, Name and Addresses of Directors and Registered Agent

What documents must be kept at the Registered Office?

The company must maintain a minute book and stock register, both of which may be maintained in any part of the world.

Is an annual return required?

No

Taxation

No tax on offshore profits

Taxation Treaties
None

ST. KITTS & NEVIS

Location
St. Kitts & Nevis form a single national federation. St. Kitts and Nevis are only two miles a part at the closest point but considerably different in their approach to corporate legislation. These two island nations are located in the Leeward Islands approximately 1,200 miles southeast of Miami. The climate is nearly perfect and the island itself is a natural garden of tropical vegetation. The capital of the federation is Basseterre located on St. Kitts. The commercial center of Nevis is Georgetown. The population of Nevis is 10,000 and that of St. Kitts is approximately 38,000.

Overview
Nevis and St. Kitts form one nation but their incorporation and trust laws are quite different. The Government of the Federation wishes to promote both St. Kitts and Nevis as a regional and international financial center. Accordingly it vigorously encourages financial activities and is making a deliberate effort to maintain the Federation's attractiveness. For the formation of companies and trust agreements Nevis is far superior from a business persons point of view, for the formation of other financial service companies St. Kitts has insurance, brokerage, and banking licensing options that Nevis does not. It is helpful to think of Nevis and St. Kitts as two different states, something like Nevada and California.

Efforts to develop St. Kitts into a qualified OFC are intended to complement services provided from Nevis. Nevis has successfully positioned itself as a notable OFC with arguably the most attractive IBC legislation and composition of corporate and trust services found anywhere in the world. Both islands offer attractive programs for offshore investors. St. Kitts focuses on attracting foreign investments that generate employment. There are no taxes levied on income or the distribution of dividends for revenue earned off island. The legal system of the islands is based upon English common law. The St. Kitts-Nevis federation is an active member of the British Commonwealth. It is not necessary to file the names of directors, shareholders, or officers with the public register.

Excellent communications facilities offer direct dialing from the U.S., Canada, and Europe. English is the official and commercial language of the island. Nevis enjoys a literacy rate of 96%, greater than the U.S. and one of the highest in the Western Hemisphere. An independent study has ranked the Federation of St. Kitts and Nevis as one of the ten freest nations in the world for seven years running.

Advantages

- Good political stability
- Law for IBC companies provides total tax exemption.
- A 98% literacy rate, the highest in the region
- Stable currency
- Economic citizenship options
- Confidentiality
- Inexpensive with minimal requirements

Disadvantages

- Annual report is required
- Corporate law is based on the Isle of Man English model.
- Listed in Group III of The Financial Stability Forum's list of 42 Jurisdictions that it considers to have significant offshore activities; "May 26th, 2000 press release, "Financial Stability Forum Releases Grouping of Offshore Financial Centers (OFC's) to Assist in Setting Priorities for Assessment". (See footnote 2)

Company Status

Non-resident domestic companies

Corporate Legislation Source

- The Companies Act 1996, which has effect in both St. Kitts & Nevis
- The Trusts Act 1996, which has effect in both St. Kitts & Nevis
- The Limited Partnership Act 1996, which has effect in both St. Kitts & Nevis
- The Nevis Business Corporation Ordinance 1984, as amended in 1995 and 1999, which has effect only in Nevis.
- Nevis International Exempt Trust Ordinance as amended 1994, which has effect in Nevis only.
- Nevis Limited Liability Company Ordinance 1995, which has effect in Nevis only.

Company Name

Name cannot be in conflict with a St. Kitts & Nevis pre-existing company. The words "Bank" and "Insurance," or derivatives are prohibited. Corporate suffix required, i.e.: "Limited,""Ltd,""Inc.,""Corp.,""Corporation." A company name can be any name provided that the name chosen is not considered misleading or otherwise undesirable by the Registrar of Companies.

Minimum Shareholders

One
One member for LLC

Are bearer shares available?
Yes

Minimum Directors
One. The director(s) may not be a corporation but be located anywhere in the world with no restriction.
- For LLC directors are optional and may be located anywhere in the world.

Minimum Officers
Must have a president and treasurer or a managing director and a secretary (Secretary may be a corporation). Each officer may hold more then one position. The officer(s) may be located anywhere in the world.
- For LLC an officer is not required

Is a registered office and/or a registered agent required?
Yes/ Yes
For LLC: Yes/ Yes

What information is available on the public file?
Registered Agent's address and Articles of Incorporation

What documents must be kept at the Registered Office?
Discretionary – documents may be kept anywhere in the world.

Is an annual return required?
No
- $200 USD annual government fee is required
- Annual Shareholder meeting required

Taxation
- Taxes depends on the company's activities, the residence of the members and their tax status for LLC's.
- No taxes on Exempt company

Taxation Treaties
None

ST. LUCIA

Location
St. Lucia is a windward island located in the Caribbean between 60∞ and 61∞ west longitude and 13∞ and 14∞ north latitude. Martinique is to the north and St.Vincent and the Grenadines are just 24 miles to the south.

It is 1.300 miles southeast of Florida and 100 miles north of Barbados. St. Lucia is known as "the Helen of the West Indies".

Overview

St. Lucia is known as a beautiful tourist destination. The tourist slogan is "St. Lucia-Simply Beautiful". Castried is the capital of St. Lucia. St. Lucia has a great transportation infrastructure.

Advantages

- Worlds first online IBC registry is at forefront of technology revolution, IBC's can be incorporated in one hour: Can do name searches, reservations, review company records, conduct company searches, request certificates and certified copies, payment for IBC with credit card,
- Large pool of qualified personnel
- Continued enhancement of education infrastructure and legislation
- Years of deliberation before entering the international financial services industry

Disadvantages

- New
- Listed in Group III of The Financial Stability Forum's list of 42 Jurisdictions that it considers to have significant offshore activities; "May 26th, 2000 press release, "Financial Stability Forum Releases Grouping of Offshore Financial Centers (OFC's) to Assist in Setting Priorities for Assessment". (See footnote 2)

Company Status

International business company

Corporate Legislation Source

International Business Companies Act, 1999

Company Name

The company name must end in "Limited", "Corporation", "Incorporation" "Société Anonyme", "Sociedad Anonima" or the equivalent suffix. Sensitive words require approval of the Minister of Finance: i.e. "Royal", "Imperial", "Bank", Assurance", Chamber of Commerce", "Chartered", "Trust", etc.

Minimum Shareholders

One

Minimum Directors

One. The director(s) may be a corporation and may be located any-

where in the world with no restriction.

Minimum Officers
Not required

Are Bearer Shares Available?
No

Is a registered office and/or a registered agent required?
Yes/Yes

What information is available on the public file?
Details of ownership and directors as this information reside with the Licensed Registered Agent and not at the IBC Registry.

What documents must be kept at the Registered Office?
Details of ownership and directors as this information reside with the Licensed Registered Agent and not at the IBC Registry. Share Register, Directors register, Minutes and resolutions

Is an annual return required?
No

Annual fee required

Taxation
Exempt from Taxes

ST. VINCENT and THE GRENADINES

Location
St. Vincent is located 100 miles to the west of Barbados. It is 133 square miles with rugged volcanic terrain, beaches, rainforests, rivers and streams. Known for the 30 plus islands that are scattered along the ocean, St. Vincent & The Grenadines have been longtime favorites of yachtsmen.

Overview
St. Vincent reverted to England under the 1783 Treaty of Versailles, has now become a British Commonwealth with a parliamentary democracy based on English common law. English is the official language; the Eastern Caribbean Dollar is the official currency. The population is 30,000. The economy is rooted in agriculture with tourism running second. St. Vincent is a member of the United Nations.

Advantages
• St. Vincent is located below the hurricane belt and is a great vacation

spot for the boater.
- Great confidentiality and Preservation protect the investor.
- No information exchange treaties with many countries.
- Confidential Relationships Preservation (International Finance) Act 1996
- No disclosure of beneficial owner to government is required.

Disadvantages
- Listed in Group III of The Financial Stability Forum's list of 42 Jurisdictions that it considers to have significant offshore activities; "May 26th, 2000 press release, "Financial Stability Forum Releases Grouping of Offshore Financial Centers (OFC's) to Assist in Setting Priorities for Assessment". (See footnote 2)
- St.Vincent is relatively new to the offshore services industry.
- Tax exempt for only 25 years

Company Status
International business company

Corporate Legislation Source
International Business Companies Act, 1996

Company Name
The company name must contain "Limited", "Corporation", "Incorporation" Societe Anonyme", Sociedad Anonima, A/S, AG, N.V., B.V., GmbH, S.A. or their equivalent suffixes or other words indicating Limited Liability. Sensitive words require approval the i.e. "Royal", "Imperial", "Bank", Assurance", Chamber of Commerce", "Chartered", "Trust", etc.

Minimum Shareholders
One

Are bearer shares available?
Yes

Minimum Directors
One (two if have more then 1 shareholder). The director(s) may be a corporation and may be located anywhere in the world with no restriction.
Minimum Officers
Secretary. The officer(s) may be a corporation.

Is a registered office and/or a registered agent required?
Yes/Yes

Is an annual return required?
> No
> • Annual fee required
> • Annual directors meeting required

Taxation
> No tax for first 25 years

Taxation Treaties
> None

TURKS & CAICOS

Location
> The Turks and Caicos are north of Haiti and the Dominican Republic and are at the bottom of the Bahamas chain in the eastern Caribbean. The capital is Grand Turk. The population is less than 12,000. The mainstays of the islands' economy are Tourism and offshore finances.

Overview
> The Turks and Caicos New Company Act of 1982 developed a foreign investment program that was really the first in the area and which set the standard for the later BVI and Bahamas legislation. Due to a lack of effective marketing, the Turks and Caicos is under utilized.

Advantages
• Very quick formation process
• Very flexible corporate structure, which allows a T&C company to be almost totally dependent upon the requirements of the client.
• A twenty-year guarantee of exemption from future taxes can be obtained.

Disadvantages
• Does not have as high a profile as many of its Caribbean cousins.
• Light professional infrastructure.
• Signed a Mutual Legal Assistance Treaty with the U.S.
• Listed in Group III of The Financial Stability Forum's list of 42 Jurisdictions that it considers to have significant offshore activities; "May 26th, 2000 press release, "Financial Stability Forum Releases Grouping of Offshore Financial Centers (OFC's) to Assist in Setting Priorities for Assessment". (See footnote 2)
• Bad marketing has brought little business to the Turks and Caicos Islands. They are currently trying to remedy this situation.
• Have not made many revisions in legislation in recent years with the

exception of amendments to trust legislation and the addition of Company Amendment Ordinance, 1999, Mutual Fund Ordinance, 1998 and a Voluntary Dispositions Ordinance of 1998

Company Status
International business company

Corporate Legislation Source
Companies Ordinance 1981 as amended

Company Name
Prior approval required. The name may be in any language and need not end with "Limited," etc.

Minimum Shareholders
One. The shareholder(s) may be a corporation.

Are bearer shares available?
Yes

Minimum Directors
One. The director(s) may be a corporation and may be located anywhere in the world with no restriction.

Minimum Officers
Secretary. The officer(s) may be a corporation and may be located anywhere in the world.

Is a registered office and/or a registered agent required?
Yes / Yes

What information is available on the public file?
Memorandum & Articles of Association, subscriber shareholders, Registered Office and Agent

What documents must be kept at the Registered Office?
No register of members or directors need be maintained. The company should have a seal.

Is an annual return required?
No
- $300 USD annual government fee subject to capitalization

Taxation
> No tax on offshore profits.

Taxation Treaties
> No double taxation treaties

< < < THE UNITED STATES > > >

DELAWARE

Location
> Small state of the United States located on the mid-eastern coast between Pennsylvania, New York, Maryland and New Jersey. It is located on the Delaware Bay on the Atlantic Ocean.

Overview
> Offshore structures have been allowed in Delaware since 1965. Delaware has been a long time favorite base for US companies and has proven its legislation to be far superior to most jurisdictions.

Advantages
- Corporate income tax exemption for companies trading outside the state
- Low costs
- Good for American trading structures

Company Status
- Limited liability company
- Corporation

Corporate Legislation Source
- General Corporation Law of Delaware
- Delaware Limited Liability Company Act (Chapter 18 Subchapters 1-11)

Company Name
> The company name for an LLC must contain a corporate ending or suffix of "LLC" or "Limited Liability Company". Words "Bank", "Trust", "Insurance", "University", "Finance", "Fiduciary" and "College" require approval along with other sensitive words.
>
> The company name for US corporation has the standard required approval for sensitive words. The name must contain any acceptable expression stating limited liability such as "Corporation", "Incorporated", "Limited" or the equivalent suffix.

Minimum Shareholders
- One member is required for LLCs
- One shareholder for corporations. The shareholder(s) may be a corporation.

Are Bearer shares available?
No for corporations

Not applicable for LLCs

Minimum Directors
- Optional Members for LLCs
- One director is required for a corporation. The director(s) may be a corporation and may be located anywhere in the world without restriction.

Minimum Officers
Not required for LLC

Secretary required for a corporation. The officer(s) may be a corporation and may be located anywhere in the world without restriction.

Is a registered office and/ or a registered agent required?
Yes/Yes

What information is available on the public file?
Name of the company, Date of Formation, Register Office and Agent, Incorporation Number, Principal activities of the company and director's details; issued capital may be voluntarily disclosed.

What documents must be kept at the Registered Office?
None

Is an annual return required?
No for corporations

Yes for LLCs
- $100 USD annual government fee for LLCs is required
- US $50 annual government fee for corporations is required
- Must file an annual franchise tax report

Taxation
Taxes on offshore profits dependent of the company's activities, the residence of the members and their tax status.

Taxation Treaties
No double tax treaties

NEVADA

Please see Chapter 11, which is devoted completely to the Nevada option.

WYOMING

Location
Wyoming is a northwest state of the United States with Montana to its north, Nebraska and South Dakota to the east, Colorado and Utah to the south and Idaho to the west. The capital of Wyoming is Cheyenne. The United States is one of the largest countries in the world in population and area. It is comprised of 50 states and the District of Columbia, which is home to the capital, Washington, D.C. The United States is a federal republic.

Overview
Wyoming is becoming a pre-eminent offshore center with its liberal legislation, which creates companies quickly, easily and for a minimum of costs while offering no corporate income tax to corporations that do not trade within the state. However, for US trading companies the Federal Internal Revenue Service will require payment of taxes.

Advantages
- Limited liability
- Flexible legislation
- Minimal corporate formality
- No capital duty
- No annual return is required
- Do not have to disclose beneficial owners to government

Disadvantages
- May not have more then two characteristics of a corporation
- No shelf companies available
- Possibility of tax liability
- No double tax treaties

Company Status
- Limited liability company

Corporate Legislation Source
- Wyoming Corporation Law

Company Name
Prior name approval required

Minimum Members
One. The member(s) may be located anywhere in the world without restriction.

Are Bearer shares available?
Not applicable for LLCs

Minimum Directors
Not applicable

Minimum Officers
Not applicable

Is a registered office and/ or a registered agent required?
Yes/Yes

What information is available on the public file?
Name of the company, Date of Formation and Register Office and Agent

What documents must be kept at the Registered Office?
None

Is an annual return required?
No
Annual government fee of $200 USD

Taxation
Taxes on offshore profits dependent of the company's activities, the residence of the Members and their tax status.

Taxation Treaties
No double tax treaties

Solutions

14

Nevis, A Premier Jurisdiction

*"We are not afraid to entrust the American people with unpleasant facts, foreign
ideas, alien philosophies, and competitive values. For a nation that is afraid to let its
people judge the truth and falsehood in an open market is a nation that is afraid of
its people."*

John F. Kennedy

Background

Nevis and its sister country St. Kitts form the Independent Federation of St. Kitts and Nevis. They are located in the eastern Caribbean,
Leeward Islands chain, formerly known as the British West Indies, now
simply referred to as the West Indies. St Kitts & Nevis are approximately
1,200 miles southeast of Miami, Florida. Although an independent two-
island nation, they retain many traditions of the British, who settled and
developed them. St. Kitts was the first British Colony in the Caribbean
and was founded in 1623. Early on Nevis was known as "Jewel of the
Caribbean and St. Kitts was referred to as the "Mother Colony of the
Caribbean," sometimes called the "cradle" of the Caribbean.

Admiral Horatio Nelson, arguably Britain's finest naval commander
of all time, married a Nevisian, made Nevis the center of British naval
operations in the Western Hemisphere, and considered it the most lovely
place he'd ever lived. Alexander Hamilton, the first Secretary of the Treasury of the United States of America, and a signer of the Declaration of
Independence and participant in the drafting of the U.S. Constitution, was
born in Charlestown, the capital of Nevis.

On Nevis, the scenery encompasses green hills, exotic gardens, se-
cluded coves and pink sands. The beautiful islands of St. Kitts and Nevis
represent the idyllic view many of us have of what constitutes a tropical
island paradise. The climate is nearly perfect for people, as well as luxuriant
tropical vegetation.

Miles of beaches facing on to aquamarine and turquoise seas encircle
the islands. The natural beauty of Nevis is breathtaking. Tourism is a major
revenue source and the Nevis Four Seasons Resort was three times rated
the Number One of the Top One Hundred Resorts for the entire world.
This particular property was rebuilt twice in two years after freak hurricanes hit the island. It was reopened for American Thanksgiving in 2000.

Nevis was sighted by Christopher Columbus in 1493, and settled by
the British in 1623. Even today, cricket is a favorite pastime, the motorists

drive on the left, and the official language is English. Formerly one of the West Indies Associated States, it became an independent state within the British Commonwealth in 1983. Nevis is a democracy based on the British parliamentary system and has an elected local assembly.

The legal system is based on English common law, served by a high court of justice and a court of appeals. A Nevis offshore company is known as an international business corporation (IBC) and although formed in a British Commonwealth country, corporate structure is based on the USA State of Delaware model.

The Eastern Caribbean Dollar is the official currency, although U.S. dollars are accepted anywhere and the banks on both islands will open a U.S. dollar accounts as easily as an EC dollar account. The East Caribbean Dollar is fixed to the United States dollar at EC $2.70 per US $1.00 and never required adjustment. A stable rate of exchange has been in force for many years.

Nevis offers excellent communication facilities, with direct dialing to Europe, the U.S. and Canada, in addition to facsimile, web hosting and dependable email services. Nevis offshore companies are exempt from Nevis taxes on all income, dividends or distributions not earned on the island.

The Nevis Business Corporation Ordinance

A Nevis offshore company, known universally as an International Business Corporation ("IBC"), is tax exempt on all income not earned on the island. An IBC need not file annual returns. Corporate records may be kept anywhere in the world, and annual general meetings or meetings of the Board of Directors are not required to be held in Nevis. An IBC has a number of other very attractive advantages:

1. There are no income taxes, social security taxes, capital gain taxes, withholding taxes, stamp, or duty taxes.
2. There are no gift, death, estate, dividend, distribution, or inheritance taxes.
3. No minimum authorized capital; bearer shares permitted.
4. A business license is not required.
5. Officers, directors, and members are not identified.
6. Plaintiff bringing civil suit must post U.S. $25,000 bond.
7. Statute of limitations for civil suits is one year.

The registration process is simple and can be accomplished with little effort. A company may be incorporated to conduct any lawful business and there is no need to enumerate the particular objects for which the company is incorporated. An IBC registered in Nevis is required to maintain a registered agent at all times. The Ministry of Finance licenses trust companies and Registered Agents.

A Nevis IBC is required to maintain a registered office in Nevis. This requirement is easily satisfied as the legislation permits the office of the registered agent to act as the office of the company.

Any person interested in forming an offshore company in Nevis need only provide the name of the corporation to a licensed trust company. The trust company will form the company and function as it's registered agent and provide a local office address.

If you would like to discuss various offshore options in Nevis you may want to contact Guardian Trust 869-469-5295, (www.guardiantrust.com), (www.gtc.com) Nevis American Trust 869-469-7168, (www.offshoreagents.com) or Morison Anderson Trust 869-469-8500 (www.morisonanderson.com).

If you seeking help in developing a strategy, want legal or accounting assistance, or are thinking through the right jurisdiction for an offshore strategy, call the Sovereign Crest Alliance at 869-466-3794 (www.sovereigncrest.com) for a qualified professional based in your country, state or province.

The Nevis Business Corporation Ordinance Act was enacted in 1984 and is modeled in large part on USA Delaware and Nevada corporate statutes. The legislation is contemporary and user-friendly. It is routinely updated to ensure that it remains progressive and avant-garde.

A particularly progressive feature of Nevis legislation is that it allows for the transfer of a corporation's legal domicile from any country in the world into that of Nevis within 24 hours. By the same token, a Nevis corporation may be transferred out of Nevis and into any other jurisdiction in the world permitting this procedure.

Nevis International Exempt Trust Ordinance

A trust is a legal relationship, as opposed to a legal entity, whereby the creator or settler of the trust provides assets and names a trustee to manage and safeguard these assets for the benefit of person(s) who are called the beneficiaries, and who are the only persons entitled to gain from the trust or in whose favor a power to distribute trust property may be exercised.

The use of trusts has rapidly expanded as both corporations and individuals apply this mechanism to fuel and facilitate a wide range of activities and as an offshoot of this, the global community is moving into an era where the use of offshore trusts is becoming increasingly imaginative and prolific. In recognition of this trend, and of the contribution that international trusts would make to the offshore financial sector, the Nevis Island Assembly passed the Nevis International Exempt Trust Ordinance in 1994. This Ordinance governs the establishment and operation of international trusts and is an amalgamation of the more progressive International Trust legislation of various jurisdictions combined with innovative provisions of a totally unique nature.

An international trust, in order to qualify as such, must have certain characteristics. These requirements are easy to satisfy and basically they stipulate that at least one of the trustees must either be an offshore company incorporated in the jurisdiction, or a trust company doing business in Nevis. And, that the settler and the beneficiaries must at all times be non-resident and that the trust property must not include land situated in the jurisdiction.

Where an offshore company is a trustee of an international trust, its registered office in Nevis may also be the trust's registered office. This provision was designed to link all parts of the offshore sector, thus ensuring the smooth interaction and working of the offshore industry.

It is possible to create an international trust with only one trustee; and the settler or trustee of the trust may also be named as beneficiary. Registration of international trusts is also made easy in that there are a minimum of requirements. Essentially, these are the names of the trust and of the registered office of the trust. A Certificate certifies that the trust, upon registration, will be an international trust, and states the prescribed fee.

The confidentiality and the privacy of international trusts are ensured by legislation. For instance, even though a trust register is maintained, it is not a public document generally available for inspection; the only exception being where a trustee of a specific trust gives written authorization to a person allowing the inspection of the entry of that trust on the register.

Additionally, the Ordinance provides that all non-criminal judicial proceedings relating to the trust shall be heard in private and that no details may be published without leave of the court. Guardian Trust 869-469-5295, Nevis American Trust 869-469-1606, Morison Anderson Trust 869-469-8500 or any of several other licensed trust companies in Nevis can arrange for a Nevis International Exempt trust by calling them. If you are seeking a consultancy referral you may want to call the Sovereign Crest Alliance at 869-466-3794 for a professional based in your country, state or province. If you are an American call Morison, Carter & Young for a referral at 503-647-7730, they work with a host of informed law firms and offshore trained accounting consultants.

The Nevis Limited Liability Company Ordinance
With the enactment of the Nevis Limited Liability Company Ordinance 1995, the island of Nevis boasts the most up to date LLC legislation in the world. This legislation is aimed at solving many of the problems that perturb lawyers and business people using, or hoping to use LLCs.

The Nevis LLC is a business entity that provides an alternative to those who might consider using corporations or partnerships. It is analogous to limited liability companies springing up throughout the U.S., to limited life companies elsewhere in the Caribbean, to GmbH's in Germany, to SARL's in France and to Limitada's in Latin America.

The owners of a Nevis LLC are referred to as members, who may be thought of in the same way as one thinks of partners in a partnership or shareholders in a corporation. Their precise characterization will depend on the nature of the LLC's management. The management might be vested in all of its members, who would have many of the characteristics of partners in a general partnership. Alternatively, the company might be run by designated managers, who may come from the ranks of the members or might be hired from the outside, making the company appear to be like a limited partnership or a corporation with general partners or officers and directors. In the latter case the members will be more like passive investors similar to limited partners or shareholders.

A Nevis LLC is formed by filing articles of organization with the Registrar of Offshore Companies. The company's operations and the rights among the members are defined through an operating agreement. A foreign LLC (or like entity), may easily convert to a Nevis LLC by simply going through the conversion procedure (no more difficult than filing articles of organization): other foreign entities, such as corporations, may convert after transferring their domicile under equally simple processes.

Only the company is liable for its debts. No member, except those who may have affirmatively guaranteed company debts has liability for any company obligations.

The United States Internal Revenue Service has indicated that limited liability companies generally may be taxed either as corporations, with potential corporate level tax, or as partnerships, with income and losses flowing through to the members without any incidence of tax effects at the entity level. The Nevis LLC Ordinance permits planners to structure their Nevis LLC in any manner that suits their situation. Hence, if partnership tax treatment is desired, the Nevis LLC could be structured to lack continuity of life, free transferability, centralized management, and even limited liability (only two need be avoided.) The latest IRS pronouncements have been taken into consideration, including Rev. Proc. 95-10 and the self-employment tax proposed regulation, in order to assure the utility of LLCs in U.S. business planning.

The Nevis LLC can be used for any business venture or professional practice anywhere in the world outside Nevis, including international financing arrangements to gather funds internationally for U.S. or non-U.S. operations, real estate holding in the U.S. or elsewhere, manufacturing concerns and operational or investment vehicles for offshore trusts.

Those structuring the popular MIPS financing arrangements will find the Nevis LLC more appropriate for their needs than LLCs formed in any other jurisdiction. This is particularly true in light of recent U.S. Internal Revenue Service pronouncements and because of the conversion provisions in the statue, which allows existing MIPS LLCs to be transferred from their current domicile to Nevis with little cost or trouble.

One concern among those employing LLCs in estate planning is the valuation issue under Internal Revenue Code section 2704(b). The Nevis LLC Ordinance prohibits members from "putting" their interests to the company unless the members agree otherwise, thereby assuring a going-concern valuation rather than a liquidation valuation for gift tax purposes.

Further Commentary On The Nevis LLC

While most U.S. LLC statutes protect company assets from member creditors (remember that an LLC has members not shareholders) through the limitation of creditors to a charging order, the Nevis LLC Ordinance specifies that this is the exclusive remedy available to the creditor and also gives the company the power to redeem the creditors' interest.

The Limited Liability Company, or LLC, has quickly become one of the most popular business entities in the United States. Once seen as a daring corporate hybrid, the LLC whether based in the U.S. or domiciled in Nevis, is now praised for its organizational flexibility and innovation. It combines the best features of corporate protection with the significant tax advantages of a partnership. It has also proven to be an effective asset protection structure as it features essentially the same shelter from personal liability and prevents seizure by a member's creditors, as do a corporation or limited partnership.

Its often said that an LLC combines the advantages of a corporation with those of a partnership, but there are other reasons why it may represent a good choice for a business structure:

- For a U.S. person double taxation can be avoided with an LLC. Since the LLC is not a corporation, there is no corporate income tax. Income is only taxed on the personal level, as with a partnership, if you so elect, on the other hand you have the option to select the taxation method by which you will be bound.
- Personal liability is limited. The personal assets of the members (shareholders) are protected from corporate creditors. The manager of the LLC and any other officers, are protected from liability due to bad choices in the administration of the company.
- There is relatively little paperwork and record keeping involved with an LLC beyond a simple operating agreement or statement of the principles of the organization.
- You can easily convert your present business to an LLC and begin receiving the benefits immediately.

Although an excellent organizational choice, the LLC is not necessarily best for everyone. There are many compelling reasons to choose a corporation or partnership structure instead.

U.S. state statutes on LLCs vary, however most conform to the model established by the Uniform Limited Liability Company Act (ULLCA) of 1995. While not actually law it is the most comprehensive code treatment available on the subject of LLCs and contains the guidelines that most jurisdictions refer to and adopt regarding LLCs.

The following highlights the general provisions of the ULLCA:
1. An LLC has a legal identity separate from its members.
2. An LLC may be organized for profit or non-profit.
3. About half of the states allow an LLC to have only one member, all others   require at least two members.
4. An LLC interest is non-transferable.
5. Any interest in future distributions and return of capital can be transferable.
6. Members of an LLC enjoy limited liability.
7. Managers are agents of the company and can bind the company to third parties.
8. An LLC may exist for a fixed or perpetual duration.
9. An LLC is dissolved upon the:
   • consent of its members;
   • dissociation of a member;
   • occurrence of a specific event described in the operating agreement; or
   • fixed date for its dissolution.
10. Members may freely transfer their rights to distributions but not rights to membership. An LLC grants rights to membership only upon the unanimous vote of the remaining membership.
11. An LLC Operating Agreement may not:
   • unreasonably restrict a member's right to inspect company records;
   • eliminate or reduce a member's duty, loyalty, care or good faith when dealing with or on behalf of the company;
   • restrict the rights of third parties; or
   • override the legal right of the company to expel any member convicted of wrongdoing, breaching the Operating
   • make an agreement making it impractical for the LLC to carry on business

Typically under corporate law shares may be freely transferred unless a buy-sell agreement is in place. The LLC, on the other hand, prevents unrestricted transfers. A membership interest in an LLC can be assigned or transferred to a third party or pledged to a creditor. However, the assignee does not become a voting member of the LLC. He or she may be entitled to receive distributions and a proportionate share of profits due the debtor-member, but the assignee is not entitled to vote or participate in the management of the LLC.

Admittance to voting membership usually requires a unanimous vote of the existing membership, or such percentage consent as otherwise stated in the Operating Agreement. Anyone assigning his or her membership may lose that voting membership.

Family businesses often take advantage of an LLC because they can take advantage of this limitation by further restricting membership transfers. Ergo transfers may be confined to within the family. A former spouse desiring to dispose of his or her membership must transfer the interest back to the family. Thus, the LLC can protect an interest from seizure by an outsider - such as a creditor - and also can protect assets in a divorce. The IRS agrees such provisions will not jeopardize the LLCs tax status provided only the right to share profits and not the authority to manage is being transferred.

Business owners frequently start their ventures as unincorporated sole proprietorships and become concerned about liability and the possible loss of personal assets only when their business experiences troubles. One answer to this problem is to quickly form an LLC and transfer the assets from the proprietorship to the new LLC as you may do with a corporation.

Another way to shield personal assets using an LLC is to owe the LLC money. The LLC can then accept a mortgage on your home or personal property (such as a car or boat), or "blanket" mortgage all your property. Should you later run into personal creditor problems, the mortgage held by your LLC can insulate your personal assets from your creditors. And, your interest in the LLC is protected from personal creditors as they cannot take control of your company because of the limited transfer provisions of the LLC.

Alternatively, you may transfer assets to different LLCs instead of transferring all assets to one LLC. The more owners there are for different assets, the harder it will be for one creditor to link and attach the assets. This insulates assets from liabilities arising from other assets.

A single LLC can be divided into separate LLCs without risking the dissolution of the original LLC. Successor LLCs are considered to be a continuation of the original LLC if the members of the successor LLCs owned 50 percent or more interest of the prior LLC. In the U.S. this is considered a restructuring and not a change in ownership.

Be careful when transferring assets to an LLC. Many people use offshore LLCs and foreign trusts for this purpose. An offshore trust may conduct its affairs through an LLC with the trust then owning the single asset — the entire interest of the LLC. This arrangement serves four important purposes:

- The trust can more easily trade and do business through the LLC.
- The LLC insulates the trust from potential liabilities.
- The LLC creates another layer of privacy.
- The LLC helps avoid U.S. income tax liability on most U.S. source income. (Speak with an offshore consultant regarding this important item)

For a Nevis LLC your trustee will usually serves as the manager of the LLC and conduct the affairs of the entire offshore program — the trust and its LLC — as one entity. It is actually the LLC owned by the trust that conducts these activities.

As with a limited partnership, a U.S. creditor who seizes a member's interest in the LLC does not become a member of the company without the consent of the remaining members. Although the creditor only receives an assignment of membership interest, the amount of membership income allocated to his share must be reported for income tax purposes. If the LLC makes no actual distribution to that member, the creditor has actually incurred an expense and received nothing in return. This will be a powerful deterrent to a creditor seizing membership interest. Moreover, the creditor must pay U.S. taxes on your share of any earnings from the LLC, whether or not these earnings have been distributed from the LLC, or received by the creditor. Your creditor cannot claim your interest in the LLC nor replace its management. More significantly, a creditor cannot pursue a fraudulent transfer claim against assets transferred to the Nevis LLC if the debtor obtains in exchange a proportionate ownership in the LLC to the assets transferred to the LLC.

LLCs are ideal vehicles for transferring real estate and other investments as gifts to children or other recipients if one is a U.S. person. If the LLC owns the property, an LLC membership interest could be gifted instead of the actual property. Parents, for instance, could retain managerial control over an LLC, receive compensation for services rendered and still depreciate the gifts. Two classes of membership could be issued. Parents may have class A membership with voting rights (regardless of percentage of ownership) and children, class B non-voting membership. If the membership interest assigned each year does not exceed the $10,000 limit, no gift tax need be paid. The flexibility of the LLCs Operating Agreement can be used to anticipate voluntary and involuntary transfers, as well as a member's death.

The LLC is much more flexible than a trust that is typically used for gifting purposes. There are no limitations as to the number of members or mandatory income distributions. Parents can eliminate third party interests by restricting membership and determine the distributive rights of members.

More advantages to the Nevis LLC:

1. The Nevis LLC requires minimal reporting to the Nevis government. It also avoids onerous reporting requirements to the IRS on legal entities such as those now required of the offshore asset protection trust.
2. The LLC can be structured to achieve virtually any asset protection or estate-planning objective and can also accomplish most business or investment objectives.
3. Ownership in the LLC can be registered in bearer form thus its owners can be anonymous.
4. If you are a U.S. person the Nevis LLC can elect to be taxed either as a C corporation or partnership for U.S. based activities.
5. Officers and directors of the LLC remain personally immune from liability.

15

Grenada, A Rising Star

There is no worse tyranny than to force a man to pay for what he does not want merely because you think it would be good for him."

Robert Heinlein

Background

Grenada is a British Commonwealth nation located in the Lower Antilles of the Caribbean, 1,500 miles southeast of Miami and 200 miles from the south tip of South America. Grenada is below the hurricane belt and has not experienced a hard hurricane since 1955. The State of Grenada is made up of the large island of Grenada and two smaller islands, Carriacou and Petite Martinique, which are located to the north of Grenada. Grenada, with a population of around 100,000, forms the southern most island nation of the Windward Islands. It is widely referred to as the Spice Isle due to the abundance of spices and flowers on the island. The island has beautiful beaches, clear blue sea, lowland forest and inland mountain rainforest. Grenada offers great snorkelling, diving, hiking and many waterfalls.

St. George's is the capital of Grenada and hosts a large natural harbor famed as a safe haven for boats racing high seas. Grenada has several beautiful natural harbours that regularly see some of the more prominent boats of the Caribbean. Grenada is also home to a deep-water port offering large ship docking and mooring capabilities. St. George's is a picturesque combination of old-world Caribbean charm and a new independent Grenadian attitude. Beautiful pastel gingerbread houses adorn the hills. St. George's hosts the Grenada International Financial Services Authority (hereinafter "GIFSA") offices overlooking the harbor. GIFSA is the offshore regulating agency in Grenada and is responsible, along with the Minister of Finance, for all activities arising under the Grenada Offshore Legislation.

Carriacou, one of the associated northern islands in the State of Grenada, offers beautiful views of the Grenadine Islands and is often a starting point for yachting trips through these famed cays. Carriacou is known worldwide for the wonderful yachting, diving and boating vacation trips it offers. A close second to the beauty that Carriacou offers is its reputation as a Mecca of fine boat craftsmanship.

Petite Martinique is the smallest of the Grenada island chain and is also the least populated. It currently hosts a private all-inclusive resort that takes up most of the island. A trip to the resort or just a trip to the island to enjoy the beaches will immediately explain why the resort on Petite

Martinique is quickly rising as one of the top exclusive Caribbean resorts. It offers privacy, some of the best beaches and water in the world, a laid back Caribbean ease and all the modern comforts of home.

Grenada was ceded by the British in 1783, becoming a Crown Colony in 1877, an Associated State in 1967 and gained its independence in 1974. In the early 80's a Socialist oriented political faction supported by Cuba, tried to take over Grenada, which lead to military intervention from the United States. The scars of this uprising will remain with Grenada for a long time to come, however this island nation is pure capitalist and highly democratic. The economy has made such a turn around that even with new construction everywhere present it is extremely hard to acquire new business space without a several month wait.

Prior to the British ceding of Grenada, these islands had gone back and forth between the British and the French throughout the 17th and 18th centuries.

In 1974 Grenada drafted a Constitution and set up its government based on the British Westminster model. The law is based on English common law. The Head of State is the Governor General, which is appointed by Her Majesty, the Queen of England. There is a Senate and a House of Representatives. The Senate consists of 13 members in which the opposition leader appoints 3 members and 10 are appointed by the government. There are 16 persons in the House of Representatives, the Speaker and 15 members. There is a Prime Minister and Cabinets of Ministers who report to the Prime Minister.

The official language in Grenada is English and the official currency is the Eastern Caribbean Dollar. However, the US dollar is widely used. The Eastern Caribbean Dollar is currently fixed to the United States dollar at EC $2.70 per US $1.00 and therefore a stable rate of exchange has been in force for many years making the economy in Grenada very stable. Grenadian banks allow for accounts to be held in either U.S. or Eastern Caribbean Dollars.

The economy in Grenada was historically agriculturally based and still retains some of its economic roots in the export of bananas and spices. Grenada is one of the largest exporters of nutmeg in the world. Today the Grenada economy is based on offshore services, tourism, and agricultural export. Grenada is on the cruise routes of several major cruise lines and is also a departure point for a variety of tourist clippers.

Grenada is serviced by a large aircraft airport and offers flights on some major, as well as minor, airlines: American Airlines, British Airways, British Caledonian, BWIA and LIAT to name a few. Telecommunication services are top of the line with fiber optic cable, USB and satellite access with worldwide services. Fax, telex and telegraph services are readily available and Grenada offers other OFC infrastructure elements such as major banking facilities offered by Barclays Bank, National Commercial Bank,

The Bank of Nova Scotia and others. There are an unusually high number of well-qualified professionals for an island jurisdiction of this size, more than sufficient to meet the labor needs of any corporate presence in Grenada.

Overview of Grenada Offshore Legislation

Grenada entered the offshore arena in 1990 with the International Companies Act of 1990. Since that time Grenada has amended that Act and drafted additional legislation adding a variety of other offshore vehicles. Grenada has a commitment to a clean, respectable zone in keeping with a desire to attract legitimate business from the international community. The offshore sector in Grenada has developed a level of respectability as a result of striking a balance between the legitimate rights of investors and the need for international cooperation. Grenada is fast becoming a leading jurisdiction for offshore banking and economic citizenships with an excellent reputation notwithstanding a scandal surrounding one particular offshore bank and its affiliates during 2000. The bank in question and its affiliates were eventually closed by the government for alleged improprieties demonstrating that the government is serious about their intent to maintain a high level of integrity in these regards. The variety of services offered in Grenada allows many opportunities for integrated financial planning and investment.

Current Offshore Legislation

International Companies Act, 1990 (as amended, 1996)
Offshore Banking Act, 1996 (as amended 1999 and 2000)
The Offshore Services (Fees) Regulations, 1997
International Trust Act, 1996
International Insurance Act, 1996 (as amended, 2000)
International Betting Act, 1998
The Company Management Act, 1996
The Citizenship (Amendment) Act
Grenada International Financial Services Authority Act
Grenada Money Laundering (Prevention) Act of 1999

The Grenada International Financial Services Authority ("GIFSA") was created in October of 1999 under the authority of the Grenada International Financial Services Authority Act to provide for a supervisory body to oversee and monitor the international financial services in Grenada. This appears to have been a good move on the part of the Grenada government because in past other offshore centers have invited problems by not having the proper supervision of the numerous entities that conduct business under their laws and within their borders.

Subsequent to the formation of GIFSA an IBM AS400 System was installed in order to provide a fully integrated IBC registry system. This new automated system expedites the registration and incorporation process of International Business Companies by conducting 24-hour name searches, name reservations, viewing files, electronically submitting name approvals and offering a messaging center.

Grenada's commitment to their burgeoning offshore service sector is clear and their early success demonstrates that although they are late to the offshore game this jurisdiction is able to compete with the best of them and move quickly ahead of many of the entrenched offshore jurisdictions.

Privacy & Confidentiality

Grenada has strict confidentiality and privacy laws regarding business and financial dealings resulting in imprisonment for their violation.

Taxation

There is no local taxation on International Business Companies for a period of 20 years.

Disclosure Treaties

USA-Grenada Taxes (Exchange of Information) Act

The Grenada International Business Companies Act of 1996

The International Business Companies Act was first enacted in 1990. Since that time there have been two amendments to the Act, both making minor changes in rates and other technicalities that helped clear up confusing terms, dates and fees. The Act has proven to be well drafted with an eye on the past and a vision for the future of the international financial center in the emerging global market. The Act will continue to be updated to ensure that it remains progressive and avant-garde.

The Act is Legislation and Authority for the creation and running of a Grenada International Business Company or "IBC". A Grenada IBC is tax exempt on all income not earned on the island for a term of 20 years and then is taxed at the local rate. An IBC need not file annual returns. There is no requirement for an annual general meeting. Meetings need not take place in Grenada at all and may take place anywhere in the world. In general, the IBC in Grenada requires little paperwork and formality. However, an IBC is a corporate entity and to protect this structure from having it's corporate veil pierced a certain level of formality should be implemented.

A Grenada IBC has a number of other very attractive advantages:

- There are no income taxes, social security taxes, capital gain taxes, withholding taxes, and stamp or duty taxes for the first 20 years.

- There are no gift, death, estate, dividend, distribution or inheritance taxes for the first 20 years
- There is no minimum capital requirement
- Bearer shares are permitted and may be authorized in varying amounts in the Articles & Memorandum of Association.
- Officers, directors, beneficial owners and members need not be identified
- Nominee Directors and Officers may be used
- Plaintiff bringing suit must due so in Grenada under the laws and jurisdiction of the Grenada Court
- Only one shareholder and one director are required
- No officers are required
- The directors and officers may be corporations

The registration process is simple and can be accomplished with little effort. A company may be incorporated to conduct any lawful business. There is no need to enumerate the particular objects for which the company is incorporated. Any person interested in forming an offshore company in Grenada need only provide the name of the corporation to someone licensed, under the International Companies Act, to incorporate a company.

Those licensed to incorporate companies in Grenada include attorneys, chartered accountants; trust administration companies and management companies. The contracted party will form the company. The appropriate party will then draft Articles and Memorandum of Association fitting a particular client's needs and desires. They will then follow the incorporation process through to its successful conclusion and will supply you with original certified copies of your Articles and Memorandum of Association and Certificate of Incorporation.

The incorporation process in Grenada consists of a name approval by GIFSA, then a name reservation. After the name has been approved and reserved, the company is submitted to GIFSA for analysis, approval and Incorporation. This process takes as little as one day. After incorporation, GIFSA sends certified original copies of the company's Articles and Memorandum of Association and Certificate of Incorporation. The company will officially become listed on the Grenada International Business Companies Register, which is a public record. The contracted party or "agent" will also function as registered agent and office. The Agent usually provides other services such as nominee directors, compliance management, bank account management, etc.

An IBC registered in Grenada is required to maintain a Registered Office and Registered Agent in Grenada at all times. The International Companies Act dictates who may be a registered agent. This list is the same as those who may be a subscriber and form companies. There are no significant requirements for the Registered Office. Normally the registered agent's office is also the registered office of the company.

If you would like to discuss various offshore options in Grenada you may want to call Morison Anderson Trust Company at 473-439-1174 (www.morisonanderson.com), Crowne Guardian Bank (www.crowneguardian.com), or Sovereign Life & Casualty (www.sovlife.com). If you seeking help in developing a strategy or thinking through the right jurisdiction call the Sovereign Crest Alliance at 869-466-3794 (www.sovereigncrest.com) for a qualified professional based in your country, state or province.

The Future

There will always be a need for offshore financial centers and there will always be a way for those centers to operate. Therefore, there should always be a need for a jurisdiction like Grenada in the offshore financial markets. During the year 2000 when most tax haven jurisdictions had their collective tails firmly between their legs, Grenada continued to take aggressive steps to affirm their place in the growing offshore arena. Faith in Grenada's industry is rising which is evident by the recent re-domiciling of many offshore entities into Grenada from their home country. What does Grenada have to offer for the future? Continuing enhancement of its legislation, offshore authority, infrastructure and country. A larger presence in the offshore market, the implementation of cutting edge computerized options to further facilitate quick and seamless corporate transactions, a network of professionals designed to protect the nature of Grenada's industry via careful due diligence, surveillance and compliance methods to ensure a safe jurisdiction for providers, investors and consumers. Grenada is in a prime location for many foreign markets and all indications are that this jurisdiction is committed to meet the growing needs of the European, Asian and other markets of the world.

16

Reclaiming Privacy

"In today's information age, personal privacy is virtually extinct.... Just a glimpse into the case files of any federal investigative, local law enforcement, or private investigative agency provides unique insight into the degree to which MILLIONS of people's private lives are being researched, scrutinized, and even exploited."
Surveillance Countermeasures

Privacy Strategies

If you have read this far, you probably have decided that privacy is a commodity you want to have. I have your attention and you have shown interest.

Regrettably, privacy is not a commodity you can buy off the shelf. It is instead a quality you acquire through a series of decisions and actions. To be successful in taking back your privacy you must organize a plan of action whose goal is the state of being we refer to as privacy.

Compare achieving privacy to wellness. It isn't something that happens overnight. To become a well person you must develop habits and behaviors that protect your health — proper exercise, rest and food. The same is true of privacy. If you have lived a life of public displays of wealth and conspicuous consumption, you can't expect to fade quietly into the woodwork. It is going to take some time.

To achieve privacy then, you must make a fundamental decision about what is really important to you. Is it more important to let the world know you are successful by touting the stuff you own? Or is it more important for you to protect what you have from marauding bureaucrats and those who will attempt to legally steal what you've accumulated through predatory litigation?

Achieving privacy is in some ways almost a spiritual journey. You must consciously decide to put aside the show and splendor that is so beguiling and live more simply. Prestige kills privacy — humility protects it. You might want to make it your ambition that the press describes you as "a private person" living "a quiet life." This approach to life is wisdom from ancient days.

Standard Business Practice

Learning humility inevitably brings you to the state of mind where you develop an alarm system regarding things that will draw the wrong kind of attention. By that I mean, the kind that will get you audited by your home country's taxation authorities, or investigated by any one of a host of government agencies endeavoring to justify their existence. Regardless of where you live, bureaucracies are pretty much the same — they justify their existence through generating work. Be careful that you do not become the object of their attentions.

The kinds of things to avoid are those that set off red flags. And by that I mean anything that isn't standard business practice. Corporations are about the only asset protection entities that do not routinely attract the attention of the authorities these days. Legal structures like forming your own private church, (don't laugh lots of people think this is a very clever strategy), creating a foundation to hold assets, certain types of trusts. These things are often suspect.

Pursue strategies that keep documentation in the main stream. Don't be cute, just because you can. Accepted business practices include such things as leases, consulting fees, loans, family trusts, family limited partnerships, LLCs and other routine structures and documents.

Part of the lifestyle of privacy is keeping a low profile politically. Major political groups are not a problem but don't get yourself on television or in the news because you are providing financial support to a candidate. Charitable groups such as orphanages, colleges, and service clubs are all acceptable places to invest your energy. But again, when you're the recognized leader, you're coming up on several people's radar screens.

Tax revolt groups, and anti-government organizations or anything that smells of the fringe is likely to cost you big-time in the privacy department. For example, I write things that some bureaucrats don't like, and it probably will come as no surprise to the reader that certain government types constantly seek to harass me. You know, the old abuse of power drill. But, this is my personal mission so I do it because I believe it needs to be done. On the other hand, I don't recommend it unless you're up for taking a lot of heat.

Assuming a low profile is best as it moves you quietly out of the targeting area. If you are committed to a cause or a movement and have a major grievance and want to lash out at the world, get a soap box and shout your message from the roof tops but forget protecting your privacy. Invisibility is the soil that privacy grows in best. The more visible you are the more likely you are to attract government investigation, predatory litigation, or both.

If you have assets to invest offshore chances are you are engaged in some sort of profitable activity. You probably do not have the time to travel all over the world looking for the right place to structure and sequester assets. You probably need help with this important task. There are those who recommend against using anyone in your home country to help you organize things offshore. This belief is based on the fact that accountant's files are available to government inquiry in most countries. And in the U.S.

these files are even available in civil litigation. On the other hand, lawyers can usually invoke the attorney-client privilege doctrine, which in most cases would put your offshore strategy planning off-limits from any form of inquiry.

In the States recent changes creating the new, "friendlier" IRS will allow your accountant some "client privilege." However, if the IRS states they are concerned about a possible criminal infraction the privilege is automatically revoked.

What you need is someone who has first-hand knowledge of the jurisdiction(s) where your assets may be held, is trustworthy, and whose records are not readily available in your country of residence. Tax and asset protection lawyers are usually the professionals of choice although there are numbers of well-trained accountant's who can steer you in the right direction.

It's always a good idea to check on the credentials of the firm or professionals that will manage your offshore activities. And yet, going to safe haven countries to meet with a potential agent may delay this kind of positive move indefinitely. Further, if you take a trip to Jersey, Guernsey, Nauru, or the Cook Islands, or some other place known only as a tax haven, you could become a target of a government agency keeping tabs on those visiting places designated as tax havens only. The automatic scanners used in some countries by immigration for passport clearance is capable of developing reports on the destinations to which you travel. Go a few times direct to the same tax haven destination and you may find yourself under government surveillance.

Of course, no matter who you deal with, there are firms or individuals who may not be worthy of your trust. References make good sense, but no legitimate trust company or offshore bank can provide you with the names of clients. However, the government where your agent is based will generally advise you with a simple telephone call if there have been any complaints registered against the trust company or bank you are considering. In addition, bank and influential third party reference letters are standard protocol all over the world.

Taking Back Your Privacy

To reclaim your privacy, I recommend you consider what information about your life you are willing to share with the world, and then take back the rest. To begin with, no one really has the "right" to know your home address and telephone number, certainly not your bank. Of course a bank requires an address in order to issue you checks. But it doesn't have to be the address where you live. In some countries kidnapping is a growing threat that requires careful consideration and event planning, whereas in the U.S. predatory litigators are tracking people with assets. Why allow private information about yourself to be out in the public domain for anyone to see?

Mail services rent private mail drops and message taking telephone numbers. The address appears as a suite number or an apartment number. With your new address, you can obtain a new driver's license and another piece of identification.

Now that you have a new address, close out the checking and savings accounts you already have. Then, choose a new bank and start over with your new address and telephone number. The bank can send its statements to the new address and your actual residence is once again your own business and off the public record. One caveat regarding such addresses — we are not the first ones to have thought of using them for confidentiality. As a matter of fact, law enforcement often uses them in their own covert or sting operations.

Remember that the checks you deposit to your account in some countries are recorded and reported. Therefore, if checks issued to you are written on a bank with a local branch, it might makes sense to cash those checks at the bank against which they are drawn. This is true of everything from paychecks to checks from clients — anyone whose dealings with you should be your business alone. You can always deposit the cash or buy a money order and then deposit the funds into your own checking account if need be.

Going to these lengths may seem over the top for many people and it is not a needed action item for most, but erasing a depository trail may save you big time if someone is out their tracking you. If you've accepted payment from someone for a service or product you've provided and you feel suspect of their downstream motives this is the time to cash their check and buy a money order before you deposit the funds. In this way you remove their ability to look to a cancelled check to determine where you bank.

If you decide to use money orders, you may want to buy them at banks other than those at which you cash checks. When checks are cashed and money orders subsequently purchased, a notation is made of what transpired. You can buy money orders at the post office, in come countries at supermarkets, and of course other banks. Because it is true that you are at risk when you stroll about with large amounts of cash on your person, it is a good idea to change your banking routines frequently when cashing checks. If you go to these lengths, the payoff is that there is no record connecting the source of your income with your bank deposits, unless single deposits are large and your bank wants you to make a statement as to the source of funds.

When you use checks to buy things in stores, you are often required to produce identification, the source of which may be written on the check. This information is also often compiled into private databases. It could include everything from your name, address, birth date, taxpayer identification number, bank account number and driver's license number. If you want to keep private who pays money to you as well as to whom you pay money, then it makes good sense to reduce the use of a checking account.

There are other, more anonymous, ways to pay bills. For example, money orders and travelers checks are non-revocable forms of payment that are accepted just like cash. Banks and other financial organizations, even AAA in the U.S. and other financial services provide these instruments to protect the recipient against loss. Travelers' checks and money orders are preferred over checks because they are guaranteed funds and cannot be returned unpaid as with a check. There is sometimes a charge for traveler's checks, but if you shop around you can get them for free. You can use these to pay rent or mortgage payments, utilities, goods and services — you name it. Meanwhile, you can move to a new neighborhood or even a new community, change your telephone number, and your financial transactions do not give you away.

An Incredible Story

My sister is one of those wonderful people that almost everyone likes immediately on first contact. She is bubbly and fun, she loves people and is interested in everyone's stories. Occasionally I tease her by calling her doctor-doctor, said real fast almost like a stutter, to remind her that I think she's spent to many years in school. (She has two Master's Degrees and two Doctorates and, as you might surmise, is a college professor and author of several books.) Anyway, as fun and well liked as she is, according to the news media and the FBI, she holds the U.S. record for being stalked the longest — well over three decades.

Her stalker has been released three times from prison after he was convicted of a double murder. During 2000 she was interviewed on over one hundred talk shows, was written about in numerous articles and books and generally is a relatively high profile person. Now it appears that a television mini-series may soon be done based on her life. But, the point of all this story is that when last the man who has stalked her all these years was released from prison the Chief of Police for the city in which she lives, came to her home and shared many of the concepts written directly above trying to convince her to drop out of sight. He even told her to get a concealed weapon's permit, buy a gun and learn how to use it, which incidentally she did. Within a couple of weeks of this convicted murder's release from prison, he was found on her street once more with loaded guns in the trunk of his car, he was arrested and returned to jail. (If you want to know more about this story her latest book is entitled "Toxic Attention" by Dr. S.L. Meinberg.)

Anyone may have a good reason to reduce visibility. It is legal, it is moral, and it is wise. You do not have to explain your reasons to anyone, and frankly if you do explain yourself you are reducing the value of what you are trying to accomplish.

Privacy Offshore

To gain even more privacy, this is the time to move your savings to an offshore bank. If you are an American you need to be aware of the Foreign Account Declaration Form — form TD F 90-22.1. Penalties for failing to report foreign accounts can be severe. However, penalties can be imposed only when you have failed to report in order to dodge taxes or cover up a criminal activity. You can't be punished for not filling out the form, as long as you report the income under "miscellaneous income" on your form 1040 and pay the appropriate taxes. Of course, you are required by law to report any interest income you've earned but in terms of privacy you will have taken a major step in the right direction.

A further caveat, not all safe havens are created equal when it comes to protecting your privacy. Uncle Sam is the big player in the world and the U.S. carries a lot of clout — especially with small countries that depend on them for trade and aid. Britain, France, Germany and the U.S. all have arrangements with offshore jurisdictions that give them easy access to private records — all part of on-going treaties and agreements between countries. If the country in question doesn't go along with ratting on their citizens — no treaty. With no tax treaty, it means people doing business in both countries can be taxed twice on earnings, thus discouraging trade with that country. In 2000 the European Union enacted rulings that provide for individual banking and documentary transparency between member countries based simply upon a request by a government enforcement agency. (I'd like to see how Germany would respond to France's request for the personal financial records of any German politician.)

The Cayman Islands are an example of capitulation to U.S. and British pressure regarding your rights to privacy. In 1989 and again in 2000, the Caymans introduced legislation that allowed U.S. investigators access to bank and the securities trading records of Americans. In 1989 the U.S. threatened to make it difficult for tourists to visit the Caymans if the changes they wanted were not made. In the year 2000 U.S. regulators threatened to freeze Cayman's major financial institution's dollar accounts held with U.S. correspondents. The amounts at risk approached one half trillion dollars! The Caymans rolled over quickly and no longer have much interest in having Americans as clients.

There may actually be more protection in Switzerland these days than the Cayman Islands. To access records there, G-7 countries must have an agent present evidence to a Swiss magistrate that the target suspect is involved in drug dealings, murder, kidnapping, money laundering, or forgery. However, the application of the new Qualified Intermediary legislation which went into effect January 1, 2001 may make Swiss banking privacy a mute point because the Swiss did capitulate and have agreed to automatically submit reports to IRS beginning in 2002.

At least for the present, the Swiss will consider requests for information —— but they do not grant it automatically. The point here is that offshore banking centers vary in the amount of privacy they offer, and here is where an offshore consultant familiar with the differences can save you a lot of headaches.

The benefits of offshore banking vary on a country-by-country and bank-by-bank basis. Some countries show a lot of backbone in dealing with overbearing big brother, others can't wait to prove they are ready and willing to help. Private lawsuits are another matter. Offshore banks are rarely subject to legal inquiry so they cannot be compelled to provide information. The exception is if the bank in question has branches in the country where the litigation is taking place. This is important because in the discovery phase of a lawsuit, especially in the U.S., a sharp lawyer will try to get his or her hands not only on your bank account records but also on your credit card files, loan applications — anything that will reveal your assets so they can be frozen until trial. With trial periods in the U.S. taking up to five years to get into court, a lawyer who gets your assets frozen has already won because you will be forced to settle in order to carry-on with your life. With an offshore account, this information is well protected. Writs of execution, or attachment orders issued by courts in your home country are rarely enforceable in traditional offshore jurisdictions and therefore have little impact on your wealth held offshore.

Further protection may be provided when you use offshore issued credit cards. Essentially you can charge to your heart's content, anywhere in the world you wish, and the information stops at your offshore bank. When you charge on a domestic or onshore bank your buying records can easily become part of a database that is sold to whoever is willing to pay the price or they can be subpoenaed in civil litigation.

Theft Control

There are others who are out to track your assets besides predatory lawyers and government agencies. Thieves can gain access to information about you by stealing identification, and cause you a world of problems. If your wallet or purse is stolen, for example, it probably contains your driver's license, credit cards, ATM card, taxpayer identification information, perhaps even a copy of your birth certificate or checkbook.

If you're lucky, you will have been hit by a low-grade thief who wants only cash and tosses the rest away. But chances are the thief will want to use your ID to make purchases on your credit cards and checking account. It's no problem to buy loads of merchandise on your credit card, and then take the stuff back for cash. A thief can even use your identity to open up new accounts, not pay the bills, and damage your credit. To protect yourself, it's best to minimize the amount of information you carry around with you. You really have no need to carry your taxpayer information, birth certificate or passport with you, unless there is a specific reason. Keep sensitive records in a safe place and do not carry them about.

If you take keys with you, it is naive to assume that putting your name and address on them will result in their return. What's more likely to happen is that a thief will go to your home and loot it while you're out looking for the lost keys.

The same is true for such things as funeral notices. If a family member has died, do not print the home address in the funeral notice, or if you do, make sure someone remains in the home during the service. There are thieves whose modus operandi is to read these notices and ransack homes while the bereaved are most vulnerable.

Keep a list of your credit cards and bank accounts with appropriate information, such as the account numbers, expiration dates and telephone numbers of the customer service department in a safe place — not your wallet or purse.

If you need a password or personal identification (PIN) number, don't use your birth date, your middle name, the last digits of your Social Security number or anything else that could be easily figured out by thieves.

Internet Security

Turn off your computer when not in use. Do not register for anything on the Internet without absolute assurance that the information will not be released to third parties for any reason. Turn off the "accept cookie" option with your Web browser. There are only two well-known web browsers: Netscape and Microsoft Explorer.

To turn off the "accept cookie" option with Netscape simply open "Options," go to "Network Preferences," then "Protocols," then tick "Show an Alert Before Accepting a Cookie."

To turn off the "accept cookie" option with Microsoft Internet Explorer open "View," then go to "Internet Options," then "Advanced," then scroll down to "Cookies," then tick "Prompt Before Accepting Cookies."

If you subscribe to a wide band Internet service that is on all the time you need to have firewall protection. Do not hesitate, this is very important.

Know Your Rights

One of the simplest routes to privacy is totally within your control. Do not furnish any more information than you have to. People may ask about your assets, but you don't have to tell them. This can be especially important to remember should you face litigation. If a creditor is suing you, you are not required to tell them anything about your assets unless or until they have a judgment against you. Assets are relevant only insofar as they relate to your ability to pay, and a court will rarely require an examination of your assets prior to a case finding against you.

Creditors may try to learn what you have during the discovery process of a court case, but in most countries it is your right to keep mum. Counsel for a plaintiff will always try to get more information from you than the minimum to which he or she may be entitled and if you are uninformed about your rights, you may wind up giving it to them. If you slip and give critical information away its pretty hard to unring that bell.

An exception to this is if you are being sued for punitive damages for wrongful conduct. A court may order you to disclose assets before a judgment rendering so they can determine if you have enough to satisfy the punitive damage award. Also, if there has been a suspected fraudulent transfer of assets, this might be examined and even set aside by court order. But such an inquiry generally relates only to specific assets in question — not about anything else you may have.

Asset Transfers

What about a fraudulent transfer of assets? This is when you place valuables in the name of someone else in order to avoid losing them in lawsuits. After all, what you don't own can't be taken from you. Getting rid of things is a good way to make yourself a smaller target and is a perfectly legitimate component of a privacy strategy — provided you handle it correctly. The key to any asset transfer is protecting you from the accusation of fraudulent transfer. Laws related to fraudulent transfers are very important, as you've read in a prior chapter entitled "Unlawful Transfers."

Placing assets offshore in trusts, corporations or other entities can be an important move towards greater personal privacy. Offshore transfers are generally beyond reasonable reach. This is an incredibly important principle.

Tax Returns

A key component of one's privacy strategy is to become protective of information about personal finances. One of the richest sources of information that can be used against you is a tax return. This document tells how much you have made and may indicate how much you have. Why share it with anyone when you do not have to?

In most countries tax returns are protected from involuntary disclosure to creditors. Tax returns are included among those things that might tend to incriminate, hence in the U.S. they are protected by the Fifth Amendment.

Judgment creditors can't force one to reveal their tax returns unless you waive your rights to keep them secret by offering or agreeing to reveal them or allowing access to them by "disinterested parties." Those are people who do not have a "need to know." People such as your accountant, banker, spouse, lawyer, are those who have a need to know. To everyone else, it is your right to keep tax reports off limits.

Clean Up Your Credit

To secure a loan, you may have furnished your tax return as evidence of your income. Make certain that lenders are aware you want to be notified if those records are subpoenaed. You can have an attorney quash the effort to learn about you through tax returns given to lenders.

If you have applied for a loan, chances are, in your effort to prove you have so many assets you don't need the loan, you may have revealed too much about your holdings or even exaggerated them. If you intend to transfer some of those assets out of your possession, it's best to ask to go back and "correct" your records.

Cash is your best friend because it cannot be traced. If you have a cash transaction over $10,000 however, never involve a bank. Divide the money into smaller amounts and process the cash on separate dates to avoid attracting attention. This is not illegal, this is prudent.

Seal Your Files

If you have had a court case in which you were required to reveal information about your assets, it's best to ask the court to seal those files. Divorces or child support cases can force you to show and tell all about income, assets, liabilities, and that information can become public record unless you act to prevent it. Your court records can be read and copied but not removed from the building. If the records are sealed, you have protected your privacy.

The Corporate Veil

Your own corporation is a great way to preserve privacy. Corporations are discussed throughout this book. If you own nothing, there is nothing to take from you. A wise goal in life is to own little, but control a lot, and a corporation can help achieve this objective.

A friendly corporation can hold a mortgage on your home, for example, and on other personal property such as cars, boats and planes. You could even give this corporation a "blanket mortgage" on everything you own and this can insulate your assets from predators. For this strategy to be effective, the corporation may need to be owned by someone other than yourself.

If you have sensitive transactions, be sure to handle them through a corporation and keep them at arm's length. If you use a domestic company make sure the corporation has its own taxpayer identification number, to keep transactions from showing up in your name. If you are using an offshore corporation to handle certain transactions, public record reporting is not required. Most developed nations provide citizens with social insurance or social security identification. Provide this information as sparingly as possible because this number is a way your movements and activities can be traced.

Liquidity Buys Privacy

Bank accounts are great because you can access money when needed. That's liquidity. But onshore or domestic bank accounts are problematic because they rarely offer privacy. Until 1982, Americans were allowed to own "bearer bonds," which were securities not registered to any individual — they could be transferred like cash. As of that date, however, they were outlawed, and the ones still existing, when they are redeemed, elicit a Form 1099-B to the IRS from the brokerage firm. If you could acquire some of these securities, you could send them abroad for safekeeping and redemption — but beware. Sending more than $10,000 outside the U.S., without reporting it to U.S. customs, is against the law.

If you are willing to pay in the coin of liquidity, however, you can purchase anonymity. By that I mean that you can have a substantial portion of your wealth in semi-liquid assets, such as collectibles, including rare coins, stamps, gemstones, art. They are easily transported, are a good store of wealth and are usually liquid enough for most purposes. Often they also offer some appreciation, but best of all, they are totally private. There is no bank reporting how much of these things you have in your possession, or where you have put them, or to whom you have given them.

If you want even more privacy, you can buy and sell these things through your own privately held corporation. The problem with them is security — depending on where they're kept they may be easily stolen.

Gold is often considered a good private investment. It is redeemable virtually everywhere for the local currency, and it is essentially untraceable. It is the ultimate currency for protecting privacy. Gold can come in the form of coins, jewelry or even bullion. You can buy it many places with no record of the transaction.

Collectible coins may have high value. There are thousands of international coin dealers who could help you turn coins into local currency. Diamond is the same. Unfortunately, both rare coins and diamond are usually bought retail and sold wholesale, so you can take a beating in a flat or down market. The other disadvantage of coins is that gold and coin dealers must report large or unusual transactions to the government.

Stamps can be a good store of value and can appreciate, but require knowledgeable buyers to reclaim value. There are other collectibles that are good anonymous ways to transport wealth, such as baseball cards, autographs, some photographs, artwork, and rare comic books. If it is possible to do business using these means of conveyance without attracting attention, make it your practice to do so.

One way to store wealth anonymously is to rent a number of safety deposit boxes registered to corporations or trusts. Then buy gold coins in small quantities and stash it away. Make sure all ends of the transaction — including rental of the boxes — is done in cash to avoid a paper trail making the connection. Incidentally, bank vaults are less secure than private vaults or secure home safes.

Silver may be especially attractive these days. It is relatively cheap compared to gold, especially as it relates to historical ratios, and its highly divisible for local exchange. On an individual level almost anyone will accept pure silver medallions or small silver ingots on private transactions. The novelty feature alone seems to interest an unusually high amount of average folks. And, of course, there is always barter. Can I slip in a plug here for one of my prior books entitled "Barter & The Future of Money?"

Wire Transfers
If you're working in U.S. dollars a regulation that took effect in January 1996 requires that when a wire transfer is issued, the originator and the beneficiary must both be identified and this information must travel with the transfer. Experts have great concern that foreign banks, which are not entirely bound by these regulations, will not include the identity of the originator because of bank secrecy laws within their countries. Trying to track all of these wire transfers is a bureaucrat's nightmare but it guarantees job security for more government employees, at least until the U.S. Congress wakes up and throws these regulations out. On the average business day, about 80,000 separate transactions totaling nearly $500 billion pass through the wire room at Citibank alone!

How Much Is Enough
How much privacy do you need? How far are you willing to go to protect yourself? As pointed out in the beginning of this chapter, you can achieve a great deal of privacy through sticking with "standard business practices." But there are those who want to go underground and have made a study of how to do it. For you, the select bibliography is included below:

How to Legally Obtain a Second Citizenship and Passport — and Why You Want To, by Adam Starchild
International rules regarding dual citizenship vary from country to country. If you are French, for example, and want a second citizenship, you must proceed according to French law. But it can be done, and this book tells how. It also discusses the pros and cons of dual nationality and nationalities that are for sale. Also, it highlights the best second nationalities for Americans and how to get them.

Reborn In The USA: Personal Privacy Through a New Identity, by Trent Sands
The second edition is said to be the best and most complete guide to

building a new identity. The book features control of information about you in computer data bases.

Understanding U.S. Identity Documents, by John Q. Newman

This book is described as a reference for anyone concerned with their official identity and how it is maintained and manipulated. It deals with the most important documents for establishing an identity, such as birth certificates, Social Security cards, driver's licenses and passports. It shows how each document is generated and used, and explains the strengths and weaknesses of the agencies issuing them.

How To Disappear Completely and Never Be Found, by Doug Richmond

This book is for the individual who wants to completely drop out, telling how those who are searching for you might be looking and how to evade the pursuit. It tells how to plan for your disappearance, how to arrange a new identity, how to make it appear you have left the country when you haven't and even how to make it appear that you are dead. It tells how to find a job, establish credit and find a place to live and how to avoid creating a paper trail.

The Heavy Duty New Identity, by John Q. Newman

This is for people really on the run. It tells the down side of starting anew — the problems of mental stress, making sure all the bases are covered, avoiding traps and discovery and bonding with your new identity.

Reborn Overseas: Identity Building in Europe, Australia and New Zealand, by Trent Sands

With an identity in any European nation, you can live and work in any of the twelve. And you can penetrate that system without leaving the U.S. Or, you can do the same in Australia or New Zealand. The book shows how to get all the documents you need to become another nationality.

Reborn in Canada: Personal Privacy Through a New Identity, Expanded Second Edition, by Trent Sands

Canada is the easiest foreign country for the U.S. citizen to adapt to. This book explains how the identity systems in Canada differ from the U.S. You can even have a Canadian identity in your original American name, with no connection to your American past.

New I.D. In America: How to Create a Foolproof New Identity, by Anonymous

This is a step-by-step book on creating a new identity, from birth certificate, drivers license, passport, Social Security, credit cards. The author is a private investigator who has spent a career locating missing persons and helping others disappear.

SCRAM: Relocating Under a New Identity,
by James S. Martin, attorney at law.

Many people would love to make a fresh start in a new location, under a new name. He answers questions such as whether to divorce before leaving, or declare bankruptcy first. The author discusses how the Justice Department creates new identities for criminals.

The Paper Trail: Personal and Financial Privacy in the Nineties, by M.L. Shannon

This book tells how to get a new ID and create a past to back it up; how to disappear and never be found— even by skip tracers. It details secret ways to communicate that can't he traced. It even tells how to make false trails to throw off pursuers.

All of these books can be ordered through Loompanics Unlimited, P.O. Box 1197, Port Townsend, WA 98368 USA.

17

Strategy

"Forty-seven of the world's top fifty banks are either located or have substantial business presence offshore. So are most of the world's largest companies. To ignore the benefits the offshore world has to offer would be financial suicide for these corporations."

Matt Blackman

What Constitutes A Strategy

A good business definition for the term "strategy" is "a long term action plan for achieving a goal." The questions who, what, why, when, and how are all vital queries to the development of a good working strategy. Contained within this chapter are some ideas and sample concepts that may have application to your circumstances, but once again I caution you to not implement an offshore plan before you've spoken with a qualified advisor.

Generally speaking, those considering shifting some portion of their assets or business activities offshore tend to earn more money than they require for day-to-day living. Taken as a group, these people seek greater privacy in their financial affairs and are determined to protect and grow their surplus. For these people there are as many as a hundred different types of core strategies designed to suit various client needs. Normally it is a combination of the elements from some of the more basic offshore plans that eventually constitute a personalized program.

Who Is Going Offshore

Virtually every major company in Europe has offshore operations, just as some of the biggest and best names in American industry have gone offshore. Companies like Boeing, Weyerhauser, Sears, Firestone, Exxon, Caterpillar, Monsanto, and most of the Fortune 1,000 companies.

American Express, Citibank, Chase Manhattan, Bank of America, and literally hundreds of mainstream financial institutions depend upon tax-free offshore profits. Take a look at the financial statements of the most substantial banks and financial institutions in Europe and America and you'll discover that their largest profit centers frequently come from offshore activities. Banking and financial service profits in an offshore financial center are virtually tax-free because dividends, interest and capital gains are not considered taxable income to these organizations. According to Offshore Outlook magazine:

"Currently half the government revenues in the British Virgin Islands, Cayman Islands, and Jersey are derived from offshore financial services. The world's leading financial institutions have all increased their offshore financial services, including Chase Manhattan, Citibank, Goldman Sachs, Fidelity Funds, Charles Schwab, Rothschilds, Royal Bank of Canada, Deutsche Morgan Grenfell, Credit Suisse, Lloyds Bank, Barclays Bank and Bank of America."

Many people mistakenly believe that tax avoidance and asset protection tools that are not well known by the majority of people are somehow less effective or not legal. This is simply not true. The question was posed earlier in this book as to why it is that we instantly believe it's perfectly legal for the Rockefeller's or Rothschild's to implement an offshore strategy but have suspicions if it's our next door neighbor. If it's legal for one it should be legal for all.

In the opening address of the 6th Annual "Money Laundering, Cyberpayments, Forfeiture, Offshore Investments, & Securities" seminar held at the Marriott Marquis in New York City in mid May of 1996, Walter H. Diamond, offshore expert and world renowned economist said this:

"Within the past decade, the once eye-catching words "Tax Havens" have given way to the far more acceptable term of "Offshore Financial Centers." Reflecting its increasing importance in the world of international finance, the Offshore Financial Center has vastly improved the global image of the continually popular "Tax Haven." Today, the offshore financial base with $5 trillion of investment funds is a powerful necessity in the daily operations not only of financial institutions but also multinational corporations, small and medium-size companies, and executives in the legal, accounting and investment counseling professions."

"Of the $5 trillion in offshore financial centers today, approximately 40% or $2 trillion is estimated to represent offshore trusts, principally handled by financial and trust companies acting as trustees. Latest surveys indicate that the rapidly growing asset protection trusts account for about one-half of trust funds, or $1 trillion. The remainder covers the original foreign trust that began to attract funds in the early 1970's. However, because of the tremendous onslaught of attorneys and management service firms to protect their clients from malpractice suits, insolvency claims, and creditors in general, the ratio is expected to rise to 60% of the total trust funds by 1997."

Walter Diamond concluded his 13-page keynote address with the following:

> "In conclusion, it is my firm conviction that offshore investment operations are here to stay and will expand rapidly in the future. This is predicted despite threats heard in Europe that government restrictions and additional negative lists currently taxing income of residents of countries whose parent companies have tax haven affiliates will be the downfall of offshore centers. In fact, I believe that the 21st Century will be known as the era of offshore domiciles."

An Economic Equivalent to the Berlin Wall

The Berlin Wall will be remembered as an icon that spoke of absolute tyranny. It was built by the communist bureaucracy to keep its citizens from escaping to freedom. In Chapter 6 the reader will have learned something of the efforts expended by the former Clinton administration, its European partners, and the OECD, to construct the equivalent of an economic "Berlin Wall" to keep citizens from placing income streams and other assets outside their respective taxable domains.

Following U.S. leadership the G-7 countries enacted legislation to thwart citizens from moving assets to safe havens. Liberty and personal property rights are now at some jeopardy in many countries that heretofore have championed freedom. But the good news is that the OECD has finally come under steady attack and their attempt to establish an international tax cartel is suffering direct assault by world-renowned economists and freedom lovers everywhere.

The U.S. Small Business Job Protection Act of 1996 passed into law on August 16, 1996, contained significant changes to the formation, reporting, and application of tax rules dealing with foreign trusts with U.S. connections. Section 6048 of the Internal Revenue Code requires that Form 3520A be completed and submitted if you are associated with a foreign trust.

The current, plausible interpretation of this requirement is such that foreign trusts must now be rendered "domestic" by either transfer of jurisdiction or by appointment of a U.S. registered agent. It is possible that this interpretation could yet go against the IRS depending upon court rulings, which ultimately are the real test of U.S. law. It is also quite possible that the Bush administration will unravel some of the more onerous requirements forced upon U.S. persons during the Clinton years. Nevertheless, to be wise, one should assume that the IRS will get their way and that eventually their taxing counterparts in other G-7 jurisdictions will follow suit with this approach.

Under this law, if you are connected in any way, either as grantor or beneficiary, to an offshore trust, the trust itself shall be considered a U.S.

revocable trust. If you are a U.S. person the complications and reports now required may make the value of a foreign trust obsolete. Internal Revenue had earlier taken the position that all foreign trusts were considered revocable grantor trusts regardless of the irrevocability of the document itself. By definition this would make all offshore trust earnings taxable to the grantor.

Lest a U.S. person should consider not reporting their position as the grantor or beneficiary of an offshore trust, you might consider that were the IRS to assume you were one or both of these they might assert their right to "estimate and assess." (Read this as meaning you are guilty until proven innocent.) It is then up to you to prove they are wrong, which in turn would require both you and the target trust's trustee to provide documentation to demonstrate your innocence. Not fun at all.

Current U.S. legislation (Foreign Grantor Trust Information Statement) requires that every offshore trust report their assets held in trust, the earnings of the trust, and the name of the trustee. This overreaching by the IRS reminds me of Fred Goldberg's rather famous quote:

> "The IRS has become a symbol of the most intrusive, oppressive and non-democratic institution in our democratic society."

What makes this such an interesting quotation is that Mr. Goldberg was a former Commissioner with the IRS.

Wings for Cows

Over the years we have heard that taxpayers are likened to "sheep waiting to be shorn," or "cows ready to be milked." It is unfortunately true that governments increasingly treat their citizens as little more than cows to be corralled and milked when, and as, they see fit. Perhaps those working in the offshore arena could be considered "angels of mercy" giving wings to cows.

Some interesting strategies that give wings to cows — wings possibly strong enough to clear the governmentally constructed economic "Berlin wall," are included below. These examples, reviewed for the first time, may seem complex, but taken step by step, particularly with the aid of a professional, you could be flying in no time. But, before we review the following sample scenarios, it might be wise to reconsider Judge Learned Hand's statement quoted in the opening Chapter of this book:

> "Over and over again courts have said that there is nothing sinister in so arranging one's affairs as to keep taxes as low as possible. Everybody does so, rich or poor; and all do right, for nobody owes any public duty to pay more than the law demands: taxes are enforced exactions, not voluntary contribu-

tions. To demand more in the name of morals is mere cant."

Before we review some of the simpler and less expensive strategies take a moment and review why and how you might want to own your own offshore insurance company, mutual fund, or bank.

Owning An Offshore Insurance Company

If you are a business owner or professional, especially a medical practitioner, you may be pleasantly surprised at how well this type of strategy might work for you. Especially when you consider there is no law against buying too much insurance and the premiums are normally tax-deductible if you own your own business or professional practice.

In the early 1900's the U.S. Congress granted tax concessions to the insurance industry similar to those available in a number of other countries. Subsequently, a concept generally referred to as "captive" insurance has become quite popular because of the special tax considerations provided insurance companies. It is not particularly difficult for a single individual to apply for and receive an insurance license from any one of a number of offshore jurisdictions.

Under the 1986 IRS code, an insurance company with up to $350,000 in net annual premium receipts pays no tax on this income. The legislation was designed to encourage companies to insure unusual or special risks and in theory help the overall economy. There is also no tax on investment income set aside for possible future claims and no limit on the size of this reserve. The insurance company may invest in virtually anything except an active business. And, even though you may be an American citizen and own your insurance company outright, you may invest in funds not available to rank and file Americans. Tax-free transfers can be made of appreciated assets to a domesticated foreign insurance company. That's an offshore licensed insurance company with a tax letter from the IRS to the American principals. (A normal part of forming and operating a captive.) And, when the company is wound up and closed down one can convert ordinary income into capital gains.

Forming an insurance captive to self-insure your own projects is much easier and considerably less expensive than trying to accomplish this task inside the U.S. The cost for legal work, application submission, business plan preparation, due-diligence background workups, a qualifying letter from the IRS, etc., typically runs around U.S. $40,000.

The Highlights

A business owner ("Client") decides to reduce his or her taxable revenue and move funds offshore where they are held in privacy, safe from predatory litigation.

Insurance premiums paid for protection of current and future business activities are generally tax-deductible. Client identifies under insured or niche specific risks for his or her domestic business or professional practice. Client elects to cover one or more of these business risks.

As an example the following three risks might be insured:
(1) economic downturn;
(2) obsolescence of the company's technology or services;
(3) internal theft of intellectual property by an employee (giving company trade secrets to a third-party.)

Because loss from any the above risks are plausible and foreseeable and because they are related to the conduct of a business enterprise, a client of the insurance company (think about yourself) would generally be considered well within the tax code by deducting premiums paid as a "before tax expense."

Benefits:

• Movement of a large pre-tax premium offshore to a no-tax jurisdiction.

• If funds are needed by the business a claim may be quickly submitted.

• Funds may be dispersed to client by loan proceeds or for consulting activities.

• Client has no offshore income to report unless the offshore insurance company makes an actual distribution of funds.

• IBC officers, directors, and shareholders are not identified in any public record.

• IBC may compound earnings free of punitive taxes. There are no income taxes, social security taxes, capital gain taxes, withholding taxes, stamp, or duty taxes. There are no gift, death, estate, dividend, distribution, or inheritance taxes.

• An IBC is essentially beyond the grasp of predatory lawyers. A plaintiff bringing a civil suit against an IBC must post U.S. $25,000 in cash. A civil court judgment from another jurisdiction is not transferable. The statute of limitations for a civil suit is typically shorter than in Canada, the U.S., England, etc.

• The ability to invest in mutual funds, hedge funds, and unit trust funds not normally available for investment by U.S. citizens.

- All the standard benefits accruing to an offshore company based in tax haven jurisdiction where laws ensure financial privacy and corporate legislation is widely recognized to be the most favorable and flexible in the world.

- Tax-free repatriation of a portion of earned income.

- Conversion of ordinary income to capital gains income thereby shrinking the tax burden on repatriated revenues.

Owning An Offshore Bank

Some years ago one of the offshore structures of choice was to own your own licensed bank. There were some terrific reasons for persons of above average wealth to secure a bank license and conduct business affairs under its charter, primarily due to the concessions granted the banking industry regarding non-domestic profits. This was true in the U.S. and a number of other countries. However, bank charters no longer provide the protection they once did for U.S. persons and are not now recommended in all but a few circumstances.

Legitimate bank charters are still available in several jurisdictions and upon careful consideration in conjunction with your offshore consultant you may yet discover owning a bank is right for you. The cost for a valid offshore Class 1 bank license, complete with business plan, due–diligence policy, legal fees and submission costs usually runs around U.S. $50,000 plus minimum capitalization deposits and government fees.

Owning A Mutual Fund

Mutual funds, hedge funds, restricted funds for accredited investors only, and other similar offshore pooled-interest investment vehicles are all the rage these days. Fees to prepare the basic plans, a prospectus or offering circular, subscription agreements and licensing fees range from US $10,000 for a non–qualifying private hedge fund, to $40,000 and up for a licensed and reporting fund, subject to the requirements of the jurisdiction and whether or not the fund is highly restricted or is open to the public. These costs do not include operational costs, fund management software, etc.

Employee Leasing (Deferred Compensation Strategy)

An offshore employee-leasing program is not what it may seem at first blush. This strategy is designed for a single individual of high annual income greater in amount than which he or she needs to service current and projected day-to-day living expenses. This program is something of the "darling" strategy now being taught to CPA's throughout America by the American Institute of Certified Public Accountants, the equivalent of the CPA's union guild. The concept is fairly simple, but the devil is in the details.

Objectives:
- To defer the receipt of personal income that exceeds current living expenses
- To defer all associated taxes
- To protect these assets from all forms of litigation
- To provide an offshore investment platform to grow the deferred income tax-free

Summary:
Most persons with a large income only require a fraction of total income to meet their living expenses. A high-income individual ("client") resigns his or her position with current employer and enters into an employment agreement with an independently owned Irish employee-leasing corporation. (Ireland has a tax-treaty that helps make this strategy work) The Irish company agrees to pay client a salary designed to meet needed living expenses, reimburse business expenses and provide a retirement plan. The Irish corporation subleases client's services to an existing U.S. based employee-leasing company. The U.S. employee-leasing company in turn sub-leases the client's services back to the client's former U.S. employer.

The original U.S. employer pays the same salary as previously but it is directed to the U.S. employee leasing firm. The U.S. employee leasing company pays a reduced salary to the client, (former employee) and the residual untaxed income is transferred to the Irish corporation where the funds are placed in a trust account with a licensed trust company. Funds held in trust are placed in a variety of quality investment funds based on client's investment profile where they grow tax-free. This is a double tax win. Whatever portion of the annual yield is withheld is not taxed, and while it remains separate from the client growing within a qualified investment portfolio, the growth is not taxed either. Unlike U.S. based deferral compensation programs (i.e. 401K or IRA's) fund dispersals are more flexible than their U.S. counterparts. The costs to organize this kind of program are variable and depend upon several details that are revealed during a consultation with a professional skilled in this arena. But, the bottom-line is it can make an incredible difference in the annual asset portfolio accruing tax-deferred to the client.

Benefits to Individual:

- Reduced income tax due to reduced taxable salary
- Can defer up to 50% of combined income
- No tax on deferred income until funds are drawn down

- No tax on funds in the Deferred Compensation Plan
- Opportunities for estate planning
- Wide range of benefits for the individual
- May be used for all regular staff thereby gaining pooled buying power for better benefits and increasing the percentage of deferrable income from 50% to a larger number.
- Premier asset protection characteristics are available within this program, which in addition to protecting assets under management, provides shelter from both litigation and taxes for future income streams.

Variable Commercial Annuity

One of the standard elements of an offshore strategy is an annuity. An annuity is essentially a group of investments, usually mutual funds, made from within a selection of pre-approved investment vehicles that are wrapped with a minimum amount of life insurance. For income tax purposes, the build-up of income under an insurance product is not subject to tax.

The variable commercial annuity is a cost effective strategy that works for those of modest wealth where asset protection, capital gains tax deferral, fair investment flexibility and/or income tax deferral is sought. The greatest short-term tax benefit is provided when an annuity is used entirely for investment in fixed income instruments or high yield dividend producing securities. For Americans, portfolios that offer significant opportunities for appreciation might better be held in some form of pass-through entity so that the long-term capital gains rate cap of 20% may be retained.

Those who anticipate an estate tax problem must be careful to secure a tax comparison for an annuity strategy versus other alternatives, taking estate taxes into consideration. For example, a life insurance trust may provide complete income tax and estate tax avoidance plus access to assets through policy loans. By having a life insurance trust based offshore in a qualified jurisdiction asset protection characteristics are greatly enhanced.

An offshore variable commercial annuity offers the same tax benefits as a domestic variable annuity with greatly enhanced privacy and asset protection and usually greater operational flexibility. In some offshore jurisdictions, such as Switzerland for example, the annuity contract is protected from creditors of the policy owner or its beneficiaries by law.

Domestic annuity contracts are not normally recorded in government databases but the information is included in the database of the insurance company. In the U.S. there are few restrictions on how an insurance company may use their database and this kind of information is regularly sold to other marketing or credit information services. And, if a policyholder is required to reveal the existence of an annuity contract in deposition or interrogatories, a judgment creditor can secure complete details from the insurance company who issued the annuity contract.

In contrast to a domestic annuity, even if the existence of an offshore annuity were to be disclosed during a deposition or by court order, few offshore insurance providers would disclose any information about the policy. Offshore insurance providers do not engage, and in many places are restricted by law, from the widespread U.S. policy of selling their customer's names, addresses, and demographic information.

A variable annuity policy may include special provisions such as a "spendthrift" clause contained within a life insurance trust that prohibits the beneficiary from assigning his or her future benefit to a creditor or making an assignment for any reason. This means that creditors cannot get an enforceable attachment and that a beneficiary designation is irrevocable, and/or in the alternative, beneficiaries may become the policy owners if there is a claim against the initial policy owner.

Assuming the issuing insurance company is based in a business friendly jurisdiction and the annuity is properly structured, there is little chance of a judgment creditor gaining access to these funds.

Private Annuity Strategy

This strategy is not expensive and has broad application to numerous persons. It does not require a large annual income only that one has assets to place into a strategy under which they may grow tax-deferred for a long period of time.

The Objectives:
- To move appreciated assets out of harms way and defer payment of capital gains tax.
- To establish a long-term investment pool of funds compounding tax-free.
- To provide a simple rationale for the transfer of negotiable assets offshore.
- To provide a simple explanation for client involvement with an offshore company.
- To provide a new, international business company, ("IBC") for use in achieving privacy, asset protection, personalized lending, access to high yield offshore investments, and tax deferral.

Essential Requirements

Client purchase a qualifying private annuity from offshore corporation owned by a non-U.S. grantor purpose trust.

Summary Explanation

Tax-deferred annuities are available in many countries and to U.S. persons from insurance and investment companies worldwide. Annuities are a safe and proven way to build long-term investments as they typically compound without punitive taxation. Unfortunately annuities and other types of retirement funds such as 401K's and SEP funds held by U.S. providers have recently come under attack by both government and civil lawyers seeking pools of assets to attach. When an annuity is based offshore with a company that is not registered in the U.S. it is essentially beyond the reach of predatory litigation (lawyers on commission), or domestic civil and governmental actions. If the annuitor is located in a jurisdiction such as Grenada, a private annuity is safe from interference whilst flexibility for a self-directed investment is dramatically increased.

An Example

Client purchases an annuity from an international business company (IBC) owned by a non-grantor purpose trust. Client may opt to exchange an appreciated asset such as a stock portfolio or real property for the annuity. The exchange of an appreciated asset for a private annuity contract is considered a non-taxable event provided it is properly structured and executed. The IBC can be controlled indirectly by means of the Purpose Trust as owner, the Client's position as protector of the Purpose Trust, and the Client's legal counsel or investment consultant acting as the fund's advisor. This allows for defacto power over the investment of the proceeds from the sale of the appreciated asset.

Step 1. An appreciated asset is exchanged for a foreign private Annuity.

Step 2. The issuer of the annuity (IBC) reorganizes the underlying portfolio in keeping with counsel's instructions and sufficient to adequately support the Annuity contract.

Step 3. Client's attorney or investment consultant acting as "Advisor(s)" to the IBC counsels with trustees as to investments and disbursements for the IBC. An offshore accounting firm provides oversight and will track, audit, and report accordingly. The annual fee for offshore trust and accounting management is usually about 0.25% for an underlying Swiss, or Swiss-like annuity not counting the embedded fee for professional money manager and general overall portfolio management. For self-directed investments the annual fee is 1.25%. Where an approved friend of the buyer of a commercial annuity provides the professional money management and is designated to administer an annuity's investments the annual charge is typically about 1.75% inclusive. The total costs for legal consultation, offshore consultancy, contract preparation, and complete implementation typically runs less than U.S. $10,000.

The Benefits:
• Asset protection for annuity investment. Both the offshore annuity and the IBC are beyond the grasp of predatory litigation.

- Tax-free compounding of annuity earnings.
- Legal judgments are not transferable.
- Shorten statute of limitations for lawsuits. In Nevis, for example, the courts will not entertain lawsuits that are more than 12 months from the date of the actionable event.
- Client has no offshore income to report unless an actual distribution of funds is made from the annuity to the client.
- Client has a clear, explainable, rationale for an ongoing relationship with an offshore business.
- Client is not required to report ownership in subject IBC to IRS, Revenue Canada, etc.
- Client is not required to report to a taxing authority that she or he signs on a foreign bank account.
- IBC officers, directors, and shareholders are not identified in any public record.
- IBC may compound earnings free of punitive taxes. There are no income taxes, social security taxes, capital gain taxes, withholding taxes, stamp, or duty taxes. There are no gift, death, estate, dividend, distribution, or inheritance taxes.
- All the standard benefits accruing to an offshore company based in a reputable jurisdiction in the West Indies where laws ensure financial privacy and corporate legislation is widely recognized to be the most favorable and flexible in the world
- Routine annuity reports on pooled fund investments.

Offshore Minority-Interest Strategy

The primary objective of the Minority-Interest Strategy is privacy, asset protection and access to offshore investments not available to U.S. citizens. The costs are relatively inexpensive and generally less than those for a private annuity strategy. Tax benefits may be available but must be considered individually and are not guaranteed. An independent tax adviser retained by client should make a determination regarding possible tax benefits and beneficial tax treatment should be confirmed by sources of "substantial authority."

Objectives:
- To provide a new, international business company, (IBC) for client use in achieving privacy, asset protection, access to high-yield offshore investments, and potential tax deferral.
- To provide a simple rationale for moving funds offshore.
- To provide a rationale for client involvement with an offshore company.
- To provide for an annual review of the reportable, taxable, consequences of the offshore company's earnings.

Essential Requirements
- U.S. shareholdings may not exceed 49.9% of IBC.
- IBC's revenue from passive income (rents, dividends, royalties, or interest) may not exceed 50% of total revenues.
- Client's shareholding in subject IBC must remain less than 10%.

Summary Explanation

Client buys common shares from an unused Nevis IBC owned by an offshore "purpose trust" (PT). The stated objective of the IBC is to "engage in global commerce" and its director/officer is a licensed trust company or its subsidiary. The company's bank account is administered by a trust officer. The new shares issued by the IBC to Client will effectively dilute the trust's shareholdings in the IBC to approximately 91%, thereby providing Client with an approximate 9% shareholding in an offshore corporation. Client receives appointment as a consultant to the company.

Example

Client purchases stock in a Nevis IBC for $100,000. IBC pays the trust company the debt accrued for initial organization and other relative charges in an amount generally in the neighborhood of around $7,000 in total; the balance of the $100,000 is retained in the IBC for tax-free offshore investment strategies recommended by Client. The trust company instructs the trustee of the PT to vote its shares in the Nevis IBC in concert with the wishes of the minority shareholder. Client is issued one share certificate representing total shares of the IBC not to exceed 9%. No other shares of stock are available for sale.

Benefits
- Client is not required to report ownership in subject IBC to IRS or other taxing authorities.
- Client is not required to report that he or she signs on the foreign bank account of IBC similar to those required of IRS Form 1040.
- Client has no offshore income to report unless an actual distribution of funds is made by IBC to Client.
- Client has no obligation to reveal his or her interest in the IBC unless under subpoena whereupon he or she merely admits to having purchased a minority interest in a foreign corporation engaged in international commerce.
- Client has a clear, explainable, rationale for an ongoing relationship with an offshore business. (Investment and consulting agreement.)
- IBC officers, directors, and shareholders are not identified in any public record.
- IBC may compound earnings free of punitive taxes. There are no

income taxes, social security taxes, capital gain taxes, withholding taxes, stamp, or duty taxes. There are no gift, death, estate, dividend, distribution, or inheritance taxes.

- An IBC is essentially beyond the grasp of predatory lawyers. For example, a plaintiff bringing a civil suit in Nevis against an IBC must post a $25,000 bond. A civil court judgment from another jurisdiction cannot be transferred to Nevis thereby forcing a judgment creditor to re-try their case in Nevis. The statute of limitations for a civil suit is one year making it virtually impossible to re-try a court case from outside Nevis.
- All the standard benefits accruing to an offshore company based in the West Indies where law ensures financial privacy and corporate legislation is widely recognized to be the most favorable and flexible in the world
- An annual report prepared by a certified public accountant in Nevis is available for a relatively nominal fee, advising client that upon review of the business activities of the company it does not appear that client has any reason to report the minority ownership or undistributed earnings of the IBC, assuming that the majority of the revenues of the IBC are not passive.
- A legal opinion by a U.S. tax lawyer is available for an additional fee.

A Concept Illustration

The strategy set forth below calls for the use of Trusts in conjunction with a limited liability company (LLC) and an offshore International Business Corporation (IBC) to achieve the benefits of privacy, asset protection, and tax deferral. This strategy takes into account the changes in the 1996 laws. For this illustration we will assume that you are a self-employed dentist in the U.S., practicing in the state of Oregon.

Calculating the Tax

The maximum personal federal income tax rate is 39.6%, the next level down is 36%, and for our example we'll use the lower of these two rates. Social security is assessed at 6.2% on the first $65,400 in earned income and must be paid by both employee and employer. In that a typical dentist is self-employed he or she will have to pay the combined amount of 12.4%. There is also a 1.45% Medicare tax, again, it is paid by both employee and employer and therefore totals 2.9%. In addition, our dentist friend gets to pay Oregon state income tax of up to another 9%.

All of these percentages add up to a whopping 63.9%, assuming we use the lower of the two upper Federal Income tax tiers. In the case of social security the 6.2% tax drops off after the first $65,400 in earned income. But, as they say on television, that's not all folks.... there's another

.62% tax on total income for TriMet, Portland, Oregon's tax for a rapid transit system. In addition, our overtaxed Oregon dentist friend is privileged to pay just about the highest property taxes in the U.S., coupled with some of the highest gasoline taxes at the pump. Okay, so why would I bother to use such an extreme example? Simply because I have such an inordinate amount of dentist friends who live in my home state of Oregon. (There is one taxation bright spot — Oregon doesn't have a sales tax.)

All the tax tables aside, let's simply assume our dentist friend is paying a maximum tax average of around 56%, and we'll forget the property taxes, the gasoline taxes, and all the taxes already incorporated in the cost of various items purchased in the stores.

The Strategy

The following example is provided to aid readers in expanding their grasp on the potential for integrating offshore planning in conjunction with a domestic business, rather than representing an actual strategy recommended by the author.

1. Form LLC in Nevada, with the Dentist as the manager.
2. LLC forms a business venture relationship with an IBC in a tax-free jurisdiction.
3. IBC forms offshore trust with the IBC as beneficiary.
4. Trustee of offshore trust forms U.S. trust.

Note: Both the offshore and domestic trusts will require that 100% of their annual income be distributed to their respective beneficiaries each year.

How And Why It Might Work

The LLC is formed in Nevada because, as pointed out in an earlier chapter, there is no state income tax in this jurisdiction, and Nevada provides greater confidentiality than any other U.S. jurisdiction. (You can locate an excellent Nevada corporate provider and management firm at www.nevcorp.com.) On the other hand if you use an offshore consultant he or she will generally make the arrangements on your behalf and use a provider with whom they feel most comfortable. An LLC, as you may recall, is a rather recent form of corporate-like structure. It can be visualized best by thinking of it as a partnership with corporate protection. The LLC is formed of members as opposed to shareholders; it takes a minimum of two members to form an LLC.

Members of a LLC can be any person or entity anywhere in the world. One of the members becomes the managing member, which is exactly the same function as president for a corporation. The manager has all the needed authority to operate the business, pay bills, hire staff, etc. In this example the domestic LLC owns and operates the dental practice, and the dentist is an employee of the company.

As the Nevada company's profits grow, the members elect to expand into other business activities, perhaps offshore financial investments. Using the services of an offshore trust company such as Nevis American Trust Company (www.offshoreagents.com) Guardian Trust Company (www.gtc-offshore.com or www.guardiantrust.com) Morison Anderson Trust (www.morisonanderson.com) or a similarly licensed trust company, they locate a suitable International Business Company (IBC) in a tax free jurisdiction to serve as a willing partner for the LLC's anticipated expansion.

The LLC is able to pay the deductible expense for this legitimate business use of the trust company for consultative services. (Contact the Sovereign Crest Alliance for a legal, accounting, financial advisor, or trust company referral at 869-466-3794, or www.sovereigncrest.com.)

Soon thereafter, the manager of the LLC (our dentist friend) receives word of his or her appointment as consultant of the IBC. He or she is then given responsibility for the source and application of funds for that company, subject to approval by the IBC's managing director.

The IBC now decides it is in its best interest to form a simple offshore trust with itself as the beneficiary and to grant the trust sufficient funds to enable it to initiate its business activities. The trustee for the offshore trust to be a qualified, licensed, trust company in the jurisdiction that the trust is formed. The terms of the trust call for the distribution of all profits to the beneficiary annually.

The trustee of the offshore trust contracts with an independent trustee or lawyer in the U.S. to form a simple domestic trust and act as its trustee. This trust will also be responsible to send its profits to the beneficiary annually.

The settlement of the domestic trust would be so structured that there were sufficient funds on hand to acquire a 90% interest in the domestic LLC involved in the dental business.

How It Comes Together

The entities are all in place and the practical application follows. Within the U.S. all sales of product or services that will be consumed within the United States will be handled by the Nevada LLC. It will report its revenues and net income on IRS form 1065 annually. Because it is taxed as a partnership it will show 10% distribution to the founding members and 90% distribution to the domestic trust. Distributions would be reported to IRS on form K-1 in concert with partnership tax law. There would be no taxes paid by the LLC, rather the tax burden is borne by the members.

The domestic trustee receives the 90% distribution of profits from the LLC and in turn distributes these funds to its beneficiary, the offshore trust. Since the trustee is required to report the profit and pay the tax, he or she would cause to be filed IRS form 1041, commonly known as the fiduciary tax form. Because the trustee had already distributed the funds received from the LLC to the offshore trust, (its beneficiary), there will be no taxable profit.

Since the offshore trust receives its funds from within the U.S. and they are therefore considered "source funds" the trustee will be required to report them to the IRS. However, since the offshore trust is also a simple trust with instructions to distribute its effective earnings to the beneficiary annually, when it files IRS form 1040NR it will also show no taxable income.

Strategy Summary

The funds received by the LLC's offshore business partner, the IBC, have come to it through an offshore trust. Therefore these funds are considered NON U.S. source funds and are therefore not subject to any tax extension of the U.S. Tax Code. In addition, any business the managing consultant of the IBC, the dentist who is also the manager of the LLC, is able to develop with offshore entities should always be done through the IBC.

If both sides of a given transaction are offshore, they are not subject to U.S. taxes. That is, assuming neither party to the transaction is an entity owned by a U.S. citizen or resident. Of course, if our dentist friend wants payment for consulting services to the IBC, he or she will have to pay taxes on all the funds received for this activity.

What has happened in this example is simply that 90% of the profits generated by the dental practice have moved offshore to a tax-free jurisdiction where they may be invested in higher yield securities than are available to citizens of the U.S.

Complicated? Yes it may sound like it the first time you come across a strategy like this. But, once in place the pieces should operate smoothly. There are initial set up costs and ongoing administrative costs for operating the IBC, and both trusts. However, the good news is that once in place the annual administrative fees are relatively low.

In the final analysis, is a strategy such as the one set forth directly above worthwhile? Well, remember that 56% tax rate way back at the beginning of this example? How do you feel about ninety percent of surplus beyond the prying eyes of predatory litigators? How do you feel about privacy guarantees? Do you want to take advantage of higher investment returns? Does it make sense for you to have a piggy bank located offshore? You be the judge.

Is there any guarantee a strategy like the one set forth above will work? In the final analysis the answer is no. However, if you have legitimate motivations for wanting to be involved offshore beyond the issue of federal income tax, the chances that a workable program can be developed to suit your needs is quite high. Once again, it is important to point out that you should avoid any attempt to replicate someone else's "cookie cutter" approach. Going offshore can be exciting, fun, and thoroughly beneficial, but do not implement a plan without seeking the aid of a competent professional.

Tax Planning Through the U.S.

International tax planning through the U.S. has become a standard for Asians and Europeans. And where properly de-coupled, or de-controlled structures are in place, for U.S. persons as well. The following are U.S. tax-neutral vehicles for non-U.S. persons:

> LLC's (limited liability companies)
> Partnerships
> Indian tribes
> Insurance & Annuities
> Charities
> Trusts
> U.S. holding companies
> U.S. licensing companies
> VEBA's (Voluntary Employees Benefit Association)
> Rabbi trusts (deferred compensation plan)

Why would a non U.S. person want a U.S. tax neutral entity?

> Treaty-based withholding tax relief
> Anti-home country CFC arbitrage
> U.S. Capital markets access
> Offshore estate planning
> U.S. political and economic stability
> Appearances

Tax-neutral entities pass taxability through to their members. Nevada, Delaware and some other States allow a single member LLC, which is treated for tax purposes as income to the owner-member. If the owner-member is not a U.S. person, then in many cases the income generated within the LLC may be tax reduced or tax free within the U.S. LLC's are generally treated as partnerships, but may be treated and taxed as a "C" corporation under check-the-box rules.

Offshore Success

To be successful, a plan will require that a specialist in this field review carefully all of your relevant circumstances and fully understand your particular goals.   He or she must be thoroughly informed as to your potential or actual legal exposures at the time the strategies are to be implemented in order to avoid fraudulent conveyances. The number of structures necessary to accomplish your needs varies according to your particular circumstances.

There are many legal and ethical devices that can and should be used to protect the assets of those in every income bracket. If you have a home, a bank account, investments, corporate securities, valuable family heirlooms, or you feel that you just cannot afford to start all over again, then your assets are at risk in today's litigious and predatory environment.

As to whether or not it is legal to develop an offshore strategy to accomplish your goals you might want to consider this pearl of wisdom from the late Louis D Brandeis, a U.S. Supreme Court Justice:

"Where I live in Alexandria, Virginia, near the Supreme Court building, there is a toll bridge across the Potomac River. When in a rush I pay the toll and get home early. However I usually drive outside the downtown section of the city, and cross the Potomac on a free bridge. If I went over the toll bridge and through the toll without paying I would be guilty of tax evasion. However, if I go the extra mile and drive outside the city of Washington to the free bridge, I am using a legitimate, logical and suitable method of tax avoidance. And, I am providing a useful social service as well."

Setting up an offshore structure can be the most practical and cost effective insurance you will ever acquire to protect your hard-earned estate. It will definitely provide you enhanced privacy and access to greater investment returns, and you may be able to enjoy the added benefit of significant tax deferral or legal tax avoidance.

Doug Casey, a co-investor in a business I founded twenty years ago, has become world renowned for several best selling books he's authored on finance and investing. He has championed the term "International Man" to describe those enlightened people who assume greater personal freedom by learning to operate multi-jurisdictionally. All of his books are excellent, but I particularly like *Strategic Investing For the Nineties*. It is an excellent text for understanding global influences on local economics even though some of the examples are now dated.

Author Dr. William Hill calls the folks that wake up and move on to become multi-jurisdictional people "PT's," which stands for "Perpetual Travelers," a term that refers to the status afforded them under various legal jurisdictions. (Some refer to PT's as "Prior Taxpayers," although no one can truly escape all forms of taxation nor would it be wise to attempt to do so.)

Lord William Rees-Moog describes the self reliant, internationally enlightened among us as "Sovereign Individuals." Personally I call them PRUDENT!

18

Planning & Review

"Whatever course you decide upon, there is always someone to tell you that you are wrong. There are always difficulties arising, which tempt you to believe that your critics are right. To map out a course of action and follow it to an end requires courage."

Ralph Waldo Emerson

U.S. Tax Review

According to the IRS Statistics for 1998 released in late 2000, there were about 125 million personal income tax returns showing a record $5.4 trillion in Adjusted Gross Income. (Curiously, this is an amount almost identical to the funds that government estimates say are now held in safe havens.) Some other interesting items:

- The average adjusted return for 1998 showed income of $43,000.
- The taxable income for the year after deductions and exemptions was $3.8 trillion — or about $30,000 per return. The total income tax due was $785 billion, which would averages to about $6,300 per return. The total income tax equaled slightly less than 15% of the AGI for all returns in 1998 or about 21% of the taxable income.
- Twenty-four percent (24%) of the total tax returns filed paid no tax due to exemptions, credits and deductions.
- Even though the average return resulted in an average tax rate of 14.6%, only 19% of the returns topped out at 15%.
- The highest 39.6% personal tax rate generated 26% of the total tax.
- The top 1% of taxpayers accounted for 17% of the total adjusted income but paid 33% of the total tax.
- If 1% of the taxpayers pay 1/3 of the total personal income taxes but earn only 1/6 of the total income, how is it that pandering politicians make the case that the wealthy are not paying their fair share?

A Chain Reaction
- A family living at the poverty level in the United States has a higher income than the median family income in 150 other countries.
- The average senior citizen today will receive $250,000 more in lifetime Social Security and Medicare benefits than they and their employers paid into the system, including the interest earned on those payments.

- The richest 1% of Americans earned 17% of the total adjusted income but paid 33% of the total tax.
- The estate tax paid by wealthier Americans at their death is equivalent to 55 percent of everything they have, this added to the tax already paid on the income which purchased these assets brings the total tax on the assets of the wealthy to about 94%!
- In the U.S. the World War II generation is now passing their assets on to their heirs, an amount which totals about $10 trillion. All the larger inheritances will be subject to death taxes.
- If the federal government confiscated every penny earned each year by every millionaire in the United States, they would only raise enough to run the federal government for six weeks.
- The richest countries in the world per capita are tax shelter nations.

Now, picture a mousetrap, pried open and set to snap. But instead of cheese at the trigger, there is a ping-pong ball. If you were to spring that mousetrap, the ball would go flying.

Now envision a vast airplane hangar full of such mousetraps, packed side by side. Now picture yourself in the middle of these mousetraps — extending far off into the distance in every direction — holding a single ping-pong ball.

You have but to drop that solitary ping-pong ball in order to set off a virtual bedlam of mousetraps snapping and balls flying. This is a chain reaction, and is the principal behind nuclear weapons.

There is no moral dimension to this phenomenon. Both the mouse-traps and the ping-pong balls are acting according to physical laws, behaving according to their natures. They cannot do anything else.

People are much the same, regardless of where the live, or what they do. There has always been such a thing as "human nature," and try as we might, people cannot help but behave in accordance with it. The argument comes in defining human nature. Are we "creatures of light and basically good?" Or is the human heart, as the prophet Jeremiah proclaimed, "desperately wicked and deceitful above all things — who can know it?"

Human nature is very much at the center of what is to come because of the mousetrap and ping-pong ball phenomenon. When there were relatively few people on earth and they were separated from one another by great distances, it didn't much matter how one individual or group of individuals behaved. Whatever action they took — for good or for ill — they generally could only affect a small number of others in the immediate area.

But after the turn of the millennium we are connected as never before due to a huge increase in population coupled with international trade and that most remarkable tool, the Internet. Whatever happens in one place now has the potential of an immediate impact practically everywhere at once. Which is why each of us must consider human nature in making long-range personal decisions.

Will the Internet ease international tensions by bringing people together in a community forum of mutual understanding? Or will it be used by international terrorists to plan nuclear, germ, or chemical attacks? Will it become a system for medical, humanitarian, and philanthropic enterprises to meet ever-greater human needs? Or will it make it easier for swindlers and pornographers to spread their corruption?

The answer, of course is, all this and more. Whatever is in the human heart — for good or otherwise — will be fulfilled at an exponential pace in coming years. The seed of human potential, now germinated and flowered will soon bear fruit. Those who took a sanguine view of human nature were dealt a devastating blow with the collapse of Soviet communism. This political system was appealing to many because it promised equal distribution of wealth — from each according to their abilities to each according to their needs.

Such an idea seems quaint today, but it has its roots in New Testament teachings, about how primitive Christianity could voluntarily organize itself as a social structure until Jesus Christ returned to Earth. The hard-nose part of the same teaching — if you do not work you shall not eat — is the part that most people under Communism chose to ignore, not to mention the need for it to be voluntary.

Understanding human nature is the only reason to once again beat this dead horse. Many people would receive something for nothing if they could(and all too frequently do), while there are others who will produce and give to the extent they are able. The Communist system did not take that reality into account. It failed because there were too many people hoping for a free ride on those willing to produce.

Of course, Communism did serve a purpose. As long as there was a viable alternative to free enterprise capitalism, the tendency of the strong and productive to accumulate a greater proportion of wealth was held somewhat in check. Now that balance is gone.

The result has been that the rich are getting richer — certainly relative to the poor. The richest 358 people in the world have net worth equal to the annual income of the poorest 45 percent of humanity, or about 2.3 billion people. The trend toward concentration of wealth in fewer hands is accelerating. Former Third-World countries (now developing nations) had something to bargain with in the past — either natural resources or votes in the United Nations. (Ironically, the vote in the UN is still a saleable commodity despite the end of the Cold War. And, the governments of some small countries have their entire budget deficits covered by wealthy governments such as Taiwan, Kuwait, and South Korea.)

History & Review

Throughout recorded history people have sought ways to protect what they've worked hard to create and accumulate. Protection is sometimes required from those that would lull you into believing that they are in fact your protector, such as the tax collector, the bureaucracy, and if you're an American your home legal system may be the culprit. Modern times require a multitude of strategies to deal with the current complicity of threats.

Many asset protection tools have become common place. The corporation is one of the most universal such strategies. A corporation is in reality a "legal fiction;" an entity constructed of paper documents, which has most of the rights and powers of a living person. A corporation can buy and sell, own and control assets of every description, sue or be sued.

Even if a single individual is the sole owner of his or her own corporation, simply conducting business through a corporation (or limited liability company) can effect considerable asset protection. The corporate entity is now so routine that most people have forgotten, if they ever knew, that corporations were originally formed solely for asset protection reasons.

Where the corporation was formed, what information is in the public record, and the corporation's legal home jurisdiction, can be extremely important. These simple facts frequently constitute the basis of a quality asset protection and tax planning strategy.

If you are properly incorporated, it is absolutely imperative that you respect the corporate entity as if it were a separate individual. One must be careful to follow the formalities of the law to ensure that the corporate shield will not be pierced. A lawsuit against a corporation may succeed against corporate assets, but a creditor will not be able to consume personal assets and bank accounts - even if you are the sole shareholder of the corporation, provided corporate formalities have been adequately maintained. This is true in almost all countries.

Seeking out a well informed professional advisor is an integral part of developing a well-designed strategy. He, she, or they, will likely review with you some of the more "esoteric" legal structures, in addition to domestic and offshore corporations, that are just as legal and ethical as those with which you may be more familiar.

As a part of your planning you will need to develop new privacy habits and be cautious with whom you discuss your overall stratagem. Many people mistakenly believe that tax avoidance and asset protection tools that are not well known by the majority of people are somehow less effective or less legal. This is simply not true. Why is it we instantly believe it's perfectly legal for the Rothschild's or the Rockefeller's to use offshore structures but highly suspect if it's our next door neighbor?

You may be familiar with a number of legal devices but are unfamiliar with their asset protection and privacy value. Occasionally legal structures, such as offshore asset protection trusts, or charitable remainder trusts, seem almost mystical and are generally assumed by most to be used only by the ultra wealthy. The fact that the very rich have been using these concepts for centuries attests that they are superb and effective asset protection tools that are capable of preserving wealth. And, although widely used by the super rich, these structures are as simple as the corporate form and can be used by the common citizen. Generally speaking, asset protection trusts are tax-neutral. That is to say, they have no inherent income tax benefits although they may have inheritance or estate planning tax benefits. At least this is substantially true in the U.S., Canada and England; however, in some countries offshore trusts may still provide direct tax benefits in addition to premier asset protection.

Legal and financial advisors have engaged in asset protection planning for many years. Lawyers regularly recommend to clients that they take advantage of limited liability vehicles. America, more than any other country, has become an extremely litigious society, which in turn has given rise to asset protection planning for the general citizenry that was previously reserved for only the best informed of the world's society. In the States virtually every state BAR association has a chapter for Asset Protection where lawyers meet and learn about legal mechanisms to better protect their client's assets.

For a legal or accounting referral call the Sovereign Crest Alliance at 869-466-3794 (www.sovereigncrest.com). They are a commercial trade association whose membership is comprised of two groups of associates. One segment is referred to as "affiliated professionals" who are lawyers, accountants, and financial advisors skilled and focused on offshore planning; and the second segment of the Sovereign Crest Alliance membership is comprised of "core service providers" such as offshore trust companies, private banks, brokerage firms, etc.

Setting up an offshore structure can be the most practical and cost effective insurance you will ever acquire to protect a hard-earned estate. It will definitely supply enhanced privacy and access to greater investment returns, and it may be able to provide the added benefit of significant tax deferral or even legal tax avoidance.

Litigation Explosion

In the U.S. dramatic journalism, radio and television, and a high concentration of government subsidized citizens who tend to comprise the jury system have given impetus to larger and larger awards. These awards are often comprised of actual reparations, with huge sums in punitive damages. U.S. society has grown to expect large punitive damage awards far outweighing the actual damages experienced by a plaintiff. Litigation, and many governments generally, are spinning out of control.

Plaintiffs and their attorneys target the wealthy, or at least those that have assets to seize, as well as professionals and business owners, who might not be considered wealthy, but are simply "better odds" for collection than other defendants. The bureaucracy targets the same group in an effort to increase revenues.

There are many legal and ethical devices that can and should be used to protect the assets of those in every income bracket. If you have a home, a bank account, investments, corporate securities, valuable family heirlooms, or you feel that you just cannot afford to start all over again, then your assets are at risk in today's litigious and over taxed society and should be protected.

A Flexible Personalized Structure

An experienced asset protection attorney or consultant will have dozens of domestic and offshore core-strategies that may be used in creating a personalized program to evoke high quality protection for client's assets, and simultaneously achieve specific estate planning goals.

There is no panacea for asset protection and tax deferral structuring. A mechanism that will give you superior asset protection may not provide privacy or have sufficient tax advantages. There is no one "perfect" structure. An experienced asset protection planner will therefore recommend a program or strategy that may incorporate several, or even many, different devices that meet the particular needs, circumstances, and desires of a client, including such things as living trusts, charitable remainder trusts, offshore asset protection trust, offshore corporations, a minority interest in an offshore structure, qualifying offshore life insurance, private or commercial annuities, LLC's, family limited partnerships, Nevada companies, a domestic trust, and so forth.

To be successful, a plan will require that a specialist in this field review carefully all of your relevant circumstances and fully understand your particular goals. He or she must be thoroughly informed as to your potential or actual legal exposures at the time the strategies are to be implemented in order to avoid fraudulent conveyances. You must tell your asset protection attorney everything pertinent to possible claims outstanding.

The number of structures necessary to accomplish your particular needs varies according to your circumstances. A cookie-cutter approach where one size fits all is rarely a legitimate approach.

Businesses Need Special Consideration

Your real property and business holdings require special attention in setting up a sound asset protection strategy. These types of holdings generate liabilities that potentially effect a company's operation, as well as effecting non-business assets. In comparison, assets such as stocks, bonds, furniture, and artwork, do not generate liability that might allow judgment-seeking creditors to reach your other assets.

The choice of the entity or entities you use for your business operation may have subtle but profound effects on you, your assets, and your overall asset protection system. Your asset protection counselor will be principally concerned with (1) limiting the reach of business-generated liability, and (2) limiting your non-business creditors from attacking business assets or personal assets.

A strategic plan must also consider the tax ramifications of these asset protection choices. Remember that there is no cure-all. A good plan requires a balancing and weighing of the benefits of any particular device, and its effect on the overall asset protection structure.

Review of Asset Protection Devices

The business form you use is an important aspect of your asset protection strategy. Trusts comprise another valuable asset protection device. Not only are trusts effective for asset protection in-and-of-themselves, they usually work well in conjunction with other devices in comprising the entire strategy.

As an example, you may decide that the most appropriate business form for your future operations is a corporation. Thus protecting your personal assets from business creditors. However, the corporation's stock is a valuable asset that a personal creditor could take to satisfy a judgment. Therefore, the stock of your corporation could be placed within a trust to protect business's assets from your personal creditors.

There are various types of trusts, such as: revocable trusts, irrevocable trusts, discretionary trusts, spendthrift trusts, support trusts, charitable remainder trusts, capital gains by-pass trusts, real estate privacy trusts, living trusts, Rabbi trusts, and an interesting hybrid trust developed by an attorney friend of mine which he calls a "Complex Trust." Various trust types, both domestic and international, may be used as devices to invoke asset protection, privacy, and tax timing strategies. Offshore Asset Protection Trusts are as "bullet proof" a device as you will find, but recent legislation has interfered with their use as an effective tax avoidance mechanism.

Jurisdictions

There are a considerable number of tax haven and asset protection jurisdictions, and each of them has their pros and cons. For example, most jurisdictions do not have treaties with all other jurisdictions. Others have laws that specifically do not recognize foreign civil judgments. Some jurisdictions have shorter statutes of limitations than others, less expensive set-up or maintenance costs, better business infrastructures, etc. Your advisor should evaluate your personal circumstances in determining which jurisdiction might be the best for you. While costs may be slightly higher for offshore corporate structures and trusts than their domestic counterparts, when properly employed and established, they provide, by far, the best asset protection and tax deferral opportunities generally available.

Offshore Banking

Offshore banking is often employed for privacy and asset protection reasons and there are a variety of issues and concerns regarding this course of action. The United States, in its drive to curb the drug trade and other criminal activities, has also curbed personal and financial privacy right out of existence. The way you hold your money, your accounts and your assets, will determine how "Bank Secrecy Acts" or "Money Laundering Control Acts" will apply to your overall strategy.

Rationale

A growing number of moderately successful individuals, business owners, and professionals are considering offshore options. Most appear to be focused on the fundamental issues of privacy, asset protection, estate and tax planning, higher yield investments and lower thresholds of business compliance. However, more recently a number of inquiries seem to be targeted exclusively on tax issues. This is a mistake.

Remember if the only reason one has for going offshore is tax avoidance I recommend strongly that one seek the assistance of a qualified tax attorney and explore the myriad of opportunities available for domestic tax deferral. Revenue Canada, the Internal Revenue, and the taxing authorities of several other jurisdictions are increasingly taking the position that if the primary reason an offshore option is invoked is taxation based, this motivation is sufficient grounds to deny tax benefits. It is important therefore that anyone considering an offshore business opportunity do so for reasons OTHER than tax issues alone. Yes, the tax issue may be a reason for going offshore but it may not be the only or principal reason for doing so.

There are a number of very important reasons for one to consider using a Offshore Financial Center such as Nevis, Grenada, the British Virgin Islands, etc., from which to base critical financial activities. Motivating factors may include:

- An offshore company can invest in global securities including top performing mutual funds not available to U.S. citizens, Canadians, and some Europeans.
- Privacy is often integral to risk planning. Offshore clients typically seek confidentiality in their affairs to protect business strategies.
- An offshore jurisdiction such as Nevis offers the best Asset Protection resources available to anyone, anywhere, in the world.
- An international business company (IBC) is TAX-FREE and there are no business activity reports of any kind required in Nevis or Grenada.
- There are no reports to your home country regarding a corporation's banking, investments, stock trading, or other financial activities provided your offshore company is based in a secure jurisdiction,

although this situation has been made more precarious for U.S. citizens with the new Qualified Intermediary legislation that went into effect January 1, 2001.

- An offshore corporation can be effectively employed in pre-planning for such things as: divorce, business break-up, corporate re-organizations, and the re-structuring of all forms of business and personal financial relationships.

- Premier offshore jurisdictions are less business invasive allowing for aggressive and unrestrained enterprise with lower overhead.

- An offshore corporation may be used to file first position liens against assets and property in your home country thereby closing the "apparent" window of vulnerability to legal predators, and stop frivolous litigation before it commences.

- By titling property into an offshore company, you can transfer real estate, cars, boats, and other titled assets easily and confidentially by simply instructing your offshore trust officer of the new owner, or handing over bearer shares in the offshore company to the buyer instead of re-titling property when sold.

- An offshore company may be used to segregate high-risk investments from other more secure holdings.

- The offshore option may be used as an effective prenuptial agreement.

- Offshore structures can protect retirement funds from possible bankruptcy or other legal conflicts.

- Informed estate planners know that offshore structures can provide the most effective mechanisms for the transfer of assets to the next generation in an efficient and discreet fashion.

- An offshore company used in conjunction with a nominee director/officer allows you to conduct business transactions and remain completely anonymous.

- By transferring assets out of harm's way, different types of insurance costs may be substantially reduced.

- An offshore company may be used as a holding vehicle for troublesome properties.

- When used in conjunction with a domestic company, an offshore corporation can reduce many kinds of taxes by shifting earnings offshore. However this may be problematic if you are a U.S. person.

- An offshore corporation can secure debit or credit cards with paper and electronic records maintained offshore under Crown Privacy Statutes, thereby providing enhanced confidentiality in ATM and credit card use.

- An offshore corporation used in conjunction with a carefully structured plan may be able to legally defer, or avoid altogether, domestic income taxes.

- But as set forth throughout this book, this kind of strategy requires an informed tax specialist, usually a tax lawyer.
- Corporations based in an offshore financial center may derive substantial tax benefits from their activities provided they know the rules and follow them carefully.

It is important to remember that the simple act of setting up an offshore corporation does not automatically reduce tax liability for the individual. For example, if you are a U.S. person the implications of your offshore company being designated a "Controlled Foreign Corporation," a "Foreign Personal Holding Company" or a "Passive Foreign Investment Company" are matters that should be addressed by an informed accountant or tax attorney. (See the 2001 Offshore Tax Guide included in the Appendices for more information on this subject.)

Notwithstanding efforts by some governments to reduce the use of offshore financial centers, they have become a critical part of the tax planning strategies of individuals and corporations in most first world countries. Remember that an offshore company can easily invest in almost any fund, worldwide, and the earnings are tax-free. However, the owner(s) of the offshore company, if resident in the U.S. for example, are required by government edict to report the gains their offshore company has earned on these passive investments and pay the appropriate tax.

The decision to utilize an offshore trust company to form and operate an offshore corporation is easy to implement. But keep in mind that if tax avoidance is your only motivation for going offshore, you really must seek legal counsel that is qualified in international tax law before you implement a strategy.

If your goal is to access new markets, take advantage of business and investment opportunities unavailable at home, regain your privacy, and protect assets from frivolous and predatory litigation, use of an offshore corporation can reap extraordinary benefits. And, until you can really fight your government, there are alternatives to losing family-built enterprises to taxation. And these alternatives often involve using offshore investment vehicles.

The offshore financial services industry has grown to such an extent that the amount of money protected in offshore sanctuaries is now greater than the entire U.S. national debt. So what do you think? Should you go offshore?

"Investing offshore doesn't have to be *all* work, you know."

T.L.N.

Appendices

The Offshore Tax Guide - 2001
Expatriation
Business Terms and Abbreviations

VI

INTRODUCTION TO THE APPENDICES

This book is focused on privacy, asset protection, and legal tax shelter, both domestically and offshore. If you are from the U.S. it should be clear to you that if you HAVE anything, or you have more than one income source, you should have at least one Nevada corporation and perhaps several. If you are from anywhere else and you want to do business in the U.S., you should have one or more Nevada companies. If you're from Canada you may be wise to apply the state-to-state strategy described in Chapter 11 as a country-to-country strategy. After all, Canadian taxes are even higher than U.S. taxes.

As you activate your Nevada Corporation with the IRS by securing a tax identification number, be certain to declare a fiscal year date ending different from that of the calendar year. This action will allow you future flexibility in shifting income between your corporation and yourself for any given year. A good date you may want to consider is having your fiscal year end January 31st.

Why is the fiscal year date important? A U.S. person filing a joint return can earn up to $40,100 and still only be subject to 15% federal income tax. And, your "C" corporation is only assessed 15% up to the first $50,000 of net income annually. Which means that with some careful planning you and your corporation can earn up to $90,100 collectively and only be subject to a maximum of 15% federal income tax. And, by keeping your company qualified in Nevada you eliminate state income tax altogether!

Your circumstances may well warrant participation with an offshore corporation or limited liability company, and you may find it advantageous to invoke a domestic or international exempt trust in concert with an offshore corporation. However, it is my opinion that regardless of whether or not you intend to enter the offshore world, in most cases you are still well advised to have at least one Nevada Corporation. As we've continually seen throughout this book, there are many advantages to offshore strategies, including guaranteed privacy, premier asset protection, various tax shelter options, reduced regulatory hassle for many types of business activities and higher and safer investment returns.

A comment about a related matter not addressed in this book — If you are an American and have not set up a Living Trust, then do so. A living trust should be established to prevent your heirs from suffering with the complicated and very expensive issues related to probate after your death. A living trust does not provide YOU with improved privacy, although it can keep particulars about your estate out of the newspaper as required by probate. A living trust does not provide YOU with asset protection although it can provide your heirs with critical protection regarding your estate. And, a living trust does not provide YOU with any real tax advantages, but again it can do so for your heirs.

As to how to invoke a Living Trust domestically I suggest that you contact a professional to prepare the necessary documents for you. It is really a rather simple process and one you can do with standard forms purchased from an office products store. But for the few dollars extra you should visit the process out with someone skilled in this arena. So, again I refer you to the Sovereign Crest Alliance (www.sovereigncrest.com) if you need a referral to accomplish this process or simply call your local legal counsel and he or she will refer you to an estate-planning specialist.

As you take the steps to implement strategies to take back your privacy, invoke real world asset protection mechanisms, reduce your taxes where possible, and simply MAKE and KEEP a great deal more money, do not forget your heirs. This means you need to address some basic estate planning issues. Interestingly enough, one little understood value to having a Nevada and/or Offshore corporation is simply that a corporation never dies, it just elects a new president!

Having two classes of stock in your corporations could allow for your future heirs to own the vast majority of the stock immediately, thus eliminating future problems with probate and punitive estate taxes. Perhaps 98% of the shares could be non-voting stock held by your children or grandchildren, with only about 2% of a family-owned company actually held in your name. The 2% of the total issued shares would represent the only VOTING class of stock and therefore keep 100% control of your business assets and activities within your power until you wish to make a change or they are passed on in your will.

OFFSHORE TAX GUIDE – 2001

MORGAN CARTER & YOUNG, INC.

Morgan Carter & Young, Inc. ("MCY") is a multi-disciplined professional consulting firm targeted to the unique needs of the wealthy and upward mobile middle class. MCY publishes educational materials for individuals and technical papers for professional service providers such as attorneys and accountants. For further information please contact us at 503.647.7730 or visit our web site at www.morgancarteryoung.com. MCY is a member of the Sovereign Crest Alliance.

DISCLAIMER AND
RESERVATION OF RIGHTS

DISCLAIMER.

The Offshore Tax Guide is a summary of the Internal Revenue Code as it relates to the treatment of various offshore legal entities, their structure, intent, and other information pertinent to their taxation. It is provided with the understanding that the authors and publishers are not engaged in rendering legal, accounting, or other professional advice to the reader. We strongly recommend that before relying on any of the information contained herein, competent professional legal advice and opinions should be obtained.

This summary contains information on the laws and regulations of the United States government and its agencies that is very technical in nature and which is subject to change at any time. Therefore, the authors and publishers make no guarantee as to the accuracy of this information insofar as it is applied to any particular individual or situation. The information contained in this summary is believed to be accurate in the opinion of the authors at the time this summary was completed.

The authors and publishers specifically disclaim any liability, loss or risk, personal or otherwise, incurred as a consequence directly or indirectly of the use and application of any of the information in this summary. In no event will the author, the publisher, their successors, or any resellers of this information be liable to the purchaser for any amount greater than the purchase price of these materials.

RESERVATION OF RIGHTS.

This information is sold to you, the purchaser, with the agreement that you have a right to non-exclusive use of these materials for your own educational purposes. Your right to use these materials is non-transferable. You agree that you will not copy or reproduce any of the information contained herein, in any form

Guide to U.S. Taxation of International Business Entities, Transactions, and Persons

By Benjamin D. Knaupp, J.D.
Phone: 503-626-7071, Fax: 503-626-7950
Email: Ben@Knaupplaw.com

Introduction

This guide is intended to serve as a summary of the most common U.S. tax laws applying to international business ownership and various common transactions between foreign business entities or individuals. For the layperson reading this guide, the most common sources of tax law are; first, the tax code or Internal Revenue Code (IRC), which is a federal statute passed by Congress and the President, second, Internal Revenue Service regulations (of which there are final, temporary, and proposed regulations), which explain the position of the IRS with respect to certain tax code sections, third, judicial opinions of tax court judges, the federal circuit courts of appeals, and the U.S. Supreme Court, fourth, tax treaties between the U.S. and foreign states (which have the same force as tax code once ratified by the Senate), fifth, the Congressional record, which is considered "law"; to the extent it offers insight into the intent of Congress with respect to a particular rule of the tax code, and sixth, various other documents issued by the IRS, such as Revenue Rulings, Revenue Procedures, Treasury Decisions, Letter Rulings, IRS Announcements and Notices, and Technical Advice Memorandums.

It is important to note that general IRS publications and instructions, such as the instructions accompanying form 1040 and other forms, or any of the more than 200 informational publications put out by the IRS are not technically "law" but are only explanations of the law based on the IRS interpretation of the law. Of course, probably 90% of the information found in IRS publications is unquestionably the correct interpretation of the law. However, the more complicated a given question, the more likely it may be that the IRS interpretation of the law may not be wholly correct. For example, a given complex business or financial transaction is never simply "legal" or "not legal" for tax purposes. Whether the transaction is "legal" ultimately may depend on what a tax court judge decides after hearing the evidence and interpretation of the law from a taxpayer contrasted against the evidence and interpretation presented by the IRS.

Now that these points of reference have been made, this guide will attempt to give a general summary of key U.S. tax laws that apply to international transactions. This guide is only an introduction to the general principles of the law, and the tax code and other citations are provided to aid the reader who wishes to undertake further study, without getting into too much detail. Always consult a licensed attorney or tax professional before taking any action or making any decision involving these laws.

PART I: OWNERSHIP IN FOREIGN ENTITIES

I. Controlled Foreign Corporations (CFC): IRC §951-964

A. Who is taxed: any U.S. shareholder of a foreign corporation that meets the ownership requirement given below.

    1. A foreign corporation is a "Controlled Foreign Corporation" if the corporation has "U.S. Shareholders" who—individually or together—own more than 50% of the total combined voting power OR more than 50% of the total value of a foreign corporation. IRC §957(a)

        a) A "U.S. shareholder" is any U.S. person who owns at least 10% of the total combined voting power of the outstanding stock. IRC §957(c), IRC §951(b).

        b) Rules of constructive ownership of stock apply to a foreign corporation in determining whether the corporation is a CFC. The rules of constructive ownership of stock are set forth in IRC §958 and IRC § 318(a). Under these rules, stock is considered "owned" by you if it is owned by your spouse, children, or an entity you control, such as a corporation, trust, or partnership. Stock is also considered "owned" by you if it is held by any other party or agent for your benefit and upon your instructions.

    2. Examples of foreign corporations that are <u>not</u> CFCs:

        a) Eleven unrelated U.S. persons each own 9.09 % of the shares.

        b) One U.S. person owns 50%, and 6 (or more) other U.S. persons own equal portions of the remaining 50% (assuming they are all unrelated parties). In this case, the 50% shareholder is the only "U.S. shareholder" of the group, because he is the only one who owns 10% or more of the shares. The corporation is therefore not a CFC because "U.S. shareholders" do not own more than 50% of the shares.

    3.   <u>Timing issues:</u> although a corporation is a CFC on any day that it meets the ownership requirements set forth above, U.S. shareholders are not required to declare the income of the corporation unless the corporation qualified as a CFC for at least 30 consecutive days during the tax year. IRC §951(a)(1).

B. How is Tax Paid: the "U.S. shareholders" of a CFC are taxed as if the CFC were a pass-through entity. Each U.S. shareholder includes in his or her personal income the sum of two major components. These include the shareholder's pro rata share of "Subpart F" income (explained below) and any earnings of the CFC from investment in U.S. property (also explained below).

    1. "<u>Subpart F income</u>": generally, it is "foreign based company income"

which includes:

a) Foreign personal holding company income (IRC §954(a)(1) and (c)). This is generally passive income such as interest, dividends, rents, royalties, and gains from sales of stock, commodities transactions, foreign currency gains, etc.

b) Foreign base company sales income (see IRC §954(a)(2) and (d)).

c) Foreign base company services income (see IRC §954(a)(3) and (e)).

d) Air & sea transportation income.

2.   Investment earnings from U.S. property: this includes earnings from tangible property located in the US; any security issued by a US payor, or the right to use intellectual property in the US. IRC §956(b)(1).

C. Exceptions: since the purpose of the CFC rules is to cut down on the use of foreign corporations as tax deferral structures, Congress created several exceptions for foreign corporations that are conducting legitimate international business activities. These exceptions are intended to give relief to foreign corporations that generate subpart F income in the ordinary course of business (e.g. interest from bank accounts or financing sales).

1. De minimis rule: the CFC rules will not apply to any corporation that has gross foreign base company income which is less than the smaller of 5% of the CFC's gross income, or $1 million. IRC §954(b)(3)(A).

2. 90% foreign tax rule: income that would otherwise be taxable as Subpart F income is exempt from the CFC rules if it is subject to an effective rate of foreign income tax which is greater than 90% of the maximum U.S. corporate tax rate.

II. Foreign Personal Holding Companies (FPHC): IRC §551-558

A. Who is taxed: like the CFC rules, the FPHC rules impose a tax directly on the U.S. shareholders of a foreign corporation if:

1. At least 50% of the stock (by vote or value) is owned by 5 or less US residents or citizens; and

2. At least 60% of the corporation's income is foreign personal holding company income. IRC §552(a)

As with the CFC rules, a "U.S. shareholder" includes a U.S. corporation, trust, partnership, LLC or estate. IRC §551(a).

Although the rules of this situation will overlap with the CFC and personal holding company rules, there are some situations in which the CFC rules or the personal holding company rules may not apply. The FPHC rules were developed to plug such a loophole. Example: the CFC rules do not apply to a shareholder owning less than 10% of a CFC. But the FPHC rules apply to any U.S. shareholder as long as the 50% and 60% tests above are met.

B. How is Tax Paid: the US shareholders include as gross income their share of the foreign personal holding company income that remained undistributed in the corporation. IRC §551(a)

C. What income is taxed: only undistributed "personal holding company income."

    1. "Personal Holding Company Income": is essentially passive, investment-type income. It also includes gains from the sale of stock (non-foreign personal holding company income does not include gains from sale of stock). IRC §553(a)(2)

★★ If the CFC tax applies, the tax under this section does not apply. Apply CFC rules instead. IRC §951(d).

III. Passive Foreign Investment Companies (PFIC): IRC §1291–1298

    A. Who is taxed: any US shareholder of a PFIC, regardless of that shareholder's individual ownership level, and regardless of overall US ownership level.

        1. A corporation is a PFIC if:

            a) At least 75% of the corporation's gross income is passive income; or

            b) The average percentage of its assets which provide "passive" income or which are held for the production of "passive" income is at least 50%. IRC §1297(a)(1), 1297(a)(2). Exceptions exist.

    B. How is Tax Paid: two methods of taxation possible:

        1. Qualified Electing Fund (QEF): if a fund provides information to the shareholder necessary to determine the income and identity of the shareholders, then the US owners are taxed currently on their pro rata portions of the company's actual income, subject to an election to defer payment of tax (plus an interest charge) until a distribution is made or a disposition of stock occurs.

        2. Non QEF: a US owner completes a current year inclusion estimate and defers payment of taxes, (plus interest) until a distribution is made or a disposition of stock occurs. IRC §1291. The owner is taxed at his highest statutory rate during the time he held the stock.

C. What income is taxed: if the corporation qualifies as a PFIC, then all the corporation's net income is taxable, and U.S. shareholders pay tax as explained in part B.

D. What is "passive" income: a group of Code sections are utilized to define the type of income that is considered "passive". Generally, it includes dividends and "deemed dividends", most kinds of taxable interest, certain royalty payments, annuity payments, and some rents. IRC §1297(b) defines "passive' income as income that falls within the definition of foreign personal holding company income as defined in IRC §954(c), except that "passive" income does not include:

    1. Banking business income: income derived in the active conduct of a banking business, either as a U.S. banking company, or a foreign corpo-

ration which obtains an advance ruling from the IRS and proves compliance with Regulations. IRC §1297(b)(2)(A); Reg.IRC §1.552-4,5; Proposed Regulations 1.1297-4. Proposed regulations IRC §1.1297-4(c) and (d) sets forth three requirements to meet the banking business income exception for foreign banks:

(i) The foreign bank must be licensed or authorized to accept deposits from the residents of the country in which it is incorporated, and to conduct one or more banking activities there (but, this requirement is not satisfied if the principal purpose of obtaining a banking license is to qualify for the banking business income exception to the PFIC rules);

(ii) The corporation must regularly accept deposits from customers that are residents of the country of incorporation, and deposits must be substantial; and

(iii) The corporation must make loans to customers in the ordinary course of its business.

2. <u>Insurance business income</u>: income derived in the active conduct of an insurance business by a corporation, which is predominantly engaged in the insurance business. IRC §1297(b)(2)(B).

3. <u>Interest, Dividend, Rent, or Royalty income</u>: if the income is received from a <u>related</u> person (as defined in IRC §954(d)(3)), and to the extent such income is properly allocable to non passive income of such related person, the income is not "passive" income. IRC §1297(b)(2)(C).

a) "Related" person: an individual, corporation, partnership, trust, or estate which controls or is controlled by the PFIC; or which is controlled by the same persons who control the PFIC. Control means ownership of over 50% of total value or voting stock. IRC §954(d)(3).

4. <u>Securities business income</u>: income of a corporation which is registered as a securities broker or dealer with the SEC, or which meets the requirements of proposed regulation IRC §1.1297-6; IRC §1297(b)(3). Proposed regulations IRC §1.1297-6 provides that income earned by an active securities dealer or broker is non-passive and exempt from PFIC taxation if either of two tests are met:

(i) The corporation is registered with the Securities & Exchange Commission as a broker/dealer;

(ii) If unregistered with the SEC, meets both of the following tests:
(A) Is licensed and authorized in the country of incorporation to conduct one or more securities activities with residents of that country, and is subject to regularly enforced securities regulations of that country;
(B) Regularly purchases securities or sells securities to customers in the ordinary course of its business, or enters into or terminates positions in securities with customers.

E. Overlap with CFC rules: The Taxpayer Relief Act of 1997 eliminates the overlap between the CFC rules and the PFIC rules. In general, if a foreign corporation is a CFC and also a PFIC, a shareholder required to include income under the CFC rules will not be required to comply with the rules for PFICs. (Effective January 1, 1998).

IV. Personal Holding Company Tax: IRC §541-547

A. Who is taxed: any corporation, whether foreign or domestic, with 5 or less individuals who own directly or indirectly more than 50% of the stock, and 60% or more of the gross income of the corporation is "personal holding company income".

1. Tax not applicable if all the stock is owned by nonresident aliens. IRC §542(c)(7)

2.   If U.S. shareholders own less than 10% of the stock, then only that percentage of undistributed personal holding company income is taxed. IRC §545(a).

B. How taxed: the corporation is assessed a 28% - 39% tax on any undistributed personal holding company income. The tax must be collected from the corporation and not from the shareholders. Because historically this was difficult to do, it led to the creation of the Foreign Personal Holding Company tax rules, which forces the U.S. shareholders to include their annual share of the corporation's personal holding company income. Because the U.S. shareholders are under IRS jurisdiction, the tax is more likely to be paid voluntarily — or at least more easily collected from U.S. residents.

C. What income is taxed: only undistributed "personal holding company income" that is derived from "U.S. sources" as defined by the code. IRC §882(b).

1. "<u>Personal Holding Company Income</u>": is essentially passive, investment-type income, including dividends, interest royalties, annuities, and rents. IRC §543. Exceptions exist.

★ Where the Personal Holding Company Tax applies, there is no accumulated earnings tax. IRC §532(b)(1).

★★ Where the Foreign Personal Holding Company Tax applies, the tax under this section does not apply. IRC §542(c)(5).

VI. Foreign Sales Corporations (FSCs): IRC § 921-927

Important Note: because of a successful legal challenge to the FSC rules by World Trade Organization members during the year 2000, the U.S. Congress will likely be forced to repeal the entire FSC tax structure. Under pressure from U.S. exporters, Congress is likely to find some alternative system to induce exporting. At the time this guide was updated, however, FSCs still exist.

A. Government Sanctioned Tax Breaks: in an effort to stimulate U.S. exports without violating the rules of the World Trade Organization (formerly the G.A.T.T.), Congress created the FSC tax rules to replace their first

attempt at encouraging exports—the Domestic International Sales Corporation (DISC) rules (see section VII below for more on DISC rules). Under
the new rules, qualifying corporations will be exempt from U.S. tax on a
portion of their taxable income. The exemption is from 15% - 32% of the
combined taxable income earned by the FSC and its related suppliers from
qualified exports. IRC §923.

B. Requirements to Qualify as a FSC: a FSC is a corporation that has
met all of the following tests:

1. Qualifying foreign jurisdiction: it must be organized under the laws
of a foreign country that meets the exchange of information requirements of U.S. law, or, be formed in one of the following U.S. possessions:
Guam, American Samoa, the Northern Mariana Islands, the U.S. Virgin
Islands. IRC §922(a)(1)(A). Many of the offshore tax havens will not
meet this test, but some will. The key is whether there is an agreement
between the U.S. government and the foreign country that provides for
exchange of information regarding the tax and financial dealings of
resident corporations. One of the most popular sites for incorporation
of FSCs is the U.S. Virgin Islands.

2. 25 shareholder maximum: it must have no more than 25 shareholders at any time during the tax year. IRC §922(a)(1)(B).

3. No preferred stock: it must not have preferred stock outstanding at
any time during the tax year. IRC §922(a)(1)(C).

4. Foreign office & books: the corporation must maintain an office in a
qualifying foreign country or U.S. possession with proper books of
accounting, and also proper books and records at a permanent site in the
U.S. IRC §922(a)(1)(D).

5. Foreign director: at all times there must be at least one director on
the board of directors who is not a U.S. resident. IRC §922(a)(1)(E).

6. No DISC relations: it must not be a member, at any time during the
tax year, of a controlled group of corporations that includes a DISC.
IRC §922(a)(1)(F).

7. Timely election: it must have made a proper election to be taxed as a
qualifying FSC within the time periods allowed by the regulations. IRC
§922(a)(2); 927(f).

C. What Income is Exempt? A qualifying FSC that has "foreign trading
gross receipts" will qualify for an exemption from U.S. tax on a portion of its
"exempt foreign trade income" (from 15% - 32%). In order to qualify as
"exempt foreign trade income", there are two additional requirements:

1. Foreign Management: except for a small FSC (discussed below), a
FSC must have certain management functions and activities occur
outside of the U.S. These include the following:

a) Meetings of the board of directors and shareholders;

b) Disbursement of cash dividends, outside legal and accounting fees,
salaries of officers, and salaries or fees of directors out of the principal
bank account;

c) Maintaining the principal bank account at all times during the year. IRC §924(b)(1)(A); 924(c).

2. Foreign Economic Processes: except for a small FSC (see below), a FSC must, either directly or by a contract, conduct the following economic processes outside of the U.S.:

a) Solicitation (other than advertising), and negotiation of the sale of goods or services which are intended to qualify as foreign trading gross receipts;

b) Incur direct costs attributable to the transaction equal to either at least 50% of the total direct costs attributable to the transaction in five specified categories of sales-related activities, or 85% of the direct costs attributable to any two of the five categories. IRC §924(b)(1)(B); 924(d).

D. Overlap with CFC rules: most of the income earned by a FSC will be subpart F income under the CFC rules. However, in general, most of the income of a FSC is not subject to the CFC rules.

E. "Small" FSCs: IRC §922(b) and 924(b) provide that any otherwise qualifying FSC with exempt foreign trade income receipts of $5 million or less does not have to meet the foreign management and foreign economic process requirements explained in section C. above. But taxpayers cannot use multiple small FSCs to avoid this limitation. IRC §924(b)(2)(B).

VII. Interest Charge Domestic International Sales Corporations:

A. Basic rules: as explained above, the FSC rules were adopted by Congress in response to charges by G.A.T.T. members that the old Domestic International Sales Corporation (DISC) rules were an unfair subsidy of American industry. Although the DISC rules were largely replaced by the FSC rules, one vestige of the old DISC rules remains. This is the Interest Charge Domestic International Sales Corporation (IC-DISC). The primary feature of the IC-DISC is that it allows domestic U.S. corporations with significant export sales to defer tax on up to $10 million of qualified export income, provided its shareholders pay an interest charge on the tax that would otherwise be due if the deferred income were distributed. IRC §995. A corporation can elect IC-DISC tax status by meeting the following tests:

1. It must be an eligible U.S. corporation;

2. At least 95% of its gross receipts must be qualified export receipts;

3. At least 95% of its gross assets must be qualified export assets;

4. It must have only one class of stock, and the par value of its outstanding stock   must be at least $2,500 on each day of the tax year;

5. It must elect IC-DISC status and the election must be in effect for the tax year;

6. It must not be a member of a controlled group that also includes a FSC;

7. It must keep separate books and records. IRC §992(a).

VIII. Sales of Appreciated Foreign Stock: IRC §1246–1248.

A. Introduction. Because some CFCs avoid taxation by earning income that falls outside of Subpart F, IRC §1248 was implemented. For example, in the absence of this section, a U.S. shareholder could avoid the ordinary income tax treatment that would occur if a CFC with no Subpart F income made a dividend to the shareholder by simply selling the appreciated stock of the CFC to a foreign party. The U.S. shareholder would thereby only recognize a capital gain. In order to prevent this result, IRC §1248 mandates that gain on the sale of CFC stock that would otherwise be treated as capital gain must be reported by the U.S. taxpayer as ordinary income to the extent of the CFC's earnings and profits (except for any portions of income of the CFC that did fall under Subpart F in the past).

B. Who is taxed: The tax applies to any U.S. person owning at least 10% of a CFC (either directly or indirectly, or by virtue of the constructive ownership rules applicable to CFCs).
    1. Timing of sale: IRC §1248 will apply to the sale of stock in a CFC if the foreign corporation was a CFC at any time during the preceding 5 years. The classification of the corporation at the time of sale is immaterial.

C. How is Tax Paid: the selling shareholder reports the gain on sale of the stock as if it were a dividend. IRC §1248(a).

D. What income is taxed: only that portion of the gain recognized by the selling shareholder, which is attributable to earnings and profits generated during years which the shareholder held the stock. IRC §1248(a), (c).

E. IRC §1246 Foreign Investment Company Stock: in cases where IRC §1248 does not apply because a U.S. shareholder holds less than a 10% interest in a CFC, IRC §1246 will apply to achieve the same result, preventing the selling shareholder from receiving capital gains treatment on the disposition of their stock. IRC §1246 only applies if:
    1. 50% or more of the CFC's stock is owned by "U.S. persons" (as defined under same principles as for CFCs); and
    a) The CFC is registered as a management company; or
    b) The CFC is engaged primarily in the business of investing or trading in securities, commodities, or any interest in such. IRC §1246(b).

IX. Foreign "Grantor" Trusts: IRC §671-679

A. Who is Taxed. Any grantor, transferor, or beneficiary of a foreign trust that has any U.S. person as its beneficiary. The grantor trust rules provide that if any U.S. person transfers property to a foreign trustee, or retains an economic interest in, or control over the trust, the U.S. person is treated for income tax purposes as the owner of the trust property, including the income of the trust. This means there is no true distinction between the trust and the grantor-owner for tax purposes. The result is that all transactions by the trust are treated as transactions of the owner. All expenses and income of the trust belong to and must be reported by the grantor, and tax deductions and losses arising from transactions between the owner and the trust would be ignored. See Revenue Ruling 85-13; IRS Notice 97-24.

    1. What is a "foreign" trust?: new rules provided in the 1996 Small Business Job Protection Act clarify whether a trust is considered foreign or domestic. The new rules provide that a trust will be considered a "United States person" if:

> a) A court within the United States is able to exercise primary supervision over the administration of the trust, and
>
> b) One or more U.S. fiduciaries have the authority to control all substantial decisions of the trust. IRC §7701(a)(30)(E).
>
> IRC §7701(a)(31)(B) provides that the term "foreign trust" means any trust other than one that meets the tests above. Trusts formed and existing before December 31, 1996 are still determined to be foreign or domestic under the old rules for determining residence, which were much more complicated and required a consideration of a long list of factors.

    2. Who is a "grantor": the IRS interprets IRC §672-679 to mean that the following persons are considered "grantors" under the rules:

> a) Any person who creates and funds a trust;
>
> b) Any person who directly or indirectly makes a gratuitous transfer of money or property to a trust;
>
> c) Any person who acquires an interest in a trust in a nongratuitous transfer from a person who is a grantor of a trust;
>
> d) An investor who acquires an interest in a fixed investment trust from a grantor of the trust. IRS Notice 97-34, 1997-25 Internal Revenue Bulletin; IRC §672-679.

    3. Who is a "beneficiary": the same IRS Notice, 97-34, also gives the IRS position that a beneficiary of a trust includes any person that could possibly benefit (directly or indirectly) from the trust at any time (including any person who could benefit if the trust were amended), whether or not the person is named in the trust instrument as a beneficiary and whether or not the person can receive a distribution from the trust in the current year. IRC §679(c).

How is Tax Paid:

    1. U.S. Beneficiaries & Grantors: a U.S. person who transfers property to a foreign trust that has a beneficiary who is a U.S. citizen or resident is taxed on any income that the transferred property generates during the year. This tax applies regardless of whether the transferor is a beneficiary or grantor of the trust. (See IRC §672(f)). Furthermore, there would be no taxable "exchange" of property with the trust, and the tax basis of property transferred to the trust would not be stepped-up for depreciation purposes.

a) An exception to this rule exists if fair market value is received in exchange for the asset transferred, and where the transferor recognizes the full amount of gain on the transfer. IRC §679(a)(2)(B).

    2. "Principal Purpose" test for Transfer: a gratuitous transfer under IRC

§679 includes any direct or indirect transfer that is structured with a principal purpose of avoiding the application of IRC §679 or IRC §6048 (see Notice 97-34, 1997-25 IRB p.23).

3. Look through rules: a foreign trust shall be treated as having a U.S. beneficiary unless (1) under the trust terms, no part of the income or corpus of the trust may be paid or accumulated to or for the benefit of a U.S. person, and (2) if the trust were terminated during the year, no part of the income or corpus could be paid to or for the benefit of a U.S. person. IRC §679(c)(1)

a) Other legal entities: a foreign trust is treated as having a U.S. beneficiary if an amount is paid or accumulated to or for the benefit of a foreign corporation (if more than 50% of the corporation is owned by U.S. shareholders), a trust that has a U.S. beneficiary, a partnership that has a U.S. partner, or U.S. beneficiary of an estate. IRC §679 (c)(2).

X. Recognition of Gain on Transfers to Foreign Non-grantor Trusts: IRC §684

A. Introduction. Section 684 was added to the tax code by the Taxpayer Relief Act of 1997 as a further barrier to use of foreign trusts, which is perceived by the IRS as one of the most utilized methods of tax evasion by U.S. citizens.

B. Who is Taxed. If a U.S. person transfers property to a foreign trust, IRC §684 treats such transfer as a sale or exchange of the property for its fair market value, and the U.S. person has to recognize gain to the extent the excess of the property's fair market value over its adjusted basis in the transferor's hands.

This gain recognition rule doesn't apply to a transfer to the extent that any person is treated as the trust's owner under IRC §671. When a U.S. trust becomes a foreign trust, it's treated as having transferred all its assets to a foreign trust. That means that the trust's appreciated property is treated as being sold on the date the trust becomes a foreign trust, and gain must be recognized on that date.

PART II: TAXES ON U.S. SOURCE INCOME

I. Taxes on U.S. Source Income of Non-resident Alien Individuals, Foreign Corporations, Partnerships, LLCs, Trusts, and Estates:

A. 30% Tax on U.S. Source "Fixed, Determined, Annual or Periodic" Income. IRC § 871, 881, and 882 impose a 30% flat tax on most kinds of income derived from U.S. sources earned by non-resident individuals or foreign business entities, trusts, and estates if the income is not "connected with a United States business". The tax applies to the following items of income:

(1) Interest, dividends, rents, salaries, wages, premiums, annuities, com-

pensations, remunerations, emoluments, and other fixed or determinable annual or periodical gains, profits, and income;

(2) Certain types of original issue discount on debt instruments;

(3) Gains from the sale or exchange of patents, copyrights, secret processes and formulas, good will, trademarks, trade brands, franchises, etc.

(4) Gains from the disposal of timber, coal, and domestic iron ore.

This tax does NOT apply to capital gains from securities trading.

B. Special Rule for 183 Day Non-resident Aliens: If the non-resident individual or business entity is engaged in a trade or business in the United States, IRC §871 and 881 do not apply because the individual or business will be taxed on all income connected to that business at the normal tax rates for individuals, corporations, trusts, etc. IRC §871(b), 882(a). For non-resident individuals only, a 30% capital gains tax applies to gains from the sale of all capital assets which are considered U.S. source capital assets, if the non-resident individual is physically present in the U.S. for more than 183 days in any calendar year. IRC § 871(a)(2). There is no similar provision found within the IRC §881 for foreign corporations. The 30% rate is higher than the top tax rate that is paid by U.S. residents and citizens (28%).

C. Exemptions: one of the most notable and useful exceptions to the 30% tax is IRC §871(h) (and 881(c) for foreign corporations), which provides an exemption from tax for "portfolio debt investments". The purpose of the exemption is to allow U.S. borrowers to compete for foreign loans on the international marketplace. A number of highly technical and legal requirements must be met to qualify as portfolio debt.

D. Tax Treaties: the United States has many tax treaties, which reduce the rate of tax to a low of 0% and a high of 25%. To qualify for the treaty benefit, however, usually means that the recipient is also subject to local tax in the country of its domicile. Because of this principle, most true "tax havens" do not have tax treaties with the U.S.

II. Collecting a Double Tax on Foreign Shareholders — the Branch Profits Tax:

A. Introduction: If a foreign corporation operates a U.S. business through a branch office in the U.S., although the income of the foreign corporation connected with the U.S. business is taxable under IRC §882, if the foreign corporation pays dividends to foreign shareholders from the earnings and profits generated in the U.S., usually the foreign shareholder fails to pay the U.S. tax due on those dividends. This is because the IRS has no realistic mechanism to collect the tax due. This allows foreign business owners to operate a business in the U.S. and only pay a single level of tax on the business profits. Contrast this to the double tax paid by U.S. shareholders on the business profits of a domestic corporation. (E.g. the corporation pays tax, and the shareholders pay tax on the dividends.)

B. Who is Taxed and How is Tax Paid: In order to try to collect the second level of tax on foreign shareholders, IRC §884 imposes a tax on foreign corporations at a rate of 30 % of what is called the dividend equivalent amount for the tax year. A foreign corporation's "dividend equivalent amount" is its effectively connected earnings and profits attributable to its U.S. business (adjusted for increases or decreases in the net equity of its U.S. trade or business.) IRC §884(b). The IRS can attempt to collect this amount by legal processes directed at the foreign corporation's U.S. branch. A tax treaty between a foreign country and the United States won't exempt a foreign corporation from the branch profits tax unless the treaty is an income tax treaty, and the foreign corporation is a qualified resident of the foreign country.

III. Taxes on Sales of U.S. Real Property (and Real Property Holding Corporations) By Foreign Persons

A. Sale of U.S. Real Property and Real Property Holding Corporations by Foreign Persons: IRC § 897

The gain or loss of a nonresident alien or a foreign corporation from the sale of a United States real property interest is treated as if the taxpayer were engaged in a trade or business within the United States during the tax year and as if the gain or loss were effectively connected with the trade or business. IRC §897(a)(1).

"United States Real Property Interest" means an interest in real property (including an interest in a mine, well, or other natural deposit) located in the United States or the Virgin Islands. This interest can also be any interest (other than an interest solely as a creditor) in any domestic corporation, unless the taxpayer establishes that the corporation was at no time during the last 5 years a "United States real property holding corporation". IRC §897(c)(1).

The term "United States Real Property Holding Corporation" means any corporation, whether foreign or domestic, if the fair market value of its United States Real Property interests are at least 50 % of its total assets. IRC §897(c)(2). Special exceptions and exemptions apply in some situations, and for Real Estate Investment Trusts.

B. Withholding of Tax on Dispositions of United States Real Property Interests: IRC §1445

IRC §1445 requires that the transferee (Buyer) of a U.S. real property interest from a foreign transferor must withhold 10 % of the sale price (amount realized). IRC §1445(a).

Withholding is not required under the following circumstances:

(1) If the transferor supplies the transferee with an affidavit stating that he is not a foreign person and supplying his taxpayer identification number. IRC §1445(b)(2)

(2) If the transferor, a corporation, supplies an affidavit stating that it is not a United States real property holding corporation or that it possesses no United States real property interests. IRC §1445(b)(3).

(3) If the transferee receives a qualifying statement from the IRS asserting that the transferor has no outstanding withholding liability and has either reached an agreement with the IRS or is exempt from taxes imposed by IRC §871(b)(1) or 882(a)(1). IRC §1445(b)(4)
(4) When the amount realized does not exceed $300,000 and the transferee intends to use the property as a residence. IRC §1445(b)(5)
(5) If the property disposed of its stock regularly traded on an established securities market. IRC §1445(b)(6)

C.   Liability of Transferee: If the transferee of property does not withhold the tax imposed by IRC §897, the transferee is liable for any tax due, thereby requiring other taxpayers to become tax collectors!

IV. Foreign Insurance Excise Taxes: (commercial annuity, life & casualty policies)

Section 4371 imposes a tax on the premiums paid for each insurance or reinsurance policy, indemnity bond or annuity contract issued by a foreign insurer or reinsurer. The tax rate for casualty insurance policies and indemnity bonds issued to or for an insured is 4 %; and for life insurance, sickness, accident, and reinsurance policies and annuity contracts, the rate is 1 %.

PART III: OUTBOUND TRANSACTIONS & REPORTING OBLIGATIONS

I. Recognition of Gain upon Transfers to Foreign Entities

A. New General Rule: Effective January 1, 1998, any transfer of appreciated property by a U.S. person to any foreign trust, corporation, estate, partnership, or LLC triggers taxable recognition of the gain in the year of transfer. IRC §367(f).

B. The Old Rule—Excise Tax: Before the 1997 Taxpayer Relief Act was passed, IRC §1491 required that a 35% excise tax be paid on any transfer of property with built-in gain to any foreign trust, corporation, estate, or partnership. IRC §1491 to 1494 were repealed by the Act.

II. Reporting of Transfers of Money and Other Property to Foreign Trusts:

A. Requirements: IRC §6048(a) requires any U.S. person who directly or indirectly transfers money or other property (with no gain built-in) to a foreign trust must report the transfer.
   1. "Principal Purpose" test for Transfer: a gratuitous transfer under IRC §679 includes any direct or indirect transfer that is structured with a principal purpose of avoiding the application of IRC §679 or IRC §6048 (see Notice 97-34, 1997-25 IRB p.23).

B. Failure to Report: Failure to report results in a 35% penalty tax on the transfer under IRC §6677(a).

C. Loans & Other Qualified Obligations Received from Trusts:

Congress was concerned that taxpayers might use trust obligations to avoid taxes under IRC §679 and reporting under IRC §6048 (see Notice 97-34, 1997-25 IRB p.23-24). Therefore, they enacted the following rules:

    1. The obligation is nontaxable (under the '679(a)(2)(b) exception for transfers for FMV where gain is recognized by transferor) if the obligation is a "qualified obligation".

        a) "Qualified obligations" must: (1) be in writing; (2) not exceed 5 year term; (3) payments made in US dollars; (4) interest yield must not be less than 100% of federal rate and not greater than 130%; (5) the transferor reports the status of the obligation including principal and interest payments on Form 3520 for each year the obligation is outstanding.

        Annuity contracts cannot be considered qualified obligations.

III. Reporting of Distributions & Loans received from Foreign Trusts: IRC §6048(c)

A. Distributions Received by a US Taxpayer: Generally, any US person who receives a distribution, either directly or indirectly, from a foreign trust after August 20, 1996 must report on form 3520 the name of the trust, aggregate amount of distributions received during the year, etc. Again, failure to report results is a 35% penalty tax on the gross amount of the distribution.

    1. "<u>Distribution</u>" includes gratuitous transfers of money or property, and includes distributions of trust corpus as well as trust income.

        a) "<u>Received</u>" includes actual or constructive receipts. For example, if a US beneficiary uses a <u>credit card</u> and the charges are paid or otherwise satisfied by a foreign trust or guaranteed or secured by the assets of a foreign trust, the amount charged on the card will be treated as a distribution to the US beneficiary and must be reported under this section. <u>Checks</u> written on a foreign trust's accounts also treated as distributions received.

B. Loans to US Grantors and US Beneficiaries: IRC §643(i) provides that (with some exceptions) if a foreign trust directly or indirectly makes a loan of cash or securities to a US grantor or a US beneficiary (or anyone related to them) of the trust, the amount of the loan will be treated as a distribution to that grantor or beneficiary.

IV. Information Returns Applicable to Foreign Trusts: IRC §6048

A. Return Required for Transfers: An information report setting forth the amount of money or property transferred to the trust, the identity of the trust, and the identity of each trustee and beneficiary must be filed with IRS within 90 days of the occurrence of: (1) the creation of a foreign trust by a U.S. person; (2) the transfer of money or property to a foreign trust by a U.S. person; (3) the death of a U.S. person who owned any portion of a foreign trust; or, (4) the death of a U.S. person whose gross estate included any portion of a foreign trust. The return must be filed by one of the following parties: (1) the grantor in the case of the creation of an inter vivos trust, (2) the transferor in the case of a reportable transfer other than a transfer by reason of death, or (3) the executor of the decedent's estate in any other case.

B. Annual Return Requirement for U.S. Owners: If any U.S. person is considered the owner of a foreign trust able year (based on the grantor trust rules of IRC §671-679), that person is responsible to ensure that the trust makes a return for such year which sets forth a full and complete accounting of all trust activities and operations for the year, including the name of the United States agent for such trust, and any other information required by the IRS.

C. Exceptions: Notice is not required for fair market value sales, or for transfers to trusts described in IRC §402(b), 404(a)(4), 404A, or 501(c)(3) (qualified employer's retirement plans and public charitable trusts).

D. Required Forms: The returns for reportable events must be made on form 3520, while U.S. owners must file form 3520-A annually.

E. Penalties: If the return isn't filed on or before the 90th day after a reportable event, or (2) doesn't include all the information required or includes incorrect information, a penalty of 35% of the gross reportable amount applies. If any failure continues for more than 90 days after the IRS mails notice of the failure to the person required to pay the penalty, an additional penalty of $10,000 for each 30-day period during which the failure continues is tacked on. However, the penalty section 6677(a) for any failure can't exceed the gross reportable amount. IRC §6677 provides the rules for penalties for the reporting required by IRC §6048.

The returns required by U.S. owners subject to a reduced penalty of 5% of the portion of the trust assets owned by the U.S. owner.

V. Information Returns for Officers, Directors, and Shareholders of Foreign Personal Holding Companies: IRC §6035

A. Requirement: IRC §6035 requires each U.S. citizen or resident who is an officer, director, or 10% shareholder of a corporation that was a foreign personal holding company for any tax year to file a return setting forth the shareholder information, the income information, and other information required by the IRS. (For the definition of a foreign personal holding company, see Part I, Section II above).

B. Information Required: Shareholder information includes the name and address of each person who at any time during the tax year held any share in the corporation, a description of each class of shares and the total number of shares of the class outstanding at the close of the tax year, the number of shares of each class held by each person, and any changes in the holdings of shares during the tax year.

The income information includes the gross income, deductions, credits, taxable income, and undistributed foreign personal holding company income of the corporation for the tax year.

C. Penalties for Failure to File: each U.S. citizen, resident, or person required to file this return by IRC § 6035, 6046, or 6046A, who fails to timely file the return, or who files an incomplete return, is subject to a penalty of $10,000, unless the failure is due to reasonable cause. If any failure to file continues for more than 90 days after the day the IRS mails notice of the failure to the U.S. person, an additional penalty of $10,000 for each 30-day period during which the failure continues applies. The increase in any penalty can't exceed $50,000. But, for a return required under IRC §6035, the penalty is $1,000 rather than $10,000, and the increased penalty for continued failure doesn't apply. Criminal penalties may also apply if criminal intent can be proved by the IRS.

D. Required Form: The information required by IRC §6035, 6038, and 6046 must be provided on IRS Form 5471, which the IRS estimates on its official instructions to be the following: Record keeping: 129.5 hours; Learning about the law or the form: 31.25 hours; Preparing and sending the form to the IRS: 38 hours;

Total time: 198.75 hours, or 8.25 days! Are they serious? Yes they are!

VI. Reporting on Foreign Transfers and Ownership in Foreign Entities: IRC §6038

A. Controlled Foreign Entities: IRC §6038 of the tax code requires every U.S. person to furnish information on any foreign business entity which such person controls. The term "U.S. person" is defined in IRC §7701(a)(30) to mean a U.S. citizen, or resident, and any domestic partnership, corporation, estate or trust. The term "foreign business entity" includes corporations and partnerships. For purposes of this reporting requirement the term "control" means ownership of 50% or more of the total combined voting power of all stock, or more than 50% of the total value of all the classes of stock of a corporation. If you are in "control" of a U.S. corporation, trust, or partnership which is required to provide this information, you automatically become a "required person" subject to penalties for failure to provide this information if the corporation, trust, or partnership which you control does not provide the information.

B. Information Required: The information required in the report includes the name, place of business, the type of business, the country of incorporation, any undistributed earnings of the corporation, and a balance sheet listing assets, liabilities, and capital. The person must also provide information on (1) transactions between themselves and the controlled entity; (2) transactions between the controlled entity and any other corporation or partnership that the person controls; (3) transactions between the person and any other U.S. person owning 10% or more of the value of any class of stock outstanding of a foreign corporation (or a 10% interest in a foreign partnership); and (4) a list showing the name, address, and number of shares owned by, every U.S. person who was a shareholder of record at any time during the year at least 5% of any class of stock of the corporation (or the partnership). These requirements force any U.S. person required to file this form to become an IRS informant on all other U.S. shareholders of the corporation, or you will face penalties for failure to provide the information "requested"!

C. Penalty for Failure to File: If a person fails to furnish the required information for any foreign business entity, then the person is subject to a penalty of $10,000 for each annual accounting period for which the failure exists. If the failure continues for more than 90 days after the day on which the IRS mails notice of the failure to the U.S. person, then an additional penalty of $10,000 must be paid for each 30-day period (or fraction thereof) during which the failure continues for any annual accounting period after the expiration of the 90-day period. The additional penalty may not exceed $50,000.

D. Required Form 5471: the IRS requires that this information be provided on Form 5471. (See Part VI above).

VII. Notice of Certain Transfers to Foreign Persons: IRC §6038B

A. Requirement: Under IRC §6038B, each U.S. person who transfers property to a foreign corporation in an exchange described in IRC §332, 351, 354, 355, 356, or 361, must provide information on the exchange or distribution. These sections mainly concern capitalization, merger, liquidation, and reorganization transactions. If a U.S. corporation or other business entity makes a distribution in complete liquidation to a non U.S. person, the U.S. person also must furnish to the IRS information on the distribution.

B. Exceptions: At the time this guide was written, transfers of cash to a corporation not falling within any of the above mentioned code sections are not required to be reported if the transferor owns less than 10% of the stock of the corporation at and after the time of transfer. Regulations IRC §1.6038B-1(b)(3).

C. Transfers to Foreign Partnerships: IRC §6038B also requires reporting by a U.S. person who transfers property to a foreign partnership as a contribution to capital (Section 721) or in any other contribution described in IRS regulations, if the U.S. person holds (directly or indirectly) at least a 10% interest in the partnership; or, if the value of the property transferred exceeds $100,000.

D. Penalty for Failure to File: If a U.S. person fails to properly file Form 926, a penalty of 10% of the fair market value of the property at the time of the exchange applies. This penalty does not apply if the person shows that the failure is due to *reasonable cause* and not to willful neglect. The penalty for any exchange will not exceed $100,000 unless the failure for the exchange was due to intentional disregard. IRC §6038B(c).
Note: Federal courts have ruled that "reasonable cause" includes transactions for which a licensed attorney (or qualified tax practitioner) advises the client that the information is not required. See Ewing v. Commissioner, 91 T.C. 396, 423 (1988), affd. without published, opinion 940 F.2d 1534 (9th Cir. 1991).

E. Required Form: The information required by IRC §6038B must be provided on IRS Form 926.

VIII. U.S. Recipients of Large Foreign Gifts: IRC §6039F

A. Reporting Requirements: This new section requires US recipients of foreign gifts to report the receipt of gifts in the following categories:

1. <u>Gifts from foreign individuals & estates</u>: although IRC §6039F does not make a distinction for reporting purposes between gifts from a foreign individual or trust and gifts from a foreign corporation or partnership, IRS Notice 97-34 states that a US person is required to report gifts from foreign individuals and estates only if in excess of $100,000 per year (IRS Notice 97-34, 1997-25 I.R.B. also see 1997 Instructions for Form 3520).

2. <u>Gifts from foreign corporations or partnerships</u>: must be reported if the aggregate amount of purported gifts from all such entities exceeds $10,000 per year (' 6039F).

B. How Reported: The recipient must report the gifts by filing form 3520 annually. Failure to file the report results in a penalty equal to 5% of the value of the gift for each month the gift goes unreported, but cannot exceed 25%. In addition, the IRS has the option to determine how the gift should be treated for tax purposes. IRC §6039F.

C. Special Rule for Foreign Trusts: Any "gift" received from a foreign trust is deemed to be a distribution, and is reportable under IRC §6048(c) and not IRC §6039F.

IX. Reporting on Organizations and Reorganizations of Foreign Corporations with U.S. Shareholders: IRC §6046 and 6046A

A. Requirements: IRC §6046 requires a U.S. citizen or resident to file a return with the IRS if the U.S. citizen or resident (1) is an officer or director of a foreign corporation of which a U.S. person meets certain stock ownership requirements (see next paragraph); (2) meets the stock ownership requirements for a foreign corporation; (3) is a U.S. shareholder under IRC §953(c); or (4) becomes a U.S. citizen while meeting the stock ownership requirements.

A person will meet the stock ownership requirements if that person owns 10 % or more of the total combined voting power of all classes of stock of the corporation or the total value of the stock of the corporation. IRC §6046(a)(2). Stock owned both directly and indirectly is taken into account when determining ownership percentages. IRC §6046(c). The return must be filed within 90 days of the date when the person meets the stock ownership requirements. IRC §6046(d).

B. Foreign Partnerships: IRC §6046A requires any U.S. person file a return with IRS if the U.S. person acquires or disposes of an interest in a foreign partnership, or whose proportional interest in a foreign partnership substantially changes. However, this return requirement only applies if a 10 % or larger interest in the partnership is involved. IRC §6046A(a). The return must be filed within 90 days of the ownership change. IRC §6046A(c).

C. Penalty for Failure to File: Each U.S. citizen, resident, or person required to file this return who fails to timely file the return, or who files an incomplete return, is subject to a penalty of $10,000, unless the failure is due to reasonable cause. If any failure to file continues for more than 90 days after the day the IRS mails notice of the failure to the U.S. person, an additional penalty of $10,000 for each 30-day period during which the failure continues applies. The increase in any penalty can't exceed $50,000. IRC §6679.

D. Required Form: The information required by this section must be provided on IRS Form 5471.

PART IV: MISCELLANEOUS SPECIAL BENEFITS

A. U.S. Possessions: There are a variety of special rules in place for various U.S. possessions. Because of the vast number of special exceptions, this guide will not cover them all here. The only way to be sure all possibilities have been thoroughly investigated and considered is to obtain the assistance of a qualified international tax attorney. In general, the rules are designed to create favorable conditions for investment, trade, or local economic development. Since 1986, the possessions that qualify for special treatment are:

Puerto Rico
U.S. Virgin Islands
Guam
Midway Island
Federated States of Micronesia
Paloa
American Samoa
Wake Island
Johnston Island
The Northern Meridians
The Marshall Islands

Any time that one is considering doing business in these possessions or with residents of these possessions there may be opportunities for tax savings that should be fully considered.

PART V. SPECIAL TAX AVOIDANCE LAWS:

I. IRC §482 Transfer Pricing and General IRS Reallocation Authority among Related Parties:

A. Introduction: When two or more parties (either domestic or foreign) are owned or directly or indirectly controlled by the same interests, the IRS may allocate income, deductions, credits, or allowances among the parties in the manner which the IRS feels is necessary to prevent evasion of tax or to clearly reflect income. Because of the extremely broad scope of this provision, the IRS can invoke this law to reallocate items of income, deductions, or credits even in the absence of a tax avoidance motive.

B. Transfer Pricing: From this rather concise code section sprang a thicket of IRS regulations, which attempt to control intercompany or "transfer" pricing. The basic idea of transfer pricing is to force the individual branches or subsidiaries of large multinational corporations to buy, sell, borrow, and lend from each other at prices and on terms, which unrelated arms-length parties would use. In the absence of transfer pricing rules, today's international corporate empires could easily isolate profits in low-tax jurisdictions and decrease income (or increase credits or losses) in high-tax jurisdictions, thus increasing the overall profitability of the corporation. When determining whether two or more parties are "controlled" by the same interests, the IRS focuses on the substance of each transaction or relationship, and ignores formal legal control measures. Under the insanity of the IRS regulations, the IRS will reallocate income to a U.S. taxpaying corporation even if a foreign law prohibits the payment of income to the U.S. corporation from its foreign partner!

II. IRC §367 Elimination of International Tax-Free Capitalization, Reorganization and Liquidation Transactions:

A. Introduction: IRC §367 was enacted to prevent the transfer across international boundaries of appreciated assets, which would otherwise be tax-free under certain provisions of the tax code. IRC §367 applies to "outbound" transfers of property from a U.S. party or location to a foreign party, as well as "inbound" transfers of property used by a foreign taxpayer which are being transferred to a U.S. taxpayer. IRC §367(a) accomplishes the main purpose of this section by providing that if a U.S. person transfers property to a foreign corporation (in an exchange described in IRC §332, 351, 354, 355, 356, or 361), then the foreign corporation isn't considered to be a corporation for purposes of determining the extent to which gain is recognized on the transfer. In plain English, if any asset owned by a U.S. resident or citizen is transferred in an exchange described in the listed code sections, the U.S. person recognizes a taxable *gain* on the appreciation inherent in the asset. However, if the asset has a *loss*, the loss is not recognized at the time of transfer. There are some exceptions to the rule that gain is recognized, including an exception for property to be used by the foreign corporation in the conduct of an active business (but NOT if the property transferred is on the list of exceptions given in IRC §368(a)(3)(B).)

B.   Intellectual Property Transactions: IRC §367(d) was enacted to address abuses involving intellectual property developed in the U.S. by U.S. residents and then transferred to a foreign corporation once the actual fruits of the property are ready to be produced. Under IRC §367(d), a U.S. person who transfers manufacturing or marketing intangible property to a foreign person is treated as having sold the intangible property in exchange for U.S. source royalties for the life of the property held by the foreign transferee. This re-engineering of the income received by the U.S. person is usually an effective deterrent to large multi-national drug and chemical companies.

EXPATRIATION AND OFFSHORE RESIDENCY

STEPHEN D. HOLMES

Holmes Greenslade
Barristers & Solicitors
Phone: (604) 688-7861, Fax: (604) 688-0426
E-mail: sdh@holmesgreenslade.com

CAUTION!!! Please be advised that the below description of tax planning matters is by no means complete from a technical, legal or tax viewpoint. The memorandum is being provided for preliminary discussion purposes only and should in no way be treated as the provision of legal advice to be acted upon in any way. The efficacy of any tax plan based on the concepts described below will be largely dependent not only upon the soundness of the underlying tax planning concept, but as well upon the proper implementation of the plan including the order of the transactional steps, special provisions contained in any implementing documents, timely filing of certain compliance documents with tax authorities, the ongoing economic substance of the relationship established and compliance with the foreign law.

It is often considered the ultimate tax plan and the dream of many, to leave behind taxes and live in a tax haven. There are many reasons why one may wish to move to a tax haven:

1. Beautiful climate;
2. Lower cost of living;
3. No or lower taxes;
4. Less filings;
5. Less or no government forms;
6. Not paying lawyers and accountants for complex tax plans, which are still uncertain;
7. Privacy;
8. Less restrictions and regulations in regard to:
   (a) how to carry on business; and
   (b) type of investments;
9. Protection of assets:
   (a) eliminate uncertainty as to asset protection structure;
   (b) minimize court orders against you for contempt; and
   (c) superior laws to protect assets against creditor;

10. Miscellaneous:
  (a) ease of travel;
  (b) anti U.S. prejudice (i.e. hijackers);
  (c) acquisition of passport;
  (d) better/cheaper health plans;
  (e) improved retirement funding from government;
  (f) safety;
  (g) political aid;
  (h) religious benefits; and
  (i) family connection.

It is often thought that by moving offshore, one will automatically avoid the high taxes of Canada or the United States. Regrettably, this may not be correct. This appendix will briefly discuss the effect of changing ones residency, expatriation, an overview of the tax consequences, planning techniques and countries one could consider.

While there are no exact numbers of how many Canadians or Americans change residency or expatriate, it is undoubtedly growing. Further, it would increase if people were accurately informed of the alternative. The media often reports when certain high profile persons expatriate, including J. Paul Getty's grandson, a Campbell Soup heir or the former chairman of Sunkist Tuna. While there have been thousands of persons who have expatriated over the last five (5) years, it is not just the ultra-rich. In fact, the not so rich have even more reasons to expatriate. If you have enough money, your lifestyle is not affected by higher taxes as much as lower income earners. Further, with enough money, you can afford the more elegant expensive tax plans and potential litigation. The less rich cannot afford the cost or risk without substantially affecting their lifestyle. In addition, the very rich can afford to buy certain privacy, security and alternate homes.

Taxation

It is a fundamental premise in regard to U.S. taxation that a U.S. citizen will be taxed on their world income, notwithstanding they may not reside one (1) day per year in the United States. If one remains a citizen of the United States, they will remain liable to file U.S. tax returns no matter where they reside.

Canada takes a different approach. Canada only taxes the worldwide income of residents. If a Canadian changes residency, he is generally not obligated to pay Canadian tax or file tax returns unless they effectively earn income from Canadian sources.

For U.S. citizens to avoid U.S. taxes and filings, they could consider renouncing their citizenship. This is expatriation. The U.S. government recognized this as having substantial tax benefits and has passed legislation attempting to restrict the benefits for former U.S. citizens.

When a Canadian ceases being a resident of Canada, they may have to pay a "departure tax". They do not have to give up citizenship. With limited exceptions, the former Canadian resident will be deemed to have disposed of his world assets and will be obligated to pay tax on any accrued profit. As such, Canada ensures that it obtains tax on any assets, which may have appreciated during the period of time while they were a Canadian resident. Thereafter, the Canadian tax system is of limited interest to the non-resident. The present United States system does not have a departure tax, though, this has been proposed.

Section 877 of the U.S. Income Tax Code (the "Code") creates a special tax for expatriates, with annual filings and penalties. It was intended to create a disincentive to expatriation. If one gave up ones citizenship with the principle purpose to avoid U.S. taxes, the person will be taxed at the greater of an alternative tax or the amount a non-resident alien would be taxed for ten (10) years or possibly longer. If income is connected with a trade or business in the United States, it will be taxed a graduated rate. If it is not effectively connected with a trade or business in the U.S., it will be taxed at thirty (30%) percent. This would generally include U.S. interest, dividends and royalties. An expatriate will be taxed on any gains from the exchange or sale of property, stock or from debt obligations of domestic corporations from U.S. persons. Further, income or gains from foreign corporations will be taxed if in the two (2) year prior period prior to expatriation, the former citizen owned fifty (50%) or more of the voting shares, or fifty (50%) percent or more of the total value of the shares. There are also special rules that deal with exchanges of gifts.

The Code provides that the presumption that one expatriated for a tax purpose is irrefutable unless you are a "prescribed" person. The presumption will apply if:

1. Within the prior five (5) years, your average net income was greater than $100,000.00. This is the 1996 figure and since, has been increased annually based upon a cost of living; or
2. Your net worth was greater than $500,000.00. Again, this number has increased from 1996 based upon a cost of living adjustment.

Even if the presumption applies, it can be avoided and therefore, potentially, the ten (10) years of filings and taxes. A prescribed person is a person who:

1. Had dual citizenship at birth or became a citizen in a reasonable period of time in the country where one was born, where ones spouse was born or ones parents were born;

2. Spent thirty (30) days or less per year in the U.S. over the last ten (10) years; or

3. Gave up ones citizenship before they were 18.5 years old.

A prescribed person must apply within one (1) year for a ruling. If they do not get an unfavourable ruling, the presumption will not apply and therefore, the potentially substantial taxes and filings of upwards of ten (10) years.

Even if one cannot avoid the presumption or is not a prescribed person, the expatriate can consider a number of strategies to avoid U.S. tax after expatriation. For example:

1. Do not hold U.S. assets or earn income directly from U.S. sources;

2. Do not sell U.S. assets for a ten (10) year period;

3. If you have a foreign corporation prior to expatriation or want U.S. assets to be held in one, make sure that it is not a controlled corporation. There are many de-control strategies which could be considered;

4. Use an offshore private annuity to potentially remove taxable assets out of the jurisdiction; and

5.   Borrow against assets.

Each of these structures are complex and there are many alternatives available so that when one expatriates, they can avoid U.S. income notwithstanding the presumption. Further, one could avoid the presumption by minimizing ones net worth and minimizing taxable income for the years prior to the expatriation.

A key planning point is that even if one expatriates and one cannot avoid the presumption, foreign assets are generally not taxed. Domestic assets and income are taxed. Therefore:

1.   Avoid U.S. source income and assets; and

2.   Consider the use of trusts, offshore corporations and foundations through de-controlled structures.

Renouncing and Change of Residency

For a U.S. citizen to renounce, they must give a prescribed oath to a U.S. consular officer. This must be conducted outside of the United States, given voluntarily and be in a precise form. There are alternative ways to expatriate, including obtaining foreign citizenship, joining a hostile army or being convicted of treason.

For a Canadian wishing to give up residency, there are no specific forms or oath required. However, it is very important that one ensures that one is not deemed a resident of Canada. Canada can consider one a resident and therefore, taxable whether or not one spends time in Canada or not. This is particularly the case if one does not have the legal right to reside in another country. There are specific issues which Canada Custom and Revenue Agency will consider in determining whether one remains a resident of Canada. These are also matters which must be considered by Americans to ensure that they do not inadvertently fall within the U.S. system as a resident alien. Matters to consider include:

1. Status of former principle residences;
2. Credit cards;
3. Bank accounts;
4. Club associations;
5. Driver's license;
6. Bank accounts;
7. Location of possessions;
8. Roots in the community;
9. Time spent in the jurisdiction; and
10. Family location.

Whether one is an American or a Canadian, one must carefully plan how they depart to ensure that they are not going to be deemed a resident of their former jurisdiction.

Going Home

A Canadian, since they are not giving up their passport, can return to Canada at anytime. This may not be the case for former Americans. Section 362 of the *Federal Immigration Act* provides that a former citizen who officially renounces and it is determined it was to avoid tax is a person "excludable". Note, this must be determined by the Attorney General and the burden is not on the former citizen. I am not aware of this section being applied. One should note three (3) further things. It will be difficult for the government, without the presumptions, to determine if there was a tax motive. Secondly, preventing the entrance of citizens of a foreign country who have not broken any laws, could affect U.S. international relations. Thirdly, it only applies when one renounces, not from a loss of citizenship for another reason. As such, if one "lost" ones citizenship by obtaining a foreign citizenship, one could argue that the section should not apply as one had not applied to expatriate.

It is important prior to expatriating that one has obtained the right to reside in a country and have documents which will allow one to travel. One should note that residency, passports and travel documents are not synonymous. Residency does not give you a passport. Often you have to reside in a jurisdiction to obtain a passport. However, in some cases, you do not even have to have ever been to the country to obtain a passport.

Choosing a Country

In choosing a country, one must consider many factors, including:

1. Health care;
2. Transportation;
3. Language;
4. Banking;
5. Hobbies;
6. Laws;
7. Stability;
8. Secrecy;
9. Asset protection;
10. Access to other countries;
11. Cost of living; and
12. Work.

Many countries have specific programs designed to provide passports and/or residency. These change constantly and must be reviewed prior to departure.

It is ironic that Canadians would leave Canada to avoid taxes, while for Americans, Canada could be a tax haven. Further, from a culture shock and convenience point of view, it is often considered the best choice to reside upon expatriation. It also has a number of tax advantages. Subject to the laws not changing, a new immigrant, through the use of trusts and offshore corporations, could potentially never pay Canadian tax on off-shore investment income. Canada's tax laws permit the formation of discretionary trusts, which if the trust is not resident in Canada will not be taxed. Further, the income once it becomes capital can be paid to the Canadian resident tax-free. If you are carrying on an international active business, the profits can be brought back to a Canadian company via an operating/holding company in Barbados and pay a maximum of two and one-half (2.5%) percent tax. Approximately $25,000.00 in dividends from a Canadian corporations can be paid from active income without the person paying Canadian income tax. The sale of shares by a Canadian Small Business Corporation which have been held by a Canadian resident is tax free for the first $500,000.00 of capital gain per shareholder. If the shares were held by a Barbados trust, there may be no tax in Canada on the sale of those shares.

To become a Canadian citizen and obtain its passport, you must first become a landed immigrant and spend approximately three (3) years in Canada. You do not have to become a citizen and can travel while an immigrant, but if you do not reside in Canada, your visa could be cancelled. A passport will not be cancelled just because you do not live in Canada. There are a number of ways to obtain landed immigrant status in Canada. There is a priority system, quotes and points. Generally speaking, investors and family members will get a priority over entrepeneurs who will get priority over retired persons. An investor will have to have a net worth in excess of $500,000.00 (Cdn) and invest an equal amount in a government sponsored fund. An entrepreneur has no dollar minimum which they must invest, but they must have the ability to start/operate a business that will employ him and contribute to the economy.

Belize does not have income tax and has specific residency and passport programs. There are many countries that you can visit without a visa if one has a Belize passport. One can "buy" residency for any individual for approximately $15,000.00 with the requirement of a $25,000.00 investment. You will obtain a passport and the oath can be taken out of the country.

The St. Kitts/Nevis program provides that for approximately a $35,000.00 fee plus a requirement to own real estate in excess of $150,000.00 or obtain a $200,000.00 / 0% interest treasury bond or invest/own $250,000.00 in certain specific programs, one can obtain a passport.

In Dominica, fees are between $15,000.00 and $25,000.00 with an investment requirement of $35,000.00 to $50,000.00. Again, it is a zero tax jurisdiction and a passport can be obtained.

Ireland will only tax income received by non-domiciled persons. It is relatively simple to obtain a residency.

Bahamas is a zero tax jurisdiction and one can obtain annual residency permits for approximately $5,000.00. To obtain a permanent right to reside, will require investments in excess of $500,000.00.

Turks & Caicos is a zero tax jurisdiction which also provides for annual residency permits. Permanent residency can be obtained if one acquires real estate of upwards of $125,000.00 depending on where it is located.

Grenada is a country which is part of the Commonwealth and you can enter many countries without a visa. These include Canada, the United Kingdom, Norway, Sweden and Hong Kong. The cost to obtain a passport will be approximately $70,000.00 (US).

Expatriation or change of residency does not have to be a permanent decision, but it is undoubtedly a major decision. There are numerous potential advantages, not all of which are tax related. However, from a tax/immigration perspective, it is very important that this is a decision that is reviewed with a qualified professional before embarking on this exciting alternative.

Appendix C

GLOSSARY OF BUSINESS TERMS AND ABBREVIATIONS

ADR. American Depositary Receipt.

ADR. An Advance Determination Ruling obtained upon application to the IRS. Used, for example, to determine if a multinational policy decision is tax compliant.

Adverse trustee. One who has a substantial, beneficial interest in the trust assets as well as the income or benefits derived from the trust. A trustee that is related to the creator by birth, marriage or in an employer/employee relationship. The term is generally found in the "business" trust or dual trust program.

Annuitant. The beneficiary or beneficiaries (in a last-to-die arrangement) of an annuity who receives a stream of payments pursuant to the terms of the annuity contract.

Annuity. A tax-sheltering vehicle. An unsecured contract between the company and the annuitant(s) that grows deferred-free and is used to provide for one's later years. All income taxes are deferred until maturing of the annuity. Capital gains and income accumulate tax deferred. Results in a stream of payments made to the annuitant during his or her lifetime under the annuity agreement. Taxes are paid on the income, interest earned and the capital gains but only to the extent as and when they are received. Currently, there is no annual limit on purchases, but there is no tax credit for purchases. An annuity is not an insurance policy.

Anstalt. A Liechtenstein entity.

AP. Asset protection.

APT. See Asset Protection Trust.

Asset forfeiture. In context of the material herein, asset forfeiture refers to seizure of assets without due process by governmental enforcement agencies operating under protection of anti-drug, anti-money laundering, and/or anti-crime legislation. The asset forfeiture phenomena is a result of legislation granting police agencies the right to seize assets based on little more than an agent's alleging that such assets may be related to a crime. In many cases the agency seizing goods is entitled to keep all or a portion of the assets to enhance their own operating budgets.

Asset manager. A person appointed by a written contract between the IBC (or the exempt company) or the APT and that person to direct the investment program. It can be a fully discretionary account or limitations can be imposed by the contract under the terms of the APT or by the officers of the IBC. Fees to the asset manager can be based on performance achieved, trading commissions or a percentage of the valuation of the estate under his or her management.

Asset Protection Trust (APT). A special form of irrevocable trust, usually created (settled) offshore for the principal purposes of preserving and protecting part of one's wealth offshore against creditors. Title to the asset is transferred to a person named the trustee. Generally used for asset protection and usually tax neutral. Its ultimate function is to provide for the beneficiaries of the APT.

Authorized capital. With respect to a corporation or company (IBC), the sum value of the aggregate of par value of all shares which the company is authorized to issue. (Also see flight capital.)

Badges of Fraud. Conduct that raises a strong presumption that it was undertaken with the intent to delay, hinder or defraud a creditor.

Bank of International Settlements (BIS). Structured like America's Federal Reserve Bank, controlled by the Basel Committee of the G-10 nations' Central Banks, it sets standards for capital adequacy among the member central banks.

Bearer shares. Shares of common or preferred stock issued from a valid corporation to bearer, meaning that the person holding the stock certificate owns the shares. Bearer shares are much like currency, if you are holding it, it generally belongs to you.

Beneficial interest or ownership. Not a direct interest, but rather through a nominee, holding legal title on behalf of the beneficial owner's equitable interest. Provides privacy and avoids use of one's own name for transactions.

Beneficiary. The person(s), company, trust or estate named by the grantor, settler or creator to receive the benefits of a trust in due course upon conditions, which the grantor established by way of a trust deed. An exception would be the fully discretionary trust. The beneficiary could be a charity, foundation and/or person(s) which or who are characterized by "classes" in terms of their order of entitlement hierarchy.

BIS. See Bank of International Settlements.

Board of Trustees. A board acting as a trustee of a trust or as advisors to the trustee depending upon the language of the trust indenture. Also see

Committee of Advisors.

British public company. See PLC.

British West Indies (BWI). All of the Eastern Caribbean Islands, such as St Kitts & Nevis, Antigua, etc., and including the UK-dependent territories of Anguilla, the British Virgin Islands (BVI), the Cayman Islands, Montserrat, Grenada, St Vincent's and the Grenadines, and the Turks and Caicos Islands.

Business trust. A trust created for the primary purpose of operating or engaging in a business. It is a person under the Internal Revenue Code (IRC). It must have a business purpose and actually function as a business.

BWI. See British West Indies.

Capital. See authorized capital or flight capital.

CARICOM. Caribbean Common Market. Consists of 14 sister-mem-ber countries of the Caribbean community. Members include: Antigua and Barbuda, Bahamas, Barbados, Belize, Dominica, Grenada, Guyana, Jamaica, Montserrat, St. Kitts and Nevis, St. Lucia, St. Vincent, Surinam, Trinidad and Tobago.

CATF. Caribbean Financial Action Task Force, a regional group comprised of 27 members states and six co-operating and supporting nations organized to combat money laundering.

Certified public accountant (CPA). A term used in the U.S. to designate a licensed qualified accountant, its international counterpart is the chartered accountant.

CFC. See controlled foreign corporation.

Committee of Advisors. Provides nonbinding advice to the trustee of a trust and/or the trust protector. Friendly towards settler but must still maintain independence. In cases where there is too close a relationship with the settler, the committee can be construed as an alter ego of the settler.

Committee of trust protectors. An alternative to utilizing merely one trust protector. Friendly towards settler, but must remain independent. See trust protector.

Common Law. The early English system of case law as opposed to statutory law.

Companies Act or Ordinance. Legislation enacted by a tax haven to provide for the incorporation, registration and operation of international business companies (IBCs). More commonly found in the Caribbean tax havens. For a typical example, read the Bahamas' International Business Company Act of 1989.

Company. A restricted corporation, i.e., an IBC or exempt company.

Contingent beneficial interest. An interest given to a beneficiary which is not fully vested by being discretionary. In theory, since they are inchoate interests, not truly gifting, they are unvested, they are not subject to an attachment by the beneficiary's creditor and are not reportable as an IRS form 709 gifting.

Controlled foreign corporation (CFC). An offshore company which, because of ownership or voting control of U.S. persons, is treated by the IRS as a U.S. tax reporting entity. IRC §951 and §957 collectively define the CFC as one in which a U.S. person owns 10 percent or more of a foreign corporation or in which 50 percent or more of the total voting stock is owned by U.S. shareholders collectively or 10 percent or more of the voting control is owned by U.S. persons.

CPA. See certified public accountant.

Creator. A person who creates a trust. Also see settler and grantor.

Current Account. An offshore, personal savings or checking account.

Custodian. A bank, financial institution or other entity that has the responsibility to manage or administer the custody or other safekeeping of assets for other persons or institutions.

Custodian trustee. A trustee that holds the trust assets in his or her name.

Declaration of trust. A document creating a trust; a trust deed.

Discretionary trust. A grantor trust in which the trustee has complete discretion as to who among the class of beneficiaries receives income and/or principal distributions. There are no limits upon the trustee or it would cease to be a discretionary trust. The letter of wishes could provide some "guidance" to the trustee without having any legal and binding effects. Provides flexibility to the trustee and the utmost privacy.

Donor. A transferor. One who transfers title to an asset by gifting.

EC. The European Commission of the European Union (EU).

Economic Recovery Act of 1981. See the Foreign Investor in Real Property Tax Act of 1980 (FIRPTA).

ECU. European Currency Unit.

EEA. European Economic Area.

EEC. European Economic Community.

EFTA. European Free Trade Area.

EMU. European Monetary Unit.

Estate. Interests in real and/or personal property.

EU. European Union; replaced by the European Commission (EC).

Euro. European Currency of the European Economic Community.

Ex parte. An application for an injunction filed and heard without notice to the other side to protect assets.

Expat. An expatriate.

Family holding trust. A trust that is created specifically to hold the family's assets consisting of real and/or personal property.

Family limited partnership (FLP). A limited partnership created for family estate planning and some asset protection. It is family controlled by the general partners. A highly appreciated asset is transferred into the FLP to achieve a capital gains tax reduction. Usually, the parents are the general partners holding a 1 to 2 percent interest. The other family members are the limited partners holding the balance of the interest in the partnership.

Family protective trust. A UK term. See Asset Protection Trust (APT).

FATF. Financial Action Task Force: agents against money-laundering.

FIRPTA. See Foreign Investor in Real Property Tax Act of 1980.

Flight capital. Money that flows offshore and likely never returns. Flight is exacerbated by a lack of confidence as government grows without bounds, the cost of government grows out of control and the federal deficit grows (over $5 billion) without the ability of Washington to cap it; it is precipitated further by increasing concerns over invasion of personal privacy, rampant litigation and the threats of further confiscatory direct and indirect taxes.

FLP. See family limited partnership.

Foreign. May be utilized in a geographic, legal or tax sense. When used geographically, it is that which is situated outside of the U.S. or is characteristic of a country other than the U.S.

Foreign Investor in Real Property Tax Act of 1980 (FIRPTA). Under FIRPTA and the Economic Recovery Act of 1981, unless an exemption is granted by the IRS, upon the sale of real property owned by offshore (foreign) persons, the agency, attorney or escrow officer handling the transaction is required to withhold capital gains taxes at the closing of the sale transaction. Unless withheld and submitted to the IRS, the party handling the sale transaction is personally liable for the taxes.

Foreign person. Any person, including a U.S. citizen, who resides outside the U.S. or is subject to the jurisdiction and laws of a country other than the U.S.

Foreign personal holding company (FPHC). Different than a controlled foreign corporation. Discuss with your CPA.

Forfeiture income. Supplemental governmental funding derived from asset forfeitures. See Asset forfeiture.

FPHC. See foreign personal holding company.

FPT. See family protective trust. Also see asset protection trust (APT).

Fraudulent conveyance. A transfer of an asset that violates the fraudulent conveyance statutes of the affected jurisdictions.

GmbH. A German form of a limited liability corporation. Gesellschaft mit beschrankte Haftung.

Grantor. A person who creates a trust or transfers real property to another entity. In a U.S. grantor trust, the person responsible for U.S. income taxes on the trust. May have a reversionary interest in a trust.

Grantor trust. A trust created by a grantor and taxed to that grantor (settlor).

High net worth (HNW) person. An individual with more than US500,000 in liquid assets to manage.

HNW. See high net worth person.

Homestead exemption. State or federal bankruptcy laws that protect one's residence from confiscation by a judgment creditor or loss in a personal bankruptcy.

IBC. A corporation. See international business company or exempt company.

IFC. See International Financial Center.

IMF. International Monetary Fund.

Inbound. Coming into the U.S.; onshore; such as funds being paid to a U.S. person from an offshore entity.

Incomplete gift. Where the settlor has reserved the right to add or delete beneficiaries to the trust, it is construed as an incomplete gift. See contingent beneficiary interest.

Independent trustee. A trustee who is independent of the settlor. Independence is generally defined as not being related to the settlor by blood, through marriage, by adoption or in an employer/employee relationship.

INTERFIPOL. International Fiscal Police. The tax crime counterpart to

INTERPOL.

International Business Company (IBC). A corporation formed (incorporated) under a "Company Act" of a tax haven, but not authorized to do business within that country of incorporation; intended to be used for global operations. Owned by member(s)/shareholder(s). Has the usual corporate attributes.

International Financial Center (IFC). A country identified as being a tax haven.

International Exempt Trust. A Nevis island term for a special type of an Asset Protection Trust (APT). Governed by the laws of Nevis.

INTERPOL. International Criminal Police Organization. The net-work of multinational law enforcement authorities established to exchange information regarding money laundering and other criminal activities. More than 125 member nations.

IRC. The U.S. Internal Revenue Code.

IRS. The U.S. Internal Revenue Service of the Treasury Department.

ITC. International Trading Company (Iceland.)

Layered trusts. Trusts placed in series where the beneficiary of the first trust is the second trust; used for privacy.

Layering. May be achieved with numerous combinations of entities. For example, 100 percent of the shares of an IBC being owned by the first trust, which has as its sole beneficiary a second trust.

LC. Another abbreviation for limited Liability Company. Also l.l.c. and l.c. are authorized in some states.

Letter of wishes. Guidance and a request to the trustee having no binding powers over the trustee. There may be multiple letters. They must be carefully drafted to avoid creating problems with the settlor or true settlor in the case of a grantor trust becoming a co-trustee. The trustee cannot be a "pawn" of the settlor or there is basis for the argument that there never was a complete renouncement of the assets. Sometimes referred to as a side letter.

Limited company. Not an international business company. May be a resident of the tax haven and is set up under a special company act with a simpler body of administrative laws.

Limited liability company (LLC and LC). Consists of member owners and a manager, at a minimum. Similar to a corporation that is taxed as a partnership or as an S-corporation. More specifically, it combines the more favorable characteristics of a corporation and a partnership. The LLC structure permits the complete pass-through of tax advantages and operational flexibility found in a partnership, operating in a corporate-style structure, with limited liability as provided by the state's laws. The LLC may be managed by members but need not be. It may be managed by a professional company manager. A caveat is in order: LLCs are in a state of embryonic evolution, without a clear body of case law and firm guidelines. They will generate much income for the legal community until they become an integral part of our tax, business and legal system.

Living trust. Revocable trust, for reduction of probate costs and to expedite sale of assets upon death of grantor. Provides no asset protection.

LLC. See limited liability company. Also seen in the form of L.L.C., l.l.c., L.C. (Utah) and l.c.

LLP. Limited liability partnership. A form of the LLC favored and used for professional associations, such as accountants and attorneys.

LLLP. Limited liability limited partnership. Intended to protect the general partners from liability. Previously, the general partner was a corporation to protect the principals from personal liability. Under the LLLP, an individual could be a general partner and have limited personal liability.

Ltd. An abbreviation for the word limited.

Mark. Abbreviation for German currency, the Deutche Mark.

Marital Partition Agreement. See Post Nupital Agreement.

Mavera injunction. A court injunction preventing the trustee for a trust from transferring trust assets pending the outcome of a law suit.

Member. An equity owner of a limited liability company ((LLC), limited liability partnership (LLP), limited liability limited partnership (LLLP) or a shareholder in an IBC.

Memorandum. The Memorandum of Association of an IBC, equivalent to articles of incorporation.

MLAT. See Mutual Legal Assistance Treaty.

Money laundering. Processes of placing "dirty money" into legitimate banks or business transactions to cleanse the money. Money laundering might be construed as a dynamic three-stage process that requires first a crime, then the moving of the funds generated from such crime and disguising the trail to foil pursuit; and third, making the money available to the criminal once again with its occupational and geographic origins hidden from view.

Mutual Legal Assistance Treaty (MLAT). An agreement among the U.S.

and many Caribbean countries for the exchange of information for the enforcement of criminal laws. U.S. tax evasion is excluded as not being a crime to the offshore countries. Nevis has not executed the Treaty.

Non-grantor trust. Usually an APT created by a NRA person on behalf of the U.S. beneficiaries.

NRA. Nonresident (of the U.S.) alien. Not a U.S. person as defined under the Internal Revenue Code (IRC).

OECD. Organization for Economic Cooperation and Development.

Offshore (OS). Offshore is an international term meaning not only out of your country (jurisdiction) but out of the tax reach of your country of residence or citizenship; synonymous with foreign, transnational, global, international, transworld and multi-national, though foreign is used more in reference to the IRS.

Offshore Financial Center. See international financial center (IFC). A more sophisticated tax haven.

OS. See offshore.

Outbound. Assets flowing offshore from the U.S.

Ownership. Ownership constitutes the holding or possession of limited liability company legal claim or title to an offshore asset.

Person. Any individual, branch, partnership, associated group, association, estate, trust, corporation, company, or other organization, agency or financial institution under the IRC.

PLC. A UK public limited company . Compare with the UK private limited company.

Portfolio manager. See asset manager.

Post Nupital Agreement. Also referred to as a Marital Partition Agreement. A legal document whereby a marial community agrees to divide its assets. Generally this type of agreement is used for asset protection and/or estate planning purposes.

Predatory litigation. Lawsuits generated and pursued on a contingency or commission basis by the legal firm representing the suing client. Predatory litigation is against the law in most countries but has become a huge boom business in the U.S.

Preferential transfer. A disposition of an asset that is unfair to other creditors of the transferor.

Pre-filing notice. Mailed by the IRS to parties (tax payers) who are believed to be participating in fraudulent trust programs. The notice requests that the receiver seek professional counsel before filing their next tax return.

Private banking. OS banking services for high net worth (HNW) persons.

Probate. The legal process for the distribution of the estate of a decedent.

Protector. See trust protector.

Pure equity trust. A special type of irrevocable trust marketed by promoters. The trust assets are obtained by an "exchange" of a certificate of beneficial interest in return for the assets, as opposed to traditional means, such as by gifting.

Pure trust. A contractual trust as opposed to a statutory trust, created under the Common Law. A pure trust is one in which there must be a minimum of three parties-the creator or settlor (never grantor), the trustee and the beneficiary-and each is a separate entity. A pure trust is claimed to be a lawful, irrevocable, separate legal entity.

Register. The register of international business companies (IBCs) and exempt companies maintained by the Registrar of a tax haven.

Registrar. The Registrar of Companies, a governmental body controlling the formation and renewal of companies created under their company act.

RICO. Racketeer, Influence and Corruption Organization Act of 1984.

Risk Planning. That element of an overall business strategy that relates to the reduction of risk. Risk reduction planning may take the form of something as simple as operating a sole-proprietor business under the umbrella of a corporate structure or entail something as complex as a series of domestic and offshore trusts, family limited partnerships and charitable foundations, coupled to corporate-type structures in multiple jurisdictions.

Rule against perpetuities. A legal limit on remote vesting of assets in the beneficiaries. May be void ab initio (from the beginning), a fixed term or determined on a "wait and see" basis.

S.A. See Société Anonyme.

Securities. Shares and debt obligations of every kind, including options, warrants, and rights to acquire shares and debt obligations.

Settle. To create or establish an offshore trust. Done by the settlor (offshore term) or the grantor (U.S. and IRS term).

Settlor. One (the entity) who (which) creates or settles an offshore trust.

Side letter. Same as a letter of wishes.

SIPC. The Securities Industry Protection Corporation. Provides up to $500,000 insurance protection for your U.S. stock brokerage account.

Situs or site. The situs is the domicile or dominating or controlling jurisdiction of the trust. It may be changed to another jurisdiction, to be sited in another country or U.S. state.

Société Anonyme (SA). A limited liability corporation established under French Law. Requires a minimum of seven shareholders. In Spanish speaking countries, it is known as the Sociedad Anonima. Important characteristic of both is that the liability of the shareholder is limited up to the amount of their capital contribution.

Sparbuch. An Austrian numbered savings account.

Special custodian. An appointee of the trustee in an APT.

Special investment advisor. An appointee of the trustee in an APT.

Statute of Limitations. The deadline after which a party claiming to be injured by the settlor may (should) no longer file an action to recover his or her damages.

Statutory. That which is fixed by statutes, as opposed to Common Law.

Stiftung. A Liechtenstein form of private foundation.

SWIFT. Society for Worldwide InterBank Financial Telecommunications.

Symbols.

§ section number, singular.

§§ section numbers, plural.

(+) Favorable attribute; (++) very favorable, etc.

(-) Negative attribute; (—) very negative, etc.

~ Tilde-used as part of an Internet URL.

Tax haven. An international banking and financial center providing privacy and tax benefits.

Tax regimen. The local tax treatment of income tax, foreign source income, nonresident treatment and special tax concessions which, when combined, form complex issues.

TCI. Turks and Caicos Islands.

Tranch. A bond series issued for sale in a foreign country.

Transmogrifying. Conversion of nonexempt assets to exempt assets.

True settlor. The true grantor is not the true settlor, and his or her identity is kept quite private by the trustee. See grantor trust.

Trust. An entity created for the purpose of protecting and conserving assets for the benefit of a third party, the beneficiary. A contract affecting three parties, the settlor, the trustee and the beneficiary. A trust protector is optional but recommended, as well. In the trust, the settlor transfers asset ownership to the trustee on behalf of the beneficiaries.

Trust deed. An asset protection trust document or instrument.

Trust indenture. A trust instrument such as a trust deed creating an offshore trust.

Trust protector. A person appointed by the settlor to oversee the trust on behalf of the beneficiaries. In many jurisdictions, local trust laws define the concept of the trust protector. Has veto power over the trustee with respect to discretionary matters but no say with respect to issues unequivocally covered in the trust deed. Trust decisions are the trustee's alone. Has the power to remove the trustee and appoint trustees. Consults with the settlor, but the final decisions must be the protector's.

Trustee. A person totally independent of the settlor who has the fiduciary responsibility to the beneficiaries to manage the assets of the trust as a reasonable prudent business person would do in the same circumstances. Shall defer to the trust protector when required in the best interest of the trust. The trustee reporting requirements shall be defined at the onset and should include how often, to whom, how to respond to instructions or inquiries, global investment strategies, fees (flat and/or percentage of the valuation of the trust estate), anticipated future increases in fees, hourly rates for consulting services, seminars and client educational materials, etc. The trustee may have full discretionary powers of distributions to beneficiaries.

Trust settlement document. See trust deed.

UBO. Unincorporated business organization.

UO. Unincorporated business organization.

Uniform Partnership Act (UPA). One of the uniform type of laws adopted by some states or used as a baseline for other states.

United States (U.S.). Comprised of the 50 states, as well as the District of Columbia, the Commonwealth of Puerto Rico, the Commonwealth of the Northern Mariana Islands, American Samoa, Guam, the Midway Islands, the U.S. Virgin Islands and Wake Island.

UPA. See Uniform Partnership Act.

Upstreaming. The process of retaining earnings offshore through the billing process.

URL. Universal resource locator on the World Wide Web. A combination of letters, numbers and punctuation that comprise and "address" for a "home page."

U.S.C. United States Code (of statutes).

USD or US$. United States dollars.

U.S. person. Any person, including a foreign citizen, who resides in the United States or is subject to the jurisdiction of the U.S. tax system (regardless of where the person is situated worldwide).

Variable annuity. An annuity in which you select the investment program that suits your future needs. The ultimate payback is a function of how well your program performs during the intervening period before the maturity of the annuity.

Vetting. It is the process used by the offshore consultant for qualifying the prospective client to determine if he or she is a good candidate for offshore asset protection; as in to "vet" the prospective client.

Web. The World Wide Web (WWW) of the Internet.

World Bank. Formed to be the bank lender and technical advisor to the developing countries, utilizing funds and technical resources from the member nations (the depositors). The headquarters are in Washington D.C.

WWW. The World Wide Web of the Internet.